"Shows that there are different ways of looking at wealth generation and … points us towards the best elements of different cultures and systems. If we could get the best elements from each system and combine them effectively maybe we could change the way the world works."

– Peter Hiscocks, Judge Business School, University of Cambridge

"Capitalism must reinvent itself. This book shows us possible avenues into the future. At its core are values. The view is holistic throughout, exactly what we need to reorient ourselves in turbulent times. The authors transcend the notorious narrowness of business books and Anglo-Saxon capitalism by learning from alternative models."

– Hermann Simon, Chairman and Founder Simon-Kucher & Partners

"Nine Visions of Capitalism challenges what we think we know about East meeting West. The authors' analysis of complex issues allows us to decide for ourselves what are the real drivers for success whilst questioning our own personal value judgements. The ability to synthesise the role of nation states such as China, Germany, Singapore and apply such thinking to contemporary issues such as crowdfunding, banking values and the Cambridge phenomenon is testimony to their ability to think differently about today's business issues. I was left, illuminated and energised, questioning my own beliefs on a number of issues."

– Dr Raymond Madden' Chief Executive, Asian Institute of Finance, former Global Head of Learning at ABN AMRO NV and Lloyds Banking Group

"At last a book that puts crowdfunding in its true human perspective. The authors understand that Alternative Finance is not just an extension of offerings from the boring and money grabbing financial services industry we know so well, but that the world of future finance might just be the brave new world in which access to finance is truly democratised. Read here about 'finance for the people and public good'."

– Professor Alan Barrell, Entrepreneur in Residence, Judge Business School, University of Cambridge, author of *Show Me the Money: how to raise the cash to get your business off the ground*

"Tackles the key issue confronting banks and financial institutions … vital not just for the established banking sector, but for the new digital companies that are also involved in financial services, who need to heed the lessons of the past."

– Charles Baden-Fuller, Centenary Professor of Strategy, Cass Business School, City University London

Sor Edward.

NINE VISIONS OF
CAPITALISM

UNLOCKING THE MEANINGS OF WEALTH CREATION

Yours in visionary policies

Charles H-T

Charles Hampden-Turner
Fons Trompenaars

with Tom Cummings

First published in 2015 by
Infinite Ideas Limited
36 St Giles
Oxford
OX1 3LD
United Kingdom
www.infideas.com

A CIP catalogue record for this book is available from the British Library
ISBN 978–1–908984–40–1

Page xvi, Anti-slavery medallion, by Josiah Wedgewood (1730–1795) c. 1787 © The Trustees of the
British Muesum. All rights reserved.
Front cover image © Quang Ho/Shutterstock.com
Cover designed by Cylinder
Typeset by Nicki Averill
Printed and bound in Great Britain by TJ International Ltd, Padstow, Cornwall

Contents

Dedicated to Gregory Bateson. This was one of his favourite poems:

Not on sad Stygian shore, nor in clear sheen
Of far Elysian plain, shall we meet those
Among the dead whose pupils we have been,
...
Yet meet we shall, and part, and meet again,
Where dead men meet, on lips of living men.

The Life After Death, Samuel Butler

Foreword

In my many years of working with global corporations implementing large transformational change programmes, most recently focusing in the complex area of cultural change, I have often been faced with the need to understand and effect change in the underlying and very personal behaviours and values that permeate an individual, their organization and the industry in which they operate. Having worked with Charles and Fons over the years and benefited greatly from their work on dilemma reconciliation, I believe this book delivers a timely, compelling and astute examination of the true meaning of wealth creation, the underlying values, its impact on capitalism and what choices this offers to us. Many of the organizations and C-suite executives I work with are facing similar challenges to those outlined in the book, not least the continual dilemma of managing stakeholder ROI whilst operating as an ethical organization in an increasingly regulated world. As the authors discuss in the first chapter, capitalism has many meanings: it provides people with a freedom within which they derive 'all manner of arrangements'; it is complex, multi-faceted and ever-evolving. Charles and Fons examine each of these facets in some detail, exploring their historical significance and evolution, and share their thinking on what this means for the new approaches to wealth creation, such as crowdfunding and financial technology, what strengths (and weaknesses) can be derived from a diverse mix of cultures (evidenced by the financial success of Singapore, for example), and how these advances can be practically applied for today's corporate challenges.

As a long-time member of the people-management community, with a career spanning many industries, most recently in the financial services sector, I have spent many a year extolling the virtues of an integrated approach to change, one that recognizes the need to integrate rather than balance the wants of the few with those of the many. As such, I find this book invites interesting debate and challenges us to think more broadly about our role in society, both as leaders and members of an organization, a community or even a 'culture'. Similarly, the challenges highlighted in respect of the more traditional approaches to capitalism raise many questions and further stimulate discussion. Charles and Fons' opinion that the sheer versatility of the meaning of capitalism means that Western economies need to learn from the extraordinary success of other cultures if they are to generate long term value, raises thought-provoking questions about the attendant complexities of other approaches to wealth creation. Throughout their book, Charles and Fons share these intriguing nuggets of clarity, contrasting and reconciling the good with the 'bad' as it were. It is a welcome and absorbing read and one that illustrates each question and subsequent reflection with specific and relevant evidence that compels one to read on. A personal favourite is the exploration of 'Hidden Champions' in Chapter 6. The characteristics of these successful but rarely hyped enterprises represent many of the features that our larger, more global corporations would truly appreciate, such as loyalty, innovation and improved diversity. To understand what can be learned from these smaller to medium enterprises and how this can be applied at the macro level is worthy of further exploration. As I read through this book, I am struck by the underlying lesson that permeates each chapter; the focus on shared values and the relationships between them. As Chapter 12 concludes 'people value a good job above all…' and 'business is above all a *moral enterprise*'. For a people manager, this is surely the best outcome one can hope for.

This robust and very relevant assessment of the nine visions of wealth creation is a forceful study; it provides a benchmark for understanding and unlocking the true meaning of capitalism and sets us on a path for continued debate. I am honoured to have welcomed Charles and Fons into the KPMG family, where issues such as these are a constant challenge in our work with clients, and to have written the foreword to this outstanding book.

Mark Spears
Global Head of People and Change;
Global Lead for the HR Centre of Excellence, KPMG LLP

Introduction

He knows he must vote always for the richer universe, for the good which seems most organisable, most fit to enter in complex combinations, most apt to be a member of a more inclusive whole...[1]

About values

This book examines the values essential to creating wealth, but we must first ask what values *are*. Only then can we appreciate how various cultures deploy and organize them. In our very materialist age we often think of values as *things*, as dollars in the bank, as diamonds around a neck. Yet values are not things at all, they are *differences or contrasts in what our minds experience*. Contrasts can be between alternative good experiences, between good and bad experiences, and between bad experiences. Contrasts between good experiences include deep sleep and refreshed awakening, competing and cooperating, the excitement of taking risks and the pleasure of becoming more secure as a consequence, patience and rewards, etc.

Those who satisfy their self-interest find they are better able to care for others. If you give to others you will often receive love and gratitude in return. A good supplier gains happy customers. A show of courage may be the most cautious act you can take for yourself or others in dangerous circumstances. If you systematically doubt a proposition you can become more certain of it. Change requires a measure of continuity or we lose our bearings. Great

---

1.   William James, *Essays in Pragmatism*, New York: Haffner Publishing Co. 1949, p. 83.

ideals need to be realized. If you assert your rights peacefully and politely, yet insistently, like Gandhi and Martin Luther King, these are harder for democratic systems to ignore.

Contrast between good and bad includes life and death, worry and relief, rich and poor, love and hate, joy and woe. The one has to be contrasted with the other for us really to appreciate either. The prospect of death can make every hour of life precious. To worry about someone we love brings a flood of relief when danger passes and a reminder of our need for each other. When we love others we may hate some of their actions. Few unloved children ever grow to full humanity, but nor do uncorrected children. The two work as one. William Blake wrote: 'Joy and woe are woven fine, a clothing for the soul divine.'

It is when we deeply empathize with the pain and misfortune of others that we come to realize the pleasure and good fortune we personally enjoy. The British author once had to sit up all night with a drug addict whose baby had been born alive but died soon after. She had suffered hours of agonizing labour. The hospital could not find a vein that had not collapsed and so was unable to anaesthetize her properly. Although the baby cried they refused to show it to her. 'It's not normal,' was all they would say. The author had sat up with his own wife in some pain from childbirth not long before, so the trauma was very real. Subsequently he went home and saw his own young son peacefully asleep and wept with sheer gratitude, so strong was the contrast. He had always taken his middle-class life and college education for granted. You have to visit hell to know what heaven is. Only those who encounter misfortune can appreciate their own good fortune

When bad confronts bad we speak of a rock and a hard place, of the devil or the deep blue sea. We think of *Sophie's Choice* – having to yield her son or daughter to be killed by a Nazi officer. Comedy has contrasting values bouncing off each other playfully and harmlessly. Tragedy has contrasting values grinding against each other in the agony of being unable to decide, for example, the complicity of a mother in her daughter's death. If you failed to laugh at the comedy festival in Athens during the winter you would weep at the tragedy festival the following spring. Humour is first aid in averting tragic outcomes. Tyrants are notoriously humourless. That theatre is a mark of a moral civilization is no coincidence. But even these terrible dilemmas are not without their value. We learn that only a creative and transformative resolution can lift us out of such an impasse, of killing or being killed, or shooting first to make ourselves less vulnerable, of curbing civil rights to fight terrorism, or deploying nuclear weapons to 'defend' ourselves from the heat-death of the universe.

Our values also resemble the humble traffic light which signals stop and go with colours chosen from contrasting ends of the colour spectrum, an example of culture borrowing from nature. What brings order to the flow of traffic is the *difference and the movement*, of green, to yellow to red and round again. The pattern is circular. We know that if we stop for others we can soon go ourselves. A light stuck on either red or green is not just useless but *lethal.* Angry motorists will run the lights and collide. Value lies in constant transition between the two, in being wise enough to encompass both ends of the spectrum and move back and forth.[2]

Cross-cultural understanding as a path to learning

It follows that moving from one culture to another, from one set of values to another, allows us to encounter people very different from ourselves and to appreciate values as never before. What are clarified are not just *their* values *but our own values.* Indeed we may be barely conscious of our own values *until* these clash and contrast with values different from our own. This process forces our own values, previously taken for granted, into conscious awareness. Numerous nations have absorbed and assimilated very different values from those they were once used to. In East Asia, for example, Hong Kong and Singapore are much influenced by the British, while Taiwan and South Korea are much influenced by the USA. East and West have mingled in a way rarely seen elsewhere. *Could this hold the clue to their competitiveness?* While many of us have only one cultural context, they have two and can switch between them. Context switching may be vital to commerce in general since the views of producers and consumers, owners and operators, management and labour, leaders and led, centre and periphery are far enough apart to be considered opposites.

Crucial to this equation are the values of diversity and inclusion. Diversity by itself is an extremely doubtful proposition. The Thirty Years' War between Protestants and Catholics halved the population of Europe. The presence of Jews in Nazi Germany led to six million being murdered. Hutus (French speaking) massacred Tutsis (English speaking) by the million in Rwanda. Muslim fundamentalists currently run amok and many European nations are rejecting immigrants with mounting revulsion. Diversity *on its own* is like the broken traffic light. We need diverse persons and their ideas to be *included* or disaster befalls us. Unless we comprehend this strange infusion in our midst

2.   The traffic signal metaphor is from Edmund Leach, *Levi-Straus*, London: Fontana Modern Masters, 1976.

we will panic. Contrasting values must be joined and reconciled to make them virtuous. Polarized values are vicious in their mutual hatred. Yet our discredited politicians aid this polarization with their sterile jousting between ideologies. The irony is that those we reject could potentially make us whole, providing the missing pieces of the puzzles.

Why immigrants succeed

At a time when politics is wracked with opposition to immigration it is useful to explain why immigrants create so much wealth and why certain subcultures have been so valuable to their mainstream cultures. Some immigrants *do* end up in prison or become welfare claimants. Being different can break you or make you. Teams of diverse people do much worse when managed badly *and* much better when managed well.[3] There is no cheap grace. But how can people subject to prejudice, racism and suspicion do *better*? A study conducted in Silicon Valley in 2000 found that one third of the Valley's wealth, over US$ 58 billion in the currency of the time, was created by Chinese and Indian immigrants entering the USA after 1970.[4] In Britain's own industrial revolution one subculture of religious Quakers *created forty times more wealth than their numbers warranted.*[5] They allowed women to chair their meetings, tithed themselves to pay for the education of apprentices and refused to doff their hats to anyone, but their strongest value was 'my word is my bond'. This was enough to create much of Britain's financial sector in a money culture where promises were often reneged upon. This book will show how values organized by cultures create, and sometimes destroy, wealth.

The advantage of some subcultures, some minorities and those with very different values and/or skin colour is that they are different perforce, a condition they cannot change. They therefore decide to *make a difference,* to put products or services in the place of their personalities and see if these will help them to survive. They both cooperate with fellow minority members in tight networks of high trust AND compete with the mainstream culture. Immigrants bring to business a wider and more *inclusive* set of values than do

3. Joseph DiStefano and Martha Maznevski, cited in *100+ Management Models,* Oxford: Infinite Ideas, 2014, pp. 231–23.

4. AnnaLee Saxenian, *Silicon Valley's New Immigrant Entrepreneurs,* Public Policy Institute of California, San Francisco, 1999.

5. See Introduction to David K. Hurst, *Crisis and Renewal,* Boston: Harvard Business School Press, 1995.

the domestic elites that so often scorn them and subject them to prejudice. In the face of rejection minorities strive to participate. They meet exclusion with values of inclusion. They emphasize education and learned knowledge as a means of aiding their emancipation. Indeed the place of education in a subculture divides those who over-perform from those that under-perform. In America, Jews and Chinese, Japanese and Indian immigrants, tend to do better than their white American peers, both educationally and economically, while blacks and Latinos do worse. Diversity can help or hinder depending on whether you are included or rejected.[6]

Wealth creation as inclusive of all parties

It is not enough for people in an economy to make money. This is because a great deal of money is made at the expense of other people. A community is only better off when it *creates wealth*, that is, when it generates more money among its members than they began with. If money has simply moved from one pocket to another then X may have outsmarted Y but no wealth has been created by that relationship. Competition is important but if this leads to a zero-sum game – wherein gains and losses total zero – then there is no gain for the society or the economy.[7] For example, banks do not, for the most part, create wealth, although their lending facilitates this and may help industry. You must repay your loan with interest so there is a net transfer of money from one party to another. Banks are *distributors* of funds which help *contributors* to create wealth.[8] If too much money is siphoned off in the distributive function industry will suffer and wealth creation will wilt. Permitting huge rewards to those who handle money is of very doubtful utility.

So what does it mean to create wealth? Wealth is created when two or more parties to a business relationship end up with *more value than they began with,* having generated this between them. They began with some silicon sand and small pieces of metal worth a few cents at best and ended up with an intelligent silicon chip which could save the occupants in a car from being killed. Note that not only is the chip worth much more than its components but it has human purpose, direction and intelligence. Similarly a Rolls Royce engine with more than a thousand components is worth much more than the sum of its parts. But

---

6. See Seth Gordon, *Tribes*, London: Piatkus, 2008.
7. Lester C. Thurow, *The Zero Sum Society*, New York: McGraw Hill, 1980.
8. Roger Bootle, *The Trouble with Markets*, London: Nicholas Brealey, 2012.

its *real* wealth-creating potential lies in what it DOES. It delivers power-by-the-hour and propels four hundred people thousands of miles to their destinations nearly every day. The contract may specify that it does this effectively. There is 'surplus value' left over at the end and the company, its suppliers, employees, customers and passengers all benefit. Wealth has been created.

What creates wealth is the *transformation* of money into products/services and the transformation of these *back* into money via revenue received from customers. The wealth is generated by this transformation. No two coins have ever created a third coin and they never will. All those who are parties to a transformation share any gains. We will be calling these stakeholders. They have a shared stake in the success of industry and they need fellow stakeholders to excel at their functions. Ironically, manufacturing creates more wealth than almost any other business activity, while speculation in a world casino creates very little, if anything. When Britain and the USA were workshops of the world they prospered. Now that British manufacturing is only ten per cent of the economy and American manufacturing only eleven per cent, they grow fitfully and slowly, while China, to which their manufacturing has been outsourced, is growing three times as fast. Manufacturing tends to double its productivity every decade while cutting hair, drafting wills and insuring lives are services that remain much the same now as they were fifty years ago.

What creates wealth are certain kinds of mutually beneficial *relationships*, not just relationships between diverse people but relationships between their diverse *values*. Suppliers are different from customers and want different things. Employees are different from owners, producers from consumers, managers are different from labour, lenders from borrowers and so on. What creates wealth is an *inclusive relationship between diverse parties*. Indeed the interests of such parties are not just contrasting but often opposite. The supplier wants the customer's money. The customer wants the product or service in exchange for money and only when *both* are satisfied is wealth created. If a customer has a choice between eating and keeping warm in a cold winter then little or no wealth has been generated. Exploitation is usually zero-sum and cripples an economy even as it makes money for predators, so that tobacco products and high interest pay-day loans almost certainly destroy wealth on a massive scale.

Another characteristic of true wealth creation is that parties benefit *indirectly*. It is because you have *given* more value to other people that you *get* more value for yourself. It is because you pay employees more that the best offer to work for you and are much more productive. It is because you train and develop your people on the job that they are more innovative and responsible and the very quality of their work repays your training costs. In the West we have been raised to believe that we should manipulate in our own self-interest. We try to *pursue* life, liberty and happiness as if they were quarries in some chase. The truth is that if we care effectively for others happiness will ambush us along the way. *All important values are achieved by indirection*, by committing ourselves to something in contrast to self-interest so that through reciprocity that self-interest is served. Unless we *first* encounter diverse people we cannot include their ideas. By first caring for customers it becomes much easier to make a profit. We succeed through their grateful contributions.

Minority cultures which are inclusive create most meaning and most wealth

This book examines nine very different forms of free enterprise, all of them effective in certain circumstances. It inquires as to how, when and why these succeed or otherwise. This includes minority cultures within nations, since it is often its creative minority that renders a nation prosperous. There is *not*, as many believe, one universal model of business success, pioneered by Britain and exemplified on a world scale by the USA. Rather there are multiple paths, some demonstrably more successful than others.

It is not a question of simply identifying and adopting 'the best way', since all ways have some validity in certain circumstances and each has something to teach us. Moreover, we cannot just change our cultures like we change our clothes. These are deeply ingrained within us via our upbringing. We need first to assert where we stand and who we really are while taking other values on board. If values are differences then we need to recognize and respect those differences yet anchor them upon our own culture. Others differ *from us* and our own culture is the touchstone for all comparisons. This is why this book begins with the Anglo-American and Northwest European culture of capitalism. We must begin with where most readers are and how we have been socialized. Only if this is valued and understood can we move on to encounter others without fear. Each of our subcultures is less a rival than an extension of our repertoire, an additional way of engaging the environment. Particular cultures are suited to particular kinds of products and if we want to be more versatile we must try to master them all. We must strive to be at home everywhere, in a variety of climes.

Josiah Wedgwood: An extraordinary entrepreneur

Is the foregoing account of capitalism ludicrously tender-minded, naïve and idealistic? In fact a major pioneer of eighteenth-century capitalism, a man credited with being 'the first tycoon', who spearheaded Britain's industrial revolution was Josiah Wedgwood (1730–1795). He symbolized nearly all the positive values discussed so far. He was the youngest of eleven children born to fourth generation Staffordshire potters. He was only nine when his father died and he was apprenticed to an elder brother. He set up an independent partnership outside the family when his brother refused him one. He became very influential, hugely wealthy and very successful in nearly everything he tried.[9]

Did he learn from foreign cultures? Indeed he did. Porcelain itself originated in China, with its manufacturing secrets being revealed in Europe in the early eighteenth century. The archaeology of the time was revealing the treasures of ancient Rome, Greece and Egypt, and all things ancient were highly fashionable. Wedgwood and his designers created highly recognizable items that combined classical motifs and references with technical innovation.

He was very much on the side of the American colonists who were fighting for their independence. But his diverse sympathies stretched much further. His whole family was in the forefront of the fight against the slave trade. His sister Sarah was a full-time campaigner. He produced a famous plate, and subsequently medallions (such as the one shown) and even hat pins with large heads, which depicted a black slave kneeling in chains, his manacled hands raised in supplication. The circular inscription reads: 'Am I not a man and a brother?' He sent specimens to Benjamin Franklin who asked for many more. He did a roaring trade in newly liberated America. There is

9.   Brian Dolan, *The First Tycoon*, New York: Viking, 2004.

extensive correspondence between Josiah Wedgwood and William Wilberforce, the merchant MP who finally succeeded in outlawing the slave trade. He seems to have calculated, like many subsequent minority entrepreneurs, that since he was diverse *in any case* he might as well act differently too, even where this involved dissent against the status quo.

Wedgwood gave his china free to many of the crowned-heads of Europe, knowing that once they graced their tables and cabinets many others would seek them out. He was the father of the illustrated catalogue. He pioneered the money-back guarantee, since his wares were fragile and could arrive broken. After the commissioning and delivery of a full tea set to Queen Charlotte, wife of George III, he was permitted to call his cream coloured porcelain Queen's Ware (pioneering the concept of brands) and was made 'Potter to her Majesty'. This was repeated in several foreign countries. He created the world's first international travelling sales force.

But if Josiah was *diverse* in his tastes was he also *inclusive* and wealth creating? He belonged to a minority Protestant sect, the Unitarians, whose belief is that all Christian sects should unite in the name of their Saviour and work together. But his unifying did not stop there. Rarely is high fashion joined to compassion but his chinaware protests against slavery accomplished this. He also believed that Christian faith could make common cause with science and he founded several churches to teach this doctrine. Barred from most universities and professions on account of his nonconformity, he turned his company into an educator and trained his people assiduously. Like all minority sects the future of each member depended on the support received from his peers. Lose your co-religionists and there is little hope of economic survival. You relate or die.

He was the epitome of wealth creation, in that products like his Portland Vase were at least one hundred times more valuable than the clay, paint, glaze, heat and craft that went into making them. Turning clay into fine porcelain is a transformation if ever there was one. Everyone connected with such enterprise was enriched by it. He went a long way to inventing modern manufacturing processes with their wealth-generating potentials. His orientation to *relationships* of every kind was what inspired his sense of aestheticism and his love of the beauty that derives from the elegant organization of the whole. He would often spend all night experimenting in the workshops. His was also the unity of mind and body, of head and hands.

Among the unities and the inclusions he sought for and achieved were the fusion of scientific knowledge and commerce. He was centuries in advance of his times. He realized early that making pots was a branch of chemistry and was prominent in societies advancing this discipline. What crowned his efforts was the invention of the pyrometer, a device for measuring the very high levels of heat involved in firing pots. For this important invention he was elected a member of the Royal Society. He met and engaged with some of the major scientists of his age. Charles Darwin wrote *On the Origin of Species* with the help of money Josiah left to his granddaughter, Emma, who was Darwin's wife.

Josiah built a model village to house his workers and looked to their welfare. He needed their craftsmanship and their utmost efforts. He had them all inoculated against smallpox, a disease he had himself caught earlier in life. Because his wares were often broken by rickety carts on rutted roads, he helped to build the Trent and Mersey canal, extended this to the doors of his factory and floated much his merchandise part-way to its destinations. If Wedgwood could be innovative, aesthetic, compassionate, scientific, diverse, unifying, international, entrepreneurial, caring, technically brilliant, wealth creating and fabulously rich, it seems strange that we so rarely combine these qualities today.

Capitalism has always been an extremely malleable system capable, for example, of both trading slaves and campaigning to stop this. Allow people freedom and they come up with all manner of arrangements. Capitalism has emancipated millions from dire poverty while affecting not to care about this. It is the sheer versatility of its meanings that we address in this book and which subsequent chapters reveal.

Chapter 1 introduces the Anglo-American linear-active model, of which Wedgwood was an example. It explains how and why Britain, America and the English-speaking dominions led the industrial revolution and where their strengths still lie, so that the Washington Consensus still tries to prescribe for people everywhere. We have researched these values for many years and we locate within them the secrets to past, present and future accomplishments. The Protestant work ethic is the foundation stone of business values across the world and we must respect this. Western economies have the power to rebound and recapture the initiative but only if they are prepared to learn from the extraordinary feats of other cultures, which are detailed in later chapters. We *must* include diverse ways of thinking.

Chapter 2 asks whether it is possible to *overplay a once-winning combination.* Could the very strengths highlighted in Chapter 1 be taken too far? In our eagerness to proclaim the *rules* of economics do we pay sufficient heed to the many *exceptions*? Does our out-and-out allegiance to individualism impede the relationships without which wealth creation flags? In our haste to consume have we ignored the need to produce? In our appetite for debt are we saving too little? In our direct pursuit of money have we lost sight of indirect wealth creation? In our addiction to the 'thing' credit, have we lost its origins in the process of believing others (*credire*) and trusting them? Are the straight-line self-interested calculations we make, really arcs of a circle which come home again to haunt us?

The problem is as old as that of the tragic hero who at first triumphs but then pushes the successful values too far and encounters *catastrophe*, literally a 'down-turn in fortune'. Our booms turn to busts, trillions of dollars mysteriously vanish and the limping gait of Oedipus (swollen foot) symbolizes values that are dangerously lopsided, uneven and more and more unequal as a tiny elite over-harvests what the rest of us have created while enriching itself.

Chapter 3 takes up the question of shareholders and of stakeholders. In one respect the Anglo-American model of maximizing shareholder value differs from every other culture outlined in this book. All the other cultures are ad hoc alliances among stakeholders, which *include* shareholders but do not give them sovereignty over all other contributors to wealth creation. It is axiomatic that maximizing any *one* value in a diverse system will eventually destroy that system, much as aggressive cancer cells destroy the human body. But it was not until the Reagan–Thatcher era and the rise of the financial sector, Wall Street and the City of London, that maximizing shareholder wealth became a stringent requirement and was rigorously pursued. Before that our economies grew faster and we shared the results more equally

The whole notion that a small group of people 'own' the development, training, innovation and the productivity of others and that in exchange for money these other stakeholders should pledge their working lives is here questioned. We are *not* concerned here with the founders of start-up companies who must and do win the voluntary cooperation of other stakeholders, we are concerned with Initial Public Offerings that put non-instigators, non-founders and uncommitted share traders into a position of extreme power over people they do not know and with whom they have no viable relationship. Ownership is privileged over those taking effective action and creating wealth.

Chapter 4 describes the *circular listening and reactive model* of the Chinese and much of Southeast Asia. It considers the quite extraordinary rise of the People's Republic of China. No one who describes values and culture can possibly ignore the fact that a country describing itself as a 'socialist market-driven economy' has out-performed every other capitalist nation in the history of economics. The second largest economy in the world is growing at seven per cent plus a year which entails leaving much of the rest of the world *ever further behind.* When Deng Xiaoping said 'it's glorious to be rich' we congratulated ourselves on having at last enlightened him, except that the word 'rich' translates into Mandarin as 'well connected'. The Chinese celebrate relationships.

The central value of Chinese business is *guanxi* meaning an optimal and beneficial relationship, not simply between people but between their values. Those successful, minority Chinese entrepreneurs in the diaspora *have brought their model home again.* The two largest IPO's in the history of Wall Street are now for Chinese companies. Ignored in this hoopla was the fact that neither undertook to put shareholders first. Alibaba whose flotation was US$ 25 billion, states 'employees first, customers second'. Its mission is to *small business* worldwide, not so much to public corporations. Were shareholders perhaps better off as a consequence of being relegated?

Chapter 5 considers Singapore as *a hybrid between East and West.* Its annual income per capita stood at $600 in 1967 and at $78,762 in 2014. It now has a GDP per capita over double that of the British. Like Hong Kong and Malaysia it was colonized and deeply influenced by the British but has large native and Chinese populations with Taoist and Confucian value systems and family-based businesses. Being the 'hinge' between East and West and including two diverse and opposed points of view seems to be a major competitive advantage. In this it is joined by South Korea and Taiwan, both much influenced by the USA. These are five of the most competitive economies in the world and also the most inclusive. They stand *between* East and West which they treat like Yin and Yang.

A very interesting role is played by the Singaporean government. Since Singapore cannot accommodate every company that wants to move there, the government can choose who to invite and selects those who have the most socially significant technologies and who treat their stakeholders with the greatest consideration, especially employees and suppliers, nearly all of whom will be Singaporean. Since most shareholders are foreigners it is less concerned with them. It also selects catalytic technologies, those like microchips, lasers or machine tools that contribute most to *other* technologies. It gives preference to knowledge-intensive products which educate the makers, buyers, users and the population of Singapore. The government acts more as a coach and less as a referee, helping rather than blowing the whistle. It regards business as a form of martial arts, less a battle to be won than a 'way' open to infinite improvement, a disciplined form of mastering human existence.

Chapter 6 looks at the 'hidden champions' of the global economy. These are small and medium-sized businesses like the *Mittelstand* of German-speaking economies. Few, if any, will become large public corporations with shareholders, rather they are family-owned. They are 'hidden' because they are rarely discussed in the media, because few make consumer goods, because they are business2business with perhaps a few dozen important customers who know them intimately. They are mostly in narrow niche markets like fish eviscerating machines, equipment to gather information from weather balloons, safety harnesses for steeplejacks, etc.

What characterizes all of them are *intimate face-to-face relationships between all stakeholders.* They have less conflict than big public corporations, many more patents per head, more new products, greater technology leadership, lower turnover, higher employee loyalty, less concern with profitability, more concern for customers and their communities, more job creation, higher growth, and better export performance. They supply considerable amounts of production equipment to China, have more women in leadership positions and outsource far less.

Chapter 7 deals with the conscious capitalism movement in the USA, spreading to other countries. Capitalism has long been a boon. The problem is how we are *taught to think* about it. We are taught to pursue our self-interests aggressively and as an accidental side effect our societies will improve without our consciously seeking this or wanting it. But even *if* these positive effects are initially accidental that does not mean we should not *intend them thereafter.* We should consciously desire everything that capitalism bestows. Research was conducted among hundreds of mostly US companies whom respondents said they *loved.* The list was finally whittled down to around thirty, many of them big, for example Whole Foods, Johnson and Johnson, Southwest Airlines and Harley-Davidson.

Those doing this research hoped-against-hope that well-loved companies had not paid too dearly for people's devotion. Might they at least have made a modest profit or broken even? They need not have worried. Loved companies were *eight times* more profitable than S&P stock averages over ten years and *ten times* over fifteen years. The success of a company depends on the positive relationships among stakeholders. These companies paid their people more than the industry average but were amply repaid by their much higher productivity, creativity, knowledge and morale.

Chapter 8 is about harmonizing companies with the cycles of nature. Since nature consists of scores of natural cycles we can only safeguard our own habitat *by thinking in the same way as nature functions.* The process is circular or helical. It is here exemplified as profitable, cost-cutting, resource efficient and earth-saving. It is far more effective to go *with* natural processes than *against* them. Whether or not global warming menaces us it is immensely valuable to give products multiple lives so that they jump from their graves to a new cradle and have second and third uses. There is even up-cycling where material increases in value. Nitrate fertilizer can be made from human sewage. Using materials up to ten times by recycling is not just cost saving but resource efficient. Why leave profits on the factory floor? We must learn to think in circles.

In time renewable energy will be cheapest for the simple reason that sun, tides and winds are free and ways of capturing them will continue improving. We are looking at an age when energy prices will only fall when Apollo becomes the sun-god of us all. It comes as no surprise that China, with its still modest income per head, has seventy-five per cent of all the solar energy technology in the world. This culture thinks long-term. The new meaning of enterprise is the survival not of the fittest, but of the finest fit.

Chapter 9 looks at the Global Alliance for Banking on Values, a rapidly growing association of twenty-five banks and credit unions, that sees the mission of financial organizations as being service to companies and customers, not trading and speculating on its own account. Members are invited to join or can apply but acceptance is only for those that adhere to its principles. First among these is people, planet and profit in that order, otherwise known as the triple bottom line. With members in Mongolia and Patagonia as well as Germany, America and the Netherlands this odd assortment of do-gooders has an enviable record of stability, sustainability, growth and return on assets. They show, beyond any doubt, that banking on shared values can pay as well as some the largest banks in the world, that one can pursue environmental and social objectives and make them pay.

Chapter 10 tells the story of the Cambridge Phenomenon, how a sleepy market town in the Fens that had waved away the industrial revolution like a noxious insect and had formed a monastic enclave of higher learning which had long scorned the vulgarities of commerce, suddenly began blooming into a US$90 billion hub of academic entrepreneurship. Cambridge is perhaps more remarkable than even Silicon Valley in having multi-disciplinary clusters, several in the process of converging. When diverse disciplines like biology, genetics, engineering, physics, chemistry and medicine fuse into new products major breakthroughs can occur. The more remote the ideas the more remarkable is their combination. Here is a minority that could change the economic complexion of the whole country.

By spinning out a new company from a parent company, by sprouting twigs from a branch and branches from a tree, Cambridge companies imitate the fractal nature of knowledge itself. The 'parent' nurtures and educates the 'child', encouraging independence and branching out on its own. Several famous entrepreneurs have spun out as many as sixty company offspring, all derivatives of the core technologies. This informs investments with rare knowledge of its possibilities. Even if the commercial venture fails the science will go on developing and new attempts can be made to find applications.

Chapter 11 takes up what is at first glance just another source of investment funds: crowdfunding. However a closer look reveals that this is an entirely new form of capitalism in the making. At the moment its value is doubling every few months. A sponsor on the Internet like Kickstarter or Crowdcube publishes a project proposal for a new venture to a 'crowd' of interested online investors. Having read and perhaps discussed it, they pledge their funds. If the project is fully subscribed the venture is launched, if insufficient funds are pledged the funds are not collected and the proposer may try again. Mistaken ideas are halted without serious loss.

In no other form of capitalism are so many investors brought in at so early a stage so that they are actually co-creating the project with the entrepreneur and being invited to respond to an ideal yet to be realized. Those who lack funds may offer to work for the enterprise, to supply it or to buy what it plans to produce. Because stakes are small and numerous very much higher risks may be taken and bold innovations essayed at an earlier stage than an established company could dare. There are large appetites for gambling in societies and crowdfunding could draw strength from this. At the moment crowdfunding is mostly for smaller projects needing only a few million or less, but if mass media take it up in the future TV may actually promote not the trailing edge of technology, as it does now, but the leading edge, launching new products in front of a million viewers with endorsements from celebrities. New business could be 'show-time' and rally viewers behind creativity as a way of life, what it means to be an 'innovation nation' and recreate the world.

Chapter 12 summarizes the main lessons from this book. Above all, people value a good job, which offers meaning and fulfilment. We must find pleasure not simply in consuming and shopping but creating, innovating and being intrinsically motivated to excel at what we do. Nearly all conventional products can be made more cheaply in poorer countries so we must innovate or perish. Our place is on the leading edges of advancing knowledge disciplines. Business is above all a *moral enterprise*. So far from profit being the ends of enterprise, profit is the means to do whatever we most love and what people and our society want from us and will pay for. Virtue lies neither in this value *nor* in that value, but in *the relationships between them*. Reconcile values and you help to create virtuous not vicious circles and wealth for everyone involved. Discover diverse wants and needs and include these in a larger whole. Arthur Miller once put it well:

What are needed are people who quite simply know how to think, who know how to synthesise knowledge and find connections between distantly related phenomena, who seek constantly to relate rather than to isolate experience.[10]

10.   Quoted in Charles Hampden-Turner, *Radical Man*, New York: Doubleday, 1971.

CHAPTER 1

The Anglo-American linear active model of capitalism

This chapter will try to understand how Britain, America, the English-speaking white dominions and much of Northwest Europe were the first in the world to undergo industrial revolutions. These cultures essentially set the pattern for the rest of the world which has tried to emulate them with mixed success. What values distinguish cultures in these parts of the world and why did they succeed so spectacularly for so long? We will look at the six cultural characteristics that gave these nations a head start and still give them important advantages to this day.

1. Universal rules .... Particular exceptions
2. Individuality.. Community orientation
3. Specific/reductive... Diffuse/holistic
4. Achieved status .... Ascribed status
5. Inner-directed .... Outer-directed
6. Sequential/linear .... Synchronic/circular

In each case the pioneer capitalists preferred the first of these over the second. That does not mean they ignored the second entirely. Rules need to be tested by exceptions. Individuals do compete for the approval of the community and we talk of vicious or virtuous circles, but there is little doubt as to which is deemed more important in each pair. The tone of this chapter will be upbeat and confident as befits the cultures we describe. These promulgate rules for themselves and everyone else, extol the dauntless individual, examine specific data and monitor results, award status to those who achieve, insist that we are propelled from within, and that we think in straight lines, from cause to effect, from means to ends, in sequences.

All pioneer industrialists share one common heritage, that of the Protestant religion. Although many of us today are godless and this piety may appear outmoded, in fact it has shaped the way we think and act most profoundly. Protestantism has formed our social characters. If we look at the most successful economies in the world during the eighteenth, nineteenth and twentieth centuries, then this roster brings us Great Britain, the USA, the white dominions, Switzerland, Germany, Holland and Scandinavia including Finland – Protestant nations all. Recently the gap between Protestant and Roman Catholic/Orthodox churches has been widening. Spain, Portugal, Italy, Ireland, France, Greece and Russia have somewhat lagged economically, although Austria, influenced much by Germany and Belgium, centre of the EU, are partial exceptions. We will now examine these value-differences in turn.[1]

1. Universal rule orientation preferred to particular exceptions

The first verse in John's Gospel reads, 'In the beginning was the Word, and the Word was with God and the Word was God.' The Protestants believed that this and the other gospels were literally the word of God and the issuance of his instructions to those who could read for themselves and had no need for popes, bishops and kings as intermediaries. A divine CEO had written down his orders which the faithful must follow and obey. This is a strong contrast to the ethic of the family and particular and unique relationships as taught by Confucius. It also differs from those who regard God as mysterious, magical and supernatural as does much Roman Catholic liturgy.

What advantages has this orientation to rules conferred upon Protestant cultures over the centuries? While it all began with moral rules and codes it did not end there. God had bequeathed to man a wondrous clock which he

---

1. The effect of Protestantism is explained at greater length in Charles Hampden-Turner and Fons Trompenaars, *The Seven Cultures of Capitalism*, London: Piatkus, 1993 or New York: Doubleday, 1992. The original thesis is by Max Weber, *The Protestant Ethic and the Spirit of Capitalism*, New York: Charles Scribner, 1930 or London: Allen and Unwin, 1977. See also R. H. Tawney, *Religion and the Rise of Capitalism*, Harmondsworth: Penguin, 1997.

had wound up and left for us to appreciate. This was the precursor of the market mechanism and similar concepts. The natural universe was his gift to us and humble and holy men of heart must uncover his creation. This was holy work and many of the early Puritans were also scientists. God's Kingdom must be built on *this* earth by his agents. This helps explain why Protestantism could be so quickly secularized. The laws of God and of nature were one. All inquiry was a search for his dispensation.

Business companies and business relationships are a nest of legal contracts and agreements, We write down our own promises and obligations so that people behave predictably. Of course the process of making rules must pay some heed to exceptions but this is done to improve the rules so that they cover more particulars. So a culture that puts rules first may be more enterprising than one which considers most events and people as exceptional and one-off. If everything is particular then it is hard to make sense of our environment and the emperor's 'mandate from heaven' explains little. Codifying is also essential to the *transmission* of information to the rising generation. Only codified knowledge can be passed on. China has a brilliant history of innovation but several discoveries never made it from one dynasty to the next.

It should go without saying that companies function on the basis of rules, whether scientific or man-made, and if a rule is first prescribed then the rest of the world must accommodate itself to your standards, so that the World Wide Web is a universal reality and Windows sets the protocol for all users. Such tools have the characteristics of the culture that invented them and imparts to them a decided advantage. The rules of engineering, operations, mass-production, finance and accounting, manufacturing, research and development and even human resources rely on standards and on their wide acceptance by others. It pays the originators to push for universal adoption.

But how do we *know* that Protestant nations are different? After all it has been some time since churches were full in much of the West. It seems barely credible that this influence might linger on. We know because we have measured it. We pose a dilemma between values at each end of a dimension or contrast and see which end respondents in different cultures choose. For example we pose the following situation:

You are driving down the road with your best friend who is driving too fast in a district where speed is restricted to 20 mph. He hits and injures a pedestrian. He is arrested and taken to court. You are the sole witness. If you testify that he was keeping to the limit he will probably be released. What right has he to expect you to testify in his favour?

Lying in court makes nonsense of the rule of law and would deprive us of justice. It is in fact perjury. On the other hand a friend is a friend. It was mistake and he needs you. Should your friend be jailed for your scruples? The results are set out below. On an issue that features religion not at all, the eight leading nations that would refuse to lie in court are all mainly Protestant, with Calvinist Switzerland heading the lot. The middle group is mostly Catholic and Muslim. Most of the respondents who would support close friends are Confucian, Greek Orthodox or Catholic.

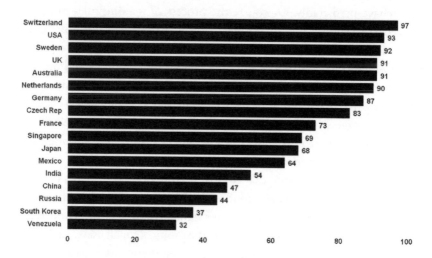

Figure 1.1 My friend has some or no right and I would not testify in his/her favour

While ninety-three per cent of all American respondents would tell the truth and ninety-two per cent from the UK, with British influenced Australia and New Zealand close behind, only forty-four per cent of Chinese would (see Chapter 4) and only thirty-three per cent of Koreans, two very successful economies.

How might a culture high on universalism behave? It would dominate most international bodies and associations, refer to itself as a New World, insist that its own beliefs were self-evidently and universally true and that everyone should obey them. It might set up an International Court of Justice at The Hague. It would institute and win most of the Nobel Prizes for science, especially for economics which is a codification of its own cultural beliefs yet certainly has some validity. It might urge nations to modernize, by which it meant following its own practices.

The computers, Internet, software it had developed would cover most of the world. It would set up the World Trade Organization and feature World Trade Centres and oblige much of the world to speak English. It would dominate and try to regulate global finance. It would be the reserve currency for much of the world and huge swathes of trade would be denominated in dollars. Its film and entertainment would sell across the globe. Its Common Law tradition would be greatly admired. It would symbolize democracy and parliaments which purport to embody freedom and human rights. The United Nations would have its HQ there. It would see itself as the guarantor of world order, willing to intervene to set things right. It would insist that its deadly weaponry was a force for peace and was in the interests of all concerned. On principle, it would steadfastly refuse to ransom captured hostages, despite the threat or reality of their execution, in the belief that if you give way to extortion more innocents will be taken hostage. The agony of the particular captive is secondary.

Indeed different industries have respondents which are more or less concerned with the values of universalism. Industries high in universalism are, as we might expect, those of the leading Protestant countries which originally created them, banking, computing, insurance, retailing, etc. Cheapness is a near universal value since no one wants to pay more than necessary. Size and scale tend to bring down prices so some of the largest corporations in the world, wealthier than whole nations, are American, British, Swiss, Scandinavian, etc. Retailing in the manner of Wal-Mart tends to universalism since tens of thousands of products dissolve into common money transactions and obey the rules of mathematics. There is no doubt that universalism is a massive competitive advantage and we should never abandon it.

2. Individuality preferred to community

An essential part of early Protestantism was that each person approached God as an individual supplicant. Just as the individual could read his Bible to learn God's will without going through priests and congregations so the individual was solely responsible for the correctness of his own reading and for his subsequent conduct. As Kipling put it, 'the sins that we do by two and two we pay for one by one'. In Bunyan's *Pilgrim's Progress,* a seventeenth-century book then second only to the Bible in its popularity, the protagonist, Christian, shook off his imploring wife and children and left his house shouting, 'Salvation I will have salvation!' and set out on a lone pilgrimage. What happened to his family is not revealed, although Mr Obstinate follows him and begs him to return, he is but one of the temptations Christian meets along the way, which include Worldly Wiseman, Sloth, Simple, Presumption, Formality, Hypocrisy, Timorous and Legality, villains all. Christian treads his lonely path, despite all beguilement, until he reaches the Celestial City. The very word Protestant comes from individual protest and as Martin Luther put it, 'No man should do ought against conscience. Here stand I. I cannot do otherwise.'

Yet the case for individualism is powerful, whatever might be its religious origins and their early quirks. It has elevated humanity to an amazing degree. We will look at its effect on the idea of progress, on creativity and innovation, on the self-fulfilment of human aspiration, on monitoring the vitality of societies, on the effectiveness of individual dissent and finally on the stark realism of human self-interest. We will see that it has propelled economies to the forefront.

Bunyan's book was not called *Pilgrim's Progress* for nothing. The whole idea of progress as a lone journey through life and its myriad distractions has its popular origins here. 'There's no discouragement can make him once relent/ His first avowed intent to be a pilgrim,' was Bunyan's hymn, full of 'hob-goblins and foul fiends' prepared to 'daunt his spirit' given a chance. Note that the Puritan saint was predestined for salvation *from the start,* provided of course that he acted out his destiny. Hence, those around him were not to be trusted and were probably damned. God's agent on earth must complete his journey and reach his destination.[2]

More important perhaps are the sources of creativity. We are creative when two or more pieces of information are joined within our minds in ways that are new, meaningful and valuable. These pieces may have been known for years and been taught to the individual. What is new and creative are not the elements themselves but their artful *combination.*[3] It is this that makes the arguments between freedom and determination so tiresome. *The pieces determine us but their combination frees us from this determination.* What passes through an individual mind can be transformed for ever in its passage. The fact that milkmaids rarely if ever got smallpox was known; that the milder disease cowpox, which they were exposed to and often contracted, was an immunizing agent against smallpox was a medical discovery.

2. For a wonderfully written description of the Puritan temperament see Michael Walzer, *The Revolution of the Saints,* Cambridge, Mass: Harvard University Press, 1965. I am also indebted to conversations with George Lodge, then professor at Harvard Business School for some of Bunyan's more bizarre writings.

3. We know of no better description than that of Arthur Koestler in *The Act of Creation* New York: Macmillan, 1964 and London: Hutchinson, 1976.

This putting of two and two together occurs in the minds of *individuals* and only there. Even if the bits and pieces came from outside their *combination* comes from playing with concepts, aligning and realigning them, pondering upon them and reflecting, then feeling a rush of growing excitement and finally coming up with a new synthesis. The brain cells communicate with each other *inside* a single person better and more artfully than in public discussion, although such discussions can supply the pieces. Thanks to half-conscious processes, our brains mull over these puzzles even in our rest or sleep, which is why Archimedes jumped out of his bath as the water rose around his body. Now he knew how to estimate the volume of the king's crown and determine whether the silver was pure![4]

Without listening to every individual, however strange and different from ourselves that person might be, creativity cannot become innovative and be shared with customers. Without allowing the creative person to *act* on what they have conceived nothing new can emerge. In order to create we have to take the disputes of society into our own souls and let these wrestle within us. 'I will not cease from *mental* fight nor shall my sword sleep in my hand till we have built Jerusalem…' wrote William Blake. Note that the 'fight' was inside him, amid values he believed were positives and complements if he could but work out their relationships. Brilliant images and poems emerged from his work.

A third vital role for individuals is that human beings learn, develop and grow their powers over time. There is no constant 'unit of labour' so beloved by economists. Individuals who are empowered, trained, nurtured and educated show increasing competence and can be transformed by their experiences. Their productivity can soar. They can both generate new ideas and realize them. They can dream and awaken, aspire and excel. We know from research by David McClelland that high-achieving individuals have an abundance of *achievement fantasies* which they proceed to act out. The more elaborate the fantasies, the greater the achievements. They do *not* do this for extra money, which affects them not at all, but to realize their visions of themselves.[5]

The roster of great American entrepreneurs speaks for itself: Rockefeller, Vassar, Stanford, Vanderbilt, Carnegie, Mellon, Ford, Getty, Roebuck, Birdseye, Kellogg, Armour and Grace among others. What characterizes these people is *not* their selfishness, but that both their self-aggrandizement and their later generosity were individual paths freely chosen. If they joined themselves to their nations, and all of them did, this was because they alone decided to do

4. Koestler, *The Act of Creation.*
5. David McClelland, *The Achieving Society*, Princeton: Van Nostrand, 1961, p. 203.

so. They were testaments to their own individuality. *The Gospel of Wealth* was Carnegie's attempt to get people to emulate him, a hand-up not a hand-out. It remains true that every worthwhile idea must be tested in action to assess its worth. 'The man who dies rich dies in disgrace,' stated Andrew Carnegie. He endowed more than one thousand public libraries. More recently the likes of Steve Jobs, Jeff Bezos, Mark Zuckerberg, Richard Branson, Anita Roddick and Elon Musk have revealed that this trend continues.

A fourth aspect of individualism is the absolute necessity for personal dissent within any community. Members of a group like to remain agreeable. It makes day-to-day living relaxing and serene. When someone disagrees and speaks out things get tense and anxious. Propriety is disturbed. Those who disagree often hide this for fear of making trouble and embarrassing others. Privately they may be appalled but do not want to make a scene and risk their acceptance by colleagues. What can they do in any case?

But there comes a moment when the most independent person speaks out and awakens the private doubts of millions, as did Martin Luther when he hammered his ninety-five theses on the church door. Nearly all those we admire were such persons: Socrates, Luther, Calvin, Sir Thomas More, William Wilberforce, Henry David Thoreau, Mahatma Gandhi, Martin Luther King, Dr Spock, Daniel Ellsberg, Desmond Tutu, and Nelson Mandela; all said out loud what their followers were thinking and were widely acclaimed for their courage. Even a small boy can see that the emperor is naked so it is unwise to ignore the least of us. Without dissent from individuals communities can commit atrocious acts. As Socrates pointed out the gadfly keeps the ox awake. His reproach rings down the centuries:

> But why do you who are citizens of this great and mighty nation care so much about laying up the greatest amount of money and honour and reputation and so little about wisdom and truth and the greatest improvement of the soul?... I do nothing but go about persuading you all, young and old, not to give care for your persons or your properties but firstly and chiefly to care about the greatest improvement of the soul. I tell that virtue is not given by money but that from virtue come money and every other good of man. If this is the doctrine that corrupts the youth then my influence is ruinous indeed. But know that I never change my ways, not if I have to die a thousand times.[6]

6.   Plato, *The Apology*, available at www.bartelby.com/2/1/1.htlm

We come last to the role of self-interest in an economy. We shall have some criticism of its excess in the next chapter. But suffice it to say that when Adam Smith first proclaimed it, its truth and power were liberating. The urban bourgeoisie was gradually gaining against the landed gentry and their tenanted estates, which they preserved as their duty to the public good. That they were looking out primarily for themselves had to be said loudly and clearly to cut through the hypocrisy of those times. They were rich not on account of what they did but on account of what they owned. Tenants working on their estates were in lifelong subjugation for no better reason than that the land was not theirs. Democracy, such as it was at that time, answered to property not to people.

That we are all to some extent self-seeking and self-preserving is something attested to by how our nervous systems react to crises, our heart and breathing rate increases, and we get sweaty. It is foolish to pretend otherwise. We can help others only if we look after ourselves. We have Adam Smith to thank for this sobering realization. We also need a concept of private property to protect the places we occupy. This is included in the notion of freedom to which much of the world now resonates, especially where this is short of being attained. Ask the demonstrators in the streets of Cairo. To test the allegiance of different cultures to freedom vs. concern for others we asked the following question:

> Two people were discussing their ideas of what it means to work to improve the quality of their lives. One said, 'Individuals work to get as much freedom as possible and to maximize the opportunity to develop themselves.' The other said, 'If individuals continuously take care of the needs of their fellow human beings everyone's quality of life will improve.'[7]

The scores for various nations are set out in Figure 1.2. We see that Israel and the same set of Protestant nations tend to head the advocates of freedom. Russia is tenth, with Catholic, Muslim and Confucian nations preferring dedication to others. France is prominent in this preference as are China and Singapore. India, Hindu by religion, is also communitarian rather than individualist. We can understand why Germany, Italy and France are more committed to the European Union than the UK, which prefers a looser arrangement of free-trading. Over the thirty years we have been posing this question individualism-as-freedom has gained ground.

7.   See Fons Trompenaars and Charles Hampden-Turner, *Riding the Waves of Culture*, Chicago: McGraw Hill, 1998.

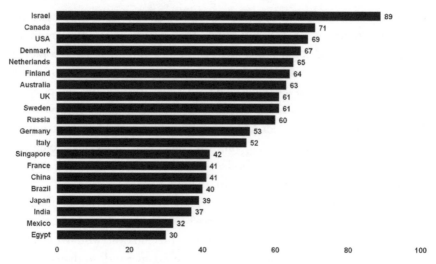

Figure 1.2 Who opts for 'as much freedom as possible'?

We might also ask whether one kind of industry offers more freedom than another and so might be preferred by citizens of more individualistic nations. Unsurprisingly, individualist industries are headed by electronics, software, banking, investment, entertainment, media, insurance and consumer products. That Wall Street and the City dominate financial services is not that surprising, and neither is their leadership of the digital revolution.

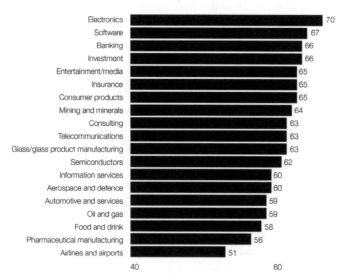

Figure 1.3 Individualism vs communitarianism by industry

3. Specific analysis preferred to diffuse, whole relationships

A third major cultural preference has to do with how we handle complex phenomena. Do we reduce these to specific bits and pieces by means of analysis, or do we relate events and people into whole constructions? Do we break down phenomena into data or build-up phenomena into patterns and contexts? Once again Protestantism has had a profound influence. It abhorred idolatry or images. It preferred the lean, the spare, the shorn, the parsimonious, the words of the sermon, rather than the ambience of the service. Early Protestants were christened according to the specific value they personified, like 'Flee Fornication'. Calvin preached the Doctrine of the Objective Word, claiming that the words of the Bible resembled objective things.[8]

Specificity was also very much the world of Sir Isaac Newton, shorn of doctrine, superstition and all belief that could not be verified by observation or instruments, he purged science of excess baggage and used scepticism as a scythe or a razor. The real world was totally apart from our beliefs, out there in the dead, freezing void of space; a universe of stellar objects utterly indifferent to our existence, our wants or our beliefs.

The Anglo-American business model is overwhelmingly specific and data-driven. We gather as many facts as we can, analyse these statistically and then act upon these indicators. It is considered objective to reduce appearances to facts, or hundreds of small atoms or units and examine these in detail. This data is thought to precede decisions, policies or strategies. Such facts supposedly guard against bias or prejudice, from excuses and from window dressing.

If we listen to Western managers and their words this orientation to specificity is most pronounced. They refer to hard facts, the numbers, the bottom line, head-hunting, brain drains or gains, databases, value-capture, checklists of items, multiple choice questionnaires, the small print, doing it by the book, benchmarks, bullet points, piece-work incentives, jobs, tasks, and units of labour, tips, bonuses and pay-for-performance. They refer to 'firing' people as if they were bullets, or 'letting them go' as if they sought freedom. They speak of financial products, 'keeping your word'(singular), human rights, human resources, financial analysts, human rights as bits of personal property, entitlements, forecasts, projections, PowerPoint, getting to the point, job descriptions, tasks, the key to the executive washroom, perks (prerequisites), share options, digitalization, computing, and so on. Older generations called 'a spade a spade' and 'got down to brass tacks' and did not 'beat around the bush'.

8. Walzer, *The Revolution of the Saints*.

Specificity has some obvious advantages if you seek to create wealth and run a company. Numbers and accountants keep track of the solvency of the organization using the very specific language of mathematics. It is essential to keep track of the revenues, the costs and the profits and only abstract digits can do this. Specific cultures would be more likely to invent computers, calculators and software programmed via algorithms. Since a machine is the sum-of-its-parts working together, specific cultures were much more likely to inaugurate the Machine Age, and did in fact do so. If the machine goes wrong you take it to pieces, replace the defective part and reassemble.

Specificity has other important if less obvious advantages. It is better at making fine yet crucial distinctions between image and reality, map and territory, words and things, persons and their performances. Hence a person criticizing your idea as 'crazy' is not trying to get you certified insane. Smart people can have foolish ideas on occasion. Specific cultures make fewer *ad hominem* attacks, conflating the message with the messenger. They do not regard a cartoon image of the prophet as a direct assault on a god, but a joke on some of those who worship him. The ability to make such distinctions may be essential to democracy itself, which consists of verbal conflict in a theatrical mode before an audience of voters. The angry rejection of policies is not to be confused with a physical attack on the author of that policy. The authors are assumed to be doing the best they could, however mistaken their policies might be.[9]

We measured specific vs. diffuse orientations by asking managers about their image of the organization. The first item is full of specific terms which we have italicized for the sake of clarity, while the second item uses diffuse terms which we have also italicized. The original questions had no emphases.

1. One way is to see a company as performing certain *functions* and *tasks* in an efficient way. People are hired to perform these functions with the help of *machines* and other *equipment*. They are *paid* for the tasks they perform.
2. A second way is to see a company as a group of people working *together*. They have *social relations* with other people and with the *organization*. The functioning is dependent on those relations.

9. For a longer and illustrated account of the Specific-Diffuse dimension see Charles Hampden-Turner and Fons Trompenaars, *Building Cross-Cultural Competence,* Chichester: John Wiley, 2000 pp. 123–159.

Once again a group of mostly Protestant nations reveal the highest levels of specificity, with the USA and the UK near the top. Note that diffuse cultures can prosper too, namely Singapore, South Korea and China. Switzerland and Germany are also more diffuse than other European cultures while being strong economies.

Table 1.1 Preference for specific over diffuse ways of thinking

Nation	% preferring specific
USA	91
Netherlands	86
UK	83
Canada	72
Australia	69
Finland	65
Sweden	64
Turkey	62
Belgium	58
Germany	54
France	51
Denmark	50
Malaysia	41
Singapore	38
South Korea	27
Japan	25
Indonesia	23
China	17

Here we can see that the differences are very large, with the response from the USA being five times that of China, with some very diffuse nations performing well economically. The top seven nations are all Protestant, once again, with Confucian nations all diffuse and Catholics in the middle.

A difference which causes endless problems is the way we greet strangers when travelling in a country foreign to ourselves. The Anglo-American data-driven model has us starting with the purpose of our meeting, which is to venture jointly. We therefore come with figures, projections, PowerPoint presentations and logical linear presentations which establish that only a fool would fail to see the profit potential here. Our hard sell presents the facts which guide us and should guide them in their decision to go into business with us. All this is very sensible and very objective. We should both be enthusiastic about the prospects for our joint enterprise. Whether we like each other or not is secondary to whether we should do business, which if successful would probably lead to our liking one another anyway. We want them to express their interest promptly so that we can see other prospects on this same trip. The idea is to make the best use of time.

Alas, diffuse nations approach this issue the other way around. The scarcity is of those you like and those you can trust. They want to know all about us *apart from business* since profits can make people greedy and deceptive leading to a bending of the truth. They have no intention of getting hooked on gain before they have decided whether to believe us. They will talk about things *other* than business and bordering on irrelevance just to try to understand our characters. They are *also* interested in saving time and for that reason they do not want to get engaged with a rogue and discover this four years from now. Our apparent hurry and impatience is to them a bad sign.

In Figure 1.4 the Anglo-American managers start in the middle with specifics and then circle outwards. The East Asians start at the outer rim and slowly circle inwards to 'the point' while the Anglo-Americans look at their watches![10]

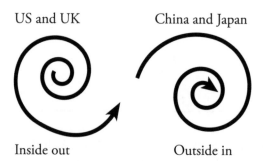

US and UK   China and Japan

Inside out   Outside in

Figure 1.4 The best way of getting to know a stranger. Do you first 'come to point' and present your proposition or do you first establish a diffuse relationship?

10.   Hampden-Turner and Trompenaars, *Building Cross-Cultural Competence*, p. 157.

4. Status by achievement in preference to status by ascription

There are essentially two ways of awarding status within a culture. In accordance with what people have actually *done* and their degree of success in essaying this, and in accordance to who and what people *are*. For example, they could be white, male, good-looking, come from a good, upper-class family and hold a position in a company that promises much. Ascriptions *can* be racist and classist but not necessarily so. Someone may be considered to have great potential despite not yet having excelled. That our three highest scoring nations on achievement are all immigrant nations is not surprising. When you migrate you often leave family, friends, homes and special relationships behind you. If your neighbour is Jewish and your landlord Estonian neither will care that you come from a 'prominent family in Kent'. In a land of strangers you are defined by what you *do*, not where you come from. You cannot rely on being liked, you must make yourself useful. You may be first among your fellow ethnics if you can engage effectively with the larger culture.

The early Puritans believed in *justification through works*. While God's elect had been chosen in advance and did not need to perform in theory, that they *had* been elected from the beginning was proved and justified by what they achieved in building God's earthly Kingdom here and now. Only visible successes could allay the fear that the call you thought you heard might be some other noise. Many Americans believe they must get an 'even break' and then 'make it'. Horatio Alger went from rags to riches and as an orphan had no one to thank but himself, so that achievement fuses with individualism. We see achievement celebrated in ticker-tape parades, the Hall of Fame, popularity contests in schools, Miss America, grades, the flag planted at Iwo Jima, Nobel Prizes, the man-of-the-match, presidential elections, high-flyers, employee of the month, management-by-objectives, up-or-out promotions. According to this view we should have divine discontent, always wanting to do better and never being satisfied with what we have. 'When the going gets tough, the tough get going.'

America's strong orientation to rules has turned much of the society into so many games played on 'level playing fields' with vigorous rivals in competition with one another. Achievement is easier to grasp where a contest has been clearly defined and has many fans in attendance. A victorious football team will be known to millions. Achievement also appeals to those seeking riches. How much someone is 'worth' becomes a source of comparison. It is clearly in the interests of the corporation that their best employees should rise to positions of greatest influence and their less successful brethren should leave.

We seek a culture of winners and star-players.

The USA, Australia, Canada and New Zealand were largely peopled by immigrants from Great Britain who found a huge canvas of near deserted plains on which its people could build monuments to their own industry which scraped the sky. Roads, bridges, tunnels, cities and factories dotted the landscape, where formerly there were only woods and fields. Such cultures would confer status on their achievers, which is what we find. In Figure 1.5 we show those who *rejected* the proposition that you should 'think and act in the way that suits you, even if you don't get things done'.[11]

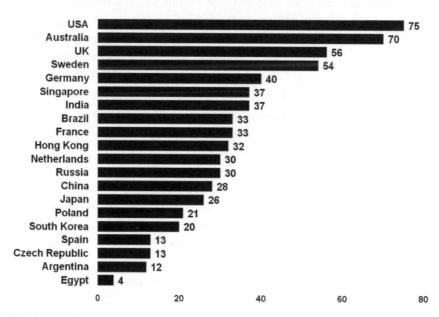

Figure 1.5 Those rejecting 'act in the way that suits you even if you don't get things done'

Interestingly enough, only four nations score above fifty per cent, and the first two of these are immigrant nations, Perhaps the reason only the USA, Canada, Australia and the UK score fifty per cent or above is that status by achievement is not the choice of most countries. Perhaps they feel that they are too different to be rank ordered and that what people do is incomparable.

11. The Trompenaars Hampden-Turner database is periodically up-dated. These are the 2015 figures, available from KPMG Amsterdam.

5. Inner-directed in preference to outer-directed

This dimension might seem similar to individualism but is crucially different. It inquires as to what drives us and from what point we are driven. Does virtue come from *inside* us and sally forth into the world, or does it come from *outside*, from the beauty of nature or from the needs of fellow human beings to which we must respond? Are we inner-directed with a locus of control inside us or outer-directed with the locus of control outside us? France is an interesting case because it is more communal than individual, yet its drives come very much from the souls within people. Historically, the French have formed protest groups, often enraged ones, which have surged out onto the streets with the aim of altering the status quo.

Yet again, the origins of much, if not all, inner-direction are Protestant. God elects his saints. They read their Bibles with objective accuracy and strongly object to a sinful world at odds with scripture and their own convictions. As God's agents on earth they act on his authority. In 'Sonnet 12' Milton expressed his scorn for his critics:

> I did but prompt the age to quit their clogs
> By the known rules of ancient liberty,
> When strait a barbarous noise environs me
> Of owls and cuckoos, asses, apes and dogs.

William Earnest Henley in *Poems of the Empire* spoke of his own 'unconquerable soul' proclaiming himself 'master of my fate' and 'captain of my soul'.

An interesting contrast is between two generals Alexander the Great, symbolizing inner-direction, and Sun Tzu, representing outer direction, both of whom won fame but by contrasting means. Alexander conquered the known world to his east and got as far as India. Sun Tzu wrote *The Art of War.* We know little of his actual feats although his book is a classic. While Alexander pushed opponents off the battlefield with his phalanx of pointed spears, Sun Tzu did everything by indirection, altering the flow of rivers, setting fires in his opponents' camp at night, intimidating his enemies by misinformation, triggering landslides, and never being predictable. He argued that a battle must be won before it starts and wars must be as short as possible or there is too little for the winning side to gain![12]

How Americans became inner-directed is hardly a mystery. Theirs was an 'errand into the wilderness' in which they left the only homes they had ever

---

12. Hampden-Turner and Trompenaars, *Building Cross-Cultural Competence,* p. 241.

known and crossed an ocean to an unknown land. Once arrived there were vast treks westwards and incredible riches to be harvested including free land, one million buffalo that had never see a gun, an endless stream of settlers to whom to sell produce and thousands of acres of fertile farmland. There may never before or since have been so many celestial cities for the taking, all culminating in the twentieth century in the new frontier of space. This is what Harold Evans called the American Century.[13] American business schools extolled the 'mastery' of business administration, a pattern emulated across the globe.

Where two cultures meet, one very sure of its rightness and one used to yielding to forces outside, then there is little doubt which will prevail over the other when they first meet. In their mutual anxiety one will shout orders, discharge weapons and try to dominate and the other will try to pacify, temporize and ultimately submit to dictation. It helps of course if you arrive in ships with guns. But that Britain became an imperial power and the US dominates the world commercially is not perhaps surprising. That both of them educate much of the world and hundreds of thousands come as students to study in both countries is not surprising either. We profess our knowledge and convictions loudly.

The clearest evidence of inner-direction comes from the huge preponderance of storytelling and novel writing in the English language and similar dominance of film in the case of Hollywood and theatre in the case of London, where there are more productions than in most of Europe combined. Any novel is narrated by the 'I' that runs through it. Novels are the inwardly generated experiences of the individual passing through serial dilemmas or crises and trying to cope with them. They ask, like Dickens in *David Copperfield*, whether the protagonist can be 'the hero of my own life'. The answer is generally 'yes'. Free enterprise may be considered an unfolding narrative as biographies of Nikola Tesla, Bill Gates, Steve Jobs, Richard Branson, Anita Roddick and Jack Welch attest. History, literally 'his story', is also a strong Western legacy to the world, assuming as it does that people seek to master events by conscious reasoning based on the Enlightenment and often succeed in doing so. Again the pilgrim's journey is very much the template for such narratives.

To test the level of inner-direction we asked respondents for agreement with the statement, 'What happens to me is entirely my own doing.' Inner-directed people dismiss anything to do with luck and insist they will create their own opportunities through sheer determination.

---

13.   Harold Evans and Gail Buckland, *The American Century*, London: Jonathan Cape, 2000.

Once again the US and the UK are to the forefront accepting responsibility for their own success or the lack of it. Th Protestantism and Judaism is again in evidence, as it was in ii They share in rejecting idolatry.

With enough determination they can gain their objectives. W Frank Sinatra 'doing it my way', Gene Kelly building a 'stairway to paradise with a new step every day', Martin Luther King and 'I have a dream', or John Kennedy and his *Profiles in Courage,* inner-directed cultures march on undaunted, guided by an inner light of soul or conscience.

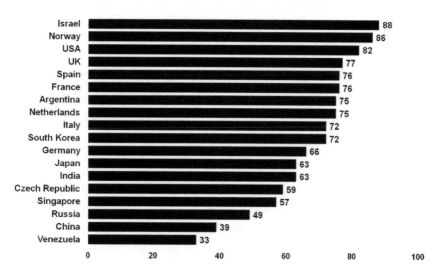

Figure 1.6 Those agreeing that 'What happens to me is my own doing.'

6. Sequential-linear is preferred to synchronic-circular

A legacy of the Enlightenment is our linear-rational approach to the world. We approach issues in a straight line. We use logical means to secure the ends we seek. We do one thing at a time in strict sequences. In the face of superstition and supposition we say 'show me!' and if we cannot predict and control the subsequent events they are consigned to happenstance or accident. Richard Lewis, a fellow cross-cultural researcher, coined the phrase, 'linear-active and data driven' to describe the approach of Great Britain, North America, Northwest Europe, Australia and New Zealand. He compared this to the 'circular-listening and reactive mode' of China and much of East Asia.[14]

14. Richard D. Lewis, *When Cultures Collide*, London: Nicholas Brealey, 1996, pp. 36–51.

Linear cultures tend to do one thing at a time, in sequence and by successive steps. These are often scheduled in advance and people who are late or miss appointments lose us money and cause offence. Puritans felt short of time. God's Kingdom had to be built in the relatively short life-spans of that age. As Andrew Marvell, the Puritan poet, complained in his 'To His Coy Mistress', 'Had we but world enough and time, this coyness, lady, were no crime ... But at my back I always hear Time's winged chariot hurrying near.' He needed to get into her knickers speedily before they were both dead. Other cultures see time as synchronized. Important people are waited upon so that *their* time is made the best of and others await their pleasure. Time is circular and re-occurring. Toyota automobiles are made just-in-time, while Americans want to 'make a quick buck'. The quicker they make it the more bucks can be made. Wristwatches show time both in circular and serial modes.

We measured the two approaches to time by asking respondents to draw circles representing past, present and future. Linear-sequential cultures drew them like successive footsteps 'in the sands of time' as Longfellow put it. Synchronous cultures drew them in the manner of gear-wheels or even telescoped. They saw past and future as within the present or interacting with it. Time and motion studies introduced by Frederick Winslow Taylor are typical of a linear-sequential culture. The faster the assembly line moves the more will be produced in the shortest possible time. 'Time is money', Benjamin Franklin explained. In the *Pyjama Game*, a Broadway musical and film, the workers sing about 'racing with the clock, when your backs all ache and your fingers break and your constitution isn't made of rock.' Rudyard Kipling urged those aspiring to manhood, to 'Fill each unforgiving minute with sixty seconds worth of distance run.' Do this and 'You'll be a man my son!' No wonder Westerners are in such a hurry, dashing from one meeting to another. Our whole industrial system appears to have been created in frantic haste by sequential cultures.

In both Greek mythology and Chinese tradition there are two versions of time. Chronos, also known as Father Time, with an hour glass to measure our years and a scythe to cut us down, represents linear and sequential time. Kairos, the god of time and opportunity, represents 'the idea whose time has come', the synchrony of supply with demand, or perfect timing.[15] The Chinese think of time as both a thread (*ji*) and as a circular track (*li*). Well-known expressions speak of both concepts: 'Time and tide wait for no man', 'as time

15. Elliott Jacques is brilliant on the subject, see *The Form of Time,* New York: Crane Russak, 1982.

goes by', 'procrastination is the thief of time', 'never put off till tomorrow' are all to do with sequential time. 'Many happy returns of the day', 'there is a tide in the affairs of men, which taken in the flood leads on' and 'what goes around comes around' are all to do with synchronous time.

Cultures that borrow from both East and West have fascinating admixtures. One author remembers buying a book at an airport shop in Singapore. The woman at the check-out desk took his credit card and attended to the person behind him in the line, scanning the barcode on her product. The author, used to a sequential culture, complained that the store employee had not yet finished serving him. But of course she was right. It took twenty to twenty-five seconds for his credit card to be validated and many of us had a plane to catch. She was doing more by allowing the serving of successive customers to *overlap with one another*, using both sequential and synchronous systems.

We are now in a position to summarize all six cultural preferences or biases in the Anglo-American model of wealth creation outlined in this chapter. A set of *codified rules of universal validity* (1) are employed by the innovative *individual* (2) driven by *specific analytical data* (3), so that s/he can *achieve* (4) goals by *inner-directed activity* (5) in a *straight-line sequence* (6) of means and ends. In preferring these values, less attention is paid to *particular people and circumstances* (1), to the *community or society* as a whole (2), to *diffuse relationships and whole patterns* (3), to the potential of value *ascribed to people* (4), to *outer-directed* responsiveness (5) and to *circular and synchronic approaches to time* (6).

We would be extremely foolish to abandon the values that have pushed us to the forefront of nations. America is once more the leader of all economies in the *World Competitiveness Report* issued by the IMD in Geneva. Both America and the UK seem to be recovering better from the recent recession than much of the European Union. It is in any case neither possible nor practicable to lay our own values aside. These are the foundations on which we build. Is everything, then, fine? Is God in his heaven and is all right with the world? Is there nothing that should concern us?

Our view is not that the values described in this chapter are wrong, far from it. They have served us well in the past and made us strong. The English-speaking developed economies are the envy of much of the world and have trouble accommodating all those who wish to live among us. It is our view that however *necessary* our cultural preferences were to past successes, these are no longer *sufficient* today in a changing, multi-polar world. They need to be qualified by the values of other nations and by important subcultures *within* our own nations which are doing spectacularly well. Generally speaking, multiple perspectives are much better than single perspectives and the better we understand views at variance with our own the more effectively can we engage them.

For the truth is that every surviving culture on earth has insight into that part of the human condition that they must currently engage. We have neither the space nor the competence to assess them all, but we will be describing some cultures which have amazed the world with their proficiencies at creating wealth, far in excess of even the feats described in this chapter. Moreover these cultures are all learning from *us*, the West, at great speed. Might it not be wise to learn from *them*, lest all the information flow in one direction? Our problem lies less with the values we extol than with the values we neglect. It is the purpose of this book to bring those neglected values to the fore and argue that they do not negate what we believe, but augment our beliefs.

Research by the Harvard Business School professor Nitin Nohria looked at a sample of outstanding leaders and successful innovators and found that they *all shared the capacity to switch from one cultural context to another.*[16] It is not necessary that anyone agrees with the views of other cultures. There may be genuine objections to doing so, but it is necessary at least to understand others if you are to engage with them effectively. This is what we aim to do in the pages which follow. We will be introducing alternative ways of thinking about wealth creation, yet we hope to show that these are fully compatible with our existing competitive advantages. We simply need to extend the breadth of our understanding and appreciation to encompass diverse points of view. We only fully discover ourselves when we encounter a different reference point. Because a lot of our business knowledge is codified other nations can learn from us at great speed. But since their knowledge is far more elusive and contextual we are not learning from them to anything like the same extent.

There is an additional point. The effectiveness of values and cultures depends very much upon the environment they encounter and over the years this environment has been changing. Successful universalism relies on the power to make your rules stick. The most successful empire-building individuals were rather larger than life, like the British and American tycoons and great entrepreneurs. The super-analysts and outstanding achievers need adoring crowds and the World Series as their platform. Inner-directed champions of new visions need vast amounts of media exposure and spiritual forcefulness on a global scale. But we have been moving to a post-colonial,

16. Nitin Nohria, *Handbook of Leadership Theory and Practice*, Boston: Harvard Business School Press, 2010.

post-capitalist, post-modernist world in which there are not just a handful of prime movers but many different moves and many relative values in a fragile ecological balance.

The values that contrast with those of the West, the many exceptions to the rule, the need of individuals to contribute to a consensus and to community, the capacity to see changing patterns and forge improved relationships, the acceptance of who people are, the ability to respond to outside shocks and disturbances and adapt yourself, the capacity to synchronize your own efforts with the social and natural environment, have all come to the fore only in recent years. These other values may be more relevant to the turmoil, the complexity, the 'white water', the plurality and radically decentralized forces of this emerging planet. We all must ride on the waves of culture and those insisting on making a big splash may swamp each other by their efforts.

CHAPTER 2

Nothing to excess: Can a once-winning combination be over-played?

At a party given by a billionaire on Shelter Island, Kurt Vonnegut informs his pal, Joseph Heller, that their host, a hedge fund manager, had made more money in a single day than Heller had made from his wildly popular novel *Catch-22* over its whole history. Heller responds.
'Yes but I have something he will never have ... enough.'[1]

Here we will explore one of the oldest ideas in the world, although contemporary policy appears to have forgotten it. Is it possible that a value expressed strongly at an early stage leads to triumph, while the *same* value expressed even more forcefully at a later stage leads to disaster because the once-winning combination has been overplayed? Might this be the reason why triumph turns to *catastrophe*, literally a 'downturn in the fortunes of the hero', a denouement borrowed from classical Greek tragedy? At the base of the statue of Athena in the Parthenon was inscribed the word *sophrosyne* which is sometimes defined in English as prudence, temperance or 'nothing to excess'. Are there characteristics of our values which are excessive and unbalanced? Can *more* lead to disaster?

In the Greek myth of the House of Thebes, King Labdakos was called after his own lameness. His son Laius had a name meaning 'left-sided',

---

1. Quoted by John C. Bogle in *Enough: True Measures of Money, Business and Life*, Hoboken, NJ: John Wiley, 2009, p. 244.

while his son Oedipus was named after his 'swollen foot'. All three walked with an uneven gait, the symbol of values out of balance.[2] We saw in the Introduction that values come in contrasting pairs: rules and exceptions, individualism and communitarianism, specific parts and diffuse wholes. Each value *needs* its contrast. It is exceptions that test rules, parts that constitute wholes, individuals that serve communities. What seems to happen when a value becomes excessive and is overplayed is that it *loses touch with its contrast.* Rules start to ignore exceptions and deteriorate sharply. Individuals disown the community in which they are rooted and run amok and parts lose sight of the whole to which they belong and that whole no longer comprehends them. What excess does is *sever the connection* between values so they behave increasingly like loose cannons.[3]

Up to this point we have largely admired the Anglo-American model of capitalism. We do this in part because it has worked well over the centuries and deserves respect and because much of the world has emulated our leadership. We also employ a methodology called Appreciative Inquiry which argues that you can only truly comprehend a culture which you are prepared to join and identify with.[4] You may even get better and fairer criticisms of that culture from those who trust and befriend you. Unless you suspend judgement for a while and join those you are studying you cannot know what it's like to be in their shoes. We will here be examining values dominant in the West to ask how exaggerated forms might actually destroy wealth rather than create it. How can trillions of dollars just disappear if they were not ephemeral in the first place? How does so much money suddenly dissolve into nothing? Why the relentless booms and busts? We will begin with a hard look at economic rationality itself. Is there a flaw?

2.   See Claude Levi-Strauss, *Structural Anthropology*, London: Penguin, 1979, p. 51–57.

3.   We derive the notion of values splitting from Gregory Bateson in *Steps to an Ecology of Mind*, New York: Ballantine, 1974. He called it 'schizmogenesis', the growing split in the structure of ideas. Two normally complementary values like being refined and being crude excite one another to extremes, so that the more Blanche DuBois behaves with the refined sensibility of a lady the cruder and rougher Stanley Kowalski, a labourer becomes, culminating in her rape in *A Streetcar named Desire*. One value provokes its opposite as each character defines the other as inferior by playing on their strong suit. Blanche is socially superior, Stan physically superior.

4.   Appreciative Inquiry was created at Case Western Reserve University by David Cooperrider. See D.L. Cooperrider, D. Whitney and J. M. Bedford Stavros, *The Appreciative Inquiry Handbook*, Heights OH: Lakeshore Publishers, 2008. You need to discover your respondent's context for thinking and appreciation makes this possible.

In the early 1980s Tom Peters and Robert Waterman wrote a best-selling business book *In Search of Excellence*. The opening chapter inveighs against the rational model of wealth creation, the process by which means were used to calculate ends and causes were mobilized to gain effects.[5] It was ill-suited to the attainment of excellence they claimed. Instead, we must *manage values.* They quoted with approval the American novelist F. Scott Fitzgerald who claimed that, 'The test of a first-rate intelligence is the ability to hold two opposed ideas in the mind at the same time, and still retain the ability to function. One should, for example, be able to see that things are hopeless and yet be determined to make them otherwise.'[6] This looks very like the integrity of contrasting values, hopeless and hopeful, helpless and determined. Can we somehow unite the contrasting values we cited in the Introduction?

Yet Peters and Waterman never explain what should replace rationality. Were they suggesting *irrationality?* Was their own book not intended to make sense? If we abandon reason, what else *is* there? We give Nobel Prizes to economists who insist that all persons in commerce rationally calculate their own self-interest. Is all this an illusion? Is an entire discipline mistaken? Do we know how wealth is actually created? Let us take a single rational sentence in the English language: 'Business is a means to the end of making money.' It is hard to deny this fact or to fault its reasoning. Business is the means and making money is the end. The more money a business makes the better. But consider another, equally rational, sentence: 'Money is a means to the end of making businesses.' Here, money is the means and businesses are the end. The more businesses money makes the better the outcome. So what we have are two *opposed* rationalities with no clue as to which should claim our greater allegiance. Choosing which of the two is a means and which is an end is a *cultural and value preference and not a matter of reason per se.* Moreover, following *either* one to the exclusion of the other is likely to unbalance us, as we shall see.

Suppose we were to follow the first logic that business is a means to make money, while neglecting the second. What would such a society look like? It would likely be awash with money, sloshing around in a world casino, not being invested in industry on sufficient scale but being used to trade and to speculate. Speculators who gained over others would have access to better information than their rivals and gains and losses would cancel out, creating no wealth overall. Some would have stakes large enough to raise the market

5.   See Introduction, Tom Peters and Robert Waterman, *In Search of Excellence,* New York: Harper and Row, 1982.

6.   The quote comes from F. Scott Fitzgerald's essay 'The Crack-Up'.

price and skew the odds in their own favour, whereupon they could sell at a profit. The big would gain but only at the expense of the small.

Multinational organizations would be sitting on cash-mountains which they could use to buy back their own shares which would spike in value allowing those with share options to cash in. There would be newspaper supplements called 'Money'. The *Financial Times* would for many years have just *one* management page on how wealth was created in the first place. Such a society would celebrate those already rich and publish Rich Lists while engineering, design or inventiveness would take a back seat. There would be much more emphasis on consuming than on producing since money can buy consumer goods. The obesity of our children would contrast with widespread malnourishment elsewhere. There would be a serious debt problem because people wanted more money in their pockets with which to buy things. They would borrow to spend immediately. Pay-day lenders would do a roaring trade with the desperately poor people as their victims.

Banking and finance would be pre-eminent in the economy because that was where the money was stored and those who handled large amounts would pay themselves lavishly. Their institutions would be deemed 'too big to fail', the rogues among them 'too big to jail' and the taxpayer would have to rescue them. The attitude to business would be short-term because people wanted their money right now and were unprepared to wait. Profits would be announced every quarter and announcements of redundancies would increase share prices because money was going from the pockets of those who worked to the pockets of those who owned. The 'bottom line' would be regarded as the distillation of all excellences. What an enterprise had done for shareholder enrichment would be regarded as the justification of all activities.

A major problem with this rational approach is that the end (money) far outweighs the means (work), so that gaining money *without* working at the press of a computer key is clearly preferable, as is inheriting the money, or renting out property and collecting rents. Since money is the ultimate end, short-cuts are permissible and scams abound, there is no good reason to trust that people will do anything except to help themselves to as much money as possible.

Note also the dual meaning of the word 'end'. It means both an objective and coming to an end. Once money has been obtained there is no reason to believe that people will do any more work since money has now been made. A nation that ceases it efforts to conduct business because its elite are so rich already is very unlikely to grow fast. Consuming will take priority over producing. There will be a vast surplus of imports over exports and debt over savings. Such a nation is abetting its own decline with its pristine rationality! Its main priority is not putting money *into* industry but get money *out* of it. Its response to recession or stagnation is to print *more* money and lower the cost of borrowing, the hair of the dog that bit it in the first place. Buy, buy, buy!

But suppose we were to choose the second rational sentence, 'Money is used to build and sustain industry.' This is similar to the previous logic only the other way around. This is the policy historically pursued by Germany and currently by China, South Korea and much of Southeast Asia. Germans learned to distrust money owing to hyper-inflation in the 1920s. Manufactured things are more tangible than money and getting people into factories gets them out of poverty. But this too can be carried too far. Some of the resources poured into export surpluses and heavy industry come out of consumers' pockets and there is some evidence that such priorities repress consumer demand. Producing ever more is not the whole purpose of our lives either! London is more fun than Frankfurt, as most single bankers will attest. Both linear rationalities tend to unbalance an economy, tilting it towards money above all, or towards industry above all. What we need is an alternative form of reasoning that manages these two contrasting aims.

Two forms of reasoning

What we are claiming is that there are two forms of reasoning. There is straight-line rational thinking with subject–verb–object, with means leading logically to ends, and there is *circular or systems thinking,* like a ship being steered through stormy seas by a helmsman. The first of these we call *technical reason.* The second we call *encompassing reason,* since it encompasses both sets of straight-line propositions into one loop. It sees supply as creating demand which then creates more supply in turn. It sees industry as creating money and money industry and so revolves for ever more.[7]

According to our view technical reasoning is *not* wrong and we should not abandon it, but it is *only half right* and such half-truths can destroy wealth rather than create it. In the Ancient Greek cosmology there was only one imperfect god, Hephaestus, blacksmith to the gods, the Olympian technician. He was the 'god who limped'. His gait, like that of Oedipus and his Theban forebears, was uneven. And this is what technical reason does: *it selectively*

---

7.   The terms 'technical' and 'encompassing' are taken from the twentieth-century theologian Paul Tillich, who in his classic *The Courage to Be* (New Haven: Yale University Press, 1952) was the first to make this distinction. See also his subsequent book The *Love, Power and Justice*, New York: Oxford University Press, 1958.

empowers parts of the human endowment while neglecting others. We can reach thousands on the Internet but those relationships may be fleeting, superficial, pornographic, predatory and often very cruel, even leading to suicides. We cannot see the tears of those we torment.

What this book urges is that those seeking to generate wealth *must learn to think in circles*. They must look economic decline squarely in the face and find the determination to reverse it, not just shaking down industry to make money but using money to nurture new industries. They must produce to consume and consume to produce. The capacity to create wealth lies in unifying these opposed rationalities. Nations growing slowly or not at all emphasize one kind of technical reason at the expense of another. Faster growing nations have achieved balances and reconciliations. Note that encompassing reason *includes* technical reason. It does not exclude it. It turns it from lines into arcs and thence into circles. Since each arc is rational the *combination* of the two arcs must be rational too. This is illustrated in Figure 2.1.

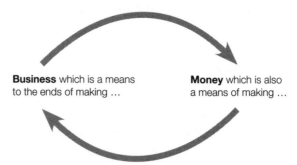

Figure 2.1 Industry and money as a virtuous circle

In this form of thinking, business and money get to be both means and ends. Neither is subordinated to the other. Is the loop above sufficient for our purposes? After all it recognizes that money is needed for reinvestment in industry. It may not be sufficient if money is given priority *over* business. It can be immaculately rational but still critically unbalanced. In the UK and the USA we are busy extracting *from* business as much money as we can. Suppose we extract too much? How would we know? When we see business as a mere instrument for money making we become more interested in harvesting than sowing. Equally rational is the statement 'money is a means to making business which is also a means of making money'. This puts business or industry in the driving street.

Does it matter which way around we think?[8] It depends on the existing balance in the culture. The UK, the USA and much of Europe needs to think much more about its industry and less about its money, while China probably needs to think more about its money and its huge levels of (over?) investment and less about industry. The art of wealth creation is to *get this balance right* and current growth figures suggest that China has it more nearly right than the West does. The fact that we have a loop or circle does not mean that the two 'handles' are equally effective. We need to strengthen whichever element of the two is weaker. Is there evidence that the UK, for one, is under-investing?

According to Martin Wolf, the *Financial Times'* associate editor and chief economics commentator, the Office of Budget Responsibility forecast that real investment would fall by 5.5 per cent in 2013[9] and the UK's current recovery is the consequence of saving less and spending more and is probably unsustainable. UK GDP per capita grew at an average 2.8 per cent a year from 1955 to 2007 but then declined to 1.4 per cent in the years thereafter. Not only has the UK lost seven years of growth but it only returned to its 2007 level in 2014; that is seven wasted years. Moreover wages have yet to rebound fully and only in late 2014 did they begin to fall below inflation. Nor will the UK return to its earlier growth trend, growth will average only two per cent. While unemployment is decreasing, so too is output per person hour; that is, we are working more but producing less and the effect will inevitably be felt in our wages.

Philip Collins, writing in *The Times*,[10] points to the fact that, in the first half of 2013, total capital investment was at its lowest for fifteen years. Business investment is at its lowest since figures were first collected in 1997. In a survey ranking nations in investment as a share of GDP, the UK came behind Mali and Guatemala in 159th place out of 173 nations. The Bank of England reported in that year that money was being withdrawn from deposit accounts at the fastest rate in four decades. Obviously, it no longer makes sense to save since interest rates are so low.

Richard Lambert, former director of the CBI, noted that British industry has a relatively low commitment to long-term investment and to research and innovation. Martin Wolf adds, 'a company like Rolls Royce could not be created today … the City would not dare'. Philip Stephens, writing in the *Financial*

8. Ellen McArthur Foundation has embarked on a campaign to make us think in circles, see their *Circular Economy Reports* 1–3.9.

9. Martin Wolf, *The Shifts and the Shocks: What we've learned and have still to learn*, London: Allen Lane, 2014.

10. Philip Collins, 'As usual we are addicted to the short term', *The Times*, 6 December 2013.

Times[11] has concluded that the big banks have essentially won. It is as if they enjoy a divine right: bankers' incomes have risen since 2008, while the taxpayer is still subsidizing the sector. And although JP Morgan has been fined up to US$ 20 billion no one has been indicted, much less convicted. Bankers' ability to choke off loans to industry put them in an impregnable position.

The dominance of banking and the ailing of much of the rest of the economy brings us back to what it means to create wealth – as opposed to making money, which is something else entirely. Wealth is something that enriches all the parties participating and the culture that gets this wrong will find that nothing else works as it should. Creating wealth requires us to first balance and then to reconcile money and industry and we do this by joining these into a circle. We will now consider the possibility that at least three of the six outstanding strengths of the Anglo-American model of capitalism have been taken too far and overplayed. We will ask what over-emphasizing universalism, individualism, and specificity/analysis means. What we mean by 'too far', 'overplay', and 'excess' is that the first value in each pair has become *severed from its contrasting value,* the integrity of the two has been shattered and the first is assailing the second. In each case the dominant value starts to assail rather than develop the subordinate one.

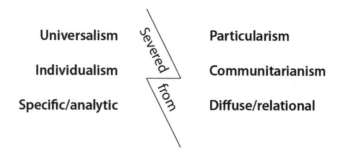

Figure 2.2 Universalism, individualism and specificity severed from their contrasts

1. Universalism severed from particularism

What might a culture that took universal rules and regulations too seriously and pushed these too far, look like? It might regard economics, the science of money, as a necessary discipline to be extended worldwide without exception.

11.   Philip Stephens, 'The neck and neck race for Number 10', *Financial Times,* 12 April 2013.

Economics does not operate in the manner of a normal science, searching for exceptions so as to remake rules and treating all conjectures with scepticism. Instead, economic beliefs are ideologically charged and highly politicized with believers in unfettered markets at odds with Keynesian interventionists. Adherence to the market mechanism is a question of loyalty to the nation, not academic research and helps define the political right and left. This mechanism is suspiciously similar to a Puritan deity, abstract, remote, faceless and mundane, rewarding the enterprising and punishing the slothful.

This discipline is considered not just best for Britain, America and their friends, but the so-called Washington Consensus, is supposed to apply to everyone. Challenging it must be resisted, even punished. It might extend its own laws to whoever it does business with, pushing for the extradition of suspects to its own jurisdiction. It would scorn attempts by other nations to make rules like the Kyoto protocol and the International Criminal Court at The Hague. Rule-making is for it and its allies alone.

Presiding over this world order requires policemen and Britain and America have both stepped into the breach. At first things went well, with the Allies helping to defeat fascism, and make a home for the Jews, with some lasting repercussions, before rescuing South Korea. But over two million Vietnamese had to die on the doubtful premise that dominoes would fall across the world if they were not subjugated. The Vietnamese have subsequently joined world markets with no hint of their supposed menace to capitalism. Wars followed in the Falklands, Bosnia, Iraq, Libya, Afghanistan and now Syria, most which have *disrupted* not restored world order. Drones controlled from thousands of miles away pick off suspected terrorists without arrest or trial along with hundreds of civilians who happen to be in the vicinity of attacks.

If we want an image and symbol of universalism assailed by its opposite, by a particular, exceptional, senseless, brutal and suicidal act then we need look no further than 9/11 and the destruction of the World Trade Center in New York. There are people who *so* despise our vision of the universal order, that they will assault it with fanatical hatred at the cost of their own annihilation. Is this universal system making us more safe, or less? Nations who default on their debts or depart from orthodox economics and suffer crises, get a short, sharp lesson in classical economics and just enough money from the International Monetary Fund to repay their Western creditors.

How else might we recognize a nation that had taken universalism too far? Does the US really need twenty-one times the number of lawyers per head of population than Japan? These destroy wealth and ratchet up the costs of disputes, while learning to trust and negotiate with people is much cheaper, as the Harvard

Negotiation Project has demonstrated.[12] Many corporations regard *not* paying corporation taxes to be a profit centre and only a small fraction of corporations pay the full rate. They simply outgun government lawyers with their own more highly paid teams. By allocating intellectual property to low-tax jurisdictions corporations get national governments to compete at letting them off the hook. The global system of avoidance wins out. There *are* moments of wonder, even admiration. What other nation save America would impeach the most powerful head of state in the world, Richard Nixon, for a breach of its constitution?

'Why are they using lawyers rather than rats for animal experiments?' the joke asks. 'Because there are more lawyers than rats, because research assistants feel less sympathy for lawyers and because there are some things rats won't do.' In the cause of winning at litigation many acts of doubtful probity can be condoned. Using the law to gain a competitive advantage is many times more costly than a friendly negotiation from which both gain.

The final distortion of universalism is the creation of a financial system which appears to have lost touch with the industry at its roots, which it is there to serve. An old adage reads:

> Some men wrest a living from nature and with their hands; this is called work. Some men wrest a living from those who wrest a living from nature and with their hands; this is called trade. Some men wrest a living from those who wrest a living from those who wrest a living from nature and with their hands; this is called finance.[13]

Finance is a giant superstructure which spans the globe. The money sloshes to and fro like an overfilled bath tub, but it has *lost its ethic of service to its industrial working roots.* It trades in what *derives* from industry and then derives even more notional money from these derivatives so that the assets are collateralized several times over and a house of cards is erected upon frail foundations. We have created a precarious universal system which *no one fully understands*, is beyond regulators' control and fails signally to recognize the needs of particular companies. It has been estimated that only three per cent of the City's wealth goes to start-ups.

Roger Bootle has contrasted *contributors* to the real economy who actually create wealth with *distributors* who are supposed get the money to where it is

12. Roger Fisher founded this whole movement, see *Getting to Yes*, Harmondsworth: Penguin, 1990.

13. Provenance unknown, quote by John C. Bogle in *Enough: True Measures of Money, Business and Life,* Hoboken, NJ: John Wiley, 2009, p. 29.

needed, but prefer to use it in a global casino for speculative purposes.[14] While distributors are not wealth creators they have considerable power in allocating money and contributors are forced to comply. It is a system of world control, but of course speculation is sterile. Winners are cancelled out by losers and investors are burdened with the cost of these activities.

We must be clear as to where the problem lies. The quest for universal solutions is a noble aim as we saw in Chapter 1 and the basis of all science. What causes periodic busts and the disappearance of trillions of notional money is the *severance* between universalism and the particular events it supposedly explains and commands. When this happens the particulars may go berserk too, witness the terrorism around the world by people who have lost all connection to any vestiges of humanity and recognize no known principle of social order. They are destructive to the point of nihilism, murdering non-combatants in cold blood, even burning them alive and boasting of this in Internet videos.

This is not the only casualty. While some people take violent exception to the rules promulgated by American law-givers and hurl themselves upon the system in a suicidal fashion, the edifice of universal legality also suffers. What we see at Guantanamo Bay is nothing less than a blatant corruption of American jurisprudence: torture, detention without trial, stamping and spitting on the Koran and the wholesale trampling of the Constitution. Once universal systems come apart from the particular instances, both values suffer. A nation imposing its own values on the world would spend twenty times more money on weapons as on the diplomacy that might negotiate agreement worldwide.

2. Individualism severed from the community

We will look at direct vs. indirect forms of money-making, at self-interest and accidental public benefits, at promiscuous competition, at the individualism of consumerism and at a fatal division of labour between West and East. So long as we compete *at* satisfying consumers we gain our own self-interest indirectly, by first satisfying other people and gaining from their reciprocity. Adam Smith saw this clearly and the picture below comes from his homilies on bakers, butchers and brewers. Here we see that the baker who bakes the finest bread and sweetmeats attracts the most custom, the most revenue and is able to expand even as his less successful rivals shrink. This is very much in

14. Roger Bootle, *The Trouble with Markets: Saving Capitalism from itself*, London: Nicholas Brealey, 2012, p. 51.

the interests of customers as a community and it reallocates wealth from the profligate to the prudent, from those who don't care for their community to those who serve it best. All this is automatic and requires no intervention by the powers-that-be.

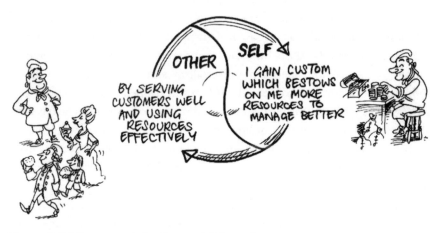

Figure 2.3 Money made by first satisfying others

The problem with Smith's synthesis of enterprising individual with grateful community is that it is *not individualistic enough for many people*. It requires the individual to first gratify others as a condition of benefiting him/herself and fails to achieve independence from the community itself. It would be much more independent to make money *directly* by clever manipulation, by out-witting or out-fighting your rivals and grabbing the lion's share of what is on offer. Yet as we argued earlier this *fails to create wealth* it simply moves money from one set of pockets to another. Moreover, serving customers violates the norm of 'making a quick buck' because reciprocity from customers may take time. Surely it is better to speculate and to win in a matter of seconds, or to charge a rent or sell energy which the tenant or customer cannot avoid paying. If s/he is at your mercy then you are independent of that person, a real individualist, not dependent on the gratitude of anyone. There is an individuality in becoming predatory. 'Never give a sucker an even break.'

In countless American films the heroic individual saves the community yet even then he does not *join* it, does not live happily in its fond embrace but rides away into the sunset, called by the faraway hills, lonely to the last. Between us the authors must have seen nearly two thousand or more American films. We cannot recall a *single one* in which a group turned out to be right and the lone hero or protagonist wrong. This is despite the fact that we have all been saved from folly by close friends. It is a common enough experience, yet it does not fit the reigning mythology. If we are in danger of stereotyping America this is because it *stereotypes itself* and concocts for audiences what they want to believe, and watch, about themselves.

Yet it is a fallacy to believe that Adam Smith counselled selfish conduct. He did nothing of the sort but he did *not*, like a good Puritan, invoke the community and intimate relationships as the counterpoint. In his *Theory of Moral Sentiments* he invoked the image of the impartial spectator that inhabited the souls of virtuous people. The desire for individual gain was partial but this was offset by an impartial and objective observer with a sense of rightness, fairness, justice and good order, who would be too enlightened to take advantage of his fellow man but would strive for the betterment of all.[15] Benjamin Franklin and Josiah Wedgwood were his contemporaries and exemplars.

But we do critique Adam Smith on another point, his curious insistence that private enterprise benefited the public good accidentally. He makes this clear in the much quoted passage below.

> It is not from the benevolence of the butcher, the brewer and the baker that we expect our dinner, but from their regard for their own self-interest...

> [The individual] intends only his own gain, and he is in this, as in many other cases, led by an invisible hand to promote an end which was not part of his intention. Nor is it always the worse for society that it was no part of it. By pursuing his own interest he frequently promotes those of society more effectually than when he really intends to promote it. I have never known much good done by those who affected to trade in the public good. It is an affection indeed not very common among merchants and very few words need to be employed in dissuading them.[16]

We have a number of questions about this passage. There is first the question of time. When the baker is preparing bread as dawn breaks would it not be wise to think about what customers liked best and purchased most over the last few days? When he visits the bank in the late afternoon is that not the

---

15. Adam Smith, *The Theory of Moral Sentiments*, 1759. Available online at Google Books.

16. Adam Smith, *An Inquiry into the Wealth of Nations (1776)*, London: Penguin, 1984, p. 651.

time to count his gains and to estimate his self-interest? But the *service precedes the counting of gains by some hours*. So if we ask what comes *first*, the answer must be the consideration of what customers are likely to buy which would be assisted by whatever benevolence he feels towards his patrons.

The second question we have is why the self-interest needs to *preclude* concern for customers, not to mention pride in his craft and his profession. *What makes these concerns incompatible?* And would not 'self-interest' include his family, even neighbours so that his thoughts were not entirely about himself? It borders on the absurd to claim that monetary gain from the provision of food and drink must override all the pleasures and the pride in doing this. What about respectability and public standing or the pleasures of baking well? We are multi-dimensional human beings after all. We can and do juggle several different desires at the same time.

But is not self-interest the *strongest* desire of all? Is it not the *end* to which sampling customer opinion is but a *means*? Possibly it is but possibly it is not. We are writing this book largely for the pleasure inherent in expressing ourselves and because what we have to say might be important to others. Getting rich would be nice but is neither very probable nor is it our main motive. Most books lose money but that does not stop them being written. The butcher, baker and brewer are specialists too and their motives are probably as mixed as are ours.

The third doubt we have is about how Smith defines the choices we make. He speaks of self-interest on the one hand and 'the public good' on the other. What is deceptive and unfair about this supposed 'choice' – assuming we *must* choose, which we questioned earlier – is that the one is very concrete and personal and the other seems very abstract, vague and elevated. *Of course* the local brewer is disinclined to worry much about the public good. He can by himself do almost nothing to advance it. He sells beer to neighbours and drinking is of doubtful public benefit in any case.

But one of Smith's acquaintances *was* concerned with this broad topic. It was his employer, the Duke of Buccleuch. It was the Duke's children whom Smith tutored when he was not writing his grand thesis. He may have seen scant reflection of the public good in their day-to-day conduct in the schoolroom. He may have felt that the hundreds of tenants and retainers on the Duke's estates were not being ruled by pure benevolence. So he made a side-swipe at his employer – hardly the first employee to do this. The claim of the ruling class to serve the public good was suspect in Smith's eyes and rightly so. He was part of the bourgeois revolution against the landed classes and was taking sides.

But however justified he was in doubting his employer's claims to benevolence, he presented his readers with a false dichotomy. It is not self-interest vs. the public good. The latter is an airy-fairy concept near impossible to define. It was self-interest vs. *concern for the customers who entered his shop and were his near-neighbours in that community.* Suppose we were to substitute customers for the public good. How would Smith's thesis read then?

> I have never known much good done by those who affected to serve their customers. It is an affection not very common among merchants…

While the public good may be near invisible, the customers who bought beer, bread and meat were *very* visible and crowded the shop of any successful merchant. They would have plenty to say about the quality of the wares they bought. They would keep him up to the mark, and in a small town or village there would be no avoiding them. But what makes this polarity between self and other unnecessary is that *the more accurately you judge the customers' needs the more money you will make and the better will your self-interest be served.* These values work much better in *combination* than apart or as alternatives. The integrity of altruism and egoism creates wealth far more effectively than some artful lure designed to trick customers into buying.

In truth *both* values, that of pleasing customers *and* that of profiting, are entirely visible and even measurable as a modern instrument called the Balanced Scorecard shows.[17] There is nothing remotely to be ashamed of in being concerned for ourselves. To that extent Smith's views were liberating. It is the *exclusive* concern for our own interests that is the problem, along with the straight-line rationalities scheming to achieve this. The Duke's possible claim to benevolence and public service would also be suspect.

Below we have illustrated Smith's 'invisible hand', the shadow hovering behind self-interest and transforming it into community service. But public benefit does *not* follow automatically or reliably from private gain. It may have mostly done so in Smith's day when most people lived in villages or small towns and the web of relationships could not be escaped even if one wished to. In those days businesses served others in face-to-face encounters. But since then we have invented thousands of economic activities that serve ourselves alone and we speculate online with impersonal computers. Business activities *may* serve others first, but all too often they deprive others and destroy wealth.

---

17. Robert S. Kaplan and David P. Norton, 'The Balanced Scorecard: Measures that drive performance', *Harvard Business Review,* January 1992.

SELF

Fierce and successful competition between businesses in serving customers assures that...

"Society as a whole, it reaps the benefit, albeit accidentally and invisibly."

OTHER

Figure 2.4 The invisible hand obscuring social concern

The truth is that the invisible hand is a metaphor, which we can neither see nor touch and the market mechanism or machine-in-the-sky may not be there save in our imaginings. It is a model and like all models includes what we value and neglects what we do not. Modern economics has an unverifiable phantom at its roots, a 'hand' no one can see. The flaw in this thinking is that benefits flow from this inadvertently. But even if the first benefit bestowed had not been intentional, the protagonist might very well welcome subsequent benefits, in which case that inadvertence would have ceased and become deliberate over time. Yet the doctrine that free enterprise should think of nothing but itself and see-saw for ever between greed and fear has done great harm to the reputation of capitalism and is quite unnecessary. It has played a part in severing individualism from all concern for the community by counselling that we forget the latter.

A pair of values badly out of kilter is *competition* by individuals as compared to *cooperation* within a company and within a community or network of companies. As Roger Bootle has pointed out, that organizations exist at all testifies to the fact that cooperation is more effective within the firm than are individuals vying with each other to get to the top. In Adam Smith's famous pin factory a division of labour paid off handsomely. The unavoidable conclusion is that business is partly competitive and partly cooperative, a means for the individual to get ahead *and* a means for the group to serve their society. What is required is that a company cooperates in serving the community and thereby competes with other companies in this endeavour, enabling the best cooperator to succeed and beat its rivals in fair competition.

The very word organization is from *organon* meaning 'instrument'. If we regard organizations as *instruments for individuals to make money* then this will neglect much of what an organization can do: educate employees, train them, grow them, give them opportunities to create, innovate and find fulfilment for their aspirations. Currently, organizations have a life-span of seventeen years, considerably shorter than that of individuals, which is precisely what we would expect from mere instruments that are easily dispensed with.

Will Hutton observes:

> Over the last decade a fifth of quoted companies have disappeared from the London Stock Exchange, the largest cull in our history. Almost no new risk capital is sought from the stock market or offered across the spectrum of companies. As the Kay Review remarks the stock market is more a vehicle for getting money out of companies than putting money in. Britain has no indigenous quoted company in the car, chemical, glass, industrial services and building materials industries, to name but a few. They are all owned overseas, with their research and development and strategic development travelling abroad as well.[18]

Hutton goes on to cite John Kay to the effect that long-term decision-making is almost entirely absent.[19] As a consequence we have lost GEC, ICI, Rover, Pilkington Glass, Cadbury-Schweppes, BTR and even the Hanson Trust which readied companies for the shareholders' table. The business best-seller of the 1960s was William White's *The Organization Man*. It claimed that organizations sapped individual liberty and circumscribed freedom, spreading conformity and compliance. Americans heartily dislike big business to this day, as recent Gallup surveys have found.[20]

But *the* major force severing competition from cooperation and the individual from the community is what we call *promiscuous competition*, that

18. Will Hutton, *How Good Can We Be?* London: Little Brown, 2015 p. 50. Also, 'British Capitalism is Broken: Here's how to fix it', *Guardian*, 11 February 2015, pp. 27–29.

19. 'The Kay Review of UK Equity Markets and Long-term Decision Making', Department of Business, July 2012, https//www.gov.uk/.../bis-12-917.

20. Gallup polls, see www.gallup.com

is competing indiscriminately with everyone, including and especially *one's own customers*. The reason is quite simple. It is hard to take on fellow banking professionals but easy to fool millions of customers, some of whom could not tell an income statement from a balance sheet. When were we last able to compare bank charges? Comparison between these is deliberately obfuscated. They do indeed compete, in how much they can take from their clients, a form of competition completely severed from cooperation. Consider the spate of recent bank scandals in the UK.

In the 1980s and 1990s financial advisers persuaded two million customers to switch from their company pension schemes to personal pensions. The administrative costs involved in doing so were at least fifty times higher because a whole company might require only one administrator but the fees paid to advisers and bankers for each individual were much greater. Clients' money was put into higher paying equities, which then under-performed. When the dust settled, they were reckoned to have cost their customers £11 billion and were forced to repay them. They also sold under-performing endowment mortgages in the same period and had to repay £1 billion. But worse was to come.

Between 2000 and 2012 financial advisers sold payment protection insurance to people afraid of losing their jobs. Many sales were to persons who were self-employed and so could never have collected anyway. The banks had to set aside £15 billion to compensate for this scam. Scores of companies sprang into existence offering to harass the banks and take thirty per cent of the money owed to customers as a reward.

From 2005 to 2011, customers with credit cards were sold insurance against identity theft, which, although rare, had been in the headlines. What the banks failed to tell them was that it was the banks, not the customers, who were financially responsible for such thefts. Customers needed no insurance at all and would merely be covering for the bank if they collected on it. £1.3 billion has been put aside to compensate customers for this fraud. Even when caught and told to refund customers, banks duck this responsibility. Lloyds, which is mostly owned by the taxpayer, rejected a large number of complaints having explained to its staff that ninety per cent of claimants would give up anyway and warned that employees might find this 'morally difficult'. The Ombudsman reversed eighty-four per cent of the decisions made as unfair. The customers of Barclays were asked to rate the bank for honesty and awarded it four out of 100. Lloyds scored twenty-one.[21]

21. Patrick Hosking, 'Bad behaviour comes back to haunt embattled Barclays', *Times*, 16 September 2013.

What all this amounts to is competing with the whole world outside your own company. You compete especially with anyone who has less information than you do and you attack the most naïve, the very customers you are supposed to be serving.

Yet another scandal erupted in the autumn of 2013. It transpired that banks had made it a condition for many small companies who wanted credit that they buy a swap that supposedly protected them against rising interest rates. They were not warned what might happen if interest rates fell, which is indeed what happened, in part because of the malfeasance of banks themselves. Small businesses found themselves with ruinous burdens. Banks were ordered to put aside £1–£2 billion to right this wrong but much of the damage was irreparable as many of the businesses had already ceased trading.[22] The banks had hit a very vulnerable yet vital part of the economy at the very moment the economy was teetering.[23]

Just as this book goes to press yet another scandal has erupted. This time it was the Swiss private banking subsidiary of HSBC helping thousands of its clients to evade tax through aggressively marketed schemes and brown bag cash withdrawals. A withholding tax of fifteen per cent had been levied on Swiss accounts by the European Savings Directive but by turning personal accounts into pseudo companies the bank got around the law even where such companies did no trading and were fronts for an individual. Lord Stephen Green, who led the Swiss subsidiary, the author of religious books on banking ethics was ennobled even after British tax authorities knew of his company's misconduct. Leaked emails discussed these machinations and left little doubt that this was deliberate evasion. Among the list of 100,000 clients suspected of malfeasance were 1,100 British subjects. Of which just one had been criminally prosecuted when the BBC and the *Guardian* broke the story in February 2015. Only £130 million has been repaid to the Treasury from this scam. The French raised double that from half the number of persons. As for the Swiss authorities they tried to arrest the whistleblower, Herve Falciani, rather than the corrupt bank executives.[24]

22. James Dean, 'Fakes, frauds and forgery in Lloyds PPI selling scandal', *Times*, 11 June 2013.

23. Martin Wolf, 'Britain's economy should not go back to the future', *Financial Times*, 11 April 2013. Philip Stephens, 'Nothing can dent the divine right of bankers', *Financial Times*, 16 January 2013. Also Anatole Kaletsky, 'Bankers are Masters of the Universe again', *Times*, 7 September 2010.

24. Martin Arnold, 'Days Turn Darker for HSBC as profits dive', *Financial Times*, 26 February, 2015.

Gillian Tett, writing in the *Financial Times*, noted that banks are now even bigger, shadow banking has expanded, qualitative easing has increased asset prices and the rich are even richer.[25] Some forms of competition are clearly sub-optimal. Sabotaging other people's work so that you, not they, will be promoted, gaining monopoly or oligopoly power and wielding this, paying suppliers late and so forcing those who can least afford it to extend you credit, 'administering' higher prices with other companies in your industry, outsourcing jobs to a cheaper contractor and firing your own people, who may end up doing the same job for less. All these are examples of competition diminishing cooperation. In the UK, energy prices and rail fares increase in tandem. Since the rail companies paid dearly for their franchises, they must now claw this money back from commuters with their local monopolies and they do!

Up to this point we have argued that cooperation is supposed to take place *within* companies and with their customers while competition takes place *between* companies. But even this is not as true as it once was. The age of individual proprietors has faded. But so has the age of stand-alone organizations. The unit which competes has expanded to cover the company, its suppliers, its sub-contractors and the whole industrial ecosystem. It is still *possible* to compete with your own suppliers, sub-contractors and customers but it is also stupid to do so, because it is this *entire system which prospers as one.*

A big company like General Motors can and did win concessions from all its suppliers and made US$4.6 billion from seizing their profits for itself, with Wall Street applauding. But do you really *want* to weaken your own suppliers? If you take their profits, how can they continue their R&D and come up with better systems or components? Since fifty to eighty per cent of the value of a manufactured product is typically contributed by suppliers, is not their strength *your* strength? If you helped and nurtured them, would you not gain in the end? In the short run GM's suppliers had to pay up but in the longer run they arranged to work for other companies. GM was digging its own grave and in the recent recession had to be rescued by the taxpayer.[26]

While large companies can and do exploit small companies in their own chains of supply, it is unwise to do so. Many small businesses go belly up as a result of such power politics. It is upon small businesses that our future

---

25. Gillian Tett, 'Insane financial system lives on post-Lehman', *Financial Times*, 12 September 2013.

26. The sad story of GM is related in John Mackey and Raj Sisodia, *Conscious Capitalism*, Boston: Harvard Business School Press, 2013, p. 116.

depends. They create most new jobs, grow faster and innova are *much* more popular with the general public. This situatic getting worse. Martin Vander Weyer writing in the *Spectator* 2015 reported that Diageo was extending its payment terms ninety days after receipt of goods, Mars, Mondelez and and A. extending theirs to 120 days. The Federation of Small Business estimates that £40 billion is owed to its members at any one time, even while the FTSE 100 companies hold net cash of £53 billion which they are not investing. Competing with your supply chain instead of nurturing your suppliers is pure folly. The big companies have too much idle cash. The small ones have far too little and when they run out of cash it often kills them.

The problem with the big exploiting the small is that small companies create more wealth than those who exploit them so that this harms the entire economy. A study by Andrew Haldane showed unquoted (private) companies have four to five times more capital assets for every pound of turnover than do companies whose shares are quoted on the stock market, a huge discrepancy.[27] This illustrates the damage wrought by the voracious short-termism of share trading.

We have been measuring individualism for more than twenty-five years and over that time it has been increasing, but not in a way that necessarily increases wealth. Our final caveat about unchecked individualism is that it *favours consuming more than producing.* The great individualists of the past were the tycoons and entrepreneurs. They worked in and with groups in organizations and in factories. But the individualists of today mostly go down to the mall and gratify themselves alone with some 'retail therapy'. This is a passive, in-taking kind of individuality catered to by a vast array of consumables and used to distinguish the individual from others.[28]

Al Gore provides some telling statistics: large supermarkets contain some twenty thousand different products; there are now more TVs in American homes than people, and five hours a day are spent watching TV; the average American is exposed to three thousand advertising messages a day; and per capita spending on clothing doubled between 1997 and 2005, much of it fuelled by household debt which also doubled to 13.8 per cent of disposable

27. Andrew Haldane and Richard Davies, 'The Short Long' presented at the 29th SUERF Conference, May 2011, cited by Will Hutton, *How Good Can We Be?*, London: Little Brown, 2015.

28. The first to draw attention to this phenomenon was Daniel Bell in *The Cultural Contradictions of Capitalism*, New York: Basic Books, 1976. The consuming et was gobbling up the production ethos.

income.[29] This may explain our growing addiction to the money which can buy these things.

We can now begin to understand how this second kind of individuality runs after the first kind and drags it down. Consider the dot.com boom and bust. Some of the innovators here were genuine enough. Amazon, Google, Microsoft, e-Bay, America Online and Yahoo were either born or grew to prominence in this era. They have survived. Unfortunately, those creating genuine wealth were *vastly outnumbered by those determined to make money from this.* After all why take years to build an organization when you can profit at the click of a mouse from a recumbent position?

The net result was far more demand for stock in innovative Internet companies than there were innovative companies worth such investment. Sucked into the vacuum were hundreds of companies that had never met a payroll, never registered a profit and had generated little or no revenue. They had intriguing concepts scrawled on the back of envelopes and sold to the credulous. Amazon was the trendsetter and it had deliberately made large losses in early years to capture such a large market share of online book and music sales as to be unassailable by rivals. Now scores of other companies tried to do the same in various industries, toys, food, pharmaceuticals and so on, yet simply crashed head on. When everyone tries to buy market share at the same time the result is an agonizing collision with cracked skulls all round.

What had promised to be a dot.com boom turned into *Dot-con: The Greatest Story ever Sold.*[30] *Wired* magazine forecast the age of ultra-prosperity. By 2020, according to Kevin Kelley, average household incomes in the USA would be US$150,000. Middle class families would have personal chefs. The Dow Jones average would be heading for 100,000. George Gilder wrote of a one thousand-fold increase in Internet traffic before the century turned. Harry S. Dent in *The Roaring 2000s Investor* predicted the Dow would reach 41,000 by 2009.[31]

The general belief was that Santa Claus was coming if only we had faith and confidence. A new paradigm had arisen where computers talked to computers, someone 'out there' would surely respond and general harmony reigned amid rational, acquisitive, self-seeking, individualist beings. The free market had reached its apotheosis at last, while Communism had failed. At the touch of key vast fortunes were possible. Similarities with the South Sea

29.   Al Gore, *Our Choice,* London: Bloomsbury, 2009, pp. 310–312.

30.   John Cassidy, *Dot.con: The Greatest Story ever Sold,* London: Bloomsbury, 2003.

31.   New York: Touchstone, 1999.

Bubble and the Dutch Tulip mania were numerous. It seems we never learn. The housing bubble and its crash were still to come.

This has not only severed individualism from community it has led to a fatal division of labour between the USA, with much of Europe, and China, which ensures that producing communities in one country serve consuming individuals in other countries.

It is difficult to see why this pattern would not repeat itself continually, so long as hordes of money-makers race hard on the heels of a relatively few genuine wealth creators and throw money at anyone who resembles them. We have far too many individualists in search of easy money rather than of hard work and its challenges. Too many want to consume as celebrity characters and too few want to work and produce quietly. That building a corporation might take years of anonymous and dedicated work which few notice seems not to have occurred to this 'publi-ciety'.

The result of too much money chasing too few goods *used* to be inflation. This was once choked off by raising interest rates, which raised the cost of mortgages, which slowed down demand and the economy. All this was before globalism and China entered the equation. What China's rise did was reduce costs and prices across the world and on such a scale that the penalty of high inflation for over-consumption was never visited upon us and interest rates were kept so low that only an idiot would save and any rational economic actor would borrow. We could buy more and more without suffering inflation because Chinese imports were so cheap they kept prices down. But this has had dire consequences. What has happened is that the Chinese have saved, invested, manufactured and exported ever more, as an expression of a cohesive community, while Britain and the USA have borrowed ever more, and have spent, imported and consumed more, as an expression of their individuality. These insights are taken mostly from the work of Niall Ferguson and his concept of 'Chimerica', pictured in Figure 2.5 overleaf.[32]

But this is not the virtuous circle of the kind we drew earlier in this chapter. This is a *vicious circle* which unbalances both nations. China produces and invests in excess so that America can consume and borrow in excess, but China is active and America passive. China has a large balance payments surplus, the USA a large deficit. China is growing fast and the USA quite slowly and unless

32. Niall Ferguson, Harvard historian, and economist Motitz Schularick, coined this word in 2006. It is drawn from 'chimera', the mythical monster composed of disparate animal parts. It refers to an excess of production in China which triggers an excess of consumption in the USA.

things change China will overtake the USA in GNP before 2020 and in GDP per capita by mid-century. But China is under-consuming and although this may suit the strategy of its leaders, it is hard on the people themselves. They are financing American indebtedness by sending abroad their savings on much smaller incomes to boost American borrowing on much larger incomes.

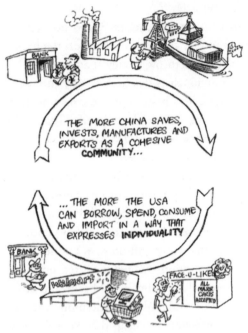

Figure 2.5 Chimerica

It also illustrates the failure of any rationality which disregards its own counterpoint. It makes absolute rational sense for Americans and Brits to borrow as individuals. Interest rates are often lower than inflation, but from the point of view of the nation as a whole this yields power to China. Nations limp precariously with an uneven gait, one excess and extreme compensated for by its opposite. These are among the dangers of globalism.

What is happening in Britain and America is that the highly individualist consumer culture is metaphorically *devouring what remains of the production* ... magazine, before its closure, retold the story of the Little Red ... ble to find anyone to manufacture her products or ship them to ... It was only when she asked who would do the advertising and ... farmyard animals clamoured to help her. Prestige in Britain is ... ate to one's proximity to consumers and consumption. Raw ... people. Selling perfume in Harrods is OK.

There is a final caveat. Not only can individualism be so over-emphasized that it destroys communities, *but community can be over-emphasized so as to destroy individuals*. This is what Communism did in much of the globe. Values at either end of our dimensions can become idols, hungry for human sacrifice. No matter how good they sound when they attack their own opposites, things come apart, the centre cannot hold, mere anarchy is loosed upon the world.[33] Individuals are members of a community. We polarize at our peril.

3. Specific/analytic severed from diffuse/relational

What might a culture that had severed the specific from the diffuse look like? It might insist that as many of its customers as possible bank online since human relationships are too costly. It might mail equipment to telephone, TV and Wi-Fi customers and insist they be their own engineers. Calls for help might be answered by automated telephone lines. Attempts to connect to a person would lead to the line going dead. They might use the words 'it does not count' to dismiss any query that could not be codified or rendered in numbers, a habit that destroys both meaning and human understanding. It might lose all sight of trust, that indefinable whole. It might refer to 'human resources', which is like money and property except for being alive, but is still a bundle of assets. It might refer to 'social capital', again like money but additionally, conscious.

It might insist that everyone is motivated by specific increments of cash and all economic activity is thereby controllable by rich persons and institutions wielding carrots. Nothing, but nothing would be more important than the 'bottom line', the specific of all specifics, the bullet point of all bullet points. This was why we came into existence. We asked whether 'A company's only goal is profitability'? The answers we received are shown in Table 2.1.

Table 2.1 Profitability is a company's only goal.

Country	USA	AUS	CAN	UK	IT	SWE	NL	GER	FRA	SIN	HK	JP	CHI
Agree (%)	40	35	34	33	28	27	26	24	16	11	9	8	2

There is still a sizeable minority which believes in profit above all. Note how much more diffuse are cultures in East Asia.

33. W. B. Yeats, 'The Second Coming'.

It is interesting to note that according to Magoroh Maruyama, a Japanese-American academic, neither Japan nor China have a word for objectivity.[34] When asked to translate this word they render it as 'the guest's point of view' (in Japanese *kyakkantekki*). This means the relatively superficial glance of a guest who upon entering a house sees separate members of a family. The 'host's point of view' (*shukantekki*) or subjectivity, sees much more. The husband can probably tell what his wife thinks of a guest by how natural her smile is. It appears not to have occurred to these cultures that treating people like objects is desirable in any way, or that they need a word to commend this habit.

Part of the problem encountered in the financial crisis was that diffuse relationships among lenders and borrowers had eroded and been replaced by 'financial products'; that is, by pretend specific objects bought from a bank and sold to customers. But these 'objects' did not remain with the lender. They were packaged, divided into 'tranches', sliced and diced, mislabelled AAA and sold on around the world, sometimes to several recipients in turn. So banks lost any relationships with those who had borrowed from them. A mortgage might have originated in London but now be in Istanbul on its way to Kuala Lumpur, for all anyone knew. It followed that the bank neither knew nor cared whether the borrower could meet interest payments since it would not lose if he or she couldn't. Its specific fee for the specific 'transaction' had been secured and that alone mattered.[35]

It is quite impossible that so many sub-prime loans could have been sold to NINJAs (no income, no job, no assets) had anyone cared for these people or their future lives. The seller was after a bonus for closing the deal and what happened later was of no concern. Teaser rates made sure the interest rate doubled or tripled in two to three years. This would lead to more sales and more fees. Forms were filled out in ways which the software (not humans) would pass and 'liar's loans' were churned out by the tens of thousands. It was assumed that risk was a *thing* that one person could pass to another and so be rid of. That the *whole system* could be at risk and that you could not indefinitely pass a specific parcel full of lies, appears not to have occurred to anyone.

When you reduce the whole to parts you almost inevitably leave out certain crucial considerations, concentrating on what is most simple, regular and reliable and omitting what is most subtle, most elusive and ambiguous. Moreover, the meaning of organizations, products and services lie in their wholeness, not their bits and pieces so that reduction into parts may rob a

---

34. Magoroh Maruyama, 'New Mindscapes for Future Business Policy and Magement', in *Technological Forecasting and Social Change*, 21(1982), pp. 53–76.
35. John Cassidy, *How Markets Fail*, London: Penguin, 2009.

phenomenon of its meaning and of its significance. Harvard-trained Daniel Yankelovich, head of the once leading research institute of the same name, has well-expressed what a descent into excessive specificity does to us.

> The first step is to measure what can easily be measured. That is OK as far as it goes. The second step is to disregard what cannot be measured or give it an arbitrary quantitative value. This is artificial and misleading. The third step is to assume that what cannot be measured is really not important. This is blindness. The fourth step is to assume that what cannot be measured does not really exist. This is suicide.[36]

The bean-counters are busy at work. Being sued for defects in an automobile would cost us X but recalling the car and putting it right would be 2 x X, so it's obvious that we save money and do nothing, since the whole, diffuse, immeasurable nature of human life and its preciousness has eluded us. The specific bottom line is what counts. The problem with specificity is that it is all measurement and no larger meaning. We lose sight of the professionalism of going to work in the first place, along with the growth and development of human beings and their relationships and the very purpose of human life itself.

This illustrates the point that *the diffuse whole can include specific parts but not the other way around*. What ultimately matters is the whole product plus service and the good use to which that product is put. The customer needs a total solution not bits and pieces. A dirty great pile of bricks does not make a house. As Wordsworth put it, 'Our meddling intellect mistakes the beauteous shape of things. We murder to dissect.' W. H. Auden wrote of the American Southwest, 'Come to our well-run desert where anguish arrives by cable and the deadly sins may be bought in tins with instructions on the label.' The author and *Financial Times* journalist, Gillian Tett, has pointed out, the word credit (which is very specific) comes from the Latin *credire* – to believe or to trust. The diffuse process of trusting is the origin of all credit and the latter will collapse suddenly and catastrophically without it. Credit is a reification of the process of trusting someone with money.[37]

To assume human relationships are a waste of valuable time and urge your customers to bank online and use ATM machines could be a mistake, despite the costs saved. Keeping people at arm's length like this can only be taken so far before all trust collapses and customers become infuriated. The reason customers cannot get what they want from banks is that the banks will only

36. Quoted in John C. Bogle, *Enough*, op. cit., p. 118.
37. Gillian Tett, *Fools Gold*, Abacus, 2010, p. 91.

sell them artificially conceived 'products' which they can sell on, so it's a 'one-year loan in increments of £5,000 or nothing'. The banks think in the form of tradable LEGO bricks not in the particular forms that customers might want. If you pay off a loan early, you incur a penalty for not being predictable.

We examined the level of trust between customers and their institutions. We did not measure it in the wake of the financial crisis because we knew it would be very low and perhaps exaggerated by recent events. So we looked at the level of trust before the crisis to see if the coming bust may have been predictable. It is clear that diffuse cultures, as shown in Chapter 1 to be China, Singapore and Hong Kong, demonstrate much higher levels of trust than specific cultures and that fast-developing economies demonstrate more trust than slowly developing ones. Banks which erode their relationships with their customers and promote financial 'products' at targeted people instead, are a relatively recent development.

Without diffuse trust, nothing else will work, least of all spending money on due diligence (examining a company's accounts and internal data) and hiring lawyers to counter every trick. Trust saves a huge amount of time otherwise spent on costly forms of surveillance and inquiry and greatly reduces the level of stress in conducting relationships. In many cases we have no choice but to trust, or else the cost of doing business goes through the roof. Table 2.2 shows our results.

Table 2.2 Level of trust in major corporations, *World Competitiveness Report*, IMD, Geneva, Switzerland, 2006 (score out of 10)

Singapore	8.04
China	8.00
Malaysia	7.62
Finland	7.48
Sweden	7.47
Hong Kong	7.43
Switzerland	7.27
Denmark	6.80
Belgium	6.14
Brazil	6.12
Australia	6.07
USA	5.77
France	5.63
UK	5.31
Venezuela	4.50
Russia	2.90

Once again we see that trust is much higher in cultures with a diffuse preference for relationships and whole systems as compared to numbers, measures, key performance indicators (KPIs) and small print. Specificity is obvious in the alphabet soup of financial derivatives – ABCPs, ABSs, CDOs, CDSs, SPVs and SIVs, otherwise known as 'weapons of mass destruction'. All in all too much specificity is in evidence.

The bank scandals we related earlier in this chapter resulted from targeting customers with the specific products banks wanted to sell. If you want a loan, you must buy a swap or risk being turned down. If you want a mortgage, you must take on personal protection insurance whether you can claim on it or not. Specific incentives are attached to specific targets and the bank employees may lose their jobs if they don't hit them. Indeed, their bosses may make more money if the employee's targets are reached. The idea is to sell those products with a high margin *not* what the relationship with the customer requires.

But the ultimate objection to run-away specificity is its inability to appreciate what life is all about. A company is not a collection of persons and things but a living whole. We are the designers of our own existences or we are nothing. We may need money but we work for meaning; our careers and our lives are dedicated to it. To reduce all this to currency units is to cast a pall over human endowments and miss out on life itself. Specificity suffers from having only one dimension, 'more'. It seems we cannot escape this. Everyone wants more all the time not because they need it or have enough days left to spend it, but because someone somewhere has more than they do.

Humanity does not belong inside the HR department, it belongs *everywhere*. One problem with HR is that it turns social skills into some kind of commodity and claims to specialize in this, so someone upset at how they are treated appeals to HR not her manager. Humanity is not just another function like procurement or legal services, unless it *pervades the entire organization* humanity is of no value to ourselves or to others. It is the crux of everything we do. It either guides the mission of the entire organization or no real accomplishment has been realized and no real wealth has been created.

Is there evidence that some of the activities described above generate low trust among members of society and that this has been getting worse? There is much evidence, most of it from the USA. In April 1979 Gallup found that sixty per cent of Americans had 'a great deal of trust' or 'quite a lot' in their banks. In 2014 this stood at twenty-six per cent, a generous assessment. It was twenty-one per cent just after the crash. In 1972 forty-two per cent trusted Congress. This is now seven per cent. In February 1991 eighty-five per cent trusted the Supreme Court. This is now down to thirty per cent, after attempts to politicize it. The presidency stood at eighty-five per cent in February 1991, but is now at twenty-nine per cent, only just above banks and business executives. There is an interesting contrast between big business, trusted by only twenty-one per cent, down from thirty-four per cent in 1975 and small business trusted by sixty-two per cent, a rating which has never dropped below fifty-nine per cent. The more remote and unequal to us a business is, the more we distrust it.[38]

Americans trust those professions that serve them and distrust those who are chiefly out for themselves. Relationships are crucial. Scores in descending and ascending order are shown in Table 2.3.

Table 2.3 Most and least trusted professions

Near the top	Level of trust	Near the bottom	Level of trust
Nurses	82%	Lobbyists	6%
Military officers	74%	Members of Congress	7%
Veterinarians	72%	Car salespersons	9%
Pharmacists	70%	Stockbrokers	11%
Engineers	70%	Senators	19%
Doctors	69%	Advertising practitioners	15%
Police	54%	Real estate agents	20%
Clergy	47%	Bankers	27% (19% in 2009)
Judges	44%	Auto mechanics	29%

It is interesting to note how accurately the public perceives the problem. The US suffers from too many lobbyists, distorting the judgement of too many members of Congress and senators who are sponsored by bankers and stockbrokers into passing laws that favour the top of the electorate. The money has come from the pockets of nurses, military officers, vets, doctors, teachers, police, clergy and judges, precisely those who are most trusted by society. It is their incomes and our taxes that bail out the banks. On the whole the professions that are trusted are those which serve and protect others, rather than focusing on profit-making. We tend to trust in those in whom we have to depend in a crisis. Those gaining at our expense are most distrusted.

38.   Gallup polls, www.gallup.com

A quite different tack was taken by Richard Wilkinson and Kate Picket in *The Spirit Level*. These researchers looked at income inequality, which has soared recently, and found that it correlated strongly and consistently with lack of trust. Those much wealthier than the rest of us have no need to trust anyone outside their elite circle and have the means to devastate those who cross them. The Pearson Correlation Coefficient between trust and relative inequality is minus 0.66 internationally and minus 0.70 within the USA when comparing states with greater or lesser inequality. The p-value is greater than 0 .01.[39]

Low-trust, unequal cultures have lower life expectancy, higher infant mortality, higher obesity, more mental illness, lower education scores, more people in prison, less social mobility, and more homicides. They spend less on foreign aid as a percentage of their income, spend less on health care, have lower child well-being, have lower female equality, more teenage births and consume more illegal drugs. We tend to trust those we know and with whom we have long-term relationships. The social problems we have cited are the substitutes for loneliness, alienation and for being marginalized by others, which makes their condition worse not better. Income groups tend to socialize with each other and the impoverished are slipping ever further away from the concerns of mainstream society. The recent Ebola outbreak was but the symptom of gross inequality.

The final fallacy of specificity has to do with extrinsic payments of incentives, tips and bonuses, otherwise known as 'pay-for-performance'. Are we largely motivated by money inducements, by carrots dangled in front of us? It should be obvious that offering such piecework incentives and bonuses for attainment is both specific and extrinsic. In contrast to this are diffuse and intrinsic motivation. This occurs when an interesting problem elicits our energies so that we may even create the solution and learn and develop through that process. There is a diffuse relationship between the person and the product, the challenge and the response, and the problem and the solution. We engage in the diffuse process of mastering our task and our profession.

One example of the power of culture over hard evidence is our stubborn belief in pay-for-performance when study after study has shown its very limited effect. After all, were it effective the USA should be pulling ever further ahead of other countries, since it has much higher bonus payments. Why is China, with a fraction of such incentives, growing three times as fast? Why is the US losing world market share? Are people motivated to do their best work by high payments? Banks have warned they could go into a 'death spiral' unless

39. Richard Wilkinson and Kate Picket, *The Spirit Level: Why Equality is Better for Everyone*, London: Penguin, 2010.

allowed to pay lavishly. They call their pay 'compensation' which sounds as if they were being paid for otherwise unpleasant work.

The evidence against the efficacy of pay-for-performance is strong and persistent over the years. We keep discovering it again and again and keep ignoring the truth as culturally inconvenient. It runs counter to what rich people with money want to believe and counter to what economists want to believe. Economists need money to be the independent variable of their discipline which predicts and controls all people everywhere and they want no truck with psychology, a rival discipline. Rich people want to believe they can buy anything and anybody they choose, that they have the keys to the universe. However the evidence from scientific research is plain. Pay-for-performance works well provided there is *no problem solving, complexity or creativity involved in the work being done.* If the job is simple, mechanical, procedural and repetitive then incentivizing it assures better compliance. Money is perhaps the only reason for doing something so dull.[40]

But the moment the task requires *even a modicum of cognitive skill,* then offering money rewards produces not better results but *worse* ones. The evidence has been gathered and marshalled by Daniel Pink and comes from reputable sources: the Federal Reserve Bank in the USA and the London School of Economics. It originates from the Candle Experiment, an old psychological test in which teams must arrange a candle to stand upright and not drip wax on a table. It takes 'creativity', if you can call it that, because the thumb-tacks come in a box and the team must realize that the box is more than a container for thumb tacks but one of the elements of a solution. (You set the candle upright in the box, impaled on a thumb-tack with the box nailed to the wall.) If you offer money for a speedy solution the team takes two to three minutes *longer* to solve the problem. With more complex definitions of creativity the results have been even stronger. The more creativity is involved the more incentives reduce performance and the more the lack of incentives increase performance. It has been repeated in rural India where the payments were three or four month's salary but the incentivized did worse than ever. Why should this be?

Pink suggests that incentives *narrow perception.* You think of the money and only the money and lose sight of the problem itself, along with the larger context. Anything creative requires you to import some new element peripheral to the task, like the box containing the thumb tacks, but incentives make you focus too intently. You hurry when you should be pondering. The

40. Daniel Pink, *Drive: The Surprising Truth of what Motivates Us,* London: Canongate, 2009. See Chapter 2.

specific 'money' usurps your attention. There is also much circumstantial evidence that paying for performance produces inferior results.

How come Wikipedia thrashed MSN Encarta, Microsoft's online encyclopaedia? The latter paid well-known authorities and experienced editors to produce their work, but were beaten by volunteers and enthusiasts contributing articles for the love of the topic. Open source software like Linux and Apache have invaded the Internet and are in wide use without contractual payments being made to the developers. The Boston Consulting Group looked at 680 open source software providers and concluded that the chief motive was to 'give a gift to the online community'. This does not mean they earn no money but it comes *after* not before.[41] Stewart Brand pointed out that the first six or seven Internet millionaires made a present of their software and asked anyone finding it useful to send them a donation.[42] These donations were generous. But they followed the gift and did not precede it. There is no evidence of anyone paying Tim Berners Lee for inventing the World Wide Web, yet we doubt he is poor. A more comprehensive job of demolishing the advocates of pay-for-performance has been done by Boston-based psychologist Alfie Kohn. There is room for only a summary here.[43]

First, 'performance' is being defined by those in authority rather than employees using their own judgement, and that of the customers, to do the job. Those at the top are usually farthest from any technological innovation and from any customers so that payments are essentially for conformity not for innovation or for helping customers. If there are incentives and rewards for selling certain products, then the employee will push that product even if the customer wants something different. The employee is focusing on their own rewards, not the individual needs of the customer, and thus is unlikely to show any initiative. Hence innovative solutions go unrewarded in favour of compliance and conformity to the powers-that-be.

Rewards also have a tendency to obscure the meaning of a particular action. For example, children who were incentivized with money to fasten their seat-belts ceased to fasten them when the incentive was removed. The reward had overshadowed the fundamental point of wearing the seatbelt, which was to save the lives to which their parents had devoted years of care. How big a bonus should a hospital pay a nurse who held the hand of a dying joyrider and then had to break the news to his parents? Would £50 cover it, or a T-shirt

41. Daniel Pink, *Drive*, p. 25.

42. Stewart Brand, personal communication.

43. Alfie Kohn, *Punished by Rewards*, Boston: Beacon Press, 2008.

with a heart? The very question insults. She does not want a pay-off. Her work is not motivated, for the most part, by money.

Paying for performance triggers a search for the easiest work with the highest relative pay off. Employees cease to do what needs to be done and start to 'game the system' for the highest rewards. They may cease to help fellow workers because only those helped benefit financially, not the helper. Relationships atrophy. Trust leaks away. Payments made *after* an employee has completed a job can be clawed back by the employer. Employees are disempowered and cannot count on receiving enough money to pay the rent each month. Pay-for-performance can be, and often is, used to divide and rule, and as a means to punish troublemakers and whistleblowers.

Pay-for-performance kills subtle communication between employees and supervisors. Supervisors need to support their *performers* and ensure they keep trying, but they also need to critique *performance* and seek its constant improvement. The giving or withholding of a sizeable bonus is far too crude a lever to communicate this subtle synthesis. The employee can see nothing but the bonus or its absence. The feedback is too gross and fails to discriminate. Pay-for-performance lends a mad momentum to bad decisions such as selling mortgages to impoverished people who cannot repay, or selling protection against identity theft when the bank not the customer would be liable in that situation. The bonus system propels booms and busts and overrides doubts, caution and acts of conscience. It does not serve customers – it targets them for institutional gain.

The system also makes for poor customer relationships because salespeople who feel manipulated and short-changed by their supervisors will pass on this treatment to customers. The product is foisted upon customers whether they want it or not, whether they need it or not, whether they can afford it or not, because it has been incentivized. Most of the banking scandals were wrought by those working on a commission-only basis or receiving hefty bonus payments relative to salary.

Evidence of the superiority of intrinsic motivation comes from companies that set employees free for a day a week or twenty per cent of their time to do *whatever they wish*. Google and 3M have led in this respect but the practice is spreading. There is a condition. Employees must share with each other what they created in this free time, an experience repeated in Australia by Atlassian who calls these 'FEDEX days' for the overnight delivery of something valuable. What has been found is that some fifty per cent of Google's innovations come from the twenty per cent free time given employees. There are no money incentives on offer. There are also a number of ROWE (Results Only Work Environment) companies in the USA who meet periodically to compare results. These employees are left totally free to manage their own time with the proviso that this produces results for their employer. Levels of innovation and employee satisfaction are extraordinarily high. People *enjoy* innovating.[44]

None of this means that money is not important. Indeed its *lack* produces angry, anti-business movements and this sense of unfairness can cripple work environments. The ideal is for *enough* money to be taken for granted so employees concentrate their minds on creative inputs and are not distracted by worry. Money is also important in the sense that it *pays to get funds quickly to where a creative breakthrough has occurred*. But money was *not* the motive for that innovation. It comes afterwards, to exploit the innovation more fully and expand activities swiftly.

All this testifies to the superiority of *intrinsic* motivation, working and creating as an end in itself and for the love of this, over *extrinsic* motivation, working because a reward has been dangled before you as a specific inducement. The implication of these findings is that paying for performance is not just of doubtful value but has been getting *more* ineffective over time. Because the simple work for which inducements work after a fashion is becoming more and more scarce and earns relatively little, while complex and creative work is increasingly in demand and earns us much more. Simple work is being turned into computer programs, being automated and being outsourced to lower-wage countries abroad. Complexity and innovation are the main hope for our future, provided we can grab it.

Let the final word be with Will Hutton, until recently head of the Industrial Society and chair of the Big Innovation Centre. He recently wrote that 'British capitalism is broken'.

> We live in a country whose banking system seven years ago was only saved by a US$ 1 trillion intervention and remains crippled by the legacy of private debt and stunning losses. Months ago the secession of Scotland, which threatened to break up the foundations of the state, was narrowly avoided; it remains an ongoing threat. Our share of world markets continues to shrink and our trade deficit has climbed to unthinkable levels. Wages have fallen in real terms, by the greatest degree in more than a century. Inequality of income and wealth have risen to desperately high levels and may soon metastasise into a serious economic and social cancer.[45]

44. Daniel Pink op cit.
45. Will Hutton, 'British Capitalism is Broken: Here's how to fix it', *Guardian*, 11 February 2015, pp. 27–29.

The severance of values into split pieces has several similarities to breakaway aggressive cancer cells in the human body which divide at runaway speed to doom the larger organism. This concludes our survey of how and why values taken too far break into lethal shards so that these broken pieces lose touch with our integrity, our shared humanity and its wider meanings. We must stop scrambling for monies and unlock the higher purposes to be found within capitalism.

CHAPTER 3

Stakeholders or just shareholders?

The second event that greatly affected my thinking was having to fight off a private equity takeover bid for the family business during the summer of 2007. There was not the slightest pretence of seeking to improve the performance of the company ... the only change they proposed was to sell off all the properties of the company and replace this with massive debt ... and walk away with £1 billion profit. This bid which had the backing of the City, due to the £100 million fees the investment banks would earn ... seemed to me a perfect example of wealth appropriation as opposed to wealth creation.'[1]

In this chapter we will explore one important consequence of the excesses examined in Chapter 2. The notion that shareholders are sovereign over the entirety of a publicly owned company is a claim to universal truth which is not well supported by the facts. It is also a doctrine which is high in individualism since shareholders are in most cases not known to the companies they own. They are scattered, aggregated, absentee owners and mostly trade in the shares they own, retaining these for less than six months on average. Their long-term commitment to the companies they fund is notable by its absence. Finally, the idea that what matters above all else are increases in the share price and dividends and that the general health and welfare of a company is indicated

1.   David Sainsbury, *Progressive Capitalism*, London: Biteback Publishing, 2014. The quotation is from the preface.

by what it pays shareholders is ultra-specific. It assumes that one statistic, quarterly reports, tell us everything we need to know. According to the universal theory the shareholders own the company and are entitled to what is left over when all contracts have been discharged. Other parties to the wealth creation process are under contract and receive what they bargained for, no more, no less. The success of the company is a function of the size of this surplus. If we assume that industry exists in order to enrich shareholders then such enrichment spells the success of the company, end of story. As the share price climbs more money becomes available for the company to continue its good work, so that more profit supposedly leads to higher investment. It is potentially a virtuous circle with the wealth-creating organization growing ever larger across the world. Why then are some well-placed individuals so critical of this arrangement?

When Jack Welch, long-time CEO of General Electric, retired he pronounced that maximizing shareholder wealth was 'the dumbest idea in the world'. He ought to know. He did it for more than thirty years at the helm of America's largest engineering company. In his early years he laid off so many thousands of managers that his nickname was Neutron Jack, in honour of the successor to the H-Bomb, the neutron bomb, which according to the taunt by Nikita Kruschev, preserved property and killed only people (it was never developed).

Why should maximizing shareholder wealth be considered 'dumb'? It is part of the rational excesses we criticized in Chapter 2. It is an extreme manifestation of the tendency of business to make money for its investors instead of using that money to create new business. It obliges all public companies to compete with each other in attracting investment in the short-term and it enables wealthy people to pay others to perform for them. It makes money into the king of the economy and elevates those who claim to act on behalf of shareholders, the financial sector of the economy. But if shareholders are not to be the chief beneficiaries then who should be? We will be exploring the role of *stakeholders* in creating wealth, of which shareholders are just one.

In order to understand stakeholding we need to consider actual business practices. Which parties are essential to creating and maintaining a business? Who owns the business and why? By what process is wealth created by those involved in the business? Looking more closely at the shareholder system itself, we will examine its roots, how it came into place, whether shareholders have increased their powers recently, and we will illustrate some of the dangers inherent in the system with the example of how Flextronics was able to extinguish its giant customer Compaq. We will explore whether shareholding is the choice of democratic countries and the role of private equity before finally turning to the startling claim put forward in a Harvard Business School publication that maximizing the take of shareholders is akin to cancer in the human body.

What parties are essential to creating business?

The truth is that business relies on quite a number of participants without which it could not survive. R. Edward Freeman, a professor of business administration, made this point at SRI International in 1983 and has championed it ever since.[2] He called these participants *stakeholders*. These are investors who supply the funds, managers and workers who produce the goods and services, suppliers who often contribute fifty per cent or more to the value of a product, lenders who supply day-to-day liquidity, customers whose use of the product generates value and who yield revenue, the community in which the company is based and the environment from which we often take without giving back. Then there are groups that might be key at one particular moment such as auditors, the media, unions and social media. For example the BBC is currently key to the tax evasion antics of HSBC. It is hard to see why, among all these actors, investors should be supreme and why a company's success should be measured by what it pays *out* rather than what employees, suppliers, communities and customers put *in*.

Where organizations are run mainly to enrich individual shareholders might not a company pay out *too much* and so weaken itself? How would we know if this was happening? Are the interests of a company nothing more than the interests of aggregated shareholders? Why should shareholders be preferred over designers, scientists and innovators who, rather than trading in company shares, may contribute their talents over the course of their whole working lives? This is not just an ethical question but a *practical* one. The relative influence of different parties in the wealth-creating process should be consistent with the facts on the ground and with the degrees of commitment required of those parties. Those who make the real difference between failure and success should be rewarded according to the difference they make. To do anything less is foolish.

If innovating, growing companies and working hard are keys to the success of an economy, should we give the power to people who may do none of those things? If A says to B, 'Here is my money! Give me your working life', then is this bargain entirely fair? If it is not fair, we can expect the wages of blue-collar workers to stagnate as they have and it looks like the managerial class may

2.   R. Edward Freeman and Jeffrey S. Harrison, *Stakeholder Theory: The State of the Art*, Cambridge: Cambridge University Press, 2010.

be next. If money for building enterprises is being siphoned off into private pockets, we can expect the whole economy to suffer. Equity markets may have recovered from the financial crisis of 2008 but most of the rest of us have hardly recovered at all and look like losing a whole decade. Something is very amiss.

The business secretary under Britain's coalition government of 2010–2015, Vince Cable, recently stated that, 'the shape of the recovery so far has not been all we might have hoped for'.[3] Engineering another housing boom and a debt-fuelled consumption boom have not been enough and could soon peter out. Exports are still stubbornly weak despite the twenty per cent devaluation in the value of the pound since 2008, business investment is poor and productivity is down. What is needed is 'long-term rebalancing at the heart of decision making'[4], with more R&D and innovation.

Who owns a business?

The idea that shareholders should own the company and receive its profits originates in how companies start up. Individuals or teams put their money at risk and recruit people to help them. Since those recruited are under contract, it seems only fair for the founders to collect any residue. They face all the uncertainty and risk. We have no quarrel with this situation and indeed the founders *should* come first, both in time and in importance.

These, usually small, companies do very well by their communities and are generally liked and admired.[5] They create most of the new jobs and are more innovative than large public corporations by a factor of five or more.[6] However, we should not fool ourselves. These are ad hoc groups of stakeholders, 'families, friends and fools'. Employees may work for nothing in the early days and get an equity stake instead, as may suppliers, customers and lenders. Over ninety per cent of the world's companies have this informal family-type structure, with founder, leader and prime shareholder as one person, allied with close friends and relatives. If they succeed they prosper as one. If they succeed exceedingly they may go public. This is where the problem starts.

The problem arises with the public corporation owned by an aggregate of

3.   *Times*, 18 December 2013.

4.   ibid.

5.   John Mackey and Raj Sisodia, *Conscious Capitalism: Liberating the Heroic Spirit in Capitalism*, Boston: Harvard Business School Press, 2013, p. 103.

6.   Hermann Simon, *The Hidden Champions of the 21st Century*, New York: Springer, 2009.

shareholders. These did *not* arrive on the scene first, did *not* conceive of the company in the first place and had nothing to do with it growing vigorously enough to justify an initial public offering (IPO). These kinds of shareholder are quite different from the original founders and they followed rather than led when an investment bank offered the shares to the market and underwrote them. That they deserve a privileged position over other stakeholders and should be treated like founders is hard to justify. Many of them will be mere speculators, ready to sell the moment the price of the shares climb. Will Hutton has estimated that seventy-two per cent of all shareholding is now speculative,[7] run by hedge funds, high frequency traders and investment banks. An indexed fund has no relationship to companies by definition. Some twenty per cent of all British companies on the London Stock Exchange have evaporated over the last decade. Between 1991 and 2015 the proportion of British shares owned by British pension funds and insurance companies has dropped from fifty per cent to fifteen per cent. British industry and finance are coming apart. Moreover in the wealth-creating process *shareholders come last* in the sequence of steps that must be taken. To this important issue we now turn.

By what process do these parties create wealth?

Far from coming first, shareholders in a public corporation 'come last' in at least two senses. They are last on the scene and only arrive when the IPO is complete. But they are also last in the *sequence of wealth creation*. In Figure 3.1 we show a wealth-creating cycle, what needs to be done in what sequence in order to create wealth. First, at stage 1, comes the loan from the bank or funds from the accumulating share price, then at stage 2 comes the purchase of components from suppliers, some of whom add considerable value, then at stage 3 the leaders of companies must inspire employees to feats of innovative and productive work. At stage 4 customers supply revenue and use the product as was intended which can also add considerable value. Finally at stage 5 lenders and shareholders are repaid. Wealth has been created at stages 3 and 4, by a whole product which is more than the sum of its parts and by the manner of customer use that could transform his life, his business or both.

The wealth-generating rectangles are white and mere zero-sum transactions are black. We have assumed that what suppliers provide is a mere transaction, but it *could* be an act of co-creation where benefits from any new component

7.   Will Hutton, 'British Capitalism is broken', *Guardian*, 11 February 2015.

are shared between the parties in a gain-sharing agreement. This is very effective but unfortunately rare. The secret of successful stakeholder and labour relations is to bargain over wealth *before* it is created, to give workers or suppliers a fixed percentage of productivity gains and the gains created by the implementation of their innovative ideas. Once the money is made everything shareholders gain, employees, suppliers and the community must lose, and the threat of outsourcing is used to beat them into submission.

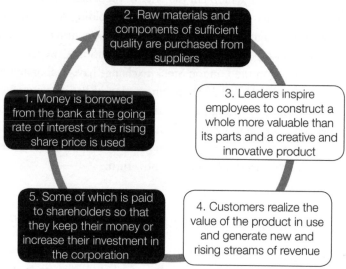

Figure 3.1 Stakeholders in the wealth-creation cycle

It is of course possible to argue that the wealth-creating cycle starts at stage 5 with the investment by shareholders of a portion of the gains they received, but that is not what typically happens. Usually shareholders have bought into an existing proposition prepared in advance. They are neither real founders nor instigators. They do *not* generally form a committed or strategic group that instructs companies how to act. Even when this is the case, the instruction is typically to buy back shares and create a spike in the price which they can exploit. By far the commonest pattern is for shareholders to react to events by buying or selling shares. Their role is passive and extractive. They are rent-collectors favouring those that benefit them most in the short-term. Moreover not everything that is received by shareholders is reinvested, especially if the ends they seek are more consumption. In this case money will be *removed* from industry over time and spent on luxuries.

There *are* a minority of activist investors who hold large blocks of shares and concern themselves with company policy whether that company is privately or publicly held. The current evidence is that such companies do much better than most. But this is because investors are behaving like managers, employees, innovators, suppliers and customers. Unlike most shareholders, they are committed to that particular company and are doing what they can to make it work better. These are, however, a very small number and our objection is not to shareholders per se but to the conduct or non-conduct of most shareholders. A front cover of the *Economist* recently featured these investors who are praised for their work. Yet the cover cartoon features *hyenas snapping at a bull,* an interesting insight into the 'dismal science'. Do not hyenas feast on dead animals? What will happen to the bull in such a vision?

The more typical shareholder is saving for retirement and leaves investment decisions to brokers, financial advisers and pension fund managers. In order to justify their keep, these managers buy and sell shares frequently so that shares in the USA are held for an average of less than a year and in the UK for even less – compared to ten years in 1946. We are becoming ever more short-term. Most shareholders do not know and therefore do not care in which companies their funds are invested. Their sole interest is receiving more money. Most pension funds spread their risks so widely that they rarely have as much as one per cent of their funds in any one company, do not sit on the board and take an interest only in share prices and dividends. They will buy shares that are performing well and dump the rest. They have little concern for any company in particular. Their earnings come from the broad aggregate of all companies in their portfolio. They are rent-collectors whose decisions are made mostly by proxies with only one purpose in mind, to trade profitably. The current relationship between shareholders and stakeholders can be depicted as a vicious circle as shown in Figure 3.2.

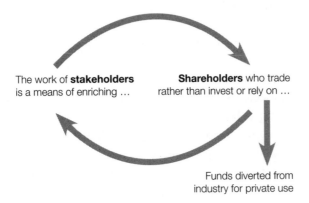

Figure 3.2 Stakeholders as a means to private gain

Stakeholders are the means to the ends of shareholder profitability and as such they are dispensable and replaceable with, for example, software or outsourced labour from East Asia.

Governments, communities and the environment are also dispensable, there to be dumped on or used up. What ultimately matters is that shareholders gain. But, as we shall see in later chapters, when stakeholders are considered as ends in themselves all parties prosper as one alliance and each benefits according to the value of the contribution made. The result would be a circle encompassing all stakeholders, investors included, in a virtuous circle, as shown in Figure 3.3.

Shareholders are but one of several kinds of ...   **Stakeholder** who between them create wealth for all, including ...

Figure 3.3 Shareholders as partners to other stakeholders

Note that stakeholders *include* shareholders in their circle of participants, while shareholders *exclude* stakeholders from their privileged entitlements. The jobs that stakeholders do for each other are ends in themselves, inherently pleasurable and valuable, yet deserving of the fruits of success. In summary, we appear to have given most power to the most passive, the least caring and least knowledgeable persons, to those most frequently absent from the companies in which they hold an interest, those who happened last upon the scene and have scant connection to the actual creators of wealth. It is their role to harvest what others have sown and cultivated. Can we be surprised that wealth creation flags?

An additional problem comes from steering a company in a way that makes it more profitable. Generally speaking profit and loss are *lagging* indicators, the result of what stakeholders have done or not done in the past few years. It is a little like trying to steer a ship by the wake left a mile astern. If we really want to know what is going wrong we need to ask employees, customers, suppliers and stakeholders. They will be the first to notice deteriorating service or quality. By the time profits dip it may already be too late!

The historic roots of shareholding

How did the shareholder system arise? It was an important source of funds for early industrialization in Britain and the USA. The risks taken by pioneering industries were very large. The first ship-builders, cargo companies, railway companies, steel mills, chemical companies and car-makers took considerable risks with untried technologies. Their investors demanded high returns and, given the risks, they deserved to receive them. But one nation's breakthrough rapidly becomes another nation's school curriculum. Other nations, Switzerland and Germany especially, started to teach the subject of manufacturing in schools and colleges.

One advantage of following fast on British heels was that the processes for creating industries were known and had been codified ready-for-use. The risks and uncertainties were much lower and industrial banks were willing to put up the money at a much lower cost of capital. This is how Switzerland, Germany, Japan, France and others chased down the leaders. Many companies also preferred to remain small or medium-sized. They never went public but were managed by founding families with large blocks of shares. In Scandinavia, most industries were founded by wealthy family dynasties and remained in their hands for generations.

The race to catch up is also responsible for the more communitarian values of continental Europe, as it created an environment in which managers, bankers, teachers, trades unions and whole industries were ready to help each other catch up with the Anglo-Americans. The main exponents of a more cooperative form of industry, Germany and Japan, had limited influence in the twentieth century, having lost two world wars in the case of Germany and one in the case of Japan. However, following the Second World War the recoveries of both countries were regarded as near miraculous. Was there perhaps something to this other kind of capitalism?

The Japanese economic miracle began in the early 1950s and lasted for thirty years or more. Japan gave a greatly reduced role to shareholders, much to the anger of Americans who had bought shares. They were entitled to dividends and to the worth of their shares but leaders of companies would not answer to their demands. Profits were lower in Japan in general and what was reported in newspapers was market share, what companies had done for their communities, not so much for themselves.[8] At the same time, several countries in East Asia were prospering, for example South Korea, Taiwan,

8.   Charles Hampden-Turner and Fons Trompenaars, *The Seven Cultures of Capitalism*, London: Piatkus, 1995, pp. 107–110.

Singapore, Hong Kong, Malaysia and later Indonesia and China, and they all chose the Japanese economic model.

Most of these countries had very high savings rates, so cheap capital was readily available. There are of course stock markets in many Asian countries – Hong Kong, Singapore, Japan, South Korea and China – but their influence is much smaller, despite Anglo-American pressure. The attitude of such nations is quite understandable. Most shareholders are still foreigners while most *stakeholders* are indigenous citizens, that is employees, customers, suppliers, lenders and the community. The various governments want to make sure their *own* people benefit from allowing multinationals to operate locally so they look to the prosperity of these stakeholders and create high-trust networks.

The People's Republic of China has stiff conditions and some US companies operating there must train their local competitors, take on and train an indigenous partner and be more generous to China than to their home communities in the USA. Thousands of trees are planted 'voluntarily' and donations to Project Hope, for the education of the peasant population, are generous. Intel mounted a Science Fair that six million Chinese attended. Volkswagen built an automobile museum. AEG was prevailed upon to set up a school for insurance agents. There is a degree of choice but you cannot choose to make no contribution at all. This kind of stakeholder oriented cooperative capitalism is growing apace.[9]

The 1997 Asian financial crisis was 'solved' by the International Monetary Fund, largely at a cost to local economies and to the benefit of foreign shareholders. Shareholders had taken fright over developments in Indonesia and billions of dollars were repatriated, even from strong economies like Singapore. As a result, shareholder-dominated capitalism was tarnished long-term, and several sovereign wealth funds were created, designed to plug the gap if international shareholders had another bout of jitters. They still accept our money but know better than to rely on it. So we have two forms of capitalism. One legal, formal and official with shareholders as supreme beneficiaries; the other is *de facto* informal and unofficial with the various parties to the enterprise getting their share by one expedient or another, underpinned by local cultures and government influence. The first extols competition, with shareholders winning. The second extols cooperation, with all parties sharing both the creation of wealth and the rewards from this.

9. Personal communication with Professor Tan Ten-Kee, 2009, at the time Visiting Scholar at the Harvard Business School and 'Case Notes on the Chinese Economy', Case Clearing House, Graduate School of Business, Harvard University.

A recent surge in shareholder power

If the shareholder-dominated economy is less effective, why, we may ask, has the USA dominated the world economy so completely and for so long? The short answer is that the shareholder system has only come to the fore in the last thirty years or so. America and the UK used to be mixed (stakeholder) economies and fared much better in that form.

Finance capitalism received a major setback in the 1929 crash and the ensuing Great Depression. America only emerged from this serious downturn in the late 1930s as a result of heavy defence expenditure as the Second World War loomed. Hardly was this war over than the Cold War commenced, alongside active wars first in Korea and then in Vietnam. The ensuing competition with the Soviet Union meant showing the world that all Americans were healthier and happier under capitalism but it also involved guaranteeing a higher standing of living for all citizens, even the poor. So if we measure socialism by the size of the command economy, then America was the most 'socialist' economy on earth at that point, outspending the Soviets several times over. In reality, the defence budget and the space programme combined to form a massive state subsidy to high-tech industries. This military-industrial complex, as Eisenhower called it, was supposed to save Americans from Big Government – but in actual fact such policies *constituted* such a government. It was an industrial policy for the growth of technology in all but name. The cost-plus contracts awarded by the Pentagon were a carte blanche to innovate at the taxpayers' expense and to their later benefit.

With the fall of the Soviet Union in the late 1980s, capitalism finally triumphed. Now *real capitalism*, dominated by shareholders, could at last be tried. Both Reagan and Thatcher as leaders championed the 'supply side' of the economy, meaning investors. The problem for America, especially, was its self-serving managers, just like the self-serving unions before them; both had to be 're-engineered' and cut back ruthlessly by an investment community demanding real returns on its money and a cutting out of waste. Assets, especially human ones, needed to *sweat*. The financial elite was taking charge.[10] Shareholders were their front and their customers, so while shareholders were officially the chief beneficiaries, in fact the financial industry acting in their name levied fees and took ever larger slices of the pie.

Both GE and Enron automatically severed ten per cent of their employees every year. The fear this practice engendered would clearly do employees good!

10. Robert B. Reich, *Aftershock: The Next Economy and America's Future*, New York: Randon House, 2011, pp. 36–39.

Money or the lack of it could do wonders. Eveready's R&D facilities were sold to Duracell by corporate raider, Lord Hanson (who'd been ennobled by Thatcher). Of course Duracell paid over the odds to take out its only real international rival and Eveready's shareholders received a huge pay-off. The only real victim was Eveready itself. What chance did it have with zero innovation? The dry-cell battery industry is sterile enough by any reckoning! This was the *coup de grâce*. A potentially creative company with a monopoly in several countries and a duopoly in the rest, turned into a money-machine for shareholders.

This bias in favour of shareholders is typically expressed with neither reserve nor apology. In his book *Firm Commitment*, Colin Mayer quotes Arnold Weinstock, head of the UK's General Electric Company, on the matter of making a profit, virtually recommending that you should attack the other stakeholders: 'The secret is to see what the market will pay for a product. You then see whether you can manufacture at that price. You then work out what you can get off costs by squeezing a discount out of the suppliers, producing in bulk, reducing your manpower – and that is your profit.'[11] Mayer's response to this approach was, 'He created immense financial wealth for his shareholders, but success for the City did not equate to success for the British electrical and electronics industry that he came to lead.'[12] GEC is dead.

In the USA, 'Chainsaw Al' Dunlap acquired businesses, carved them up, fired their managers and then sold the pieces to former competitors, like heads upon a platter. His book *Mean Business* celebrated these purges and, indeed, 'lean and mean' were the watchwords of the time.[13] He told 'arrogant' young managers stepping out of Porsches for which shareholders had paid that they were dismissed forthwith, a process that seemed to give him infinite pleasure. He made a great deal of money for shareholders, himself included, but wealth was being destroyed along with the companies he seized and the managerial class was shrinking.

That this surge in shareholder power was relatively recent is demonstrated by statistics relating to relative income. During the period of great prosperity in the USA, between 1947 and 1975, average wages climbed from US$25,000 to US$75,000. As recently as 1963, the top one per cent of Americans earned only ten per cent of national income. With Reagan at the helm, by 1983 the earnings of the top one per cent rose to sixteen per cent. The situation stayed

11. Quoted in Colin Mayer, *Firm Commitment: Why the corporation is failing us*, Oxford: Oxford University Press, 2013, p. 164.

12. Colin Mayer, *Firm Commitment*, p.165.

13. Alfred Dunlap, *Mean Business*, New York: Random House, 1996.

that way for ten years, then jumped to twenty per cent by 1993 and to 24.6 per cent by 2007.[14] This money was taken from the pockets of those who work for a living and put into the pockets of those who manage investments. As the *Financial Times* headline of 13 January 2012 declared: 'RBS plan to cut 3,500 jobs lifts share price'. No wonder productivity levels are falling among those employees remaining.

Three more developments skewed the distribution of income in favour of tiny elites at the apex of society. It became popular to award stock options to the CEO and very senior managers. On average, the top five managers in US companies now receive seventy-five per cent of all stock options.[15] This was supposed to help management identify with shareholders since they were now shareholders too. Unfortunately, it also gives them an incentive to create spikes in the share price so they can exercise their options and then sell. A favourite device is to buy back your own shares, which creates a brief spike and a profit for the favoured five but does very little for the company as a whole. GM bought back its own shares more than twenty times before declaring bankruptcy. Its option holders did well and flew to Washington in a corporate jet to ask for bailout money.

We have also witnessed an astronomical rise in the salaries of CEOs. In 1980 they received 42.1 times as much as the average employee. By 2010 this had reached 325 times as much.[16] It is hard to understand why they are worth multiples of what they were worth just twenty years ago when the economy was doing much better and why nations with a fraction of these rewards compete so successfully with the USA and UK. Surely the *real* reason for this sudden generosity is to make top managers side with shareholders against employees. Since they work every day with these employees their natural sympathies might lie with colleagues, unless large amounts of money pull them in the opposite direction.

Such rewards also place the CEO under relentless pressure to increase profits quickly and in the short-term. Profits raised through R&D, higher productivity and innovation are hard work, very demanding and take more time than the CEO has left to serve, but profits raised by cutting costs, lowering salaries, laying off people, raising prices and cutting quality are much easier and quicker and will show up in the next quarterly report. The CEOs alone can do little to boost innovation, which is achieved by others, but they

14. Reich, *Aftershock*, pp. 20–21.

15. Mackey and Sisodia, *Conscious Capitalism*, pp. 71 and 107.

16. Mackey and Sisodia, *Conscious Capitalism*, p. 19.

can sell the downtown HQ building and then lease it back and add millions to the profit figures at the stroke of a pen. There are many such tricks that increase profits and redistribute money to the investment community but create no real wealth. Only the accounting is creative.

A report by management consulting firm McKinsey found that eighty per cent of managers in the USA would cut spending in areas like R&D if it meant hitting promised targets in the company's quarterly report. They would do so even if they thought it would destroy the long-term value of the company.[17] Earnings targets for shareholders get the highest priority. Growing the company can be postponed indefinitely. No wonder major companies shed labour and that growth comes from the small and medium-sized.

From a strategic point of view maximizing shareholder income can be a serious handicap. All your rivals have to do is lower their prices, squeeze your margins and wait. This is what the privately owned German supermarkets ASDA and LIDL have done to Tesco and Morrisons, etc. If publicly owned companies feel they must make twenty per cent while privately owned companies are prepared to make half that for a few years, guess who wins? British and American profit maximizers will yield to companies willing to accept *less* profit in the short-term in exchange for higher market share. Of course when the profit maximizers withdraw from these markets the market-share seekers can *raise their margins again*. Longer-term strategies trump the short-term every time. We are repeatedly outfoxed.

Centrica, the privatized British Gas, withdrew from the bid to build the Sizewell and Hinkley Point nuclear power-stations because the government would only guarantee a 10.5 per cent rate of return. Who rode to the rescue and joined the consortium? It was two state-owned nuclear power companies from China who insisted on being the controlling shareholders. They now have a major stake in Britain's energy future. Less profit meant more power. Another way we progressively give away our industrial infrastructure is by outsourcing to lower-wage countries. This pays shareholders but costs jobs and skills.

The case of Flextronics and Compaq

That the exclusive pursuit of shareholder profits can lead to disaster is illustrated by the relative fortunes of Compaq, a once-huge Texas-based multinational, and the formerly tiny and humble Singapore-based subcontractor Flextronics.

17. Mackey and Sisodia, *Conscious Capitalism*, p. 90.

Compaq had started to outsource the manufacture of its circuit boards to Flextronics and in doing so had lowered its costs and raised its profits. The following account of what happened next was given to us by Professor Clayton Christensen at the Harvard Business School.

> It really is the pursuit of profit that is the causal mechanism behind both prosperity and failure. Disruption can occur when a company comes in right at the bottom of the market in its least demanding sector, as Toyota did, and then moves up tier by tier, or when a company starts at the very lowest tier of the value chain and integrates forward. There is an interesting illustration in the interaction between Flextronics and its customer Compaq. Flextronics started by making the simplest of the circuit boards inside Compaq computers. But the company approached Compaq with a proposition. 'We are doing a good job on your circuit boards, why don't you let us make your motherboards as well? Circuit assembly is not your core competence and we could make them for twenty per cent less cost.'

> Compaq's analysts looked at the issue and said, 'Gosh, they could! If we gave all the circuit making manufacturing to them we could get this off our balance sheet.' So they shovelled that over. Their company's revenues were unaffected and their profits really improved. Flextronics' revenues and profits increased too. It felt good for one to get in and one to get out. Then Flextronics approached them again. 'We've been making your motherboards and that's really the guts of the computer. Come to think of it, why should you be bothered by assembly? It is not your core competence and we could do it for twenty per cent less.'

> Compaq's analysts looked at it and saw that they could. 'If we gave them assembly we could get the whole of our manufacturing assets off our balance sheet.' So they moved that over. Compaq's revenues were unaffected but their profits improved and Flextronics' profits improved. Once again, it was good for one to get out and the other to get in. Then Flextronics approached them again. 'Come to think of it, we're already making your computer. You should not be bothered with your supply chain, all those components and logistics. We have the contacts, as it is. Logistics is not your core competence. We could do it all for twenty per cent less.'

Once again, Compaq's analysts looked at it and agreed. 'If we gave them this, we could get all our current assets off the balance sheet.' Compaq's profits looked really good now, particularly their return on assets because they had almost no assets left and Wall Street loves asset-light companies. Flextronics revenues were up and its profits and they were now into value-added services and Wall Street loves value-added services. Flextronics comes back once again. 'We've been managing your supply chain for you. Come to think of it, you should not have to bother with designing the computer. Design is only component selection and we're in touch with all the component suppliers anyway. Your real core competence is your brand.' So Compaq shovelled over the design as well and its profits went even higher!

So then Flextronics comes back, but not to Compaq to Best Buy, the giant retailer. 'Here we are, makers of some of the world's finest electronic products and computers. Come to think of it, you should not have to stock that brand Compaq; we can give you this brand, that brand or any brand, since we make several of them anyway and we will do it for twenty per cent less.' Bingo! One has arrived and the other is gone. And this strategy has really been an engine of prosperity for Singapore, for Taiwan and others. You start at the back, at the least profitable tier and no one takes any notice, then you integrate forward. But there are signs that Flextronics, Zeus and others are now outsourcing their lower-value components to China and Vietnam – and so it all begins again.[18]

Compaq foundered and was sold to Hewlett Packard for whom Flextronics also worked! But what is the difference between the profitability sought by Compaq and the profitability sought by Flextronics? Why was only one fatal and the other brilliantly successful? The answer is quite simple: Compaq sought profits for its shareholders above all other objectives and sacrificed other stakeholders in doing so. First domestic circuit board makers had to go, then the more skilled makers of motherboards, then the assemblers and then the logistics staff. Finally, the engineering designers were for the chop, all to boost the bottom line and get more for shareholders and the investment industry.

An economy that gives work to foreign countries and deprives its own employees and suppliers of that work will become poorer over time, while assisting the countries to which it outsources to overtake it. Singapore is

---

18. Excerpts from a filmed interview with Clayton Christensen for 'Innovation and the Fate of Nations', currently in production.

much wealthier per capita than the USA and the UK as Chapter 5 will show. Compaq 'gave away the store' allowing Flextronics to hollow it out – all so that it would look better to the financial markets. Giving away your assets to improve the profit–asset ratio is akin to a death wish. Unlike the temporary profitability of Compaq, Flextronics brought all its stakeholders with it and shared the wealth. The skilled employees Compaq shed were substituted, trained and created wealth in Singapore instead.

This is by no means the only case. The Italian silk tie industry was eight hundred years old and had always sourced its silk from China. But then their suppliers asked to dye the silk and then to cut it. Both operations were cheaper than before and raised profits. The supplier asked for the patterns and offered to print the ties. Even more profits were made. Why send all the ties to Rome? Why not send the patterns to those countries where they sold best? And that was the end of a venerable Italian industry.[19] Once you start outsourcing you are on a slippery slope because the labour pool around your company will drain away until it may not be *possible* to recruit locally. The talent has dispersed.

Underlying this whole problem is an obsession with specific costs. Yes, indeed, East Asia is a lot cheaper but it is also far away, may speak other languages and have its own plans to replace you. What matters is the productivity per man-hour and the innovativeness of your workforce and the readiness of your suppliers to co-create with you and feed you with ideas and vital new components. And all this means much more than the timely delivery of cheap circuit boards. Many products succeed or fail as a result of their components. The electric car industry is at the mercy of battery technology. At the moment the range of cars is insufficient. Those who outsource too readily may give away the most important component and find themselves the hostage of foreign suppliers.

Share prices tend to leap when companies announce redundancies. Why? It cannot be true that fewer, more frightened employees will do better work – quite the contrary. It is well known that fear kills innovation. The reason the share price jumps is because money is on the way from one set of pockets to the next. Employees are getting less, shareholders and their advisers are getting more. The irony is that, while shareholders are treated better than employees, customers or suppliers, they are *still* not doing very well. This is in part due to the financial industry which helps itself from what investors supply. But it also comes from milking the undernourished cow until it dries

19. James Kynge, *China Shakes the World*, London: Weidenfeld and Nicholson, 2006, pp. 84–87.

up. Many pension funds are ailing and, as we live longer, retirement income is increasingly inadequate while savers are losing money through rock bottom interest rates. There is a note of desperation in the acquisitive postures of many shareholders. They are trying to get more for less and are shaking down the genuine wealth creators.

Should large public companies gobble up the small?

One thing that large publicly owned companies do is acquire and gobble up smaller companies. The assumption is that the larger company is right and that seizing control of the smaller one is to the benefit of us all because its larger size spells greater success. But does it? One problem with large companies is that they are far more bureaucratic, structured and hidebound. Xerox Parc recruited some really brilliant innovators in the 1970s. Their good judgement was extraordinary. There was only one problem. *They all had to leave Xerox before they could succeed.* Large companies are far less innovative, job creating, developmental and growth-oriented as Chapter 6 will show. When Hewlett Packard acquired Autonomy disaster struck and accusations still fly. The whole problem of taking ownership of genius is that you can destroy what you grab though failure to grasp its potential. Is not just a piece of property but a complex living system all too easily killed unless you closely confer with its creators. It is like a beautiful sea-shell from which the living creature has flown. You have purchased its dead form which is merely decorative. The founder of the acquired company has received so much money that he cannot wait to do another start-up and leave a multinational to count its own digits and rationalize its own property portfolio.

We may have to radically rethink what it means to take ownership of innovative systems. You cannot order them around or deploy their powers to your own advantage, at least not without reducing their value. Indeed you cannot really deploy their strengths in any way without deep mutual understanding and without sharing power with them, which renders ownership untenable. The whole property paradigm may be out of date, an exercise in taxidermy and the stuffed trophies of the chase.

Is shareholding the preference of a democratic society?

Surely the real case for shareholding is that the electorate prefers it and the USA and Britain are democratic societies? Moreover, it enables us to vote and voting is a democratic procedure. If shareholders vote for their company to be taken over at a particular price per share, then isn't that fair and just for everyone? Well, not exactly. The takeover of a company may radically disrupt the lives of employees, suppliers, customers and so on, yet they have no say in it. The shareholders will be offered more money per share, which they will usually accept, even if they cannot remember the name of the company! They do not share and too few of them care.

Takeovers may also reward failure. The company which is the target will usually find its share price rising and the handful of senior executives with share options may want the hostile bid to succeed so they can cash in. If they mount a defence it may be half-hearted. They have private reasons for yielding their company to outsiders. Once a bidding war starts 'the markets' want the highest bidder to succeed. They have much to gain. Many acquired companies lose whatever lustre they may once have had. Small is flexible, informal, spontaneous and generative. Large is too often rigid, formal, contrived and lethargic.

As to whether shareholding is *preferred* to stakeholding, we have been asking this question for ten years of companies who share in our research agenda and pay for the information, nearly a hundred of them have responded. Table 3.1 provides the latest results from the Trompenaars Hampden-Turner database.

Table 3.1 Percentage of managers preferring the stakeholder model

Country	%	Country	%	Country	%
1. Japan	92.4	7. Indonesia	81.7	13. Sweden	72.5
2. China	91.2	8. Taiwan	79.3	14. Italy	71.4
3. Singapore	89.1	9. Germany	76.1	15. UK	67.2
4. Malaysia	87.0	10. Finland	75.1	16. Canada	65.3
5. S. Korea	86.2	11. Belgium	74.9	17. Australia	64.1
6. France	84.2	12. Holland	73.9	18. USA	59.6

The scores have moved towards stakeholding over time, but quite slowly. Note that all the East Asian nations, led by Japan who pioneered the model, choose stakeholding by a five to one majority, that Germany and Finland, Europe's most successful economies, endorse it by four to one or better, and that only in Britain's ex-colonies is shareholding supported and then by less than thirty-five per cent. So the maximizing of shareholder wealth is not even supported by most English and American managers. Of course, managers *are* stakeholders so they might have something to say about the situation. Clearly, making money for a group of people unknown to them fails to inspire their enthusiasm.

The reputation of big business reached an all-time low in 2009, with eighty-four per cent of Americans having no trust or confidence in it, up from sixty-six per cent in 1975.[20] At the same time, the reputation of small business, without publicly held shares, was high and the same survey found that sixty-nine per cent of Americans had confidence in them. Clearly something goes wrong when corporations pass into public ownership and shareholders flex their muscles.

The role of private equity

How do shareholders get hold of the monies and the value previously delivered to managers, workers, suppliers, customers and the government? They do it through private equity companies that buy up companies by offering more to shareholders than they are currently receiving. These were once called leveraged buy-outs, which sold 'junk bonds' to raise vast amounts of debt, but these were getting a poor press. American financier Michael Milken was even sent to prison for securities fraud; he was the model for Gordon Gekko (whose mantra was 'Greed is Good') in the film *Wall Street*. This led to the labels 'high-yield' bonds and private equity, but the wealth destroyed was much the same as before.

The ordinary company, whether public or private, is constantly in danger of being raided and taken over, even when it is creating wealth. For example, Cadbury was making respectable profits when acquired by Kraft.[21] Suppose a company invests in the calibre of its workforce by training it to a higher level. It pays more than the market pays but it gets much more from each employee and comes out ahead. Or suppose it invests heavily in R&D and picks the best suppliers, not the cheapest, and pays them on time. This strategy is expensive in the short-term but will pay off in spades a decade from now when the whole industry has a chance to upgrade itself.

But a hostile raider, noting these expenditures, says to shareholders – who hold their shares for an average of six to eleven months, remember – 'would you not like more money *now*? I can get it for you.' By slashing R&D expenditures, by cutting back on training, by squeezing the prices suppliers charge and paying them late, by saving on product quality, the hostile raider

20. Jeffrey M Jones, 'Americans most confident in the military', *Gallup Politics*, 23 June 2011.

21. Colin Mayer, *Firm Commitment*, pp. 151–53.

can offer more money per share to people to whom the company itself may mean nothing and is simply a minor source of their incomes.

Once a rival bid is made, the price of shares will rise to a level not far from what is being offered. The shareholder is *already* better off and may not wish the bid to fail and the price to slip back. The shareholders, or those acting for them, are likely to welcome the rise in price and thank those who occasioned it. For this reason, it becomes very hard to protect the long-term interests of the company from short-term opportunism. There is a persuasive case in hard cash for giving shareholders and the PE raider more and everyone else less. On 29 January 2014, for example, the *Financial Times* informed us that Vodafone shareholders were 'disappointed' that AT&T's takeover bid had stalled. They clearly *want* a US company to take over a British one. In this way money is moved from the middle and working classes to what *The Economist* hailed as 'the New Kings of Capitalism'.

What the many PE partners then acquire is a company weighed down with the huge debts incurred as a result of buying it in the first place. It is not the same company! And this debt effectively discourages any further investment until the debts are paid off. In any case, the acquirer is usually a finance type with little understanding of the technology the company employs. The company has its costs squeezed, its unused land sold off, its headcount reduced, its R&D expenditure slashed, its salaries frozen or reduced and its prices hiked. But, more than that, the PE firm can charge its *own company* a hefty fee for the trouble of taking it over and brook no refusal; cash is thus drained from the unit that could create wealth and placed in the hands of private money-makers – a zero-sum game if ever there was one.[22]

Indeed, the PE partners may not stop there. They can order the company they have bought to borrow even more from a bank and pay these sums directly to the partners. In a recent study, thirty-eight per cent of them did so in the first year of ownership. The acquisitions, not the PE partners, are legally responsible for this debt. They can demand their acquisition pay them dividends and pocket these too. Forty per cent of the companies owned by the fourteen largest PE partnerships in the USA paid dividends to their acquirers between 2002 and 2006. Bain Capital, headed much of the time by Mitt Romney, took over seven large companies between 1988 and 2000. Six filed for bankruptcy, after lasting an average of six years, and the seventh was prosecuted for fraud. The money moved from working people to equity partners and shareholders.

22. See Josh Kosman, *The Buyout of America*, New York: Portfolio Penguin, 2009, p. 220.

Of course, given this crushing burden, the company is unlikely to survive; it generally struggles on for six to nine years until the principal on its loan is due as a balloon payment (the balance due at the maturity of a loan). Then it will declare bankruptcy. But this takes some years and, given the present value of money, the attitude is that it probably pays to win now and lose something much later. Also there is land to be sold off and assets to be stripped and sold to the highest bidder. There is also a good chance of the creditors accepting, say, 50 cents on the dollar. Plundering the company and destroying wealth is well worthwhile for the partners and many of these costs are externalized and picked up by the taxpayer and other stakeholders.

Of course, PE firms would prefer their companies to survive and their stated strategy is to sell them at a profit having turned them around. But the time span for this transformation is three to six years, ludicrously short-term, and anything that might pay off in the longer term is not usually attempted. The aim is to make the most profit in the least time and to free up the money for another raid. If you cut back on customer service or product quality, this may not register for three years or more. If you cut back on R&D, the benefits of the earlier expenditure have yet to emerge from the pipeline. The aim is to sell before the consequences of the cuts bite and that could take six years or more.

The evidence is that PE firms cut more jobs than comparable companies. These tactics lead to a brief spurt in profits and a longer-run malaise; long before that malaise strikes the equity partners will have flown. Is there evidence for this? A study of leveraged buy-outs in the 1980s showed that fifty-two per cent subsequently declared bankruptcy, including Burlington Industries, Gillett Holdings, R.H. Macy, Owens Corning, National Gypsum and other long-established companies.

This is not a small problem. Buy-outs by PE partnerships totalled US$ 1.81 billion between 2000 and 2008 and PE-owned firms employ 7.5 million Americans. Kohlberg, Kravis and Roberts, a PE partnership, was the world's fourth-largest employer, larger than the US Postal Service, and 855,000 of its employees were working in the companies it owned. What will happen to these companies and their employees when debts fall due is anyone's guess. In May 2009 the Boston Consulting Group, which works with several PE partnerships, estimated that half of the companies they own, with 3.75 million workers, could collapse by 2015. To put this in proportion, only 2.6 million workers lost their jobs during the recession between 2008 and 2010. If this analysis is correct, we might expect many companies that were taken over to go bankrupt – and we do.[23]

23. Kosman, *The Buyout of America*.

This trend of buying, profiting and destroying wealth is encapsulated in the experience of Mervyn's discount stores. This large retail chain was acquired by Cerberus Capital Management and Sun Capital Partners. What attracted the acquirer was not merely the chain but also the real estate on which it stood, adjacent to which were unused spaces. What helped make Mervyn's profitable was that, like Wal-Mart, it paid below market rates for the space it occupied, which underpinned its discount strategy. The acquirers promptly split the company into two, a real-estate company and a discount retailer, and instructed the real-estate company to repay the debts by which it had been acquired by selling surplus property and by making Mervyn's pay full market rent. The retailer rallied briefly under good leadership and closed some unprofitable stores. It begged for the lower rents to be maintained so it could maintain its low-cost reputation and buy sufficient inventory as the recession hit.

But the real-estate company was having none of it. By this time it had repaid its purchaser the original price but not a penny was invested in Mervyn's retail stores. They declared bankruptcy in July 2008, having lost US$65 million, less than the extra rent they had been charged; 18,000 people lost their jobs, with no severance and no vacation pay. Charlene Glafke had spent thirty-five years working for the company and had risen to the position of senior marketing executive.[24] 'I gave my life to Mervyn's,' she told the *Wall Street Journal*. 'It is heart-breaking.' But there was a considerable amount of real estate to be sold off. Those who destroy wealth very soon discover that a dead company may be worth more than the lingering life of a feeble one. In any case it is the local communities and taxpayers who pick up the tab.

Another stakeholder whose funds get transferred to the PE partnership and its shareholders is the government. Under pressure, the Federal Government made interest on debt for PE partnerships tax deductible, like mortgage interest, at a cost to the taxpayer of an estimated US$2.5 billion in one decade. The transfer of money away from working people to the investment community was being subsidized at public expense! The excuse was that these deals were 'entrepreneurial'. In fact, most were purely financial and transferred money from acquired companies to investors. A move in   ~ess to stop the interest deduction caused the Dow Jones to fall sharply proposal was abandoned forthwith.

24. *Women's Wear Daily, 22* January 2007.

The race to the bottom

Another trend which maximizing shareholder enrichment precipitates is the 'the race to the bottom'. It is all very well to say that all other stakeholders bar shareholders are under contract but desperately poor countries have very little bargaining power to make those contracts even remotely fair. What typically happens is that a multinational company agrees to locate in the country that offers them the most generous terms and drives the hardest bargain it can. If it does not get what it demands it will locate elsewhere and the particular nation is desperate for an agreement. Typical demands are no unions, no environmental controls, free land, tax holidays, no social security, no pension rights and the easy repatriation of profits. The nation finds its safety net for its people shredded. When the Minister of Health earns ten per cent of the salary of the head of sales and wants a green card for his son, there is only one way concessions can flow. You hardly need to ask.

Is the maximization of shareholder value akin to cancer?

One of the most important properties of a living system is its vital balance. Human life depends upon our organs and biological systems functioning harmoniously as a whole. If just one element falls out of balance it can prove fatal to that whole.

We never expected to read a book published by Harvard Business School Press in which maximizing profits is likened to cancer in the human body. But *Conscious Capitalism*, by John Mackey, CEO of Whole Foods Markets, and Raj Sisodia, a professor of marketing, makes just this claim (see Chapter 7 for their theories on Conscious Capitalism). Neither is a rip-roaring radical and, in the case of Mackey, more the opposite. He is an ardent supporter of capitalism. Nevertheless they write,

> We find that cancer is a useful metaphor in what goes wrong with stakeholders in many businesses. The human body has about one hundred trillion cells, interacting cooperatively to stay alive, grow, and reproduce. Cancer is a breakdown of the harmonious interdependency between cells that is essential to good health. A cancerous tumor starts because some cells mutate and begin to divide and grow, ignoring the warning signals of the body's immune system that ... such growth is harmful to the larger biological system ... If the immune system has been weakened (by genetics, an unhealthy diet, tobacco, drugs, hol, toxins, stress, or negative mental attitudes), the cancer will

continue growing and spreading, eventually killing its host (and itself as well: cancer is ultimately suicidal).[25]

If one of America's most successful and innovative retailers can believe this, then we think it should be considered seriously. Cancer is a form of 'runaway' in the human body, in which certain cells grow aggressively at the expense of the rest until they encroach on a vital organ and death ensues. In order to grasp the concept of runaway we must first understand simple cybernetics. Cybernetics operates in terms of more–less, off–on. For example, the *less* warm it is in a house, the *more* the thermostat will turn up the heat. The heat is switched *on* in response to cold and *off* in response to warmth. The idea is to maintain equilibrium or a steady state. Likewise, the bulge behind the funnel of a steam locomotive (called the governor) provides *more* fuel to the engine if the train is moving slowly and *less* if the train is moving quickly. You do not want all that heavy metal to run away and cause a catastrophe.

Suppose the authors were saboteurs and sought to murder passengers on a train. We might rig the governor in the engine so that the *more* was its speed, the *more* fuel reached the engine, causing it to run ever faster and run away until it crashed. This is roughly what happens in a boom followed by a bust. Normally speaking, the more money you ask for your house, the less will be the demand. This is how markets work. But suppose house prices are rising by ten per cent a year? Then the more a buyer pays for your house in a quick cash sale, the sooner they can get ten per cent more for it. More has been followed by more rather than less. This situation is called 'positive feedback', an unfortunate term since the consequences are not positive at all! It is negative feedback, *more* followed by *less*, that keeps us all stable. The market booms when positive feedback takes hold but crashes when negative feedback returns, as it always does in the end.

This situation is exacerbated by speculation and the world casino. Would-be cash buyers for your house are not going to live there. They long ago ceased to ask themselves whether *they* would pay so much. They are gambling on the verdicts of *others* – somewhere out there is the greater fool who will pay this ridiculous sum! John Maynard Keynes likened this situation to a beauty pageant in which you had to guess the contestant whom *other* people would pick. With such a mindset you go with the crowd, however stupid and mistaken you believe it to be. We seem to have travelled some way from the rationality of the nineteenth century concept of 'economic man', honoured for his cool, deliberate decision-making.

25. Mackey and Sisodia, *Conscious Capitalism*, pp. 171–172.

Runaway can also occur when just one group of stakeholders, the shareholders, insist that they must get more money despite the fate of other stakeholders whose incomes are eroding. The more money the shareholders insist on getting, the less is available to other stakeholders. Their efforts may flag, their productivity may suffer and their revenues may fall, leading the shareholders to be *more* not less demanding. A vicious circle results

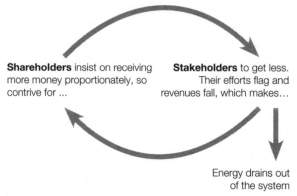

Shareholders insist on receiving more money proportionately, so contrive for ...

Stakeholders to get less. Their efforts flag and revenues fall, which makes…

Energy drains out of the system

Figure 3.4 A larger proportionate share of a starved industry

Shareholders are indeed getting less than they hoped for and many a pension pot is in severe trouble, but they fail to see the real reason. They are not getting too much overall, but too much *proportionately* from the industry and too little proportionately from the finance industry. If they allowed managers to invest more in their staff by providing training, and if they spent more on R&D, then revenues would be forthcoming. Above all, shareholders should *wait their turn* and let high quality and new knowledge attract more customers and more revenue *before* allowing the proceeds to be captured by their advisers.

It is odd that we can clearly recognize that some trade unions could wreck industry in pursuit of a singular group purpose, by growing too large and becoming too aggressive, yet we are unable to see that the finance industry purporting ⌐   ⌐sent shareholders can also push their self-interests too far and ⌐   Maximizing profits as opposed to optimizing the whole ⌐ns seizing incomes due to other stakeholders and thus ⌐as a whole. As we begin to short-change innovation, ⌐omer value, taxes due to the government, the growth ⌐ so that the finance industry gets more, the corporate ⌐ die.

⌐ize that we have *no problem with profits whatsoever.* ⌐ cannot continue its chosen activities or make its activities pay. Profit is a necessary condition but not a *sufficient* one. The problem with maximizing shareholder profit as an ultimate end is its *exclusivity* and what else is sacrificed to bring it about – just about everything that makes life worth living: other people, the environment, our customers, our colleagues, our children's children, innovation, meaningful work, the poor, equality and empathy. Maximize *any one thing* in an ecological system and every other element suffers and, ultimately, even that one thing perishes. We have scorched the earth of our own territory, wrecked our own habitat. In our public corporations and our political economy some monstrous tumours are growing. They threaten us all. Shareholders are *not* for the most part a trustful network, but a scattered aggregate of brokered interests concerned only in extracting more money from companies whose long-term fate is a matter of scant interest.

CHAPTER 4

Learning from China's
spectacular growth

Today, Washington's creed is largely ignored. History has been brought back to life by China, whose economy is now close to being the biggest in the world. And it has reached this threshold largely by ignoring America's advice.[1]

The puzzle that has to be solved is why the People's Republic of China changed so suddenly and so comprehensively after the death of Mao in 1979. It switched from being one of the poorest performing economies in the world to being probably the best of all in the whole history of economic development. We think that we have a tentative answer to this riddle. Before 1980 communism *was* pathological, because it came to regard itself as an exception to all markets and much universal science. It persecuted not only individual dissent but the whole notion of individuality. You were a 'capitalist roader' if you thought and acted for yourself. The nation believed in the diffuse, mystical wholeness of the Great Cultural Revolution. This vainglorious dream was almost entirely severed from the appalling, specific events on the ground occasioned by this folly. The grandiose ideology ignored the hunger and distress of millions.

What happened after 1979 were two simultaneous changes: first, China allowed world market forces into its economy and second, it encouraged the

---

1.   Edward Luce, 'Anglo-Saxon trumpeting will strike a hollow note', *Financial Times*, 5 January 2014.

members of the vast Chinese diaspora to come home and/or transact business with the mother country. Hong Kong, Singapore, Taiwan and minority Chinese communities across the world were welcome to invest there. What returned was not just inward investment, but traditional Chinese values from a highly aesthetic and inventive four thousand-year-old culture. This also pushed up to the surface from long buried roots within the nation itself.

Consider the difference this made. Chinese exceptionalism and particularism now had to contend with a universal market entering from the outside. Chinese communitarianism had to absorb the individual entrepreneurship of its own diaspora, not to mention strong individual objections to the conduct of the Gang of Four. Mao's errors were suddenly discussable. Chinese holism which had become totalitarian had now to contend with tens of thousands of specific market signals. No longer could the Great Cultural Revolution, deny the evidence of the catastrophic events it had wrought.

This change was not as sudden and unprecedented as it seemed at the time. By 1980 the Chinese diaspora constituted the *third largest economy in the world*, behind only the USA and Japan and larger than West Germany. Chinese culture knew how wealth was created and its overseas communities had honed these skills. Just as the Chinese abroad had steered clear of governments and cultivated their own businesses, so the Chinese at home now reverted to family-based enterprises to express a freedom newly opened to them. These newly legitimized activities took off with a vengeance.

But something else had also returned home: traditional Confucian family ethics of close relationships and more importantly *the value dualities of Yin and Yang*. All of a sudden it became possible for one nation to have two systems as Deng Xiaoping put it, capitalism *and* communism, for a cat to catch mice whether it was black or white, for socialism to be market-driven, for market forces to be let in but with key exceptions, for communities to be sustained by their individual members and for China as a whole to include its many specific parts. When Deng announced it was 'glorious to be rich' Western commentators noted this overdue obeisance to our beliefs. Except that the word 'rich' in Mandarin means *well connected*. What had happened is that contrasting values had suddenly been connected and were boosting the economy of the nation in vigorous expansion. The ancient dream of being a Middle Kingdom where opposed cultures met and joined was being realized.

What is most obvious, even infuriating, about Chinese culture is that it flatly contradicts our own in the West. Their cultural values are the *mirror images of ours*. Chapter 1 made that abundantly clear. Whereas we in the West prefer universal rules, the Chinese are more taken by personal exceptions.

While we are individualist to the core, they learned long ago that only an extended family group can sow and harvest rice. While we analyse phenomena to bits and pieces they prefer networks of diffusely related purposes. While we hanker after achievement, they ascribe value to projects yet to succeed. While we are resolutely inner directed they learn much by listening to us and letting our ideas qualify theirs. While we think in lines, they bend these into circles. The hundreds of thousands of their students studying in the West are no coincidence. *They learn from us at speed while we fail to learn from them.*

The concept of mirror image is important. When we look in a mirror a freckle or dimple on a left cheek is transferred to right side of the mirror image and vice versa. This value-reversal is pictured in Figure 4.1. So that what comes first for us, comes second for them and what is of major importance for us is of lesser importance to them.

Figure 4.1 The mirror image hypothesis

Despite the looking-glass writing we can see that particularism has changed places with universalism, the community has changed places with individualism and diffuse has changed places with specific. Does it matter which of these we put first? When we confront a traffic light does red precede green or does green precede red? It *does* matter because such values differ in their inclusiveness. The community can include its individuals more easily than individualism can include communities. The diffuse whole can include its specific parts more easily than the parts can include the whole.

In short, the communitarians have an advantage *provided* the individual is not persecuted and oppressed as still happens on occasion in political (not business) contexts. In our view by far the most important consideration is that *the values work with one another*, that rules learn from exceptions, that individuals enrich their communities and that parts join to form a coherent whole. If the People's Republic of China has a secret it lies here. They have an awareness of the interdependence of contrasting values, while we get into endless sterile arguments between left and right. A glance at the *China Daily*, which has won international press awards, shows that eighty per cent of its coverage is about *solutions* rather than conflicts and stories about successful cross-cultural ties.

For most of the authors' lives their national politics have been torn asunder by the fierce antagonisms between capitalism and communism. On the one hand was the ideal of competitive individualism and free markets, described as the 'free world' and our 'way of life'. On the other hand there was cooperation and community as an ethic and a society directed by the state for the alleged benefit of all. Despite its superficial attractions, this was *The Road to Serfdom*[2] according to its Nobel prize-winning author Friedrich von Hayek (1899–1992). Those adhering to communism would be progressively impoverished and coerced into a totalitarian existence. We confronted nothing less than an evil empire. It was self-evident that we had won except that we were in for a shock.

Russia and the Eastern bloc converted to capitalism comprehensively, quickly and chaotically. In many cases their economies lost ground. The power of the state was devolved on major industries. In Russia the commissars-turned-oligarchs put the American robber barons in the shade as piracy ruled. Yet mysteriously, with its communist government still at the helm, between the early 1980s and 2000 China achieved double-digit growth of up to sixteen per cent GNP per annum. Had we, the authors, received £100 for every article prophesying the imminent collapse of this rate of growth we would be wealthy by now. Thirty-five years on and the collapse, so confidently and frequently forecast, has not yet happened. It is surely time to ask why a country calling itself socialist has so comprehensively out-performed orthodox capitalism.

China's boom has lasted thirty-five years and, although growth has slowed, it is still seven to eight per cent while nearly everyone else was experiencing a recession and losing ground. It has also emancipated more than 600 million citizens from poverty in just three decades – a feat without precedent anywhere else in the world. Growth rates typically diminish over time because the underlying economy is that much larger and the percentage growth figure applies to a much larger economy,

2.   Friederich A. Hayek, *The Road to Serfdom*, London: Routledge, 1944.

for example, fourteen per cent of fifty is a smaller number than eight per cent of 100. The Chinese economy has doubled in size every 7.5 years. When the second-largest economy in the world has a seven to eight per cent growth rate, it is going to leave the rest of us standing. As BBC economics editor, Robert Peston, points out, 'China is creating another Greece every three or four months.'[3] He means that China's economic output creates an economy equal to the size of the Greek economy every twelve to sixteen weeks.

In exploring these extraordinary levels of Chinese economic growth, we may recall that the Chinese diaspora is a worldwide business phenomenon. China's economic growth is based less on a traditional communist system and more on the kind of East–West synthesis already achieved by Hong Kong, Singapore, Taiwan, South Korea and others. Despite the fact that Chinese values are the mirror image of our own, which should help us understand them, they tend to unsettle us.

China's real economic feat lies in learning from the 'hybrid economies' of Hong Kong, Singapore and Taiwan, all of which have successfully combined cultural influences from the West and from the East and are among the most competitive economies in the world. They have become masters of *guanxi* or relationship, not just personal relationships but relationships between ideas and processes in business. We shall see that this engenders much higher levels of trust, because in an extended relationship that trustworthiness is closely monitored.

Although it may have adapted some of our business practices, China resists our definition of democracy; so are other definitions possible? Is growth being achieved by exploiting its own citizens? Finally, we will explore the idea of a Beijing Consensus. Many readers will know of the Washington Consensus, ten principles laid down by English economist John Williamson in 1989 for assisting economies in crisis, which over the years has come to be used in a broader sense to refer to a market-oriented economic consensus. Is there a Beijing Consensus rising to challenge it and to which the under-developed world is likely to turn? This will not be a ringing declaration, American style. Indeed, the very words 'Beijing Consensus' were coined in Britain and America.[4] The Chinese know well when to maintain silence and not give things away. However, what is emerging has a clear shape and outline.

---

3.   Robert Peston, *How Do We Fix This Mess?* London: Hodder and Stoughton, 2012, p.263.

4.   This is sometimes also called the China (Economic) Model. The term Beijing Consensus was coined by Joshua Cooper Ramo as an intended counterpoint to the Washington Consensus. A report on the Beijing Consensus was published by the Foreign Policy Centre in the UK and triggered a debate joined by Arif Dirlik, John Williamson and Stefan Helper.

The not-so-sudden surge in economic growth

By 1979, when Deng Xiaoping became vice-premier of the PRC, the Chinese *outside* China had been doing extremely well for some time, notably in Taiwan, Singapore and Hong Kong, where growth in double-digits had been attained. Even more impressive was the performance of minority Chinese communities living as part of the Chinese diaspora. By 1998 the World Economic Forum had rated Hong Kong first, Taiwan second and Singapore fourth in the world in competiveness and they had been climbing in prowess steadily in the preceding years. But perhaps the most impressive performance was by Chinese minorities in countries where the native population was not Chinese.[5]

In the Philippines, for example, three per cent of the population is Chinese yet it controls seventy-two per cent of trade. In Indonesia, four per cent of the population is Chinese yet it controls seventy per cent of all business. In Malaysia, although the Chinese population of thirty-two per cent is actively discriminated against, it controls eighty per cent of wealth. Similar disproportionate success is the rule throughout the Pacific Rim countries. These immigrants, many of whom fled the Communist takeover, never suffered the attacks on traditional Chinese values mounted by Mao and took them into exile with them. They also had the dual perspectives that a minority in any country enjoys, as explained in the Introduction. They knew their own values *and* that of their adopted lands.

They were not simply traditionalists but had adapted to foreign climes using the 'life-raft values' explained by the then Harvard Business School professor John Kao. Those values typical of minority entrepreneurs include: 'thrift ensures survival', 'save much of your income – worse could be coming', 'trust the family and a network of fellow immigrants known to your family', 'obey patriarchal authority', 'portable and tangible goods are preferable to intangible goods' and 'keep your bags packed; you may have to run'.[6] Because an individual's economic survival depends on thirty to fifty people of similar background, their conduct within the network is exemplary. The slightest dispute over money could mean losing some of an individual's supporters and they could face economic ruin. Relationships of deep trust are the key to everything and mutual benefit is vital to network survival.

5.   Ming-Jer Chen, *Inside Chinese Business*, Boston: Harvard Business School Press, 2003.

6.   John Kao, 'The World-Wide Web of Chinese Business', *Harvard Business Review* 71, no. 2, March–April 1993, p. 25.

When Mao died and the Gang of Four had been arrested, the economic disasters of earlier years could at last be admitted to. The only economic model remaining then was what overseas Chinese had been doing so successfully in world markets for some years. Their money poured into the country and many returned home. Hong Kong, Taiwan and Singapore were the largest foreign investors in the PRC; they contributed roughly seventy per cent of China's capital inflow up to 2001, which dwarfed US investment. Between 1979 and 2001, 100,000 joint ventures were set up between China and overseas Chinese. Many of these were modelled on the Hong Kong, Taiwanese and Singaporean economies.[7]

The return of the Chinese diaspora

The very fast growth rates experienced by Hong Kong, Taiwan, Singapore and elsewhere were now transferred to the PRC. The nostalgia for the old country knew no bounds. Some sixty thousand Taiwanese businesses invested in the PRC. Their current estimated value is US$90 billion. The PRC is also well connected. Over twenty per cent of Silicon Valley high-tech companies are run by Chinese immigrants to the USA, including Jerry Yang, co-founder of Yahoo.

As an ethnic group, the Chinese are now on the verge of leading the world economy and being the best business practitioners in the world. There is already a worldwide network of Chinese people ready and willing to cooperate with one another, shaped by a culture several millennia in the making. If we look at the sheer size of the PRC's population, 1.3 billion people, then the coming together of the diaspora makes good sense and offers amazing opportunities.

A new 'communist' system

Much of our hostility to China results from the fear that communism is chiefly responsible for its amazing economic expansion; in truth, however, the connection is tenuous. Most growth since 1979 in China has emanated from the grass roots, from Township and Village Enterprises – largely local community initiatives, typically headed by an entrepreneur but jointly owned and boosted by local governments. Many of these are unknown to central government and operate in a *laissez faire* style under local protectors. State-owned companies, have a more patchy record and survive because of their strategic implications.

7.   Chen, *Inside Chinese Business*.

Furthermore, the theory of communism was originally posited by Karl Marx, a German Jew writing in the British Museum, largely influenced by working conditions in British factories. *Das Kapital* was a document typical of Enlightenment thinking, relentlessly rational and adversarial and purportedly 'scientific', and is not at all related to traditional Chinese philosophy and culture. In any event, a 'communist' system willing to open itself up to world markets and trade with them is unlike any other communist system we have known. This is something entirely new. The planning process survives and is often condemned by those who oppose socialism. But plans of any kind in a world market come unstuck. It is nevertheless useful to record your expectations if only to remind yourself (like Socrates) of how very little you know. You learn much by contrasting your expectations with what really happened. We learn most from being surprised and confounded. Yet without initial 'plans' these differences may not register. This is sometimes called 'indicative planning'.

The Chinese learn from us more quickly than we learn from them

Not only do the Chinese have ethnic networks throughout the world but they come to the West in their hundreds of thousands for educational purposes. One might think that their signal success in business might make them arrogant, but this is not the case. They are still eager to learn from us. I (Hampden-Turner) recall a visit with a Chinese friend to a Shanghai bookshop. The business section contained piles of books, mostly in English. And all the way down the stairs, sitting to the sides so that people could pass, were avid readers absorbing what they could not afford to buy. My friend pointed at their shoes. They were from the countryside, he told me. I found their total absorption and hunger for knowledge strangely moving.

It makes sense for the Chinese to come to the West because we are still the more adept codifiers. Even after they have overtaken us, as they are surely in the process of doing, we may still give the clearest account of why this is so. Just as the Romans employed the Greeks to teach them, so may we offer the best explanation of how or why we lost. Many traditional practices are only half-conscious. People rarely ask why they prefer to do this and not that. The difference is that the Chinese know they need to learn, while we seem content to wag our fingers at them and offer free lectures. The cruel truth, as Cambridge professor Ha-Joon Chang points out, is that the speed of economic growth on a world scale is now inversely related to the number of economists a nation employs![8]

If all that divides us from the Chinese is mirror-image values then it is hard to see why we cannot work together and why arguments about where a circle starts should detain us. Yet the truth is that the reversal of our priorities makes us uneasy. When people reverse what we perceive as the 'proper' order, our values feel subverted. In the Cold War both sides prepared for the mutually assured destruction (or according to its apt acronym: MAD), of those who reversed their values, that is, those who put the community first and those who accorded the individual supreme importance. Cold War ideology has given us the habit of polarizing values: universal markets good, exceptions bad; individualism good, communal spirit bad; bits and pieces good, whole conceptions and higher goals bad. We must free ourselves of these habits. What *really* matters is whether these diverse values can harmonize with each other.

But does it make any real difference to which value we give priority? If laws need exceptions and exceptions need laws, are we splitting hairs? Actually, it makes quite a lot of difference. Let us consider a business activity that occurs routinely, a contractual business venture between American and Chinese companies. The British and Americans come to China with several lawyers in tow, armed with universal principles of law. The Chinese greet them with party planners, who organize events intended to develop particular and exceptional friendships. The idea is to establish a mutuality of interests and long-term, trusting relationships.

Let us assume that what the Americans and Brits want is a legally water-tight contract, protective of their rights above all and drafted with great care and precision. The Chinese want warm friendship between the particular parties, the formation of a new international community and a diffuse aura of goodwill including all parties. These different premises have been labelled the Anglo-American cultural priority and the Chinese Priority. These are set out in Figures 4.2a and 4.2b (overleaf).

American and British companies are trying to drive the best bargain for themselves and their lawyers are smart in pushing their advantage and justifying their own inclusion. The advantage they seek to win might lead the Chinese to renege on the deal when they realize that foreigners are fighting them, unless the contract prevents them from doing so. In short, they must, if needs be, be *made* to comply. In part, we resort to the law because it is very highly developed in the USA and the UK and, if you have a good system, why not use it to the full?

8.   Ha-Joon Chang, *23 Things They Don't Tell You About Capitalism*, London: Penguin, 2010.

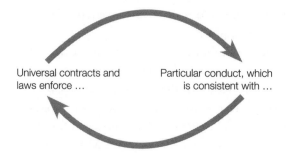

Figure 4.2a Anglo-American priority

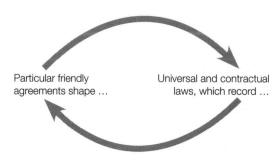

Figure 4.2b Chinese priority

On the other hand, the Chinese are used to the family model of business between persons of the same ethnicity, demonstrating high trust in a tight network. When dealing with foreigners, they must try extra hard to create an atmosphere and relationships in which everyone wants to benefit everyone else and reneging would be unethical and counter-productive. The idea is to *want* to help each other. The word *lunlixue* means 'whole policies in the place of ethics'. That the rule of law is less well-developed in China makes this procedure even more important. Not only are contracts secondary but they are little more than memoranda of friendly understandings. Those unhappy with a contract should be released from its obligations. This is what friends would do for each other.

We in the West also see *individual* rights as primary and their protection as creating a better *community*. This is a perfectly rational way of thinking but it is only *one* possible way. That individuals create communities is true but communities also nurture and develop individuals. So once again we can contrast the Anglo-American priority, putting the individual first with the Chinese priority of putting the community first.

Individual rights, well
protected, assure better...

Communities of persons,
all of whom have ...

Figure 4.3a Anglo-American priority

The Chinese reverse this thinking. Here, it is the *community* that protects the rights of each *individual*, who in turn upholds the community.

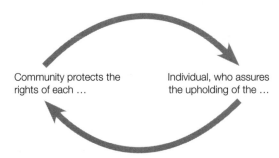

Community protects the
rights of each ...

Individual, who assures
the upholding of the ...

Figure 4.3b Chinese priority

Another reason we prefer written contracts and the rule of law is that they are *specific* and clearly spelled out so *no one* can renege or claim ignorance. There is no wriggle room and expectations are clear. Since both parties are out for themselves any ambiguity will lead to conflict unless the small print is precise (Figure 4.4a).

In contrast, a verbal agreement amid a party atmosphere is far vaguer and more *diffuse*, depending as it does on the social context of that time, which might be differently interpreted by the parties. Will greater clarity and specificity reduce misunderstandings or is it better to settle such issues with goodwill on both sides, as expressed in the Chinese preference shown overleaf? Surely what is most important to a long-term relationship is that both parties are satisfied with the agreement and that they remain satisfied over time, which may require flexibility at both ends?

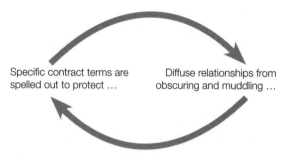

Figure 4.4a Anglo-American priority

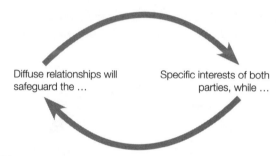

Figure 4.4b Chinese priority

If we look at these three pairs of values, all involved in negotiating and signing a contract and living up to what was agreed, then we have little hesitation in claiming that Chinese values contribute to better outcomes. Why is this? First, the Chinese way is considerably *cheaper*. It saves on all that legal work that tries to make cheating impossible yet it might still be outwitted by a costlier lawyer. Second, it is much *quicker* and cuts out the haggling, manoeuvring and bluffing. Third, it is less *punitive* should anyone have second thoughts. Fourth, it is much more *flexible*, since it aims to benefit both sides and there may be several creative ways of doing so. Fifth, since its ultimate purpose is mutual gain, it *creates wealth* as opposed to taking money from the other party and simply moving resources from one side to the other. Finally, it is much more *meaningful* since several alternative arrangements vie with each other to improve the chances of attaining a shared superordinate goal. All in all, people can achieve much more when they *trust* each other to reciprocate.

Clashes between these viewpoints have occurred in the past. Lehman Brothers filed a suit for US$100 million against China's three largest trading companies for failing to pay debts from foreign exchange trading. It won. The outcome is unsurprising. The law was drafted with such protection in mind and Lehman relied on this fact. It got its money back, but the company lost much, much more in the PRC as a result of its 'victory'. The prospect of good partnerships with Chinese companies vanished and it became a pariah and later succumbed to its own ambitions. In contrast McDonald's negotiated amicably about an arbitrary decision to move it, at great expense, from its largest facility in the world, two blocks from Tiananmen Square. The Beijing Municipal Authority finally agreed to pay it US$12 million for the inconvenience. Had it sued it would probably have won but it knew better. Relationships matter more.[9]

Does this mean that the Chinese are somehow morally 'better' than we are? No, it does not. It happens that the tightly networked minority groups that have served the Chinese so well in exile have concentrated their minds on business in the same way that the Quakers and the Huguenots, two groups discriminated against by the then authorities, were; these groups succeeded in areas that were still open to them. Indeed, the Communist Party, with its old habit of oppression lingering from earlier times, may have actually *helped* businesses in the same way that the governments in Britain and France kept religious minorities in their place and barred them from many professions, which ultimately allowed them to excel in new areas of enterprise.

All cultures have a tendency to overplay their dominant values, as we saw in Chapter 2. Where Americans and the British err, it is with approaches that are too legalistic and adversarial, by trying to claim that business and economics are 'sciences', by excessive individualism-turned-to-greed and by analysing everything to the consistency of broken shards, which lack any meaning or ideals. Where the Chinese err is by taking a too-particular approach to near-magical leaders and 'fathers' of the nation who command a dangerous degree of obedience, so that any mistakes made are magnified. The risk is that the power of the community is exaggerated until it resembles a juggernaut. Visions of the future and superordinate goals can become coercive in their intensity and crush criticism or dissidence. That China has made such mistakes in the past is hard to deny.

However, there *is* a moral dimension to economic development. Values are circular, as we have seen. Hence understanding *other* business cultures, bringing migrant values to a new country, understanding how others see things, trusting relations within small networks and emphasizing the value of education are all related to fast economic growth, as we explain in the next section.

9. 'McDonald's Amicable on Dispute over Beijing site', *South China Morning Post*, 10 December 1994.

Integrating rival views

In contrast to the West, the Chinese have always been comfortable with paradox. The word for 'dilemma' is comprised from the Chinese characters 'spear' and 'shield' juxtaposed with each other. It is a dilemma from one moment to the next whether to defend with your shield or attack with your spear, yet it is blindingly obvious that you must rely on *both* and few warriors could survive without the two implements. Hence *both* sides of the dilemma are vital to survival and what we in the West think of as either/or choices the Chinese see as a choice combination, a spear advancing defended by a shield and both deployed strategically.

SPEAR   SHIELD

Figure 4.5 The Chinese for 'dilemma': within every dilemma is complementarity

In the words of novelist Maxine Hong Kingston, in *The Woman Warrior*, 'I learned to make my mind large, as the universe is large, so that there is room for paradoxes.'[10] It is a view expansive enough to unite East with West, competition with cooperation, capitalism with communism, two systems with one, free trade zones with non-free trade zones, being with non-being and, of course, Yin with Yang.

It is somewhat galling to realize that a methodology which we have been trying to put over in this book and several previous ones is *so* familiar to the Chinese that they have two words for it. *Buhe louji* has no two-word equivalent in the English language but can be rendered as 'Thinking in circles holistically in a logic of diversity and contradiction.' It is also rendered as 'non-logical'. What we have tirelessly tried to explain to Western colleagues is known to a properly educated Chinese adolescent in just two words! While Chinese sages don't necessarily agree with each other, all deal in paradoxes. Confucius was famous for seeing that self-government could complement the role of government. You

10.   Maxine Hong Kingston, *The Woman Warrior*, New York: Vintage, 1975.

would have less need of a master if you could master yourself and the best ruler was one who taught this doctrine. He also taught that the superior man was, above all, modest. 'He conceals himself, yet every day grows in stature. The inferior man shows himself and every day loses stature.'

Confucius also taught that any value taken too far turns into its opposite; you can become what you hate. When you burn witches or martyrs, your righteousness becomes an evil worse than the crimes alleged against them. Should we be surprised that, in pursuance of a Cold War, America would become the largest command economy the world has ever seen? 'To win without fighting is best.' Who else but a Chinese general (Sun Tzu) would argue that you accomplish most by doing least, that the best victory involves the least violence, that you should win a battle before it starts and that, if you must have a war, it should be as short as possible or you will ruin both sides, destroy the terrain and cause starvation. Strategy should always be indirect, doing the opposite of what your opponent expects. Sun Tzu's 'bloodless battles' make him almost a pacifist warrior. American presidents are allegedly given *The Art of War* as a briefing document – we seem willing to learn from China if the wisdom is ancient enough.

Perhaps the best-known Chinese paradox in business studies is the word for 'crisis' – *wei-ji*. This word involves two parts, *wei* meaning 'danger' and *ji* meaning 'opportunity', which together mean 'danger in which there is an opportunity' (shown in Figure 4.6). It turns what appears to be bad into something good, while not hiding the risks inherent in doing so. It is the nub of wealth creation.

DANGER   OPPORTUNITY

Figure 4.6 The Chinese symbol for 'crisis'

Hong Kong has its own '*wei-ji* hero', Yu-Tung Cheng, famed for making quick moves in turbulent conditions and coming out on top. He was the first to re-enter the PRC after the Tiananmen Square tragedy, in which hundreds of demonstrators were killed and injured on 4 June 1989, and so earned gratitude for caring about his home country. He purchased the Hong Kong Convention and Exhibition Centre in the run-up to Hong Kong's restoration to China and then made millions when it became the site for many of the reunification celebrations. In 1994, during a property slump, he bought from Donald Trump 'the last piece of land in Manhattan'.[11]

As Ming-Jer Chen, Professor at the Darden School of Business at the University of Virginia, has pointed out, the West thinks in terms of *either–or* while China thinks in terms of *both–and*. The West wants victory while the Chinese prefer accommodation. In the West, polarities are exclusive of one another and the middle ground is just a trade-off, a lacklustre compromise; in China, opposites fuse and melt into one another and achieve harmony and synergy.[12] The West thinks in lines or arcs; the Chinese think in circles or helixes. The West thinks in objective quantities of things; the Chinese think in terms of subjective qualities, contexts finely fitted together in one whole.

The West's sense of time is linear: seconds, minutes, hours, days, amid rapidly passing events. The Chinese sense of time is circular: everything comes round again if you wait patiently. If you cannot stop time and stare at the lotus flower, what is life worth? Chen quotes Jack Ma, head of Alibaba.com, when he says, 'One must run as fast as a rabbit, but be as patient as a turtle.'[13] Hong Kong will not fully merge with China until fifty years after its return by the British (in 1997). By then, the two systems will have been carefully studied and their relative merits borrowed from each. Taiwan will ultimately return too, just give it time.

Hybrid economies

Is it a coincidence that economies influenced by both the West *and* the East are among the strongest in the world? Hong Kong, Singapore and Malaysia were colonized by the British; Taiwan and South Korea were substantially shaped by US Cold War policies. Not only are these five among the most successful economies in the world,[14] they also greatly influence the policies of the PRC. Indeed, Taiwan, Hong Kong and Singapore in some ways act as 'pilot fish' for the Chinese 'whale', showing how ethnic Chinese communities can achieve affluence using the Japanese stakeholder model. South Korea also testifies to the fact that governments can create large businesses and make these viable and competitive worldwide, for example Samsung and Hyundai.

11. Ming-Jer Chen, *Inside Chinese Business*, p. 99.
12. Chen, *Inside Chinese Business*, pp. 85-87.
13. Chen, *Inside Chinese Business*, p. 100.
14. *The World Competiveness Report* is issued annually by IMD in Geneva.

The mixture of Chinese cultural values and Western business techniques appears to be unusually effective. It is as if West and East had shared the truth between them and a Taoist belief-system had healed the broken halves, thus bringing the enmity between communism and capitalism to an end. These four cultures now form the hinges between East and West; speaking Mandarin, Cantonese and English, they could become world business educators, not by universalizing American practices but by hosting a dialogue among nations, drawing on the original inspiration of the 'Middle Kingdom', namely the idea that China is the point of balance and harmony among nations. We examine how Singapore balances these influences in Chapter 5.

Guanxi, the premier value of Chinese business

The Chinese characters that form the word 'humanity' symbolize 'persons' and 'two'. Everyone is seen as related and concepts of virtue are applied less to individuals than to their relationships. It is these relationships that are seen as the root of all possibility. Even an inventor needs a customer and succeeds only when connected to that customer. The West thinks in terms of transactions, things to be counted. China thinks in terms of *guanxi*, or relationships to be further improved. *Guanxi* is difficult to define because of what it includes, that is, not just people, but ideas, knowledge, values and processes that form larger meanings.

Guanxi is especially prevalent in networks, but much more than connection is implied. There is the norm of reciprocity, the obligation to return favours, the feeling of being indebted. But there is also the virtue of harmony, similar to the Japanese *wa*, testifying to the aesthetic almost symphonic nature of the satisfaction attained. *Guanxi* involves trust and honours shared experiences, like veterans surviving the same battles. *Guanxi* flourished in the anti-capitalist years because it compensated for the rigidities of Communist Party bureaucracy. It was an informal, supplementary economy, which had only to be legitimized after 1979 to thrive in the open. Mutuality is also a vital recourse where the rule of law is weak.[15]

Gift-giving is frequently the beginnings of *guanxi* and, while it *can* constitute a bribe, it is usually too small and too personal for such purposes. It is more likely to be the prelude to virtue than to corruption. You will be expected to reciprocate, but over time not straight away. As relationships

---

15. Ming Zeng and Peter J. Williamson, *Dragons at your Door*, Boston: Harvard Business School Press, 2007, p. 107.

develop, mutual favours become more significant, so that 'if someone gives you a droplet of generosity, you repay them with a gushing spring'.[16] Who you know may be every bit as important as *what* you know – connecting people and knowledge results in mutual benefit.

The largest advantage resulting from an orientation to human relationships, however, is that moral value can be attributed to relationships far more readily, coherently and intelligently than it can be attributed to individuals. Values characterized by individuals tend to clash in irreconcilable conflict. For example, should an individual be trusting? Is trust a virtue? Yes, if it helps to create a trusting relationship; no, if it tempts other people to exploit you. If someone is known to be trusting, they may be taken advantage of. The same applies to being generous, obliging, kind, truthful, innocent or vulnerable. You may be taken for a ride. If you bare your throat, you must watch out for vampires! Should you never cheat? What if you encounter a card-sharp who is cheating you?

But there is no doubt at all that *relationships* of trust benefit the participants and are much better for business than a lack of trust. Verifying and supervising relationships can be expensive. Those who reciprocate generosity, obligation, kindness, truthfulness, innocence and vulnerability are much better off than those who do not and make their money by depriving others. *Provided* they are mutual, kindness and respect may know no bounds. Relationships specify the context in which values are appropriate; for example, truthfulness in the context of inquiry, generosity in the context of sharing. *Without trust in reciprocity values fail to work.*

It is possible to extol a relationship without extolling yourself and claiming all the credit for it. To give thanks for a wonderful relationship is not to elevate yourself above others but acknowledge their contribution to whatever success you have enjoyed. Relationships keep you modest. You owe much to other people and to good fortune.

Each party to a relationship has responsibility for improving it and each can only change it from their own end. I (Hampden-Turner) studied Human Relations at Harvard Business School and in no single case did improved relations not reap benefits. Of course, when you reach out to another human being, there is the prospect of misunderstanding and failure to connect and money may be lost. Yet if the attempt is successful, you will gain more knowledge and rarer insights. Reaching out to strangers is one of the risks of enterprise. There is no cheap grace.

16. Chen, *Inside Chinese Business*, p. 50.

Guanxi also addresses the problem examined in Chapter 1 about rational ends being valued above the means of attaining them. Since the supplier is offering a product as a means for getting money and the buyer is offering money as a means of getting the product, a good relationship guarantees the equality of means and ends in a way that economic rationality does not. There is reason to believe that wealth actually inheres *within* relationships. If someone is paid three times more than a subordinate, they are then three times more responsible for that relationship and are thus charged with improving it. If three subordinates ask for a transfer due to poor working relationships, we do not have to apportion blame among the disputants. We simply note that the requisite relationships have not been formed and the person paid most for forming them must account for this outcome.

Alternatives to traditional democracy

The shadow that haunts China most of all is the deficit in democracy. We need to ask what democracy is before accusing China of lacking it. We also need to ask whether the Chinese *want* our kind of democracy and whether being 'democratic' may take other forms more suitable to Chinese culture. Western democracy stems from the Golden Age of Greece and the leadership of Pericles. He may have ruled because he was a general and an aristocrat but he was also wonderfully articulate and chose to rule by words. Rather than *physical* conflict he utilized *verbal* conflict and led by his greater eloquence.

The Western ideal is that it is much better to fight verbally than physically and that debate is a theatrical performance with which the most verbally astute will win over most of the audience. Both Athens and Britain were famed for their theatres. The most articulate and moving have the right to rule and winning the most votes demonstrates the widest agreement. What this model tends to lack is any sure avenue to consensus, so that Labour and Conservative, Democrat and Republican can barely tolerate each other and resort to hurling insults. Their jousting becomes a form of public entertainment and the least disliked combatant tends to win, while all or most politicians are losing public favour. For example, Prime Minister's Question Time has nothing to do with real questions and answers, but with accusations and excuses, heightened by sound-bites and point scoring.

It is of note that no attempt was made to render Hong Kong democratic until the Chinese takeover loomed. The PRC can be excused for doubting Britain's sincerity in this matter. Initially, there was also very little pressure from the population in this regard. The British ran the civil service, while the Chinese prospered in business: freedom was exercised through enterprise. Even more significant is the example of Singapore, whose population can vote for an opposition party if it chooses to do so, yet the People's Action Party has received most votes at every election since 1967, and an opposition barely exists. Malaysia also has the right to vote in the opposition but has never exercised this. Taiwan has a Western-style government but when the Members of Parliament start hurling insults they end up wrestling on the floor of the House!

The fact is that substituting verbal conflict for physical conflict, the major principal behind Western democracy, does not work well in Chinese cultures which put a high premium on maintaining 'face' and where insults leave near-mortal scars. So far from verbal taunts *substituting* for physical violence they may help *trigger* it. Verbal fisticuffs are offensive in this part of the world.

The Chinese tend to move from *consensus to conflict* rather than the other way around. The Singaporean government sues MPs who insult government ministers and several have had to leave the country before they ran out of money. Chinese communities overtly support consensus – they put it in the shop window – and covertly manage conflicts in the corridors of power because they are a little ashamed of these. Western governments do the opposite and place conflict in the shop window; but they often fail to achieve consensus, even privately. They agree only on matters above the fray like the monarchy, Remembrance Day, the Constitution, the death of Princess Diana and the destruction of the World Trade Center.

That voting is the sure mark of democracy is not supported by the facts. Hitler was elected. Elections have been held in Vietnam, Iraq, Afghanistan and the Crimea, without democratic outcomes, while those in Russia and Africa are often the occasion for demonstrations, riots and charges of vote-rigging. It is little use electing a government that refuses to speak to those who disagree. The Chinese path to democracy is to expand just the one party until many of those who disagree are included within it, hence Deng Xiaoping reclassified intellectuals as 'proletariat' and encouraged them to confer with him. There are also elections for local party officials in an attempt to build democracy from the bottom up in the belief that the more people who take part in the deliberative process the better. This is then celebrated as consensus.

We, the authors, think that China needs a different approach to democracy, and we would wish their efforts well. The British Parliament has been embroiled in expenses scandals, influence peddling, perjury and slanging matches that reflect little credit upon it. The US Congress is more unpopular now than at any other time since polling began, as we saw in Chapter 3.

Elections involve vastly expensive advertising campaigns aimed at tarnishing the opposition's reputation. Running for office costs millions of dollars and is mostly financed by corporations with their own agendas.

The two approaches to democracy are illustrated in Figures 4.7a and 4.7b.

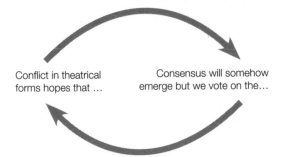

Conflict in theatrical forms hopes that ...

Consensus will somehow emerge but we vote on the...

Figure 4.7a Anglo-American priority

This style of democracy greatly exaggerates conflict at the expense of consensus. This is a potentially serious flaw *because wealth creation is in part a consensual and trusting process*. Moreover, exaggerating conflict may cause democracy to break down as it has done in many parts of the world. China takes the opposite view, with what the West regards as show-events contrived in advance to pretend that everyone is in agreement. In this case the theatrical performance features thousands clapping on cue to celebrate consensus while, behind the scenes, pressures are being applied.

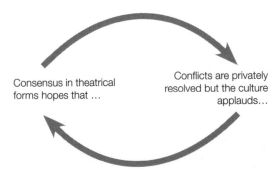

Consensus in theatrical forms hopes that ...

Conflicts are privately resolved but the culture applauds...

Figure 4.7b Chinese priority

This style of government has yet to be acknowledged as even remotely democratic. The West tends to regard any orientation towards consensus as 'totalitarian' and has yet to work out what Singapore is trying to do or how it should be regarded. What does one do if the electorate and the culture dislike speech that is considered insulting? However, there is no doubt that this style of democracy, if you can call it that, greatly exaggerates consensus at the expense of conflict, with the result that people with views that anger or distress others, however true, will not get a hearing. Genuine democracy creates consensus out of conflict and/or creates a consensual arena in which people are free to argue and disagree on what is best.

Do policies of fast growth exploit Chinese citizens?

A frequently voiced complaint is that China short-changes its own consumers in pursuit of export-led economic growth. This point is made repeatedly by BBC economics editor, Robert Peston, in print and on television. He believes China might be not the answer but 'the next big problem'. According to this thesis, China exports far more than it imports, much of which are raw materials to feed its industry; its consumers cannot afford to buy luxury goods made in the West and as a result, China has accumulated a US$3 trillion balance of payments surplus. It has also held down the value of the yuan so that foreign-made goods are less affordable but exports are boosted.[17]

While wages for working Chinese have risen rapidly, they have declined as a proportion of the economy, dropping from almost sixty per cent in 1998 to forty-eight per cent by 2008. This compares to sixty-one per cent in the USA, sixty-four per cent in Europe and sixty-two per cent in Japan. Rewards accruing to labour in a communist country are lower than in most other nations! State-owned companies make as much as eleven per cent profit, which they promptly reinvest instead of distributing to pensioners and shareholders; while privately owned companies make twenty-one per cent profit on average, most of which is also reinvested rather than enjoyed.

Because workers still feel insecure, they save more; their savings are then used for investment but at an interest rate so low that they must save even more to provide for themselves in old age. Peston cites economists who call this situation 'financial repression'. Why are furious revolts not occurring? Possibly because living standards are higher than ever before and employees are immeasurably better off. They recall the periods of mass starvation prior to 1978. For the Chinese government, climbing living standards serve to justify the Communist Party's power and it dare not remove its foot from the accelerator. What the Chinese need, in Peston's view, is some 'instant

17. Robert Peston, *How China Fooled the World*, BBC2, 18 February 2014.

gratification' rather than investment spending, which has reached forty-nine per cent of GDP, the highest in its history and unprecedented in the world.[18]

So, is this criticism valid? Is China on the cusp of a catastrophe? Peston accuses China of spending excessively on resources that will pay off in the long term – on education, homes, offices, roads, railways, bridges, ports and factories. But can we *ever* spend 'too much' on education, on the resource between our ears, the greatest boon to wealth creation and human self-fulfilment? A better-educated person enriches every other person they encounter. Likewise, a road and bridge can save hours of time for vast numbers of people; they are thus well worth the investment. If the price of building roads and bridges is missing out on Western consumer goods, might it not be worth it?

Even if wages are falling behind investments, isn't it investment that boosts the economy and raises wages? The exact ratio between investing, saving, buying and indulging remains undiscovered and most parents would sacrifice much to obtain a better life for their children. Where an economy has grown twenty times since 1978, might it be worth waiting a year or two and forgoing some Western trinket? When the authors visited China we were amazed to see the penetration of companies like Starbucks, McDonald's, Dunkin' Donuts and Kentucky Fried Chicken. Moreover, there seemed few domestic equivalents. Then, a horrible thought struck us. Were they letting *us* celebrate the finger-licking culture of the West while they built solar-powered vehicles and high-tech shipping containers? Is fast food and the accompanying obesity the fodder of economic decline?

There comes a point, as we have seen in earlier chapters, when a culture of production, saving, thrift and commitment to work yields to a culture of consumption, possessiveness, indebtedness and self-indulgence. Perhaps this shift is inexorable and will slow us all down in the end, even the PRC. But wouldn't China be wise to *postpone* this outcome for as long as possible? The longer it can keep what Americans call 'divine discontent' at bay and postpone the feeding frenzy, the faster it will grow, much as did the American economy under the Puritan work ethic. China may have achieved a better balance between these two than we have. Geert Hofstede measured various cultures on their short-term and long-term orientations, on a scale of 0 to 120 with the top end of the scale indicating the long-term.[19]

18. Peston, *How Do We Fix this Mess?* pp. 284–286.

19. Geert Hofstede Cultural Dimensions, Database, http://geert-hofstede.com

Table 4.1: Long-term and short-term orientations

Long-term													Short-term	
CHI	HK	TAIW	JP	KOR	IND	THA	SIN	NL	SWE	GER	USA	ETH	KEN	UK	PHI
118	96	87	80	75	65	61	56	48	44	33	31	29	25	25	19

As we see, the West is mostly short-term, particularly the USA, UK and the Philippines under US influence, while East Asia is more long-term, with the top three being culturally Chinese countries. Recall that the long term *includes* many short-terms and pays off daily, while the short-term *excludes* the longer. Long-term thinking entails trust that the future will be better than the present if we work for it now and that sacrifices will be repaid. Current investments will ensure future returns.

What is the cause of the short-term attitudes? Possibly it is the desire to consume *now*, the same indulgence that puts us deeply in consumer debt. Hofstede also measured self-indulgence against self-restraint. The comparisons are shown in Table 4.2, with indulgence at the top end of the scale.

Table 4.2: National attitudes to indulgence and restraint

Self-indulgence														Self-restraint	
AU	UK	USA	CAN	NL	SWI	IRE	HK	FIN	MAL	NOR	TAI	JP	GER	KOR	IND	CHI
71	69	68	68	67	66	65	61	57	57	55	49	42	40	29	26	24

Is instant gratification the answer for *any* of us, or did the Puritan work ethic give us the discipline and self-restraint needed to grow? We in the West still think the Chinese should be more like us and embrace our indulgent and consumerist lifestyles, but should they? Is business about providing cures for 'tired blood' (Geritol), pay-day loans (Wonga) and indigestion remedies (Alka-Seltzer)? As Steve Jobs once asked John Sculley when appointing him CEO to run Apple, 'Do you want to sell soda pop [Pepsi] for the rest of your life? Or do you want to come with me and change the world?'[20] While we dunk donuts, China has a seventy-five per cent market share of the world's solar energy production, mostly through sponsoring this technology. When the cost of producing solar energy matches that of fossil fuels, the price of energy will fall as technology improves. Are we blind? Can we not imagine what is coming? Such an opportunity is worth trillions.

20. John Sculley, *Odyssey*, New York: Doubleday, 1991, p. 26.

The historical lesson is that long-term thinking and self-restraint, Puritan style, makes short-term gains and self-indulgence possible too.

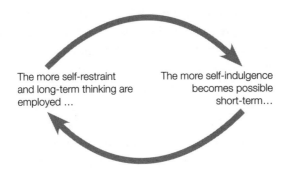

The more self-restraint and long-term thinking are employed ...

The more self-indulgence becomes possible short-term...

Figure 4.8 Long-term self-restraint includes its contrasting values

Is there an emerging Beijing Consensus?

As it continues to grow at an incredible pace, China has become the model for developing nations around the world. The 'Beijing Consensus' does not emanate from Beijing. The Chinese government is not in the habit of making universal declarations, as we tend to do in the West, and makes no claims to economic 'science'. Fewer 'truths' are 'self-evident' to them than to us. As we might expect, the notion of a Beijing Consensus first emerged from a think-tank in the UK, the Foreign Policy Centre, and in articles written by Joshua Ramo, ex-senior editor at *Time* magazine, and Stefan Halper, Director of American Studies in the Department of Politics, Cambridge University. The issue has also been taken up in the USA by historian, Arif Dirlik, and economist, John Williamson.[21] The PRC is keeping quiet.

However, a professor at the University of Peking, Yang Yao, and his co-author, Linda Yueh, have addressed the topic and their remarks are to the point.[22] They do not deal directly with Ramo's indictment of 'ruthless' innovation – whatever that is – and they sidestep Williamson's accusation of 'authoritarianism' as an

21. See Wikipedia entry on the Beijing Consensus: http://en.wikipedia.org/wiki/Beijing_Consensus.

22. Yang Yao and Linda Yueh, 'The China Model and its Future', *China: Twenty Years of Reform and Development*, Peking University Press, 2010, available on *Foreign Affairs Online*, February 2010.

ingredient of 'state capitalism', but they do offer useful insights. They explain that China has moved towards market capitalism with a heavy emphasis on infrastructural development. Eighty per cent of China's state-owned enterprises have been privatized and many are now publicly listed. The government has taken a step by step approach to institutional reform and judges each change in the light of results rather than in terms of ideological purity. It set out ways to make all stakeholders in an institution support changes.

For example, Township and Village Enterprises (TVEs) were owned by local governments but driven by entrepreneurial individuals. They generated considerable revenues for the townships and turned local governments into eager participants in economic growth, often legitimizing successful new enterprises retrospectively. Local government and local entrepreneurs prospered together and became adept at developing a culture of enterprise and efficiency at the grass-roots level. The contrast between official output and prices set by state-owned enterprises (SOEs), which were far more modest than market output and prices may have even incentivized the SOEs to produce much more and pocket the difference.

A World Bank report on the *East Asian Miracle* points out that Chinese government officials are paid and promoted on merit. However, that merit is frequently defined as the economic gains made by the industrial sector in which that official is coaching and advising. The role is typically facilitative rather than regulatory, closer to the coach than to the referee. The behaviour of government officials is less rule-following and more opportunity-seizing. Much science and technology belongs to the government and it is possible to grant strategic industries access to it.

The pay scales of civil servants depend on the prosperity of that particular region of the country, so that there is considerable incentive to raise the income of one's region. The closer a department is to the real economy, the better it is paid and salaries are sometimes attached to tax revenues. Much activity is extra-legal and discretionary. It is hard to see how the accusation of authoritarianism holds up in the face of so many spontaneous, extra-legal initiatives that are helped rather than hindered by government officials. China's officialdom is radically decentralized: seventy-seven per cent of total government spending goes to local governments and they are usually vigorous proponents of economic growth. Local governments also compete with each other for resources using ambitious project plans on whose success they will be judged.

What appears to have happened is the importation of Western economic ideas but allied to Chinese networked family-style relationships to create a *developmental state*. It combines the idea of rational self-interest with incentives to work for the common good. Yao and Yueh refer to *volitional pragmatism* and constant experimentation with wealth creation as the focus.[23] Nothing is permanent or perfect. Everything can be improved. The truth is that authoritarianism cannot survive the operations of a market economy. Precise plans tend to fail; the question is by how much and what should be done to correct your aim? No government is either large or intrusive enough to capture and make millions of market decisions. If the government is arbitrary in some of its dealings, then it drives citizens further into private business activities, as it once drove the Quakers, the Nonconformists, the Huguenots, the Jews and the Indian and Chinese commercial minorities.

China is of course haunted by the spectre of social disorder, which has so often in its history meant civil war and mass starvation because rice cannot be harvested amid disorder. A population of 1.3 billion constitutes a big challenge for any government. In Tiananmen Square in 1989 this nightmare came to a head. Yet change so sudden as to disrupt continuity is doomed. Revolutions devour their own children. China's gradualist approach has been an extraordinary lesson for the world. It is high time to recognize its successes and try to learn from its example.

23. Yang Yeo, 'Beijing Consensus or Washington Consensus? What explains China's economic success?', *Developmental Outreach*, April 2011.

CHAPTER 5

Singapore and the hybrid economy: the infinite game

People are and always will be our most precious resource. Most of all it is the effort and drive of Singaporeans that have made the country what it is today. Overcoming great odds as a newly-independent nation without natural resources, we have turned our city state into a thriving and modern economy.[1]

Singapore *does* have a natural resource, the one between its people's ears. Like Hong Kong, it is an East–West synthesis and the forerunner of the Chinese feat discussed in the last chapter. Indeed, China has largely followed the path it has pioneered. Singapore is one of the most extraordinarily successful economies in the world. It is rarely out of the top six in the *Global Competitiveness Report*. It also represents the vanguard of what the Chinese economy could develop into and charts the voyage to affluence. In 1967, GDP per person in Singapore stood at US$600. The UK had left it poor. Singapore had become part of Malaysia in 1963, but Singapore's government disagreed with the Federation on certain issues, such as whether Bumiputra (native Malays) should receive special rights to compensate them for being less wealthy than the Chinese minority. There were race riots in 1964 and the Malaysian Parliament voted to eject Singapore on 9 August 1965. Lee Kwan Yew, Singapore's first prime minister, had wept on television when

1. *The Next Lap EDB Yearbook,* 1996.

the news was announced. It was exclusively among the Chinese population that Malaya's communist revolt a decade earlier had occurred, so that the Chinese population was suspect. Few expected the small nation to survive economically much less militarily. It had been overrun in three days by the Japanese in 1942.

In 2013, its GDP per person qualified by purchasing power stood at over US$78,672. It was, according to the IMF, the third richest economy in the world behind only Qatar and Luxembourg and considerably wealthier per head than the USA, which is tenth with US$53,001. Germany whose *Mittelstand* we will look at in Chapter 6 is sixteenth in the world with US$ 44,469 (World Bank estimate), while the UK, at one time Singapore's colonial master is twenty-eighth in the world with US$36,208. This means that Singaporeans *have over twice the purchasing power of Britons*. According to *Economist* rankings, Singapore grew by 3.4 per cent in 2014, faster than the USA (2.3 per cent) and Britain (2.8 per cent).

While Singapore is self-evidently capitalist, its economy is fundamentally different from those of the UK and the USA. Rather than pioneering capitalism, it 'came from behind' and has outperformed its mentors. We need to distinguish pioneer capitalism from catch-up capitalism. The first originates products and is highly competitive. The second emulates, refines and facilitates and is much more cooperative. The first creates innovative technologies of many kinds. The second can select among these tools what it most likes and what best educates its people.

Singapore has few major brands but it is the Asian HQ for many world brands and its well-educated population earns a good income for the nation. It is a fast-follower and an excellent platform from which to introduce Western-made products into East Asian markets. It is more in the development and marketing of new products that wealth is created, than in the initial introduction. There is a race to create a world standard in which Singapore has often participated on behalf of the multinationals to which it has played host. The distinction between pioneers and those catching up is illustrated in Figure 5.1.

PIONEER CAPITALISM — CATCH-UP CAPITALISM

Figure 5.1 Two kinds of capitalism

The men on the left are slowed down by having to clear a path through the elephant grass, whereas the car can travel quickly down the already established road. Growth rates during the British industrial revolution were slow, one to two per cent or less per annum, but growth of *any* kind was a new phenomenon. The fact is that it's much easier to grow fast when the technologies are already developed, when investors are rich and when other nations are growing too. Catch-up capitalism tends to be *stakeholder oriented* since shares tend to be held by the pioneer capitalists and catching up uses domestic savings and government policy. The modern world offers a cornucopia of technologies; it's just a matter of utilizing the best. This explains why every wave of economic growth is more rapid than the one preceding it, and why China and Singapore are growing much faster than Britain or the USA.

Singapore is the pre-eminent stakeholder economy, and this chapter will consider its strengths. One reason is that many foreign companies wish to locate there and must bargain with the government for the privilege. The government acts as a 'coach' to such companies, trying to ensure that they win out in Asian markets. In return they are expected to train indigenous employees and nurture local suppliers and customers. There is a preference for catalytic and horizontal technologies – those that enhance *other* technologies and ramify the most widely through the economy. Products and services containing considerable knowledge are preferred to those containing less knowledge, a process called 'knowledge intensity'. Clustering is encouraged, as is the idea of economic growth as a game or discipline to be perfected and mastered, akin to Asian martial arts.

The pre-eminent stakeholder economy

Coming from behind is more rapid and more effective if you practice stakeholder capitalism, in which power is shared between all those with a stake in the outcome of the business. If new technologies are to be rapidly deployed, everyone has to help in the process. Singapore may be the world's chief exponent of this practice. We use the word 'practice' advisedly because stakeholding is not yet a doctrine or a dogma, although it may soon be. Indeed, like the Beijing Consensus, described in Chapter 5, stakeholding is more practiced than discussed. East Asians codify and proclaim much less than we do.

How does stakeholding differ from maximizing shareholder value? Stakeholding, according to US philosopher and professor of business administration, R. Edward Freeman, includes all those with a stake in the success and survival of the company: employees, customers, suppliers, investors, lenders, the community, the environment and the government.[2] They create wealth between them and should share the results. Currently, stakeholding is less a legal entity than a voluntary ethical commitment. Those most responsible for the success of a company should be in receipt of the benefits. Stakeholder economies are doing *much* better across the world and in the course of this chapter we will see why. In the meantime, most East Asians are not advertising their advantage or claiming to have a superior system.

The existence of stock markets in Shanghai, Singapore and elsewhere does *not* signify a preference for maximizing shareholder returns. Equity capital is much less important in these parts of the world, where savings provide a lower cost of capital and offer smaller returns than shareholders are seeking. Nor do equity holdings by founding families denote shareholder maximizing policies. Families typically look to the long-term survival of the dynasty. They are thinking of their grandchildren and may treat employees, suppliers and customers as family members. Countries like Sweden and much of Scandinavia favour continued family influence and ownership. They will grow their companies for the long-term.

In the early days of rapid growth in South Korea, Singapore, Hong Kong and China, most shareholders were foreigners. The rights of those providing equity funds would be respected, but the chief concern of governments was rather naturally the prosperity of their own people, employees, customers, suppliers, communities and tax authorities. National policies favoured the latter and sending large profits back home to shareholders in the USA and Europe was not considered the pinnacle of achievement.

Stakeholding is, in any case, how most companies start and grow. Over ninety per cent of the businesses in the world were started by families and most are owned by their founders. Investors, employees, customers and suppliers are typically related by kinship, friendship, ethnicity, knowledge and/or community and form networks of mutuality. Even large companies may be private, such as Virgin, Dell and Chanel. Others may preserve the ethics of their founding families, as well as retaining enough shares to be influential, such as Johnson & Johnson and for many years Motorola. Small and medium-sized companies in Germany, Austria, Switzerland and the Scandinavian countries – the *Mittelstand* – are highly successful and mostly still in family hands. What turns such companies into publicly-owned corporations are initial public offerings

---

2.   Edward Freeman, *Stakeholder Theory*, Cambridge: Cambridge University Press, 2010.

(IPOs), whereby shares are offered for sale to the general public. At this point, the company passes to the control of shareholders.

However, this situation does not automatically mean that the company thinks only of its shareholders. The Singaporean government makes skilful use of publicly-owned multinational corporations and it has many in the world to choose from. These may be shareholder dominated in the UK or the USA but in Singapore they must play by its rules as the price of being admitted and being allowed to operate. They must undertake to be members of a prospering community and, in exchange, may be better situated in East Asia than their world rivals, with the many advantages Singapore offers as a business location. Wages must be maintained by training and upgrading employees. Singapore sanctions companies for paying workers too little. Fines are paid into a pool, from which companies can borrow to upgrade skills. There are no excuses for falling behind in the development of your workforce. They must learn more so that they can be paid better.

Singapore is a privileged location

Singapore is a tiny English-speaking enclave with infrastructure and logistics second to none and a highly trained, cooperative workforce. It is also a bastion of English common law, with a first-rate reputation for the fair judgement of commercial (not political) disputes that Westerners can understand and count upon. Singapore has been referred to as 'Asia-lite', because although you are in East Asia, so strong is the Anglo-American influence that many foreigners feel 'at home' there. Its port has the fastest turnaround time in the world and is strategically situated on the main sea-route to China. The capital city is beautifully maintained and elegantly landscaped. If you were looking for an Asian HQ for your Western company, you could hardly do better. There is even a local journal, *HQ Asia*, for the many taking this step.[3]

So attractive is Singapore as a location that companies must negotiate hard to be admitted. Many more companies would *like* to be located there than can be accommodated and Singapore makes overtures to the kinds of highly sophisticated companies it seeks. It is not possible to know the terms under which a company is allowed to establish itself in Singapore since such negotiations are private and our attempts to inquire into the criteria have been rebuffed. The Economic Development Board (EDB) is primarily responsible for the acceptance or rejection of applications. The young staff members of the EDB are mostly top

3. Published by the Human Capital Leadership Institute, Singapore.

scholars educated in the West or in Japan, who have studied abroad on scholarships but have pledged to return after graduation and repay their nation. They are also experts in the technologies of the particular companies seeking admission, and will undertake most of the negotiations with them.

The referee and the coach

It is possible to *infer* the terms of admission from the subsequent conduct and policies of those companies admitted. What follows is our educated guess. It begins with understanding that the Singaporean government is not simply a referee, guaranteeing fair competition, who will blow the whistle on you when you misbehave. The government is the national *coach* for more effective business practices whose advice and encouragement you can expect to receive and whose wishes you should heed; less an instruction than a nudge in desired directions. This means that the government tries to earn your trust through being a mentor. The decision to admit a company is not an easy one.

In the West, governments are widely considered ignorant of business innovation. Politicians are often arts graduates and wordsmiths in the UK and lawyers in the USA. But the governments of catch-up capitalists tend to be very well informed. They have had several years to judge the viability of new technologies invented elsewhere and are negotiating free lessons in their use from competing multinationals. Singapore's judgement as to whether it would benefit from hosting a particular world-class technology is often intelligent, even inspired. For example it admitted Hewlett Packard at the height of its creative surge, when its expenditure on R&D was ten per cent of total product costs. This has sadly declined.

Governments tend to play one of two roles in regard to private companies located in their nations. The 'referee' oversees fair play. Companies compete but on a 'level playing field' that gives all-comers an equal opportunity to defeat their competitors and prosper at their expense. Such governments are rarely popular since they award penalties against those who have erred and infringements are dealt with in court. They act *after* an error has occurred and punish the malefactor. All governments must act as referees to an extent to avoid corruption. But governments who *also* 'coach' their star players can earn popularity and gratitude by advising them *before* they make mistakes. As any football fan knows, the coach of a winning team is applauded, even loved, while the referee is verbally abused for contentious decisions.[4]

4.   Bruce R. Scott and George C. Lodge, *US Competitiveness and the World Economy*, Boston: Harvard Business School Press, 1985.

Allowing the government to coach you provides many benefits. It can show you why laws were made and how to fulfil their spirit rather than their letter. It can help you find the staff and the resources you need. Your coach and adviser is paid and promoted in relation to how well *you* do, so wise counsel is in the interests of both parties. As a foreigner in the country, you need to learn quickly how things are done and where allies might be found. Having let you into the country, your coach needs to have his or her judgement vindicated by your success. Grants are available from the government for various purposes and the leading universities are mostly public not private and access to them can be negotiated.

Your coach is also on the lookout for benefit to *all* your stakeholders. Are your employees happy and fulfilled? Are your suppliers up to the mark? Have you considered training them alongside your own staff? How satisfied are your customers? What might you do to improve customer relations? How great is the level of trust between contracting parties? Funds may be available for joint projects. Fate-sharing or gain-sharing projects allow a customer and a supplier to agree to share the revenues from jointly created initiatives and there are consultants available to set these up.[5] The government is there to help, to understand and to facilitate new developments. It has lists of the most reliable sub-contractors in various fields and can make them available to you. It is prepared to manage the managers for the greater benefit of all concerned and for Singapore as an economy. Introductions to joint venture partners are available, as is joint university–industry research.

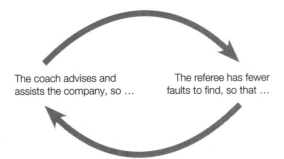

The coach advises and assists the company, so …

The referee has fewer faults to find, so that …

Figure 5.2 The coach and the referee

5.   See Charles Hampden-Turner and Fons Trompenaars, *Mastering the Infinite Game*, Oxford: Capstone, 1997.

Selecting the best companies

There is a great deal of information on various multinationals and, thanks to American business schools, much business scholarship on what companies are best at, plus reports in business media. It is possible to find out which companies are most innovative, how and why this has occurred and in what ways they excel. Most successful Western or Japanese companies would regard representation in Singapore as an added bonus, so the EDB is in a position to choose which to invite. We are in touch with several high-tech companies in and around Cambridge University who, despite their small size have received inquiries from the EDB regarding expanding into Asia, using Singapore as their springboard.[6]

The EDB studies the *100 Best Companies to Work For* to inform decisions on which companies to invite to Singapore. It also checks out the *100 Best Companies for Minorities to Work For* to gauge how their citizens will fare working for such companies. Other criteria applied to identifying suitable firms are whether they are chosen by ethical investors, their reputation in relation to stakeholders and how they are rated as customers by suppliers.

The EDB will only give consideration to those companies that score highly against these criteria. Its motto is 'EFCS': 'Employees First, Customers Second'.[7] The needs of employees must be attended to first because only happy and fulfilled staff can provide high levels of customer service. Shareholders are not even mentioned! The EDB might be criticized as 'picking winners' rather than heeding markets but this is not the case. It *already knows* how the markets have responded and identifies those companies that are successful as a result of proven excellence. Although there are some accusations of cronyism, the EDB is in fact picking *teachers*; that is, those companies that will help them learn about world-changing technology and place them at the cutting edge.

The human resource policies of applicant companies are carefully scrutinized and those with a track record of making employees redundant or cutting wages or benefits are not admitted, while those in the process of growing and expanding are more likely to be welcome. While picking companies in advance of proven success or propping up ailing industries and banks because they are 'too big to fail' wastes public money; choosing the world's major innovators is unlikely to go wrong.

6.   Personal communication with The Technology Partnership. A Cambridge-based technology transfer consultancy (see Chapter 10).

7.   Personal communication with the editor of *HQ Asia*, journal of the Human Capital Leadership Institute.

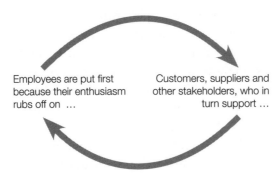

Figure 5.3 Employees first, customers second

Catalytic quality of 'horizontal' technologies

If you are going to pick and choose companies to be located in Singapore then it might be wise to ask what their technologies might contribute to that economy. Products and technologies vary considerably in their influence on *other* products and technologies in general. It helps to distinguish between *vertical* technologies with a single intended use, such as an oil drilling rig, and *horizontal* technologies that are utilized by several industries. Consider steel production. South Korea selected the steel industry as a key ingredient in its economic development, however, it was unable to gain financial backing from the West as it had no iron ore, Australia was considered too far away to be a viable source, and there was no tradition of metalworking in South Korea. Luckily, recognizing the potential benefits of successfully creating a steel industry, South Korea ignored this advice. Using the money the Japanese had paid them for reparations in regard to the Second World War, especially for the prostitution of 'comfort women',[8] and sourcing the iron ore from Australia, it went on to create a steel industry second to none, and every product *made* from steel also benefited.

Or consider number-controlled machine tools. Those machine tools with keyboards attached which can change their calibration in seconds instead of hours. The more highly developed this industry, the better tooled are nearly all that nation's factories, the quicker you can change tools and the cheaper it is to customize and undertake short runs. Better machine tools will create benefits for several industries and make them stronger than before. Roughly

8. Ha-Joon Chang, *23 Things they don't Tell you about Capitalism*, London: Penguin, 2010. pp. 126–128.

the same applies to industrial robots, photovoltaic cells, liquid crystal displays, universal joints, graphene as a material, alloys, metal ceramics, lasers, smart phones, three-dimensional printing and, of course, microchips. A 2008 survey identifying numbers of industrial robots per person per country listed Singapore second in the world and the UK seventeenth.[9] Metal ceramics with heat conserving properties could potentially revolutionize engine use and construction across whole economies.

There are now far more microchips in the world than people. These tiny 'brains' inside a vast array of products mean that Texas long-horn cattle can now broadcast their location to the rancher trying to find them and people can activate their central heating remotely so that their house is warm when they return from work or holiday. In whole industries, such as car manufacturing, sixty-five per cent of all innovations are electronic, and most machines in factories are now electronically regulated and monitored. Photovoltaic cells are clearly a catalyst for all forms of solar energy, while battery technology will make or break the electric car.

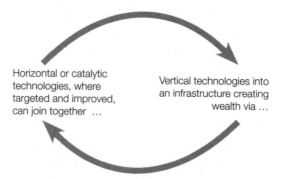

Horizontal or catalytic technologies, where targeted and improved, can join together ...

Vertical technologies into an infrastructure creating wealth via ...

Figure 5.4 Horizontal and vertical technologies

We earlier cited an oil-rig as a 'stand alone' vertical technology. Yet microchips, a horizontal technology, can now detect how much oil and water remain in a well, leading to enhanced recovery of the oil. Digital film-making is a new technology that has been supported by the EDB. What if entrepreneurs could demonstrate their ideas about new ventures to potential investors, employees and customers using digital prototypes? Would this not be more powerful than a business plan? The richer the prototype the more innovative is the product. Singapore has budgeted millions for this very purpose.[10] Armed with

9. Hampden-Turner and Trompenaars, *Mastering the Infinite Game*, p. 85.
10. Personal communication with Cine Equipment Ltd, Singapore.

the English language as well as Cantonese and Mandarin, Singapore aspires to grow into a world leader and educator in business prowess. It is certainly well situated to do so.

Questing for knowledge: The perpetual feast

A crucial flaw in classical economics is that customers and *only* customers decree the value of a product. Customer preferences are subjective but the resulting price and volumes demanded at that price are objective indices. Where governments or any other authority claim that one kind of product is 'better' than another they usurp the role of the customer and substitute guesswork for price information. The result is white elephants that no one wants to buy, like Concorde with its magnificent feats of engineering but a cabin too small to be profitable. It lost money on every flight it made. It follows then that industrial policy of any kind is a snare and a delusion – but is it?

You have to be trained in economics to believe that US$1 million worth of potato chips or wood chips are as valuable as US$1 million worth of Pentium chips. The claim is palpably absurd even if the price is identical. The first expands your stomach; the second your mind. The first renders you fat and lonely; the second connects you to a global network. The first satiates you quickly; the second helps to make you insatiable for yet more knowledge. All products have greater or lesser *potential* and that potential can be estimated by how much knowledge is contained within them. A map of your genes will be of more value in saving your life than a Post-it note. Of course, a complex product *may* turn out to be of little use to anyone. These things happen. But provided enough people want it, a knowledge-intensive product is superior to a simple one, ramifies more widely and may help to change the world.

When a computer or an electronic tablet is manufactured, distributed, bought, used and maintained, everyone involved in the process is being educated. They inform one another. In addition, the knowledge being communicated is scarce and scarcity enhances value. There are a limited number of people who can produce anything so complex and full of knowledge, which gives the educated a big advantage. There will be fewer competitors at the leading edges of knowledge and therefore higher profit margins. All in all, knowledge intensity is highly compatible with free markets. You can make whatever you like, *provided* it is packed with knowledge, and import the simpler things you need from less-developed nations so they gain too.

When the Singaporean government prioritizes intelligent products, it makes its people more independent.

In the West, the advance of knowledge has rendered entire industries obsolete. The unskilled fall further and further behind, as do the technologies they are trained in. Unemployment rises, as does the cost of unemployment benefits. How much better it might have been to move simple operations to cheaper countries *before* they started to fail commercially and to have trained citizens to do the increasingly complex work of the future. A new economic world order would have nations producing goods in accordance with the educational level of their citizens. Developing nations, with less higher education such as Vietnam and Cambodia, would thus supply the simpler necessities even while upgrading themselves and learning apace.

Such a policy is avidly advanced by the EDB. Companies wanting to locate in Singapore must do their most advanced research and development there. They must estimate in advance how many Singaporean research scientists they will employ and the government will see that universities prepare them for the task in hand. They do not want a labour shortage to push up salaries. The government will also be interested in the size of the training budget. How many Singaporeans will this company be educating? How much better off will the community be as a result? When PepsiCo asked to locate a bottling plant in Singapore, it was politely referred to Vietnam. Singaporeans have better things to do than dilute syrup with water. Of course, the Pepsi HQ is a different matter. By the time you are admitted to Singapore, you are guaranteed to be a *very* useful addition to the community of stakeholders!

Higher knowledge intensity also boosts innovation. Where two or more disciplines are operating at the leading edge, the opportunity to make novel innovative combinations increases exponentially. Bodies of knowledge within a community are self-generating and ceaselessly expanding. Products, like people, come in 'generations' except that these are much closer together than human generations with one giving birth to the next within two or three years as seeds of knowledge germinate. We can rarely predict *what* will be discovered but we *can* predict that discoveries will occur when, say, genetics mixes with medicine or three-dimensional printing meets prosthetics. It is not difficult to foresee the advent of many cross-connections. The virtuous circle is shown in Figure 5.5.

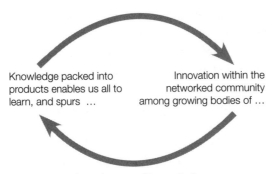

Figure 5.5 Cross-connected packages of knowledge

All stakeholders in a company are connected by skeins of knowledge, which is why they prosper together. Singapore aspires to be the innovation nation. Employees are key to such a vision and to subordinate them to shareholders would be folly. It is employees who receive components from suppliers, engage customers, seek investors, engage partners and create whatever wealth the company generates. If strategies are to triumph, productivity to improve and innovations to be designed, then employees must be involved. Well-trained and educated employees make a country prosperous.[11] It is not money flowing to owners but skills honed by employees that make a nation competitive. Singapore has few multinationals of its own and few famous brands, yet it is a star performer among already affluent countries.

The exciting thing about knowledge is that it is a truly new paradigm that can raise us above the scarcities of what Carlyle dubbed the 'dismal science' of economics. Knowledge is *something you can give and yet keep*. We are paid for *sharing*. An economy powered by knowledge is no longer materialist but communicative and moral. Knowledge is a perpetual feast, self-generating and self-renewing, in which what each of us knows joins together to create more than we began with and together we develop new meanings.[12]

When the EDB intervenes in the economy, not on behalf of cronies, but on behalf of rendering the economy more knowledgeable, does this diminish freedom? Is this the 'road to serfdom'? No, the result is quite the opposite, for in greater knowledge and complexity lies the greatest freedom known to humankind. Nations who oppress their creative minorities shoot themselves in the foot; witness the growing tendency of Americans to excoriate 'liberals' and the sad decline of

11. Robert B. Reich, *The Work of Nations*, New York: Vintage, 1992.
12. Conversations with Dr Jay Ogilvy, the author of *Many Dimensional Man*, New York: Oxford University Press, 1978.

Muslim scholarship over the centuries. Those encouraged to think freely are as essential to human development as they are to economic development.

So important is the role of the teacher that in traditional China teachers were at times rewarded or punished depending on the conduct of their students. If we wish to estimate the role of minorities in wealth creation we need only look at the role of education within those groups. In the USA, more Jewish, Japanese, Chinese and Indian minority students attend college than do Americans as a whole, while fewer African-Americans and Latinos do so. To be in a minority network *and* value education is a ticket to the top. Not to value education has consequences that impoverish. This is why Singapore, Hong Kong and most of East Asia pay their teachers generously. In contrast, in the West market forces tend to subtract money from professions in which intrinsic pleasure is found. People will agree to do it for less because they enjoy it and their paymasters take advantage of this situation! Yet this is almost certainly a foolish policy. We have to get the money to where the genius is, not exploit their intrinsic pleasure by paying them less.

If truth be told, the UK and the USA have sponsored high technology and the knowledge needed to produce it by way of defence expenditure. In the days when it spent four per cent of its GNP on space programmes and twice that on the Cold War, America was booming as a mixed economy. The national highway system was built for defence purposes, without which cars would have had nowhere to go. Troop carriers developed for the Second World War were converted to passenger jets. The Pentagon very wisely gave its millions to outstanding professors and not to their institutions and thus effectively sponsored pure research in all but name. Defence spending not only boosted the development of computers, microprocessors and robots but also led to the creation of the Internet, which was originally a network set up for the Department of Defense to communicate in a national emergency.[13] In the UK the development of jet aircraft happened in a similar way, sponsored by a military project that led to the Comet, the world's first passenger jet. British pharmaceuticals are strong thanks to the National Health Service.

What Singapore has done is sponsor knowledge intensity *without* the rationale of needing to kill those who oppose us. Government spending to defend the country is the only knowledge many conservatives in the West are prepared to pay for. It is time we faced the fact that economic development is a form of intellectual development and social learning, which is why it

---

13. John Gray, *False Dawn: The Delusions of Global Capitalism*, London: Granta Books, 2009, see especially Chapter 2, 'The engineering of free markets'.

is increasingly taking place in the vicinity of universities in knowledge communities and in cosmopolitan urban centres, an issue we take up in Chapter 10.

The policy of clustering

Knowledgeable people must have access to each other. And not only remote access via email but intimate access in which new relationships can be developed. It is for this reason that innovative companies tend to *cluster* within a few miles of each other. Singapore is rarely the first culture to develop new ideas but it is often the first to *act* upon the ideas of others. In 1990 Michael Porter published *The Competitive Advantage of Nations*.[14] In it he drew attention to the fact that innovative industries formed clusters, whereby businesses, supply chains and customers develop in close proximity. The high-tech cluster in Silicon Valley is an obvious example, as are the publishing clusters in New York and London, and the cluster of start-up companies in Cambridge, known as the Cambridge Phenomenon (see Chapter 10).

The advantage of such clusters is that skilled employees form a pool in such places and are readily available for recruitment. The resources and specialized services this industry needs are readily to hand. Customers come from all over the world to visit competing companies and find these conveniently grouped within a few square miles or so, making comparison and choice easier. Information and knowledge can be shared. The leading players can be emulated and best practices observed. Competition means literally 'to run together' and it helps to keep an eye on the opposition.

Porter's book had been out only a few months when Singapore began to create its own clusters. These were not of the kind Porter had described, which had evolved spontaneously, but were contrived by government to produce the same effect. For example Biopolis is a custom-built biomedical research facility in Buona Vista, close to the National University of Singapore and Singapore Polytechnic, with tenants including Glaxo Smith Kline and Novartis. It cost US$100 million. It was this hub which discovered the SARS virus of which there is even a statue in the pedestrian square below. Biomedicine now forms six per cent of Singapore's economy. Almost next door is Fusionopolis, a recently completed electronics and technology cluster, and Mediapolis is under construction nearby, which is intended to make a

14. New York: Free Press.

multi-lingual Singapore into Asia's media and education hub. There are also clusters for financial services, aeronautics, shipping and green technologies.

New companies admitted to Singapore are steered towards a cluster of similar companies. Sometimes the adoption of American ideas is accomplished in weeks. The American press ran stories on 'coffee bar creativity', whereby entrepreneurs had met by chance in coffee bars and decided to go into business together, and when we visited Biopolis only a few months later there were new coffee bars on almost every corner! There have been important questions raised by Peter Williamson as to whether contrived clustering really works. Many foreign companies have subsidiaries in Singapore more responsive to their foreign HQs than to local opportunities in Singapore. They may have their 'tails' in Singapore rather than their 'heads' and these outposts often lack the decision-making powers to take initiatives.

Yet the cluster is tantamount to an admission that wealth is *not* created by excellent companies alone but by an ecosystem or group of fellow stakeholders. The reason for being so close, even in the age of the Internet and even when Singapore is just one town of over four million people, is the important effect of proximity on innovative solutions. The company, its employees, its suppliers and sub-contractors need to congregate in one place for innovation to occur and for the company to share its visions of the future with its stakeholders.[15]

This is known as 'open innovation', where instead of being kept secret, your strategy is shared with other stakeholders so they can help you launch it successfully. Getting the best components and new materials that your suppliers can furnish may often be crucial. For example the performance of a solar roof depends on the quality of photovoltaic cells and the heat-absorbing qualities of the material used to make panels. Of course, the danger any company risks with this approach is that those in which it confides may reveal the secret to a competitor, so once again it is close, cooperative relationships among stakeholders that make companies competitive.

It is also important to know government policy. If the price at which a householder can sell unused energy to the national grid is raised, which happened in Singapore recently, then your roof contributes to your household income. It serves the public interest for the government to pay generously for the energy if doing so speeds up households' voluntary conversion to solar power. It is stakeholders working together which creates wealth, as shown in Figure 5.5.

15. H. W. Chesbrough, 'The Era of Open Innovation', *MIT Sloan Management Review* 44 (3) 2003, pp. 35–41.

Knowledge packed into products enables us all to learn, and spurs ...

Innovation within the networked community among growing bodies of ...

Figure 5.5 Building networks of knowledge

One might think that clustering or huddling together might *close* minds but thanks to the hundreds of suppliers involved, sometimes in three or four tiers, the number of potential combinations of materials and components multiply. Hundreds of consultants have sprung up to orchestrate these clusters and to elicit novel combinations from them. The wealth-creating unit is growing larger and larger before our eyes. A company is more likely to be successful in Singapore than elsewhere because of the assistance it receives from other stakeholders, including the government, and the knowledge that joins them all. Clusters form around universities, for example Harvard, Cambridge, Stanford and the National University of Singapore, because knowledge joins its stakeholders.

Finite and infinite games

Time was when human tribes were largely predatory, attacking and seizing the territories of others and devouring their booty. It was a huge step forward when trade replaced battle, and over time contests were staged in satisfying customers more effectively than rivals could. Yet the element of conflict was still present. Companies could use their prowess to put rivals out of business and acquire their resources. In this sense business was a *game*, a mock combat undertaken according to the rule of law, which tried to guarantee that the conflict contributed to the welfare of customers, patrons and protagonists. The combat could get rough on occasion but the gains outweighed the pains and were considered beneficial to the society as a whole.

James B. Carse called this arrangement a *finite game* insofar as there are periodic clashes between combatants, in which some win and some lose, and then that particular bout is over. It is more about wealth distribution than contribution, more about zero-sum games than positive-sum games. The winners wrest more and more resources away from losers until the latter are bankrupt or sell up. Such games are witnessed, even cheered on. We learn from observing winning ways how to do better. By and large the skills of the combatants increase over time and winners make money, although there are periodic bust-ups in which much wealth is destroyed. Because money moves from the less effective to the more effective such games are considered benign.

But is there perhaps another kind of game? An infinite game that goes on forever? Carse, an American theologian, described such a game in *Finite and Infinite Games* published in 1986, which is played for the sake of the game itself.[16] The game is seen as a discipline, a way of life, a calling and a challenge to human mastery, as are martial arts. The suffix 'do' means 'way of', hence 'the way of archery' or 'the way of swords'. You can still win or lose these games, yet the prime purpose is the *game itself* as a disciplined way of life. Winning or losing are mere episodes along the way, indicators of progress. Since East Asians practice martial arts as ways of life rather than ways of winning, a similar attitude to business should not surprise us. Business excellence becomes an end in itself to be perfected, not just a means to make money. The contrasts between the finite and the infinite game are shown in Table 5.1. We have 'fighting snakes' on the left and infinity on the right.

Table 5.1 The contrasts between the finite and infinite game

Finite game	Infinite game
The purpose is to win	The purpose is to improve the game
Improves through survival of fittest	Improves through evolving the game
Winners exclude losers	Winners teach losers better plays
Winner takes all	Winnings widely shared
Aims are identical	Aims are diverse
Relative simplicity	Relative complexity
Rules fixed in advance	Rules changed by agreement
Rules resemble a debating contest	Rules shape language like grammar
Compete for mature markets	Grow new markets
Short-term decisive contests	Long-term enduring processes

16.   James B. Carse, *Finite and Infinite Games*, New York: Ballantine Books, 1986.

We posit that shareholder-dominated capitalism plays finite games while stakeholder capitalism plays infinite games, and that the latter is much more effective. The infinite game is a way of life, an exercise of conscience and a form of autonomy and mastery to which whole lives can be dedicated. A glance at the columns above reveals that, while the column on the left *excludes* the column on the right, the right-hand column *includes* the left-hand column. An infinite game can consist of many finite games joined together, so as to learn from the outcomes of them all. Those who survive, that is, the fittest, can preside over the evolution of the game itself to improve the way it is played for the benefit of all players.

Ironically this ethos was once very much alive in Britain and the USA. The battle of Waterloo is said to have been won on the playing fields of Eton; although the authorship of the statement is disputed it has been attributed to the Duke of Wellington. As recently as 1941 the American sports writer Grantland Rice wrote approvingly of the 'One Great Scorer' who would write against your name not whether you 'won or lost but how you played the game'. By 1963 this was being recited as a *joke* by the *Beyond the Fringe* satirists touring the USA. The whole notion of good form has been eclipsed of late.

Winners can start to share their gains with losers and teach them winning plays. Aims that were identical can take on diverse characteristics so that both parties are satisfied by different outcomes. Rules, like contracts, can be temporary and changed by agreement later on because the parties trust each other. Rules can circumscribe freedom or they can promote novelty, as in original statements which obey the rules of grammar or rules of blank verse as do Shakespeare's plays. That the plays are in verse does not diminish their originality but *elevates* it. All those brief contests can form one enduring process stretching to infinity, a tribute to the creation of wealth in all its forms. Figure 5.6 illustrates this process.

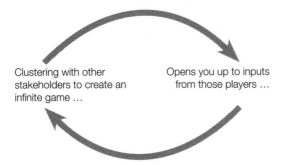

Clustering with other stakeholders to create an infinite game …

Opens you up to inputs from those players …

Figure 5.6 The infinite game created by the cluster

Short finite games become the means to the end of developing an infinite game. Victory and defeat may both be seen as lessons for improving the calibre of the game and making the players more masterful. Instead of simply cheering on our winning side, we could ask why this particular side won and what we might learn from it. Bearing in mind that entrepreneurs frequently have three or four failed businesses behind them before they succeed, we need people to learn, not be eliminated and give up as a consequence. Failures are frequently the prelude to success and only those who persist are in a position to learn.

One problem with seeking to win above all and caring little or nothing for the game itself is that one stakeholder, say shareholders, wins, but loses sight of the need to serve customers, employees, suppliers and their community. They may win several finite games in succession but the game itself deteriorates. As in the natural world, the game *itself* needs to evolve and those who fit most finely need to survive, not the 'fittest' in the sense of the most predatory.

Instead of everyone wanting the same thing, like money, players can desire different outcomes and work to achieve them. Rules don't have to be fixed and obeyed but can be changed by mutual agreement to enhance everyone's experience as both players and spectators. One side does not have to win at the expense of the other. If what they excel at is incomparable, both can win.[17]

We need to appreciate that creating a product, producing it and finding ever better ways of serving those who buy it is a calling infinitely more important than winning a particular round and making off with the spoils. Each finite game is petty compared to the enduring lessons to which it contributes. What we are searching for, and we must never forget this, is the *logic of innovation itself*. All those victories and defeats hold lessons if we can but find and explain them – this is the greater truth we are searching for.

Finally, we need to consider the role of game-playing in society. Games allow us to simulate contests yet do so in a way that minimizes suffering and *maximizes learning*. It is no surprise that great civilizations, such as those of the ancient Greeks and the Romans, had strong theatrical traditions. Finite games are mere simulations from which we draw lessons. What ultimately matters is developing our human endowments, and finite games are but stepping stones in this direction. Another virtuous circle arises from this...

17. Hampden-Turner and Trompenaars, *Mastering the Infinite Game*.

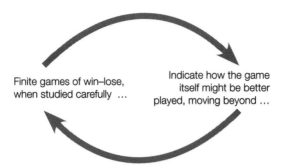

Finite games of win–lose, when studied carefully …

Indicate how the game itself might be better played, moving beyond …

Figure 5.7 Finite games as rehearsal for the infinite game

Finite games alone are for those who want to make the most money in the shortest period of time and with the least physical and intellectual effort. The infinite game is for those who want to create a legacy that will outlive them. Which game we play involves a moral choice indicative of the kind of people we are and what we stand for. A book describing the role of the EDB is not called *Heart Work*[18] for nothing. In this edited collection of essays, each author describes their own role in helping Singapore to develop into the innovation nation it is today. This is the work of a government and party so well respected that it has been re-elected ever since the founding of the nation!

18. Chan Chin Bock (lead author), *Heart Work: Stories Of How EDB Steered the Singapore Economy From 1961 into the 21st Century*, Singapore: EDB, 2002.

CHAPTER 6

The hidden virtues of small and medium-sized companies

We often hear that China will become the 'factory of the world', an assertion that will probably come true. But hardly anyone asks the ensuing question 'Who builds the factories?' The answer is The Hidden Champions! These little known mid-size firms play a key role in constructing 'the factory of the world.' China is the market of the future for industrial suppliers, engineering companies and equipment manufacturers. A French study views Germany and China as the chief beneficiaries of globalization: China as the supplier of consumer goods, Germany as the supplier of industrial equipment.[1]

We have a seriously distorted view of capitalism, in part because we are looking in the wrong places. We are over-exposed to some of the excesses of capitalism and are seriously under-exposed to where its true virtues lie. The companies we know best are those that make the most noise and intrude into the living rooms of consumers to secure their attention. Yet ironically, few of the products competing so strenuously for our custom are of major importance to the economy. They constitute mostly undifferentiated mass-produced and mass-marketed products, with little to choose between them.

1. Hermann Simon *Hidden Champions of the 21st Century*, New York: Springer Verlag, 2009, p.108.

Indeed, much of the purpose of advertising is to distinguish the otherwise indistinguishable. If something is genuinely new and fascinating, like Apple's iPad, people queue up to be among the first to buy it. The media can be relied upon to bring genuine novelty to our attention and word of mouth will do the rest. It is not the leading edge of technology that is most advertised but the trailing edges.

The underlying malaise of most mass marketing is the very different levels of commitment demonstrated by suppliers and consumers. The supplier is highly committed and invariably wants to sell as much as possible, however humdrum the product; the consumer feels low commitment almost to the point of boredom. Few consumers are much interested in scouring pads, indigestion remedies, skin creams, the squeezable nature of toilet rolls, the sounds made by milk being poured on breakfast cereals, the red lines of mouthwash in toothpaste and other gimmicks. The fact that we care little, but the company cares a lot, makes for an asymmetrical and manipulative relationship between suppliers and their 'targets'. Large amounts of money are spent on trying to change the unreflective buying habits of a largely indifferent public and to control their half-conscious conduct.

Apart from the intrusiveness of advertising, the second major source of public interest in business is the way the price of shares rises and falls on stock markets. The battle royal between hostile bidders and the target companies is a form of financial blood sport, with many hunt followers. Owners of shares standing to gain from the strife are riveted by the action and invited to support the highest bidder. We are naturally concerned with how our pension funds are faring and publicly owned companies are obligated to keep us informed. Public ownership allows companies to grow very large and we assume that the gobbling up of smaller companies is evidence of the power, superiority and success of big companies.

But suppose that it is in some of these smaller companies the true virtue of capitalism lies? Suppose we are ignoring the strength of this near invisible network? This is the contention of Hermann Simon, Chairman of Simon Kucher and partners, cited as Germany's most influential management thinker. He is the author of *Hidden Champions of the 21*st *Century* from which much of the information is this chapter is taken. He has selected around thirteen hundred companies worldwide, but more commonly in German-speaking nations, which he calls 'hidden champions' on account of our knowing so little about them and sadly under-estimating their significance.

In this chapter we will first consider the problem of size. This is vital to establishing trust. We trust those with whom we have informal, spontaneous relationships, not those with whom we have engaged officially and routinely.

Are large companies doomed to impersonality, formality and bureaucracy? Is it better to be small, intimate and cohesive? We will then look at the *Mittelstand,* the German term for a medium-sized or small company, often unknown to the general public because it keeps a low profile and sells to other companies. Its virtues are often considerable but hidden from our scrutiny because it mainly deals with other businesses and operates among fellow stakeholders. Such companies are in many cases highly innovative, more so than large companies, and strongly competitive. They are much keener than most companies on developing and keeping their employees. They achieve very high world market shares and are unusually profitable for their owners. Their continuity over time reveals them to be highly sustainable

The problem of size

Sheer size is a doubtful blessing. Only nineteen per cent of Americans trust *big* business, while a majority, sixty-four per cent, still trust small businesses, perhaps because respondents know these businesses personally.[2] These are not in the public realm. The acquisition of the small by the large may therefore do us no favours. They have very different cultures, as we shall see, and having to yield to those with more money discriminates against those who are lean, youthful and still growing organically. The 'bear hug' of a large company's bureaucracy has squeezed the life out of many acquisitions that were more nimble on their own.

Many once-small companies enjoy a spell of paradise before the Fall. The creation myths are very similar. Once there were two enthusiasts in a garage, a couple in a bicycle shed or people who met in a coffee bar and asked 'Why not?' The resulting business boomed. In those early days everyone knew everyone else by their first name and every Friday the founders bought beer or doughnuts, assembled all employees and thanked them for a successful week. Life was vibrant and exciting. They were building a new world. Customers scrambled for anything they made, adapted this and co-created.

The technical name for this situation is 'span of control'. A company of less than about 120 people is self-organizing and within the span of control of one or more leaders. Relationships are informal, operations ad hoc, and you 'manage by wandering about' among innovative individuals collecting and absorbing their ideas. You do not require formal titles, job descriptions, qualifications, pay scales, HR departments, forecasts, budgets, time-sheets or procedures. At this

2.   'Americans most confident of military, least confident of Congress' in *Gallup Politics*, 23 June 2011.

stage, you not only have vital knowledge of your own, you also know who *else* knows and can tap into everyone's expertise. But as the company grows larger, hierarchy, formality and bureaucracy creep up on you. Everything is divided into separate departments and it becomes difficult to do anything that isn't formally expected or required of you. Having new ideas is the job of R&D and that department may not even admit you. The once vibrant organism has become a machine for making money by rote and very little else.

This does not mean that 120 employees are the limit. Much depends upon the size of the *business units* and what disciplines HQ imposes on each unit. Richard Branson divides companies approaching 200 people into two and then encourages them to compete in a friendly manner, so that they can then discuss and adopt the secrets of the company that is doing better.[3]

Even large companies can set up teams championing new ventures and seeking new directions. Within each team informality reigns, so that it is possible to retain the virtues of a *primary group*; that is, any group adhering to the norms and values of a family: intimacy, respect, affection and nurturance. A *secondary group*, in contrast, is allocated pre-set tasks and follows formal procedures. In companies of up to a thousand or more, the spirit of the family can often linger and the hierarchy can be kept at bay. Many large East Asian companies utilize familial metaphors. There are 'elder brothers' and 'sisters' to show you the ropes, as well as 'fathers, mothers, aunts and uncles'.[4] In Japan, the nickname for the Ministry of Trade and Industry is 'worried auntie'. In the USA, Johnson & Johnson has retained much of its former family feeling. John Lewis in the UK is an exemplar of such an approach.

The *Mittelstand* and its low profile

The meaning of the German word *Mittelstand* is somewhat ambiguous. Its literal translation is 'middle estate'. It means both small and medium-sized companies (SMEs) and 'companies still run by the founders or their heirs'. It is the first meaning we will use in this chapter, although the large majority of SMEs are also still run by founders and families. *Mittelstand* are especially common in Germany, where they constitute 75 per cent of private sector employment, two-thirds of all exports, 99.7 per cent of all companies and provide 80 per cent of all jobs. They constitute roughly half of German GDP

---

3. 'Richard Branson', *Forbes*, March 2012.
4. Gordon S. Redding, *The Spirit of Chinese Capitalism*, New York: Walter de Gruyter, 1990.

and train eighty-three per cent of all apprentices. There are an estimated 3.5 million *Mittelstand* in Germany alone. Close on ninety per cent of what they make is exported. They are both diverse and beneficiaries of globalization; they have close relationships with universities and academics and utilize modern business tools such as total quality management (TQM) and lean manufacturing. There is nothing amateurish about them.

Mittelstand are also plentiful in Switzerland, Austria and Scandinavia. In Sweden, the *bruk* goes far back in history and although few if any remain, their ethos lingers. It was the isolated company town that traditionally sustained its community through long winters and paid the salaries of the priest and the local schoolteacher. *Mittelstand* are common in Sweden and much of Europe but are found as far afield as North America, South America, Africa and Japan. They constitute an alternative, family-style business culture.

While fifty per cent of Americans work for SMEs, there the ideal is to be an entrepreneur. In Germany, in contrast, it is to invent a high-tech machine or vital component that helps to make things. The nation's terrible experience of inflation in the 1920s has led Germans to trust machines, what they make and the engineers who make them, and to distrust money. They regard machines as the engines of growth and, unlike Britain and the USA, have retained their manufacturing sector. While most people in the West want businesses to make money, Germans prefer money to make business and contribute to industriousness.

Hermann Simon is the world's foremost expert on *Mittelstand*. He defines 'hidden champions' as those companies ranking first, second or third in their industry globally, with revenue *below* US$4 billion, of which the public is barely aware. Companies of amazing quality exist in this category, 'plough horses' rather than 'show horses', but the better for getting on with their tasks quietly and being of human scale and local significance, not large bureaucracies interested in power relations.

Our attitude to *Mittelstand* might be considerably more positive had they not been championed by Germany, loser of two world wars and tinged by moral disgrace. For some time after the end of the Second World War, anything stemming from Germany was viewed as possibly suspect, and the Anglo-Americans enjoyed far greater influence in the world. However, a dispassionate look at economic growth suggests we disparage Germany at our peril. Germany came from behind economically but caught up with the UK using a very different model. Since it was creating industries, such as steel and chemicals, already pioneered in Britain and the USA, investors incurred lower risk.

Germany created a highly decentralized network of regional and cooperative banks to lend to local industries; the German habit of saving money enabled the financing of many SMEs, especially in engineering. Long-term, low-interest loans were plentiful, while shareholders, who expect much higher returns, were unaffordable. A stakeholder economy emerged, backed by local politicians, industry associations and supported by universities who had studied the practices of British and American industrial pioneers. One of the advantages of coming from behind is that labour relations are much better as a result of workers' wages rising year by year as the economy improves, catching up with the leaders. In contrast, British companies, afraid of being overtaken, tried to *cut* the wages of workers, which led to the development of an angry and adversarial labour movement and to political parties who took sides with either workers or managers. Indeed, intimacy and solidarity became associated not with companies themselves but rebellious workers in large companies fighting for fair shares.

To catch up, German universities, governments, industry associations, regions, towns and trade unions worked together in the national interest. While Germany's industrial might equal that of Britain by 1890, defeat in the First World War and subsequent reparations took their toll. By 1938 its industrial strength was restored only to be destroyed once more by the Second World War. By 1951, however, barely six years after their total destruction, German industry and the German economy had overtaken those of the UK and have stayed ahead ever since. Germany's GDP per person, even though much reduced by the absorption of East Germany, stands at US$44,469 (sixteenth in the world), while other *Mittelstand* cultures such as Switzerland (eighth) and Austria (fourteenth) score US$56,565 and US$45,493 respectively. UK GDP per person is US$ 36,569, leaving it in twenty-first place.

A word should be said about the approach to capitalism of the German-speaking world in general, since it is very different from the Anglo-Saxon approach. In *Progressive Capitalism: How to Achieve Economic Growth, Liberty and Social Justice,*[5] British businessman and politician David Sainsbury stated that this model of the economy is less derived from Adam Smith than from Friedrich List, the nineteenth-century German economic philosopher and advocate of the customs union (*Zollverein*) that led to German unity. List taught that each nation should find its own path to economic and industrial development, which was a particular form of cultural and national self-expression. He regarded Smith's views as overly abstract, pseudo-universal and too deterministic. They had more to do with trading than with industry. Britain's recent de-industrialization would not have surprised him. He would

5.   London: Biteback Publications, 2014.

probably have applauded the exceptional paths to economic development adopted by China, Singapore and South Korea.

List was a sceptic on the subject of free trade, pointing out that powerful nations demanded it only once they had reached the top – free trade was not how they had got there initially. Britain's colonial markets had first been captured. Sainsbury sees in List a progenitor of progressive capitalism. List was a strong advocate of infrastructure and of banks serving industry and not merely themselves. He stressed the importance of manufacturing and believed that it should be protected until it was strong enough to stand on its own. He was the apostle of close coordination and trusting relationships between industry, trade, banking, government and agriculture. This is important because many of the successful *Mittelstand* discussed in this chapter have characteristics favoured by List and belong in this context. The following sections discuss the strategies and characteristics of these companies, which take the form of a cybernetic learning loop, as shown in Figure 6.1.

Here we see a virtuous circle beginning with 1 and ending with 6 with an assembly of informal stakeholders, cohering in family-type relationships around a technology to which they are committed and of which they are proud. There are egalitarian, engineer-to-engineer relationships to customers, with no tolerance for puffery. Innovation provides for human fulfilment. The prime purpose of such companies is to serve children and grandchildren long-term and sustain their extended family.

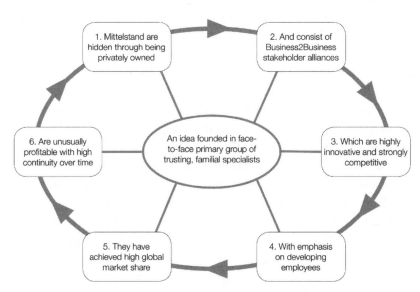

Figure 6.1 The process of wealth creation for 'hidden champions'

Mittelstand are hidden through being privately owned

Why are the *Mittelstand* hidden and under-appreciated? Let us give you the names of some companies singled out as especially successful, fast-growing, innovative, job-creating, profitable, high performing and transnational: Baader, McIlhenny, 3B Scientific, Tetra, Hamamatsu Photonics, Petzl, Ulvac, Orica, Gallagher, Webasto, Essel Propack, Technogym, Plansee, Top Glove, SEAG, Delo, Jamba and Sappi. Typical is Flexi, with a seventy per cent world market share of retractable dog leads. How many of these names did you recognize? Even our Microsoft spell-checking software objects to nearly all of them! Yet they were singled out by Hermann Simon as especially notable for their sustained excellence over many years. So why have we not heard of them?

One reason is that they are privately owned and keep a low profile. It is not necessary that we know them – they are content to be unknown to the general public as the fewer people who know they are on to a good thing, the better. The second reason is that they are mostly supplying capital goods. What is important is that their business customers know and appreciate them. Sappi is a South African company that makes coated fine paper and dissolvable cellulose pulp; it manufactures in forty-six locations. Ulvic makes ninety-six per cent of the world's coatings for liquid crystal displays and most of us didn't know that such a product was even needed. Gallagher, based in New Zealand, is a global leader in electrical fencing. These are not large companies and they are narrowly specialized. The wider public is not much interested.

The third reason we have probably not heard of them is that, since there is no consumer market to which to appeal, there is no brand to be advertised. There are very few shareholders outside the families that own most of these companies. There is little occasion to be regaled by advisers or newspapers and just a handful of customers to be talked to quietly and technically in a language few others would understand. Plansee produces 'high performance materials made with refractory metals and composites' – not exactly dinner party conversation.

A final reason these companies are little known is that many of their operations are located in rural communities, with which they have established close relationships of mutuality. In these remote locations fewer public appearances are necessary, fewer business rivals exist and there are fewer investors to woo. Strangely, the local plants seem to grow no bigger, but this is because ninety per cent of expansion is abroad. The companies grow apace, scattered across the globe, but their growth isn't visible as mostly the foreign units also remain small, human scale and informal.

A majority of Simon's hidden champions are still owned by their founding families. In situations where at least some outsiders have a stake in the company, they are known and trusted by the family, which usually still holds controlling shares. But even in the minority of cases where such companies are publicly owned, the family ethos lives on. The company is still run by say, the founder's grandchildren. Employees are 'family', as are suppliers, sub-contractors and the local community. Often people are on a first-name basis. The culture is informal. Everyone knows everyone.

Research has shown that such family firms are more person-oriented and less task-oriented, more friendly and spontaneous and focused on coming generations in the long-term. The founder is typically a parental figure, powerful but also responsive to those around them. There are many more female executives than in shareholder-driven corporations. These kinds of companies encourage strong networks of relationships and employees tend to stay for a long time. Such firms are very much run by and for a small number of people. They must form very honest and accommodating relationships, because they rely on each other for their future. Without fellow specialists, they'd be out in the cold. Journalist John Ardagh pens a vivid portrait of such a company in his book *Germany and the Germans*:

> The typical Swabian factory is still likely to be owned and actively run by a self-made man, or the son of one. He may earn 300,000 DM [€500,000] a year, but he lives very simply, probably works a 70-hour week, knows exactly how to turn a lathe or adjust an engine and will readily go to the shop-floor and discuss technical details with his workers. He has a close and benevolent contact with them, usually knowing them all by name: and he is anxious to avoid his firm becoming too large for his personal supervision and thus less efficient. … [H]e has a blithe disregard for showy public relations, believing that sheer quality will win through – as usually it does.[6]

B2B stakeholder alliances

None of the clowning involved in marketing to consumers occurs in business2business relationships. Both parties are typically deeply committed and deadly serious. The explosives made by Orica either work in the way they're

---

6.   John Ardagh, *Germany and the Germans*, London: Penguin, 1991, p. 110.

intended to or result in serious injury or even death. Nothing but total honesty and transparency will do. Clear instructions for safe use are mandatory. B2B operations are typically conducted between engineers, scientists or experts of some kind. Petzl sells to people operating in the vertical world of building, window-cleaning, mountaineering and caving. The equipment must be up to standard or disaster ensues.

Discussion is between professional stakeholders. Those people involved know value when they see it. It is even possible to demand certain results; that a knitting machine produce two thousand or more cardigans per day, or that a generator produce so much power-by-the-hour for a specified period. The customer's customer must also be satisfied. There is no room for excuses. B2B relationships tend to be more egalitarian and more authentic. The equipment either works as warranted or it does not. There are no gimmicks, silliness or the manipulation of images.

Most of these companies have avoided flotation on the stock market, although it is conceivable that this might occur in the future. Hence they are run by and for an assortment of people with a stake in the companies' fortunes: founders, investors, employees, suppliers, lenders, customers and the community. What characterizes these companies is the presence of committed equity holders – a handful of people who have invested their money in the business and are determined to make it pay. Suppliers, customers, friends and relatives may have stakes too. These people are free to offer their advice to the CEO and may pull out if it's not heeded. Essentially, everyone who makes a difference to the success or failure of these companies must be consulted. We can trust commitment of this magnitude.

This situation is in sharp contrast to publicly owned corporations in the UK, the USA and former dominions. These are legally obliged to maximize the returns of just one party, the shareholders, even if doing so adversely affects employees' salaries, squeezes suppliers and delivers less value to customers. In the wider world in general, stakeholding economies such as China, Singapore, Indonesia, Sweden, Finland and Germany are out-performing shareholder economies. Once companies pass into the hands of shareholders through an initial public offering (IPO), growth will typically slow or even stop, the number of employees will begin to shrink and the corporation will become a means of enriching its owners, as more money is given to shareholders and less and less invested in the future. It is SMEs who create most new jobs, undertake most innovation and have the highest growth rates.

It is of particular interest that the companies in Simon's sample of hidden champions don't prioritize profits in the way that public corporations are obliged to do. If we take it that profit for shareholders is the number one priority for 100 per cent of companies in public ownership, the identified priorities of the 1,300 hidden champions are very interesting: when their senior managements were polled, 89.4 per cent of respondents put 'company survival' first. This is consistent with the corporation *being an end in itself*, a recipient of money rather than a mere source of money. Its purpose is to support the family dynasty. Capacity utilization was cited by 53.6 per cent; employee satisfaction was voted third by 53.5 per cent; profitability fourth by 38.8 per cent; and cost reduction was the fifth priority for 25.5 per cent. Since it is blindingly obvious that a company will not survive long if it doesn't generate profits, we can safely infer that hidden champions believe that engaging employees in company goals and ensuring the long-term survival of the company are actually the best means of doing so. This approach seems to work.

The average growth rate of the hidden champions is 8.8 per cent per annum, which means that they double in size every eight years. The Fortune 500 companies hardly grew at all, at 1.9 per cent. Hidden champions provided 4.7 per cent more jobs per annum, or fifty-eight per cent more over the decade from 1999–2009, while the Fortune 500 companies *shed* 4.6 per cent of jobs. Overall, there are fewer and fewer jobs in large public companies, so start-ups and *Mittelstand* are the chief hope in reducing unemployment and providing meaningful work. Some six per cent of British companies, all small in size, are responsible for fifty per cent of new jobs.[7]

Highly innovative and strongly competitive

Relationships deteriorate sharply with organizational size and, without a proper hearing, innovative persons founder, according to Peters and Waterman. Innovation needs support but often gets nothing but opposition, even strikes. Back in the seventies, during Britain's industrial problems, Professor John Child looked at relationships among unionized plants with up to twenty-five employees and those with one thousand or more. The number of lost days per thousand employees was fifteen for the smaller units and two thousand for the larger ones. Peters and Waterman claimed that smaller companies are many times more innovative but did not cite their source. This lack of innovation was despite the fact that big companies have more financial resources to spend

7.   Patrick Hoskin, 'Are SME's the Key to the economy?' *Times*, 28 October 2013.

on innovation.[8] It is exciting to work with innovative people. The West needs to innovate urgently and it may at last be rising to the challenge. According to Start-Up Britain, 380,000 businesses were created in the UK in the twelve months up to December 2013,[9] and there are now 4.8 million companies in the UK. The UK Enterprise Investment Scheme of 1994, revised in 2012, offers tax relief to those investing in small unquoted companies on both income tax and capital gains tax. It claims to have received considerable praise from other countries.

In the Netherlands, the town of Eindhoven claims to have more patents per head of population than any other city in Europe. The diversified technology company Philips is based there and has created hundreds of patents which it shows to potential entrepreneurs while offering to act as both customer and joint investor. What big companies can do for smaller ones remains an unexplored area; in this section we look at R&D expenditure, patents, new products and then ask what drives innovation among hidden champions and larger public companies.

Of the hidden champions, eighty-five per cent regard themselves as 'technology leaders', seventy-nine per cent call themselves 'quality leaders' and seventy-four per cent believe they lead in 'market awareness'. The ratio of R&D spending to revenue for the Fortune 500 companies is 1.8 per cent; for the hidden champions it is 5.9 per cent, although one-fifth of them spend over nine per cent. The hidden champions' average is fifty per cent more than the top one thousand companies by size in the world. Even if we take the top one thousand overall spenders on R&D, their average spending still only amounts to 4.2 per cent.

Patent applications for the hidden champions amount to 30.6 per one thousand employees, but only 5.6 among Germany's largest technology-intensive companies (for example, Bosch and Siemens). Patents are much less expensive for hidden champions, only $725,000 per patent per one thousand employees, as opposed to $3.7 million per patent for larger companies. Clearly, hidden champions get more out of their work-forces in the form of innovation. Among hidden champions, eighty-five per cent of revenue derives from products that are less than four years old. The comparable figure for larger companies is twenty-three per cent; according to Hermann, on average, innovation has not stopped in larger companies but it has slowed appreciably,

8.   John Child, *Organization: A Guide to Problems and Practices*, p. 124, quoted by Peters and Waterman, *In Search of Excellence*, p. 31.

9.   See Start-up Britain website, http://www.startupbritain.org, founded by Emma Jones.

either because of size or because shareholders are not prepared to wait so long for their rewards, or for both reasons.

When asked what drives innovation, sixty-five per cent of the hidden champions credited both technology and markets. Most declined to separate them – only thirty-five per cent were prepared to cite just one of these. The dominant point of view is holistic. Among larger, publicly owned organizations, only nineteen per cent do not separate these influences and eighty-one per cent are prepared to cite either one or the other as the dominant force driving their innovations.

Simon also found that his hidden champions were much faster in their R&D and were typically first to market with their innovations. They were closer to their customers and hence more aware of unfulfilled needs, of new market niches opening up and of the chance to co-create with customers. Westfalia Separator achieved an eighty per cent market share of bio-diesel centrifuges because it entered this new renewable energy market before others and held on to what it had gained.

Simon reminds us that an important aspect of innovation is that 'uniqueness comes from within'. It is for this reason that hidden champions make much more of their product and outsource far less of it to suppliers. They are more vertically integrated than most large companies, making their own components rather than buying them in. We can measure vertical integration by the amount of value added by a particular corporation. Hidden champions add forty-two per cent of the total value of the product manufactured and sold. German industry as a whole adds twenty-nine per cent, and this is on the high side compared to other economies. Large companies have outsourced on a vast scale. Doing so is very much in the interests of shareholders because it cuts the wage bill and threatening to outsource further keeps employees in line. Less money is spent on employees' wages and is diverted to shareholders. But if you do not make the product yourself how can it be unique and stand out from other items in the marketplace?

If components and sub-assemblies are outsourced, then those parts of the finished product that are in the supply chain will be available to other companies too. Assembled standard offerings can be copied by rivals, perhaps more cheaply. Ex-suppliers may start to compete. If a company *really* wants to be original, then it must make innovative products with its own new tools and new components. That way, together with its unique work culture, no one will be able to imitate it. Hidden champions are vertically integrated, making not only, say, the camera tripod, but the tools for making the tripod; not only garden watering equipment but the machines that make the garden watering equipment.

While outsourcing may benefit shareholders, it is often calamitous for employees, for the industry in general and for the nation at large. The pool of skills within and around major corporations disappears as unemployed workers scatter. The tax base shrinks and it becomes impossible to recruit locally, even for those companies that didn't outsource originally. The skills are gone. And once those skills are in another country many more industries and innovations can arise from this base. The loss is irreversible. If we *wanted* China to catch up and overtake us, we could hardly do better than send them the blueprints for various components, enabling them to discover more and more about the final product and finally construct it themselves.

One very obvious reason why hidden champions do not outsource is that the small rural communities in which they are mostly located would be devastated by this development. They are often the biggest employer in town and it is a symbiotic relationship. Moreover, the highly specialized skills they seek are often unavailable elsewhere and they must typically train their own employees in them. Their talent is home-grown. Several hidden champions have three generations of the same families working for them.

When asked about their competitive advantages, the hidden champions are much more likely to cite the elements of a trusting relationship, product quality, the economies offered by using the product, on-time delivery, service and advice, and their ability to integrate client systems with their own so that they work together. They are also more likely to cite their people, culture, qualifications and processes, which are unique. Educating the customer is part of the package and products and services tend to be bundled together. Word of mouth and endorsements are considered the major reason for preferring a supplier. Simon found that larger, publicly owned companies are more likely to mention advertising and PR, distributors, the influence of vendors, price cutting and patent protection. They are also more likely to consider their technology as superior and stress the size and reach of their organization and its market power. They also claim to be better informed as a result of their position in the centre of the industrial ecosystem. They stress brand, reputation and push.

A major advantage enjoyed by hidden champions stems from the lack of internal resistance and opposition to new ideas that occurs in most bureaucratic organizations. Simon asked what percentage of employee energy was dissipated by internal conflict. For mid-size companies in general, the response was twenty to thirty per cent. For larger organizations it was more than double, at fifty to seventy per cent, suggesting that size alone can exhaust new initiatives. For the hidden champions, in contrast, the response was that ten to twenty per cent of energy was wasted by conflict, less than one-third of the waste in large companies. His champions declined to work for money alone. They worked for 'overarching goals and values' shared by all.

Emphasis on the development of employees

Among the hidden champions, twenty-eight per cent more jobs had been created over the previous decade in those countries where the companies were headquartered. In countries to which the companies' activities had spread, there were 110 per cent more jobs. The number of jobs in multinationals with their headquarters in Europe or North America had declined during the same period. Asked what it was about employees that they most valued, the hidden champions cited loyalty (79.5 per cent), excellent qualifications (seventy-two per cent), motivation (72.7 per cent) and flexibility (58.4 per cent). Motivation in hidden champion companies is largely *intrinsic*. Motivation in public companies is largely *extrinsic*; studies have emphasized pay for performance, bonus payments and fear of being fired.

The engagement of employees is very important. A recent UK survey found that a high degree of engagement reduces absenteeism by two-thirds, raises the number of creative ideas by a factor of ten and reduces the number of employees seeking employment elsewhere by a factor of five. Those fully engaged in their work report much lower levels of stress.[10] A survey by Gallup found that only thirty per cent of American employees were engaged in their work. The hidden champions report far less sick leave than the average for German industry; turnover among them stands at 2.7 per cent annually compared with nineteen per cent for US industry and 7.3 per cent for German industry as a whole. Seventy-five per cent of hidden champion employees are trained by the company in-house, but only thirty-nine per cent in larger companies, whose preference is to buy in talent from universities and competitors. It is clear that hidden champions see themselves as developing employees over time while most public companies see themselves as buying in and deploying talent engendered elsewhere.

10. Employee Engagement Factsheet UK (http://www.cipd.co.uk/hr-resources/ factsheets/employee-engagement.aspx), August 2013. See also Gallup Consulting 'What's your Engagement Ratio?' (www.gallup.com).

High global market shares

An impression that hidden champions are very local, very provincial and hidden in the rural climes of one country needs to be disabused. Recall that they are all first, second or third in the world market in their particular niche. Far from being provincial, their international scope is extremely wide. The average world market share of the hidden champions is thirty per cent, that is, higher than Fortune 500 companies. Some hidden champions even have a 100 per cent share of the world market, for example a company that makes large theatre curtains.

These companies are especially welcome and successful in China because a great deal of manufacturing is done there and the champions sell machinery and components that sustain manufacturing. How is lipstick inserted into tubes? There are only three world suppliers of the necessary technology. Who makes instruments that record data from weather balloons? These B2B products tend to be narrow technologically, wide internationally and deeply embedded in the work of their customers.

In contrast, large corporations run into strong headwinds in China. When Motorola launched its mobile phone in China it had no domestic rivals. Within six years it faced 100 rivals, mostly offering a cheaper product. While the rarer products of hidden champions are welcomed, mass-manufacturers face head-to-head competition from indigenous companies that re-engineer their products at frightening speed.

Hidden champions attain their high market shares almost entirely by high performance rather than low-cost production or low price. What a machine is worth depends upon its subsequent performance and for this reason a company must have confidence in its supplier's ability to eliminate any bugs or shortfalls. The company's fate is tied to that of the supplier and there may be no other supplier available. Of the machinery and components sold by hidden champions, 78.9 per cent is described as 'high-tech', which is over three times as much as larger companies.

Unusually high level of profitability and continuity

The 1,300 hidden champions achieved a 13.9 per cent pre-tax return on investment compared with an average 3.7 per cent for Fortune 500 companies. Return on equity was 24.2 per cent for the hidden champions and return on revenues was eleven per cent; for the Fortune 500 companies, return on revenue was 3.5 per cent. The implications are clear. Companies actually make *more* profit when they aim for something beyond the bottom line: the satisfaction of customers, the engagement of employees, the support of suppliers and good relationships with the community of stakeholders.

It is in the years *before* any IPOs that companies grow apace and most never intend to go public at all. Once shareholders take over, companies tend to change as enriching shareholders becomes their chief aim. The family behind Hewlett-Packard discovered this to their fury but could do nothing about it. Richard Branson took Virgin back into his own hands after falling out with shareholders, as did Michael Dell of Dell computers. Companies managed in a way to enrich shareholders cannot take a long-term view because shareholders keep their shares for less than a year and regard them as chips to trade with. The necessity of producing quarterly reports means that short-term gains are everything and managers refuse to accept the short-term losses that investment in the longer future entails.

Increasing revenue and innovating are hard work, but slashing pay-rolls, cutting costs, buying back shares and compromising on quality are easy. Unfortunately, the effects of such actions are only revealed in the long-term, by which time the shares will have been sold and the protagonists retired. The finance people now in charge will have little understanding of technology and the company will become a mechanism for making money for its owners.

In contrast, a majority of the hidden champions are reluctant to go public. Should they choose to do so, the easiest route is via a private equity partner. But these are also considered to be more interested in money than in growth and in quick profit rather than in high technology. The more complex the technology and the narrower the niche, the harder it is for equity funders to understand and appreciate what's on offer. Most hidden champions complain that their financial worth is under-estimated by non-specialists and outsiders.

An IPO is even worse. It obliges a company to report more information than it wishes to and opens it up to publicity and scrutiny. Letting people know how valuable your niche is invites rivals to enter the business. It makes it impossible to maintain a low profile and shareholders may resist any investments that fail to pay off in the short-term. Going public does of course create vast riches and allows sellers to fund whatever other activities they choose. It is sometimes seen as the ultimate success. However, it is not in the long-term interest of the corporation and its survival as a profitable incubator of human development.

Hidden champions were also paragons of continuity. Over ninety per cent of the hidden champions identified by Simon are still prospering and growing. This contrasts with the very spotty record of large publicly owned companies identified as 'excellent' by Peters and Waterman in the early 1980s. These included Kodak, Western Electric, Delta and K-Mart, nearly all of them casualties. Most of the companies identified by Jim Collins and Jerry Porras in *Built to Last*,[11] published a decade later, have failed to shine or, indeed, even last; these include Motorola, Sony, HP, Ford, 3M and Boeing. Collins selected some superlative companies in *Good to Great*, published in 2001, yet by 2012 this select bunch had *lost* more money than they made and were not even above the Standard and Poor's stock averages.[12] Being identified as 'great' or 'excellent' appears to be a curse.

Why is this? Perhaps these companies refuse to change, believing they have arrived. Perhaps they are mobbed by shareholders who now expect too much and milk them. Perhaps their products are widely imitated and they are trapped in a war of attrition. Perhaps maximizing *anything* is fatal to the balance of a whole system. Whatever the case, the success of such a company may ultimately be fleeting. A company famous for its profitability may start extracting too much from other stakeholders. Even as it is acclaimed, it has already gone too far, hence the mortality rate among large corporations with stellar reputations.

The casualty rate among hidden champions is exceptionally low. The average tenure for a leader at the top of a 'champion' company is twenty years. Compare this to 6.6 years in the USA, 9.4 years in Japan and 5.5 years in Germany for publicly listed companies. The founders of hidden champions commit their whole lives to their ventures, hence their long tenure. Simon noted a tendency for big companies to think of their decisions as either/or, while hidden champions tended towards both/and, considering both new technology and demanding customers, customer satisfaction and profitability, gains for the customer and gains for the supplier.

On this last issue Simon looked to see to what extent customers had been able to muscle suppliers into lowering their prices, often using threats to replace them. He asked suppliers how far they had conceded on price to see whether relationships which hidden champions had formed were more nearly equal. Hidden champions had lowered prices by only 1.4 per cent, while others had conceded 3.8 per cent. They were in a weaker position, perhaps; easier to replace and less trusted.

---

11. London: Century, 1994. An exception is Johnson and Johnson, which is still going strong.

12. Jim Collins, *Good to Great*, New York: Harper Business, 2001.

Face-to-face primary group of intimate, familial specialists

We now move to the centre of Figure 6.1, which argues that face-to-face human relationships are what holds all the other elements of the *Mittelstand* together. The *Mittelstand* and its values are more a practical philosophy and an art form than a description of the conduct of companies of any particular size. It is not that size is irrelevant but that limited size plus expansion abroad, rather than domestically, makes possible small business units scattered across the world. The whole company can be quite large without any of its units being too big for visionary leadership and for people to be held together by ideas, values and human bonds. The *Mittelstand* is more of an ideal of how people can better work together as stakeholders in an enterprise.

The power of the *Mittelstand* ideal comes from the informal, spontaneous, familial and intimate clustering of the primary group *around* exceedingly intelligent machinery, designed by superior minds. The narrowness of the focus ensures that the company retains its human scale and intimacy. Yet the breadth of its appeal to producers everywhere makes it relevant on a global scale too. It competes with rivals yet is inherently cooperative insofar as it renders production more effective in hundreds of venues and makes factory systems more efficient.

The conclusions we can draw from this chapter can be summarized in four vital balances or creative syntheses which enable the hidden champions among the *Mittelstand* to excel (see Figure 6.2, overleaf).

Mittelstand are committed *emotionally* to their employees and customers and yet are *technically* proficient and highly disciplined. They are simultaneously very *global* and very *local*. They have been able to fuse these contrasting values. They refuse to make *either/or* choices and achieve *both one and the other*. Finally their Socratic dialogue among *equals* leads them to *excellence*. Equality is the harbinger of both trust and excellence. In contrast, unequal, exploitative relationships, in which the buyer must beware of being cheated, lead to mediocrity. Alibaba is the world's largest network of buyers and sellers and is China's answer to eBay, Gumtree and so on. What is less well known is that it is largely dedicated to B2B relationships, in which the protagonists are near-equals, exchanging expertise and discovery.

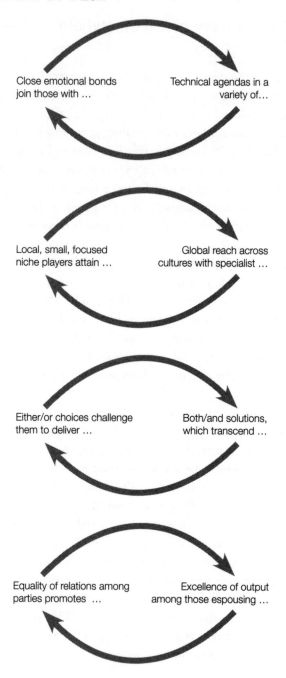

Figure 6.2 Four creative syntheses

This relational way of working closely together means that *both* parties benefit and customers buying machines or components have confidence in the fact that their investment will pay back within a stipulated period. This raises the whole question of power, especially 'market power'. Is it the capacity to foist on customers products they do not want at prices they cannot afford, or is it power *through* rather than *over* people; that is, what modern management literature calls *empowerment?*

If we can empower other people, we become powerful ourselves but in quite another way. We have the power to teach, develop and sustain others, especially other stakeholders, so that the whole industrial ecosystem grows more effectively. This type of power resembles the family ethic we discussed in Chapters 4 and 5, but shows that it also works in a European context. Indeed, *The Economist* recently pointed out that the growth of *Mittelstand* vies with the growth rate of China.[13]

Hermann Simon conducted two studies of *Mittelstand* roughly ten years apart. Some companies that had been small enough to qualify in the 1990s had grown beyond the US$4 billion mark and were too large to qualify for inclusion in the second report. He created a new category for these companies: big champions. What is fascinating to observe is that the big champions did not stop growing as they became larger. Indeed, Simon found no correlation between size and rate of growth. What this strongly suggests is that the term *Mittelstand* encompasses more of an ethos rather than being simply a question of size, although being smaller does help. But a company that has grown large under its family founders and is wisely led doesn't lose the spirit that made it great. Bosch is an example, with 400,000 employees, US$85 billion revenue and a family shareholding of only eight per cent. We take this to be an illustration that a *Mittelstand* is many things but, above all, it is a new 'ecology of mind'[14] and a special set of human relationships.

13. 'Beating China: German family firms are outdoing their Chinese rivals. Can they keep it up?' *The Economist*, 30 July 2011. Accessed online, http://www.economist.com/node/21524922.

14. Gregory Bateson, *Steps to an Ecology of Mind*, New York: Jason Aronson, 1978.

CHAPTER 7

The conscious capitalism movement

The myth that profit maximization is the sole purpose of business
has done enormous damage to the reputation of capitalism and the
legitimacy of business in society. We need to recapture the narrative
and restore it to its true essence: that the purpose of business is to
improve our lives and to create value for stakeholders.[1]

What is meant by 'conscious capitalism'? As used by John Mackey, co-founder
and CEO of Whole Foods Market, and Raj Sisodia, Professor of Marketing
at Babson College in Massachusetts, it seems to imply that capitalism is semi-
conscious of itself or even unconscious of some of its best attributes, relying
as it does on phantom hands to restore public benefit. As we have seen in
previous chapters, insisting that economic behaviour is 'rational' leads us
to make an assertion and ignore the equally rational counterpoint to that
assertion. For example, we get very excited about business serving our own
self-interests but are far more reticent about how it serves the interests of
other people, seeming to believe that acknowledging this issue will weaken
our prime purpose. We seem to believe that social benefit happens accidently
and inadvertently and that we should adopt a *laissez faire* approach and not
try to question the alleged benefits.

But taking this approach makes us only half-conscious of the benefits
capitalism can offer to our society. The problem, then, is not capitalism per

1. Mackey and Sisodia, *Conscious Capitalism*, p. 20.

se, but the *incredibly narrow* way in which we think and speak about it. We see capitalism in terms of the exclusive rights of shareholders, while ignoring other stakeholders; as chiefly about money, ignoring wealth creation; as all about private enrichment while rubbishing the public good; and all about competing but forgetting the cooperation behind it. By ignoring the 'other half' we remain semi-conscious of the world in and around our companies and especially the amazing value potential that the capitalist system can contribute to our welfare.[2]

Consider that two hundred years ago eighty-five per cent of the world's people lived on less than $1 a day. Today that figure is sixteen per cent. During this period average per capita income has increased by 1,600 per cent. In South Korea, GDP has grown 260-fold since 1960. In the same period, average life expectancy has risen from thirty to sixty-eight years. From a world in which almost everyone was illiterate, eighty-four per cent can now read. Fifty-three per cent of the world's population now enjoys democratic systems with universal suffrage; 120 years ago the number was zero.

The heroes and heroines of these developments were innovative entrepreneurs, without whom few or none of these developments would have been possible. They used 'their dreams and their passions as fuel to create extraordinary value for customers, team members, suppliers, society and investors'.[3] It is high time we became fully conscious of just how much capitalism has provided and why. It's time to make visible the so-called 'invisible hand' and comprehend its largesse. Business activities have widespread ramifications. They create and they destroy. Unless we become aware of this entire spectrum of activity we will remain unable to improve our situation or halt our apparent decline. Marc Ganfi coined the phrase 'conscious business' but Mackey and Sisodia have done most to illustrate it. The authors explain:

> Lifting people out of poverty was never the conscious purpose of business; it was the by-product of a business well enacted. Now business is awakening to itself and becoming conscious. It is recognizing that it is a force with enormous power and responsibility. By becoming conscious, it can do what it does even better .... It can create more community, more mutuality, and paradoxically more profit, by engaging everyone in the system.[4]

2. Mackey and Sisodia, *Conscious Capitalism*, pp.11–25.
3. Mackey and Sisodia, *Conscious Capitalism*, p.15.
4. Mackey and Sisodia, *Conscious Capitalism*, p.22. See also http://uniqueself.com

Behind this awakening is the aging of the baby boomers of the 1960s and 1970s. A participant in the 1964 Berkeley student revolt would be around sixty-nine to seventy today and a veteran of the anti-Vietnam War protests outside the US embassy in London in March 1968 would be not much younger. With the onset of age comes a yearning for meaning, a desire to provide for the welfare of one's children and grandchildren, consideration about what, if anything, one is leaving behind and the awareness that knowledge, development and love can be three such gifts. Older people seek integrity. The alternative, according to Harvard psychologist Erik Erikson, is 'disgust and despair'.[5] Is this all that life is – a dirty great pile of loot you cannot take with you?

No company can exist, much less survive, without stakeholders to whom the visionary leadership of the company relates.[6] These stakeholders are employees, suppliers, partners, customers, society, the environment and investors. There is a reason for putting investors last. Until leaders have inspired employees, until employees have gathered in supplies and contracted with other partners, there is nothing to offer to customers. Until customers and the local community have responded to this offer, creating revenue for the company, there isn't anything to *give* investors. Investors can only be paid if and when other stakeholders have effectively completed their work and have produced more than they began with, in a climate of mutual trust. If these other stakeholders fail, shareholders will suffer.[7]

What we have here is the confusion of means and ends, discussed in Chapter 1. If employees, suppliers, partners, customers and the community are nothing but means to an end, that is, shareholder enrichment, then there is a very real danger that these means will be sacrificed to the all-important end. But it proves almost impossible to create this situation because these stakeholder 'means' need to generate money initially. We can, if we wish, decree that shareholders are the most important and deserve all the rewards from successful work, but this will not alter the fact that other stakeholders must operate first *in time*. They must first excel if shareholders are later to benefit. If you cut back on employee pay, if you restrict pension contributions or announce redundancies, if you substitute machines for people, then employees might not work as hard or be so innovative – we have already seen

5.   Erik Erikson, *Insight and Responsibility*, New York: Norton, 1964.

6.   R. Edward Freeman, *Stakeholder Theory*, Cambridge: Cambridge University Press, 2010.

7.   James C. Collins, and Jerry I. Porras, *Built to Last*, London: Century, 1994.

that fear saps innovation.[8] Likewise, if you squeeze suppliers' margins and pay them late, they may find better customers and cut back on their R&D. What they supply may be of declining quality and originality. And if you save money by downgrading the quality you deliver to your customers or raise prices, they may buy less.

Shareholders may *initially* do better because you have saved on what you pay to other stakeholders but in the longer run they could do worse because less wealth is being created and less revenue generated. Moreover, by the time productivity and quality deteriorate it is too late to do much about it. The whole system has slowed, employee morale is low, suppliers have switched, customers are complaining and revenue has plummeted so that even the privileged investors suffer. Figure 7.1 illustrates how the system could work at its best with stakeholders earning high returns in a cyclical process and a virtuous circle.

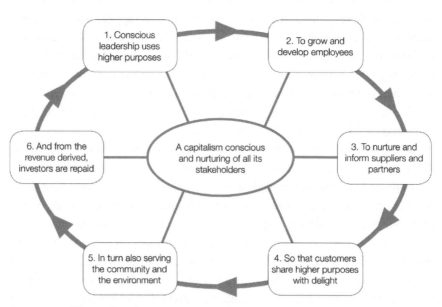

Figure 7.1 The cycle of conscious capitalism

It starts with higher purpose and clear meaning and grows employees in this context and for this reason. These employees nurture suppliers and set out to delight customers by serving them, the community and the environment. *Only at this juncture are there any revenues from which shareholders can be repaid.*

8. Teresa M. Amabile, Constance Hadley and Steven J. Kramer, 'Creativity Under the Gun', *Harvard Business Review,* August 2002.

This model is our take on Mackey and Sisodia's approach. They insist that the interests of all stakeholders must be *aligned* and that none take precedence over another. In short, every stakeholder is both an end in him/herself and a means to an end beyond. In relation to his business, Mackey stated his fundamental disagreement with Milton Friedman with whom he debated.

> While Friedman believes that taking care of employees, customers and business philanthropy are means to the end of increasing investor profits, I take the exact opposite view. Making high profits is the means to the end of fulfilling Whole Foods' core business mission. We want to improve the health and well-being of everyone on the planet through higher quality foods and better nutrition, and we can't fulfil this mission unless we are highly profitable. Just as people cannot live without eating, so a business cannot live without profits. But most people do not live to eat and nor must business live just to make profits.[9]

When Brits and Americans say 'shareholders come first' they are talking about their own priorities. A glance at the cycle above shows that, in fact, 'shareholders come last' in the temporal process of wealth creation. There is a case for arguing that investors come first when a family founds a company with its own money and sweat but there is no case at all for claiming that those who responded to an IPO came first in any sense of that word. Since they are last in this process, putting them first in importance disrupts and confuses the very process of wealth creation. Non-active investors should keep out of the way until customers have been so well satisfied that revenue climbs.

The interests of stakeholders, of which investors are just one group, should *not* be traded off. Rather, their interests should be reconciled. If you look for trade-offs, you will always find them; but if you look for synergies or symbiosis, you can find these too, and the best solutions are those that benefit *all* stakeholders. John Mackey found this out by accident during a crisis suffered by his company. In 1981 Austin, Texas, experienced its worst flood in seventy years. Thirteen people died; damage was estimated at $35 million ($100 million at today's prices). The flood wiped out Whole Foods' one and only store, which was deluged by seven feet of water. Incurring losses of US$ 400,000, the business was bankrupt.

The next day was a public holiday and, to the amazement of the destitute owners who were surveying the damage, scores of customers and members of the local community turned up with mops and buckets and began clearing

9.   Mackey and Sisodia, *Conscious Capitalism*, p. 4.

up the mess. Nearly all the employees turned up too, although there was no prospect of being paid. 'Stop moping and start mopping' was their advice. In the days that followed, thousands of hours of work were gladly donated. Suppliers offered to extend credit and to postpone payment for months so the store could be restocked. In response to the generosity of others, investors dug into their pockets and provided more capital. Mackey never forgot this experience and would always remember just who it took to save the store when it faced catastrophe.[10]

Origins of research into conscious companies

Study into fully conscious companies was initially undertaken at Bentley College, Waltham, Massachusetts, by Raj Sisodia, David Wolfe and Jagdish Sheth in the mid-2000s. They published their results in *Firms of Endearment: How World-class Companies Profit from Passion and Purpose*.[11] Their search for an unusual kind of company began in a curious way when they asked their study cohort to 'Tell us about companies you love, not just like, but *love*.' Hundreds of companies were nominated, many of them small family businesses.

Criteria for inclusion in the list of endearing companies included longevity; treatment of employees and temporary staff; treatment of customers; and willingness to pay tax. Profitability was *not* a criterion for selection, although it was later investigated. Ultimately, many publicly owned companies were included in the final list because discovering the profits made by small private companies is not easy. The companies researched included, among others, Caterpillar, Whole Foods, Wegmans, Costco, Google, Starbucks, Southwest Airlines, JetBlue, Patagonia, L.L.Bean, Harley-Davidson, Commerce Bank, IKEA (USA), IDEO, Toyota (USA), Honda (USA), New Balance, Trader Joe's, the Container Store, UPS, REI, Johnson & Johnson, the Home Depot and Jordan's Furniture.

Only when the list had been whittled down to twenty-eight 'endearing' companies was profitability and contribution to investors studied. Expectations at this stage were modest. The researchers hoped to discover that very little was lost and perhaps something gained by treating all stakeholders in an exemplary manner. What they actually discovered astounded them. Compared with Standard and Poor's 500 stocks, firms of endearment returned 1,026 per cent over a ten-year period, compared with 122 per cent for average stocks, eight

---

10. Mackey and Sisodia, *Conscious Capitalism*, p. 5.
11. New Jersey: Wharton School Publishing, 2007.

times higher. We shall see later in this chapter that recent results have been even better. We will now examine one by one the stakeholder relationships illustrated in Figure 7.1, the conscious capitalism cycle.

Leading consciously towards a higher purpose

Among the chief characteristics of the conscious or visionary leader is an appeal to a higher purpose. This is the reason the company exists. It engages employees and customers, catalyses creativity and innovation, and elicits organizational commitment. This higher purpose is above petty disputes and is a reason for finding agreement and creating a sense of common allegiance. For example, a company called Medtronics creates pacemakers. Under the leadership of Bill George from 1993 to 2003, its profits grew from US$1.2 billion to US$60 billion. But the prime purpose of the company was never to make money, but to prolong the lives of its patients, which it did for ten million people, a great source of pride for everyone in the company. Medals awarded to outstanding employees feature a patient rising from an operating table.[12]

A higher purpose can transform an entire company. Originally, Waste Management was recognized as the company that owned most landfill sites. It was synonymous with waste removal and burial. Then it learned how to extract value from waste in the form of energy and materials. It consulted on waste reduction and created machinery to separate technical from organic waste for better recycling. Today it supplies enough clean energy to heat over 1.1 million homes. It estimates that the waste it handles is worth US$10 billion. It has started *paying* companies to dispose of their waste rather than charging them to remove it. Waste Management's slogan is 'think green' and it defines itself as providing 'integrated environmental solutions'. Where a goal is sufficiently uplifting it will cement trust among those striving for it and become a common cause and touchstone.

Google seeks to 'organize the world's information and make it universally accessible and useful'. Henry Ford once strove to 'open the highways to all mankind'. Muhammad Yunus' Grameen Bank strove to hasten the day 'when poverty is something you see only in museums'. And Whole Foods Markets, which some would see as little more than a grocery chain, holds 'tribal gatherings' of delegates from all its stores at which it renews its core purpose: to 'help evolve the world's agricultural system to be both efficient

---

12. See Bill George's foreword to Mackey and Sisodia, *Conscious Capitalism*, pp. ix – xiv.

and sustainable'. Its concerns include livestock and animal welfare, seafood sustainability and organic agriculture. It seeks to promote healthy eating as a means of reducing cancer, heart disease, obesity and so on. It seeks to make micro-credit loans to millions of the impoverished, including potential suppliers and to help these improve their businesses. Finally, it seeks to make conscious capitalism into a new business paradigm.

A second objective of such leadership is stakeholder integration. This involves creating win–win relationships among all stakeholders rather than win–lose relationships in which what one stakeholder gains another must lose. Take, for example, employee pay. The usual instinct is to pay employees as little as possible or, if this approach doesn't work, to outsource to China or a local contractor with access to migrant labour. But regarding labour as a commodity or a 'resource' is counter-productive. You get what you pay for. Paying decent wages means you attract higher calibre workers, who will potentially learn more on the job, be more productive as a result and remain loyal to the company. You incur fewer recruitment and induction costs, and avoid expensive mistakes made by inexperienced employees. If in a company of a hundred employees just ten people leave, that is scores of interpersonal relationships lost in which knowledge and information had been stored.

Conscious and endearing companies commonly offer wages fifteen to twenty per cent *above* the industry average. Jordan Furniture is one such company, yet sales per square foot are *six times* the industry average and its sales per employee nearly double. In such cases, *everyone* gains: the employee, the customer, the investor, the community where the higher wages are spent and the government, which receives more taxes from higher incomes. The same applies to money spent on training: if it leads to higher productivity and innovation then all concerned benefit. Footwear manufacturer New Balance outsources some of its simpler products to China but keeps the more complex in-house and challenges its manufacturing employees to be ten times more productive than the Chinese – a challenge they have met – so that it pays investors, not to mention their American workers, to create wealth at home.

The third essential quality of an endearing company is a highly conscious culture in the workplace. Here, culture refers to the accepted behaviours and practices within an organization framed by the values it adheres to. So for example, Southwest Airlines has set up a culture committee of employees, while the Container Store has a 'fun committee'. Values fail to make sense if they are not embedded throughout the company culture. For example, it is impossible to argue that leaders should always trust, be so transparent that everyone else has an advantage over them, show care even for those attempting to exploit them or be loyal even to a failing cause. Values applied to individual conduct face so many exceptions and qualifications that the situation becomes impossible.

But it is quite different to apply these values to a culture or workplace relationship because here values are confirmed, reciprocated and upheld. A culture in which people trust each other is demonstrably superior to one in which they do not, and much less costly. Just consider the time and effort expended on checking up that people are not lying to you and have really done what they promised to do. Of course *some* verification is in order, that is what supervision, auditing and due diligence are all about, but these are expensive processes and the longer you can wait between supervisions, the more money you save.[13]

The values of the company, manifested in its cultural behaviour, guide the conduct of everyone in it. The conscious leader shapes the culture and the culture guides its members in being accountable for their actions, in being open or transparent with each other, in being loyal to the company and its purposes and in being egalitarian. This last value is an example of something that well describes a culture but can only with great difficultly be applied to an individual. If you are 'equal' to everyone else, can you also be better? If you are the same as them, can you be best? When applied to individuals, equality must forever vie with excellence.

But applying egalitarianism to *cultures* makes sense. You treat every member of that culture *as if* they are your equal. This does not mean that this person *is* your equal. It means you respect that person; to treat someone as an equal is the greatest respect you can show to them. To treat them as inferior is to discourage them and to treat them as superior is to disparage your own position and feedback. Egalitarian cultures facilitate the best contributions their members can make and they increase their readiness to make them.[14]

Growing and developing employees

John Mackey does not use the term employees. He prefers 'team members'. This preference points to the fact that all employees in Whole Foods join teams, often more than one, members of which are as accountable and loyal to one another as they are to the wider organization and its mission. Newly

13. See Jacques Elliott, *The Form of Time*, New York: Crane Russak, 1982, who suggests that if employees are checked too rarely, their mistakes could prove expensive, but if they are monitored too often, efforts can be duplicated and trust dwindles.

14. For the high social cost of inequality see Richard Wilkinson and Kate Pickett, *The Spirit Level* London: Penguin, 2009.

hired people are considered probationers until at least a two-thirds majority of the team to which they are assigned agrees to work with them. Close bonds within a team are developed by members appreciating and caring about each other and through the sharing of information and knowledge. Similarly, each new recruit at the Container Store is interviewed by eight different people. It wants to ensure that the interviewee will have the integrity to fit into its company culture and, hopefully, stay.

Monday morning is the most likely time to have a heart attack. Too many people face their working week with a sense of fear or even despair. A Gallup World Poll found that the chief determinant of human happiness isn't wealth, health or even family – it's having a *meaningful job and good relationships with colleagues.*[15] This is hardly surprising. One-third of our waking hours are spent working. Yet a Conference Board survey found that only fifty per cent of Americans are satisfied with their jobs and only thirty per cent experience training programmes as useful.[16] Our work can be 'a job', 'a career' or a 'calling'. It's the latter that conscious companies insist upon.

Fairness is usually very important to employees. No one employed at Whole Foods earns more than nineteen times anyone else's salary, a ratio that compares with 350 times on average for large US corporations and up to 500 times in many cases. Everyone at Whole Foods knows what everyone else earns. The company needs people who care as much about the company and its purpose as they do for private enrichment, and very few of its top executives leave despite receiving better paid offers elsewhere. Any team that comes up with a new idea can propose it and, if it's successfully implemented, the team shares the gains made by the company, divided according to the hours worked on the project by different members.

Johnson & Johnson decided it was much cheaper to keep its staff healthy than to pay sickness benefit. Its Wellness programmes actually made it money by cutting back on medical insurance premiums and reducing absences from work. Every dollar spent earned the company an extra US$1.40 in reduced costs. It is cheaper to watch your weight than to undergo major surgery; cheaper to drink less than to have a liver transplant. Doug Rauch, ex-President of Trader Joe's, and now chief of the Conscious Capitalism Foundation summed up the situation:

15. Gallup World Poll, Jim Clifton, *The Coming Jobs War*, New York: Gallup, 2011.
16. http://www.forbes.com/sites/susanadams/2014/06/20/most-americans-are-unhappy-at-work/

When people come to work, they bring their worries, their sickness, their anxiety or their sadness, and customers feel that. For us it's win–win; you pay for these crew-member benefits, and the crew members are grateful, appreciative and happier – and when they're happier customers will feel that happiness and enjoy being in your store more.[17]

Every employee at Whole Foods is given a wellness check-up and their health insurance costs rise or fall depending on their score. As a result, each employee knows what risks they are taking and ways in which they must improve to pay less. Twenty per cent of employees' premiums are paid by the company. Its overall sickness rate is well below average.

Wegmans is a family owned company that compares very well with the likes of Wal-Mart. Wegmans believes that more intelligent and ambitious employees will better help its customers, and has a policy of attracting high calibre employees. Unlike Wal-Mart, which pays many workers so badly that they also have to receive benefits, Wegmans pays wages twenty-five per cent above the industry average. It also contributes fifty cents in every dollar to health insurance and retirement plans. As well as insuring its employees, it also insures their children, grandchildren and parents. As a result, it gets a large number of applicants for jobs; in fact the company hires just 1.5 per cent of the people who apply, so it gets the pick of the very best. For its part-time baggers, it contributes up to US$6,000 towards their college education, and contributes US$54 million in college scholarships for its 17,500 employees. It gets all these costs back through higher performance. Costco employees also make a vivid contrast with those of Wal-Mart. They earn twice as much and generate three times the revenue!

In contrast to an industry average of twenty per cent, Wegmans' turnover rate for full-time employees is six per cent. Viewed in terms of the cost of turnover, Wegmans' is forty per cent lower. Promotion is always from within. Extensive training pushes its direct labour costs to sixteen per cent, well above the industry average of twelve per cent. However, Wegmans' operating margins are *twice* the industry norm and its sales per square foot fifty per cent higher. Walter Wegman explains his company philosophy thus: 'I have never given away more than I got back.' Sadly, financial analysts rarely see these things, because being conscious is more qualitative than quantitative. Were Wegmans a public company, it would be roasted for 'wasting' money on employees and their education and the takeover kings would start to sniff around their quarry. Just think of the money they could siphon off for shareholders! As for

17. Quoted in Mackey and Sisodia, *Conscious Capitalism*, p. 96.

Wegmans' deliberate policy of hiring single mothers, well, shareholder power would soon put an end to *that*!

Conscious firms also have a strong track record of working with trade unions. Harley-Davidson operates a joint management–union safety programme second to none, and records a profit per vehicle of US$200, very high for that industry. Within a day of 9/11 and the destruction the World Trade Center, Southwest Airlines, America's most successful carrier, had ruled out any furloughs for its staff. 'It would have been more profitable short-term,' explained Herb Kelleher, 'but shortsighted; you want to show your people that you value them.'

There are plenty of other innovative practices and policies that such companies have introduced. Google is famous for allowing its employees to take off twenty per cent of their work time for thinking up their own proposals as we saw in Chapter 1, an approach that has paid off with projects such as Orkut, for social networking, Google News, and AdSense for content. Google also provides onsite doctors, free massages, a games room, showers, subsidized childcare, free gourmet lunches, dry-cleaning and advice on tax matters. Creative consultancy IDEO allows employees to design their own work stations and contributes to the cost; a recent work station included an airplane wing. Timberland sets aside rooms to feed babies and has onsite childcare for both employees and customers. Patagonia mixes employee benefits with green policies and pays US$2,000 towards hybrid vehicles together with free parking. It also offers onsite childcare and the parents using it can lunch with their children in its subsidized cafeteria. It receives 10,000 applications a year for 100 positions.

Firms of endearment train their staff assiduously. The Container Store, continually voted as among 'the best companies to work for', spends more than *thirty times* the industry average on training – 235 hours compared to seven. And this is just in the first year. Employees receive 160 hours a year thereafter. Southwest Airlines has its own University for the People, as does Commerce Bank. Toyota (USA) provides 'continuous improvement' training, while United Parcel Service (UPS) provides 1.3 million hours of training to 74,000 of its drivers. In 1999 UPS also launched its 'earn to learn' programme and over the next two years it helped over twenty thousand part-time workers to attend college. It paid US$9 million in fees, tuition and books and arranged with 242 colleges to defer tuition fees while their employees earned it back. These efforts continue.

Nurturing and informing suppliers

Treating your employees well so that they increase your productivity and innovation is not enough for the simple reason that employees create only part of the wealth creation chain. In the case of a retailer like Whole Foods, around eighty per cent of the value derives from suppliers and how these are treated is crucial to success. But even in the case of original equipment manufacturers, components go a long way to define the product itself, like the disk drive in the computer or the battery in the electric car. Increasingly, manufacturers don't buy components but whole systems, such as the cockpit of a car or the bed-like seats on a plane. How well suppliers perform is crucial to the product and service as a whole. People Express, America's first cut-price airline, failed because of the late delivery of software used to book its seats. Rival companies were dropping their prices if their cabins looked to be under-booked on future flights. For a few fatal weeks PE lacked the software to do the same, and, during a recession, it was the selective low prices that prevailed.[18]

Large companies paying suppliers as little and as late as possible and appropriating their profits was accepted as conventional practice by academics such as Michael Porter.[19] This situation prevailed because smaller suppliers could not afford to lose their business; the big bullied the small. This explains why so many domestic suppliers have collapsed, and the resultant job losses, and why so much business has been outsourced to China.

An example of this folly is provided by General Motors. José Ignacio López de Arriortúa, global purchasing czar, gouged US$4 billion out of GM's suppliers in 1992 to 1993 and was roundly applauded, especially by Wall Street. In the short run GM 'won', but the reckoning was yet to come. Desperate to survive, the suppliers had no choice but to cut quality, reduce service, push the problem down the supply-chain to *their* suppliers, court Japanese car-makers who treated them better and cut back on the R&D they could no longer afford. The better suppliers were in a position to switch customers if they chose and reduce their exposure to GM, which is what they did. For GM, bankruptcy was then merely a matter of time. Unfortunately, the US taxpayer has had to pick up the bill.[20]

Conscious companies behave quite differently. Whole Foods has tens of thousands of suppliers and prides itself on sourcing fresh food locally. Suppliers are partners in every sense of the word. It is the *suppliers* who innovate, not

18. Personal communication with PE's founder, Don Burr.

19. Michael Porter, *Competitive Strategy*, New York: Free Press, 1980.

20. Mackey and Sisodia, *Conscious Capitalism*, p.116

Whole Foods. It is upon *their* diversity that the astonishing range of produce, much of it organic, depends. Whole Foods is 'a mile wide but only inches deep'. Most novelty is bought in from the outside, thus nurturing small, start-up companies is vital to originality and to encouraging better agriculture, land-use and sustainability. The company sponsors experiments of all kinds and provides suppliers with data from its stores to help guide strategy. Creating win–win partnerships and trustful relationships with suppliers is Whole Food's sixth core value.

Ways in which to create win–win partnerships with suppliers are legion. Designating a company as 'sole supplier' and giving it a five-year 'rolling contract' (meaning that every year is the first) gives that company long notice of any termination and the confidence to borrow funds from the bank to improve its operations. If a company can be sure of a certain volume of future orders, it can drop its price. Indeed, as efficiency improves prices may fall by five per cent a year, so customer and supplier both gain. Via gain-sharing agreements it is possible for the customer to pay a proportion of the costs of new machinery providing it gains the benefit of the fall of prices which results. Unless the supplier makes a profit, he cannot serve you well and you'll soon need to turn to another, sacrificing the rapport and trust you established with the existing supplier.

Unfortunately, paying suppliers late is very common, despite the fact that a retailer is usually flush with cash and suppliers are desperately short. Indeed, lack of cash flow has wiped out more small businesses than any other cause, all while the bigger customers sit on their cash-piles. Late payment forces the cash-poor to lend to the cash-rich, which kills some of our most innovative companies. Those paid late cannot pay *their* suppliers in time and the whole chain disintegrates. The British supermarket Tesco is currently under investigation for a deliberate policy of late payment and charges for product placement at eye-level not agreed.

POSCO, the South Korean steel-maker, pays its suppliers in cash within three days. It also has a Win–Win Growth Bureau designed to develop the industrial ecosystem shared with suppliers. It runs sixty-seven programmes that offer technology assistance, low-interest financing, human resource development and joint training programmes. (Many small suppliers cannot afford training without assistance.) It began sharing its employee benefits with tier one suppliers a few years ago and has recently extended this arrangement to include tier four. It has signed agreements with 459 partner-suppliers who have received US$70 million in profit-sharing as a result of joint gains made between customer and supplier. In this way, the whole value chain becomes conscious.[21]

One of the firms of endearment nominated in 2004 was Starbucks, which has recently been accused of not paying corporation tax in the UK and declaring its profits in lower-tax jurisdictions. We must expect that at least some of these firms will slip from grace in some respects. However, the reason Starbucks was included originally was largely due to its treatment of coffee growers, many of whom are poor farmers in the developing world. It used its knowledge about the prices of some of the more specialized and exotic coffee beans to train farmers in how to grow, store, ferment and refine some of the rarer varieties. Under its CAFÉ (Coffee and Farmer Equity) programme, farmers increased their incomes substantially by following quality and sustainability guidelines and upgrading accordingly. Their standards were verified by Scientific Certification Systems – an independent judge.

Starbucks gained expert suppliers in whom it could trust, while its share price increased ten-fold. AMSA (Agroindustrias Unidas de Mexico), a commodity trader, acted as an intermediary, as did Fair Trade, and both the income and skills of coffee growers were substantially improved. The life of those who supply commodities can be hard, as prices fall when harvests are good and they have nothing to sell when harvests are ruined. Starbucks taught farmers how to specialize and preserve flavour and, by ordering in advance, took some of the volatility out of prices.

The concept of partnership spreads beyond suppliers. Even trade unions can be partners. Southwest Airlines, whose success amid the troubles of most airlines is legendary, is among the most unionized airlines in the USA. It works *with* the pilots union, which signed a ten-year contract in 1995 freezing pilots' wages for five years in exchange for stock options. ROPA (Ramp Operations and Provisioning), which includes cabin staff and baggage handlers, is also unionized and quite assertive, but is vital to Southwest's quick turnaround times. Unions are stakeholders too and contribute to the highest on-time performance and safety record in the industry. Planes have to be cleaned overnight and those who do it belong to the Teamsters Union. As Tom Burnette, president of trade union branch Local 19, said of Herb Kelleher, CEO and co-founder: 'How many CEOs do you know who come into the cleaners' break-room at 3.00 a.m. on Sunday morning, passing out donuts or put on a pair of overalls to help clean a plane? If employees feel they are respected and dignified, cared for and loved, then they will take good care of outside customers.'[22] It is to customers that we now turn.

22. Mackey and Sisodia, *Conscious Capitalism*, p. 159.

Serving and delighting customers who share your higher purposes

When employees have done their best and made good use of what suppliers have contributed, the product is then offered to customers. It is great to be served by people who demonstrably like each other and the pleasant atmosphere rubs off on customers. In the words of Peter Drucker, hailed by *Business Week* as the man who invented management, 'There is only one valid definition of a business purpose: to create a customer.' Doug Rauch, ex-President of Trader Joe's, views employees and customers as two wings of a bird. You need both to fly.

While many customers just want the product and never mind who is selling it, an increasing number like to shop with companies whose values, commitments and wares are a seamless whole, where the product and services attached to it *mean something*. This is very much Whole Food's stance. It seeks to satisfy not just customers' wants but also their *needs*: good nutrition and a long and healthy life. Customers should be led and educated if a company truly cares about them. If you know that certain foods are better than others, you should say so, as any good friend would do for another. Too many people are addicted to foods that are bad for them. Of course, customers will make the final choice but you must tell them what the consequences will be and then leave them free to choose.

When Whole Foods began to recommend organic food only five per cent of customers responded; this has now grown to thirty per cent and is climbing. A few products are even banned from Whole Foods: tobacco products, foods with artificial ingredients, hydrogenated oils, meat and eggs produced using low standards of animal welfare and fish caught beyond the level of sustainability. What is being communicated to the customer is not just the product and not just the excellence of the service but the higher purpose behind the company's very existence. Whole Food's mission is to improve its customers' diet so that they remain healthy and enjoy a longer and better life as a result of what they eat.

The company *does* sell some products to which it objects because these are in high demand, but rarely without providing a warning about them and attempting to initiate conversations on cutting down. It has created a Wellness Club for customers, via which its views are circulated. It is the breadth of thinking involved in being conscious that gives such companies an advantage. The challenge of simultaneously providing what consumers want *and* what they need makes for a broader canvas, with more possibilities.

Perhaps the most surprising aspect of conscious companies and firms of endearment is how relatively little they spend on marketing and advertising. This is because a higher purpose is significant in itself and needs no bells and whistles. Customers either understand you or they don't and gimmicks aren't necessary. You are not trying to infiltrate the minds of customers, you are seeking to engage their hearts and heads on the subject of their own betterment and, if you do that sincerely, they'll listen.

What conscious companies sell is not just things but a wider context of trust and caring for the customer and these need no trumpeting just quiet communication. One trillion dollars a year is spent on advertising in the USA, or US$3,200 for every man, woman and child, much of it for sugary and fatty products. Real marketing must have a higher purpose. It must try to solve not just personal problems but social problems too. It is searching for answers. What people need is rarely simple. You are not just selling them an object but showing them how best to use it or cook it so that it's right for them. Value lies not in what the seller provides but in what the customer uses and unless you care they may not use it to their best advantage.

The customer you have served well becomes your advocate, and the best and most credible advertising of all is word of mouth from grateful customers, which is only credible if those who testify haven't been paid to do so.[23] A sentence spoken by someone who cares about you is worth a hundred intrusive commercials competing for your attention. The woman who realized her credit card had been stolen and that the thief had been on a huge shopping spree, will always remember the customer services manager at Commerce Bank who offered her a tissue and said the bank would cover the theft. The man who lost his contact lenses on a plane will never forget the calmness and kindness with which the stewardess located what his bleary eyes could not. Conscious capitalism knows we are here for one another, but the usual tendency is to only look for what can be counted and in doing so we miss the immeasurable. As Albert Einstein was reputed to have said: 'not everything that can be counted counts, and not everything that counts can be counted'. The numbers game of the financial analyst is just a skeleton without flesh and blood.

The truth is that for every *legal* contract between a seller and a buyer there is also an *emotional* contract, an often unspoken promise to serve and help the buyer. It is this larger contract that conscious companies seek to fulfil. Toro makes large mechanical lawnmowers, but one day it discovered a problem with its products. When the engine breaks down there is the possibility that

---

23. Mackey and Sisodia, *Conscious Capitalism*, pp. 80–81.

parts may go flying. Fearing huge litigation expenses if users were injured, the company embarked on a policy of providing immediate help, apologizing to anyone injured and suggesting non-legal arbitration that would save both plaintiff and defendant a lot of money. Since it embarked on this policy, Toro has not been in court for a single personal injury case. The emotional contract with its customers was the most important thing to the company.

A supplier of pizza ovens to restaurants hit upon the idea of offering to replace the oven at any time during the first two years, with no questions asked. Lawyers condemned this idea. They warned that restaurants would simply turn in a two-year-old oven, however well it worked, and demand a new one. The lawyers turned out to be partly correct, and certain restaurants did indeed wait until the two years were almost up and then demand a replacement. However, less than one per cent of customers behaved in this way, while the offer inspired trust and confidence in the remaining ninety-nine per cent. Once again, the emotional contract was stronger than the legal one.

Similarly, Costco operates a policy of refunding dissatisfied customers under all circumstances. They don't even have to produce receipts so the store cannot be sure the product was even bought there. Does it get cheated? Undoubtedly at times, but the company still feels strongly that it gains overall. People who are not trusted will never be trustworthy, and will plot and scheme instead. Someone must be the first to start trusting. Pursuing a higher purpose and explaining this leads customers to let you know when you are not living up to your ideals. Trust is a necessary risk in conducting business.

Many conscious companies deliberately hire people who are hobbyists for what they sell and can give customers the benefit of their experience. Patagonia, L.L. Bean, Whole Foods and Wegmans employ staff who are enthusiasts in climbing equipment, outdoor life, cooking and nutrition, etc. What is being sold is the experience to be enjoyed and knowledgeable staff can help the customer access it. Moreover, since the customer gets the product anyway, why not *also* enjoy the humane conditions under which it has been produced, the sustainability of the supply, the generous treatment of the supplier, its local sourcing among people you know and the knowledge that it is good for you? All of these reinforce the customer's belief that they've made the right purchase decision. We all need to eat, exercise and survive but if we can serve *additional* causes by doing so, then surely that is even better? Conscious companies give customers fresh reasons for buying their products that support their higher purpose and that reinforce the idea of citizenship, to which we now turn.

Sustaining community and society

Opposition to businesses exercising corporate social responsibility (CSR) is based on the fact that the money does not belong to businesses but to shareholders. If managers wish to be generous and help other people they should use their own money. Mackey and Sisodia regard this attitude less as wrong than as myopic. There are hundreds of ways of helping the local community that *also* help shareholders; to miss out on this is to remain blinkered and only partly conscious. If you serve their community, your employees will be proud and enthused, your customers will be grateful and your business will prosper. Much of what you can do would cost you very little and earn you a good deal, so to not even try is senseless.

CSR is not the point in any case. Many of these programmes function as appendices to the main purpose of the organizations, which is to make money. CSR becomes an afterthought, a nice gesture on the side. The point of conscious capitalism is that service to the community is inseparable from the purpose of the company as a whole. It should be part of the corporate strategy not a voluntary donation, public relations expense or conscience money. Conscious capitalism is a harmony of integrated virtues, a form of citizenship, a shared strategy, a demonstration of trust. CSR is too often just a trade-off.

Whole Foods designates several 'five per cent days' a year. On those days, five per cent of the profit for that day is donated to a local charity or non-profit selected by employees. The recipient is asked to drum up shoppers from among its supporters, to increase the store's revenue on that day and thus increase their cut. Having been introduced to the store, the supporters may continue to shop there. All concerned contribute more and gain more. The company also has two global foundations: the Whole Planet Foundation and the Whole Kids Foundation. The Whole Planet Foundation supports micro-lending under the auspices of the Grameen Trust. This foundation has improved the lives of some 1.2 million people by providing US$130 million worth of loans in fifty-plus countries. Because the loans are mostly repaid the money can be 'recycled' by being loaned to a new recipient, meaning that the money goes much further in helping others. Whole Foods trades in ninety-one countries, and it aims to lend in every country in the world. Customers are told about the foundation in a six-week campaign and are invited to contribute. The company raised $5.6 million in 2012.

Employees (team members) are also invited to volunteer to work for the Whole Planet Foundation, assisting with micro-lending in India, Kenya, Peru, Ghana, Guatemala and Brazil. Their expenses are covered and Whole Foods has created its own little peace corps. These trips are often a transformative experience and they have helped convince employees and the company that among their higher purposes is helping end poverty. They have moved the company forward in this respect. The Suppliers' Alliance also contributes to this cause. While it is near impossible to calculate accurately, Mackey reckons the return on the investors' money from such activities is one thousand per cent or more. Whole Foods is by no means alone in this type of venture. IBM has created a Corporate Service Corps that uses volunteers to teach technical and business skills to people in emerging economies. This is part of IBM's Global Citizen's Portfolio, which is designed not just to help the poor but also develop IBM's future leaders. Volunteers have proved to be the high-flying executives of the future.

The Whole Kids Foundation aims to encourage children to eat more healthily. It has created a thousand salad and fruit bars in schools and planted hundreds of gardens in school grounds, on the basis that pupils will eat what they have grown. Whole Foods has also joined 'Let's Move', Michelle Obama's campaign to deal with childhood obesity. Does the company gain from doing so? Of course it does, but then altruism and egoism are not exclusive motives. We can reconcile our interests with those of others and eschew claims of nobility.

Another major way in which firms of endearment differ from the usual run of public companies is in their attitude to paying corporation tax. Time was when corporations, spurred by a sense of patriotism, paid their taxes in full. In 1943 US corporations paid 39.8 per cent of their profits in corporation tax. In 2002 the General Accounting Office revealed that sixty-one per cent of US corporations paid *no corporation tax at all* between 1996 and 2000, most of them boom years. The official rate is thirty-five per cent, but avoiding it is the work of thousands of lawyers who receive far better fees than the enforcers. Ninety-four per cent of large American corporations paid five per cent or less in taxes – victory!

Many companies have turned tax into a profit centre and many spend more on tax lawyers than on taxes in a battle with their own government. Money is moved around the world into low-tax jurisdictions. Pharmaceutical company Eli Lilly paid one per cent in 2004, although most of its revenue is made in the USA. It helps spend the US$30 billion a year contributed by the National Institutes of Health from taxpayers but gives almost nothing back. There could hardly be a clearer example of the adversarial relations that blight US society – a thirty-five per cent tax rate that almost no corporations pay, having forced the government into a position of stalemate!

The twenty-eight firms of endearment are very, very different. Just one of them, Johnson & Johnson, paid half of all taxes received from the pharmaceutical industry in 2004. Between 1996 and 2004 none of the firms of endearment exempted themselves from paying tax. Their average payment was thirty-three per cent. Whole Foods paid forty per cent, UPS thirty-two per cent, Timberland thirty-five per cent, Google thirty-nine per cent, Southwest Airlines thirty-six per cent, Toyota (USA) thirty-nine per cent, Harley-Davidson thirty-six per cent, Costco thirty-seven per cent and Starbucks thirty-seven per cent. They made no effort to avoid tax. Google pointed out that the Internet had been paid for by the government. How do you explain the fact that these companies were hugely more profitable than those avoiding paying tax?

More recently some of these companies have failed to live up to their past tax records, especially outside the USA. Starbucks, Google and Amazon have all been rebuked for not paying the British government its fair share of their profits. Starbucks offered to donate the difference. Has their success spoiled them and rendered them less endearing? Is there a tendency to become complacent? Are foreign governments considered fair game? It is clear that national communities need to keep them up to the mark.

Repaying and enriching investors

We come to investors last as they are last in the temporal sequence of wealth creation but this is in no way to disparage their importance. Yet there *are* serious costs incurred by shareholders asking to be prioritized and demanding that their profits rise quarter by quarter. Nearly everything that pays off in the long-term involves costs in the short-term. This is what investment means. Long-term investment is a tautology. If you are *not* there for the long-term, you are trading or speculating, not investing, and you are useless to most other people.

The reverse proposition is also true. Most things that pay off in the short-term incur long-term costs. Individuals are living longer and longer but corporate life-spans are becoming ever shorter, especially in the USA. We work our companies to death and then discard the people inside them. Companies are the mere instruments of our enrichment. This helps to explain the extraordinary mortality rate among companies that are supposed to be 'excellent' and to grow from 'Good to Great'.[24] These companies were picked based on their profitability, but where that profitability was gained at the expense of other stakeholders the decline had already begun and quite soon became manifest.[25]

For example, the retail chain Kroger was designated 'great' in 1996, but it had halved its stock price six years later. Its 'value capture' had proved precisely

24. Jim Collins, *Good to Great*, Random House Business, 2001.
25. Rajendra S. Sisodia, David B. Wolfe and Jagdish N. Sheth, *Firms of Endearment*, Wharton School Publishers, 2007, p. 141.

that, value seized from other stakeholders. Such companies harvest too much and sow too little. By picking them just after their profitability has peaked, their longer-term decline is assured. As Jack Welch argued, *profitability is a result but not a strategy.* Or as Peter Drucker stated, 'Profit is not the explanation, cause or rationale of business decisions but rather the test of their validity.' Profit tells you *after the fact* how well you have managed those stakeholders who create your wealth.

It is really quite easy to manage a short-term rise in share price and, if you have large stock options, it is very tempting to do so. It resembles taking steroids to help you run faster now, although they will ultimately wreck your body. Hewlett-Packard reduced its expenditure on R&D from ten per cent of total product costs to six per cent and then to three per cent. Doing so freed up a lot of money for equity holders but subsequently the company suffered a steep decline and is no longer considered innovative.

A study by the National Bureau of Economic Research in the USA found that most managers would not make an investment that would result in a good return if it meant missing a quarterly earnings target. Eighty per cent of executives said they would cut R&D and marketing expenses for the same reason, even if they believed doing so would hurt the company. These targets are set by boards, and bonuses and stock options are often attached. By hitting the target, you make money for your boss. Think of the longer term and you may not have a job through which to do so![26]

So how do the conscious capitalists and the firms of endearment fare, compared with the majority of public companies? The original twenty-eight firms of endearment out-performed the market eight times over. Six years later, with a slightly longer and amended list of conscious companies, the difference was a factor of 10.5 as shown in Table 7.1.

Table 7.1 Investment performance of firms of endearment (FoE) led by conscious capitalists vs. Standard & Poor's 500 (1996–2011)[27]

Return	15 years		10 years		5 years	
	Cumulative	Annualized	Cumulative	Annualized	Cumulative	Annualized
FoE (%)	1646.1	21.0	254.4	13.5	56.4	9.4
S&P 500 (%)	157.0	6.5	30.7	2.7	15.6	2.9

Note: Returns are total returns, with dividends re-invested and compounded.

26. Mackey and Sisodia, *Conscious Capitalism*, pp. 281–282.
27. Mackey and Sisodia, *Conscious Capitalism*, p. 278.

The first thing to notice is that conscious companies do even better in the long term; they are only three times better over five years, but over fifteen years this jumps to 10.5 times better. Even if we take excellent relationships with just *one* stakeholder, employees, and we pick the companies selected each year for America's Great Place to Work list, then their returns to shareholders are 10.32 per cent between 1997 and 2011, nearly three times higher than those of the S&P 500 companies, which are just 3.71 per cent.

Companies selected as 'ethical' by Ethisphere, an American NGO, outperform the S&P 500 by an average of 7.3 per cent annually. A study by John Kotter and James Heskett at Harvard Business School selected 207 large US companies in twenty-two industries and looked at their performance over eleven years. They were focusing on 'strong and flexible business cultures that included all stakeholders and empowered all managers'.[28] Compared to a control group, these companies experienced higher revenue growth of 682 per cent compared to 166 per cent, a stock price increase of 901 per cent compared to seventy-four per cent and a net income increase of 756 per cent compared to one per cent.

Finally, the comparison between companies chosen for their caring attitude and Good to Great companies chosen for their profitability is stark, as shown in Table 7.2.

Table 7.2 Investment performance of firms of endearment compared to Good to Great companies (1996–2011)[29]

Return	15 years		10 years		5 years	
	Cumulative	Annualized	Cumulative	Annualized	Cumulative	Annualized
FoE (%)	1646.1	21.0	254.4	13.5	56.4	9.4
GtGs (%)	157.0	7.0	14.0	1.3	-35.6	-8.4

Note how very badly Good to Great companies performed a few years after they were nominated on the basis of their profitability. They actually *lost* an average of 8.4 per cent a year. We see where the relentless pursuit of profit leads. Indeed, were we to include the cost to the economy of Philip Morris (now Altria), the figures would be far worse. Smokers have a reduced life expectancy of fifteen years, stretch medical resources to their limits and

28. John Kotter and James Heskett, *Corporate Culture and Performance*, New York: Free Press, 1992.

29. Mackey and Sisodia, *Conscious Capitalism*, p. 283.

one *billion* people are expected to die from tobacco use this century. Philip Morris destroys wealth on an epic scale, even if it was briefly 'excellent' for stockholders.

It is stakeholders, not shareholders alone, who create wealth out of what shareholders have contributed and increase that wealth over time. Profits are recorded *after* stakeholders have excelled and are verdicts on, and verifications of, their success. Profitability is *not* a good motive or a sound aim since it is *reduced* in the short term by sponsoring the efforts of stakeholders. Profit targets or the attempt to wrest money *away* from other stakeholders are counter-productive and catastrophic in their consequences. You can no more pursue profit as a singular objective than you can pursue happiness. Both result from sustaining other people, employees, suppliers, customers and your community, who then reciprocate. This indirect path to profitability is illustrated in Figure 7.2.

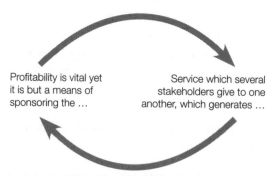

Profitability is vital yet it is but a means of sponsoring the ...

Service which several stakeholders give to one another, which generates ...

Figure 7.2 The indirect path to profitability

Whole Foods made the interesting distinction between what customers *want* and even crave and what the conscious capitalist supplier knows that they *need*, including a healthier and longer life for consumers, the sustainability and welfare of the animals they eat, the welfare of those who supply the retailer, the support of their local community, better nutrition for society as a whole and continued reduction in world poverty. There is no reason why such aims should not be served by the way in which we shop and buy. We must eat to live but, once alive, can achieve much more by *how* we purchase what we want and what we need. The act of purchasing can be turned into a conscious decision to help build a better world and improve the condition of humans, animals and the environment.

The wants of customers are met but this is not all, we can also care for the ...

Needs of customers, suppliers, animals, society and locality while supplying ...

Figure 7.3 Buying for a better world

Finally, we have provided further proof that what shareholders receive must first be generated by what stakeholders produce and create. Diverting funds from stakeholders to shareholders will inevitably lead to stakeholders being less successful and to shareholders receiving less. What we need instead is illustrated in Figure 7.4.

Stakeholders receive all available funds so they can generate more for ...

Shareholders, who cannot get a really good return unless and until ...

Figure 7.4 'Shareholders come last'

This is what Johnson and Johnson mean by 'shareholders come last'. They are last in the *temporal sequence* of wealth creation and only weaken themselves by pushing to the front of the line and appropriating the shares of others.

CHAPTER 8

Harmonizing the cycles of nature

We now stand where two roads diverge. But unlike the roads in Robert Frost's familiar poem, they are not equally fair. The road we have long been traveling is deceptively easy ... but at its end lies disaster. The other fork of the road, the 'one less traveled by', offers our last, our only chance to reach a destination that assures the preservation of our earth.[1]

Throughout this book we have stressed the need to think in cycles; nature consists of many of these. Indeed our straight-line rationality of cause-and-effect, means-and-ends has clashed with nature and has brought about our present environmental crisis. Our traditional attitude to nature is that it besieges us. We are pitted against threats to our survival and must overcome them. While the Bible instructs us to 'multiply and subdue the earth', it is not clear what a 'subdued' earth would look like, nor whether it would be fit for habitation. We are on the verge of a fifth 'great extinction', this time man-made.

A brilliant evocation of our error is dramatized in the novel *Moby Dick* by Hermann Melville. The Great White Whale symbolizes God's creation. Captain Ahab, who lost a leg in a previous encounter with Moby Dick, is bent on revenge. He abandons the commercial logic of whale hunting and the search for the lost son of a fellow whaling captain and scours the seas for his mortal enemy, armed with long-boats and straight-lines, barbed harpoons

----

1.   Rachel Carson, *Silent Spring*, Boston: Houghton Mifflin, 1962.

to be plunged into the body of the creature. Moby Dick is totally quiescent and indifferent to Ahab *until attacked* by the linear technology of harpoons, at which point he goes berserk. Ahab's remaining leg becomes entangled in the coiled rope that joins the boat to the harpoon embedded in the whale's body. He finds himself *strapped to the body* of the whale and dragged down into the ocean to his death. Moby Dick then attacks the whaling ship and all its boats and only one crew-member survives. We are, it seems, *joined with nature* and we assail it with our logic at our own peril.

Yet the view that we are in a struggle *against* nature retains some validity and we cannot dismiss it out of hand. The earth holds many hazards for us: earthquakes, tsunamis, volcanoes, forest fires, meteor strikes, even ice ages. We must rule or *be* ruled. Microscopic creatures invade our bodies, and evolve into new strains immune to our medicines, while cancer cells seem determined to proliferate and kill us.

On the other hand, nature is in many respects our friend, not to mention our origin. That the earth supports life at all is amazing; all around us in the universe are celestial bodies, cold, silent, colourless, objective and dead. But in the last 100 years we have been using up resources that took millions of years to generate. At this rate of depletion we will leave our children's children with a plundered planet, replete with poisonous waste that will be lethal for tens of thousands of years.

A powerful case exists for cleaning up our environment, whether or not some of the specific threats, like rising sea levels, actually occur. To do nothing would be plain stupid given the huge advantages inherent in taking creative action to preserve the world's natural resources and lower pollution levels. But markets cannot look that far ahead. They will only register strong demand when solutions are close at hand. Indeed, markets can make things worse by raising the prices of threatened species as extinction approaches so that the 'rational' approach seems to be to grab all we can and profit from the collapse of whole species. (Ivory poachers are very rational!)

While our industrial system lifts the siege in *some* respects, it worsens our situation in others by spewing poisonous waste into rivers, oceans and the atmosphere. The negative effects on people's health resulting from such waste are increasingly evident. This chapter will *not* enter the debate on global warming. Indeed, debate is part of the problem. The subject of ecology is so complex that sceptics will never be satisfied. We may talk our way to oblivion. We face a choice between cleaning up after the mess we make or creating sustainable systems which avoid making such a mess in the first place. Clearly, the second option is the more viable; and for those who care only about money – it is also the cheaper option.

This chapter will contend that we should not be focusing on the survival of the fittest but the *survival of the finest fit* into our living environments. Nature consists of many natural cycles and we would benefit from imitating nature, in particular recycling what we produce. Industries are potentially symbiotic and can co-evolve with other natural processes, and should do so given the environmental challenges we face. All this constitutes a challenge to our ingenuity and can trigger feats of innovation in everything we do. We must improve resource efficiency, not just machine efficiency, by using evolution, the outcome of nature's successful experiments over the course of millions of years, as our model.

Survival of the finest fit

Early attempts to understand the concept of evolution stressed the 'survival of the fittest', the idea that in the struggle for life, the strongest would prevail, rather than concepts of differential reproduction, in which the most successful genetic traits were passed on. There's no denying that plants and animals compete for light, air, moisture and territory, as any gardener extracting weeds will tell you, and some plants and animals are clearly parasitic. However, this is by no means the end of the story. Recently we have discovered many ways in which species co-evolve and so 'parasitic' may be the wrong description for systems that appear rather to be cooperating. The human body makes extensive use of 'friendly bacteria'. A particular type of ant lives in the hollow core of bamboo and rushes out to bite the lips of foraging creatures, thus protecting the bamboo. The goby fish picks parasites from the teeth and gills of larger fish and avoids being viewed as prey by them in return.

A business also operates in two ways. It competes with other businesses, but what it competes *at* is fitting ever more finely into the needs of customers and other stakeholders. The ultimate test of survival is being the 'most fitting', not just in relation to customers but to physical and social environments. How does business achieve this fine fit? In this chapter we will answer this question by focusing on an outstanding, fast-growing, profitable business that serves all its stakeholders *and* has a beneficial effect on the environment. It should go without saying that we hold the environment in trust for those coming after us.

At the age of sixty, Ray Anderson was winding up a modestly successful career as the CEO of Interface Carpets. Asked to make a speech about the environment, he picked up a book, *The Ecology of Commerce* by Paul Hawken,[2]

---

2.   New York: Harper Business, 1993.

and was so affected by its message that he changed his life completely. He suddenly saw himself as a plunderer of the earth, helping to burn up a cubic mile of oil every year, a resource that had taken millions of years to evolve. He was despoiling a treasure chest at a rate that could never be sustained. He thought, 'My God, someday ... they'll send people like me to jail.'[3]

Anderson was reassured by Hawken's book in one respect. His company sold carpet *tiles*. Carpets rarely wear out evenly; they become scuffed near doorways and under chairs, for example. Using tiles extends a carpet's lifetime three to four times over as areas of wear can simply be replaced. Yet, as he read through the book, Anderson realized that he hadn't done enough. He vowed to produce zero emissions by 2020, even if doing so meant he didn't retire until he was eighty. Anderson didn't live to see that day, he died of cancer in 2010, but his company is still well on its way to reaching that target, and a great deal was achieved within his lifetime. By 2009, when his book *Business Lessons from a Radical Industrialist* was published, he'd reduced landfill waste by eighty per cent, total energy use by forty-three per cent and fossil fuel energy use by sixty per cent, with thirty per cent of the company's energy provided by sustainable sources. Thirty-six per cent of raw materials were either recycled or could be used to nourish the earth; eighty-nine per cent of electricity used was renewable; 200 million tons of worn carpet had been reclaimed from users; and 106,000 trees had been planted to offset airline flights.

Does it pay to serve a higher purpose such as this, as claimed in Chapter 7? You might expect that all this would cost a fortune and cut into revenue and profit, but between 1994 and 2009, reducing waste resulted in cost savings of US$443 million. During this same period, sales doubled and profit margins increased. Anderson's environment-saving Cool Carpets were a big hit, and *Time* magazine hailed Anderson a 'Hero of the Environment'. He was appointed co-chair of the President's Council on Sustainable Development and led Barack Obama's Presidential Climate Action Project. He featured in three documentary films and was written about in the *New York Times*, *Fortune* and *Fast Company*. Environmentalism had become economically viable after all.[4]

One step Anderson took to make the product fit the needs of the customer better was to turn his product into a process. Instead of selling and delivering 'a carpet', he provided high quality *carpeting* through leasehold agreements with his clients for a period of years. He maintained the carpet in perfect condition by

3.   Ray Anderson, *Business Lessons from a Radical Industrialist*, New York: St. Martin's Griffin, 2009, p. 10.

4.   Anderson, *Business Lessons*.

replacing the tiles as they wore out, and by retaining ownership of the carpets he could then recycle those tiles. If the customer owns the carpet, they are likely to take it to the dump when it wears out; if Interface reclaims it, the company can strip the acrylic backing from the nylon tufts using a separator machine and thus recapture two valuable components. These components can then be used to manufacture new carpets, saving a great deal of money in the process. Not only is recycling in this way ecologically efficient, it also reduces costs and increases profits. And the more worn tiles that are reclaimed, the more can be recycled.

Employing natural cycles

To say that nature is cyclical is a bit of an understatement. Consider biochemical cycles, of which photosynthesis is an example. Take rock cycles, marine cycles and temperature warming and cooling cycles. Even if we ignore the National Academy of Sciences and the Board on Atmospheric Sciences and Climate, and deny global warming, the cyclical nature of most natural processes is not disputed.

Nothing is wasted in these natural cycles, and when industry recycles it imitates nature. Recycling takes place in two principal ways: down-cycling and up-cycling.[5] To down-cycle is to produce something less valuable than the original resource; for example, high quality steel goes into cars but the scrap-steel left over when vehicles are crushed is full of bits of plastic, cloth and rubber from their interiors and is worth less. While this doesn't mean the recycling process is without value, it does mean the resultant product is worth less than the original materials. Value has been lost. Up-cycling is more ambitious. Here, the original object is made *more* valuable to the company and the environment, not less. A prime example of up-cycling is the way that modern science has learned how to convert human waste into valuable phosphate fertilizer. Given the vast amount of human waste that is produced, and its public health implications, such a conversion would be immensely valuable on a global scale.

McDonough and Braungart also cite roof gardens as an example of up-cycling. They cool the building in summer and warm it in winter; absorb rain and heat from the sun; replenish the atmosphere; *and* make the roof last longer. A roof garden on a civic building will provide valuable recreational space, solar energy, vegetables for consumption and flowers for enjoyment. A roof garden on

5. William McDonough and Michael Braungart, *Cradle to Cradle*, New York: North Point Press, 2002.

someone's home will also usually raise the value of the property. In time, our cities will have farms, trees and roof gardens to counter the effects of global warming.

For Ray Anderson, the tree is an important metaphor. A man approached him after a lecture and said: 'Isn't it strange how we call our factories "plants"? They don't look like plants and they don't work like plants. A plant runs off solar power, rain and soil... What if our plants worked more like that? Isn't that what you are really talking about?'[6] Anderson also quotes Jim Hartzfeld, a researcher from his West Coast facility, who explained to his boss:

> A plant's waste (e.g., dropped leaves) is 100 per cent biodegradable. In fact some other plant probably uses its waste as food and turns it right back into soil, and more plants. Nature functions cyclically and with essentially zero waste. One organism's waste is another's food. I used to say that nature was the model. I realize now that nature is the real thing, and our poorly designed industrial system is a deeply flawed artifice.[7]

Making industrial 'plants' imitate real plants is vital to Anderson's vision. He ran several of his factories on the methane gas produced by landfill sites that would otherwise have been piped into the atmosphere. Because the landfill within the site shrinks when the methane gas is removed, it increases the waste capacity of the site. So both ventures gain: one from cheap energy and one from added capacity.

Anderson refers in his book to the Recyclebank, set up by entrepreneur Ron Gonen. Gonen calculated that each family in Pennsylvania threw away 1.2 tons of recyclable material every year. He created high-tech bins with an integral microchip that records the weight of aluminum, tin, plastic, glass and so on. He pays each household that uses these bins in Recycle dollars, redeemable in more than 1,200 businesses in Pennsylvania that are seeking new and more responsible customers. As a result, recycling has risen statewide from twenty to eighty per cent and even higher.

Everybody wins in this situation – the household members, the companies redeeming scrap, the environment, Recyclebank and its investors and employees, local government and the environment as fewer virgin materials are unearthed, fewer landfill sites are required and so on. By imitating nature expensive problems have been turned into income streams. By 2009 Recyclebank had served 300,000 customers. By 2014 this had doubled. Gonen describes his business ethos thus:

6. Anderson, *Business Lessons*, p. 87
7. Anderson, *Business Lessons*, p. 110.

In nature there's no such thing as waste. Everything is used. We are just following Nature's lead when new products are made of glass, metal, paper that's been captured from old ones... In an era of expensive oil, gas and electricity, our approach to recycling saves cities and companies money, and drastically cuts greenhouse emissions... We are making healthy profit and growing, doing the right thing for the planet.[8]

In terms of recycling, *closed-loop recycling* is the ultimate aim. This means that a product uses 100 per cent recycled materials and no new materials are injected into the loop. No new resources have been dug up and nature's bounty has not been depleted. A favorite maxim of industrialists concerned for the environment is 'Reduce, repurpose, reuse, recycle and redesign'. Gonen achieved this and so did Anderson with his Cool Carpet manufacturing process. Care must be taken to recycle organic and synthetic or technical ingredients separately since these adulterate one another. The organic components can return to the earth, feed animals and create fertilizer, for example. The technical components can be used for entirely different products, and can be recycled several times over. Since the natural cycle is our inspiration it is appropriate that we create a cycle for the sequence of this chapter.

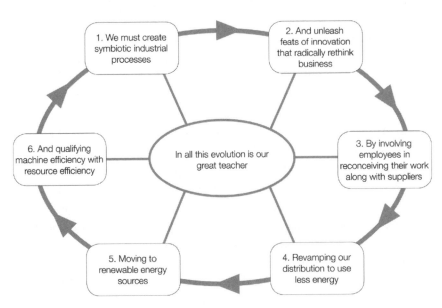

Figure 8.1 The sustainability cycle

8.   Anderson, *Business Lessons*, p. 127.

We must create symbiotic industrial processes

The capacity of nature's creatures to help one another never ceases to amaze. But for the birds picking crustaceans off their shells, turtles would capsize beneath their weight and perish. Termites make mounds from their own excreta of such elegant design that architects have been inspired by them, but they are only possible due to the micro-organisms in the guts of the termites which ensure the excreta coheres. A relationship of mutual advantage between two organisms is called *symbiosis*.

The relationship between the clown fish and the sea anemone is another classic case of symbiosis. The fish feeds on the small invertebrates that would otherwise hurt or even devour the anemone, and the fish's faecal matter nourishes the anemone; the clown fish, meanwhile, is protected from predators by the stinging cells in the leaves of the anemone, to which the fish itself is immune.

Of course, contests still exist within nature, but these may strengthen a breed without hurting its members. Hence stags battle for a mate so that the winner passes on his genes and the entire herd benefits. The losing stag withdraws from the contest, but usually without serious injury because his ability to fight again is essential – he may get the better of another stag. Nature is organized so as to renew itself from an aggregation of the best genetic material available.

Industrial symbiosis occurs when several products are produced at the same time, often inadvertently. British Sugar, based in the Fens near Cambridge, is the second-most profitable and cost-efficient sugar producer in the world; only its own subsidiary plant in China betters its performance. British labour costs aren't the cheapest and general productivity lags behind much of Europe, so how does this company gain its advantage? It is an exemplar of industrial symbiosis, selling products that naturally emerge from the production process. It grows sugar from sugar-beet harvested from the heavy soils of the fens. The sugar beet is uprooted by large machines that pull up a lot of soil and stones along with the roots that are the source of the sugar. During the manufacturing process, the soil, stones, lime in the soil and leaves must be separated from the beet itself, as the sugar needs to be free of such contaminants.

British Sugar removes, cleans, debugs and then sells the topsoil to garden centres, together with the stones; it filters out and sells the lime; and it collects the leaves and sells them as animal feed. The manufacturing process also produces betaine, a substance used in fishing bait and indigestion remedies. The same process also creates bio-ethanol, a green substitute for petrol, also readily saleable; and it generates considerable amounts of carbon dioxide, which by itself isn't valuable but can be piped to greenhouses to help grow tomatoes. This process has produced Britain's second-biggest source of fresh tomatoes. Finally, electricity is generated during the manufacturing process that is often surplus to requirements, and this too is sold on to the national grid.[9]

Usually these products would be regarded as, at worst, waste and, at best, by-products in which a sugar manufacturer has little or no interest. But since these products are an inseparable part of the manufacturing process, why not supply them all? They have the same market price whether produced deliberately or accidentally, so why not take full advantage of this symbiosis? Not to sell them would be pure waste, while selling them creates seven additional sources of revenue over which to spread fixed costs and overheads.

Unleash feats of innovation that radically rethink business

One reason that the environmental challenge is so important to the future of an economy is that it entails renewing and recreating the entire infrastructure. Products must be reconceived and redesigned from the ground up. The processes by which they are made must be improved. Industrial symbiosis must be built in. Second or third 'lives' must be created for products so that the substances from which they are made are not wasted. All employees must be enlisted in joint efforts for improvement. Products must be designed in such a way that they can be taken apart easily so that technical and organic components can be separated for recycling. Products may be leased rather than sold. Customers must be persuaded to support the environmental goals of the supplier.

Waste must initially be reduced and ultimately eliminated. Toxins must be removed from the supply chain. Less wasteful forms of distribution must be devised and we desperately need to move as soon as we can to using renewable sources of energy. We need to rethink the whole notion of what constitutes wealth, otherwise we may wake up to the realization that, for the last half century, we have been *destroying* wealth not creating it, once environmental costs are factored in. For example, a recent study estimated that it takes fifty litres of water to create one litre of Coke.[10] It is a cheap and profitable soft

---

9.   From a presentation by Professor Steve Evans, 'Industrial Symbiosis', Institute for Manufacturing, Cambridge University, March 2014.

10. Peter Senge, *The Necessary Revolution*, London: Nicholas Brealey, 2011 pp. 204–205.

drink, but if the world ran out of fresh water and animals and humans died in their thousands what would Coke have cost us? Many costs only register with hindsight. We are still in thrall to GNP estimates that add the mess we have just made to the cost of trying to clean it up and then pronounce ourselves better off! According to this calculation the Exxon Valdez oil spill actually did us a favour.

Innovation to save the environment is *radical* in the sense that it means going to the very roots of business itself and rethinking and redesigning business models. It must occur everywhere in concert, since it is little use improving the quality of your manufacturing processes if your suppliers are sending you raw materials and components full of poisonous substances and much of your total energy is taken up by trucking and airfreight. You need to be a conscious capitalist – as discussed in Chapter 7 – and take responsibility for the whole network of stakeholders.

Involving employees in reconceiving their work along with suppliers

Your employees are the people who will succeed or fail to deliver greener products created by greener processes. No one knows more about waste, duplication, unnecessary operations and correctable faults in the system than the people actually *doing* the work. Without these people and their enthusiastic backing, nothing else will work. Toyota famously implements multiple suggestions per annum made by each of its factory workers. In a Malaysian factory we visited, each suggestion was printed on a piece of paper next to a photo of the originator and pasted on the walls and ceilings of the building. They extended as far as the eye could see![11]

Anderson implemented QUEST – Quality Utilizing Employee Suggestions and Teamwork – teams at Interface. Their focus was on eliminating waste, saving energy, increasing quality and challenging the take–make–waste culture of an industry that delivers a *billion* tons of used carpet to landfill each year! Anderson described waste as 'profits left on the factory floor' and 'putting good money in a dumpster'. He took his campaign to Wall Street but discovered in the mid-1990s that it hated 'greentalk'. It took three years and a share price that climbed from US$6.75 to US$15 to gain its attention. *Now* he was speaking their language![12]

11. Visit by author to Motorola plant in Penang, July 2007.
12. Anderson, *Business Lessons*, p. 44.

Anderson also described waste as 'the measurable cost of anything that does not help the customer'. It was discovered that fifty per cent of the packaging the company used wasn't needed and that boxes could be used several times over. 'You cannot produce a green product if you are a brown company,' he said, 'brown' meaning that there is still waste that has not been eliminated. Next he measured the cost of imperfect tiles, clerical errors and misdirected shipments and found that they amounted to ten per cent of sales, or US$70 million a year. QUEST teams set out to reduce this figure and the goals were at first modest – just ten per cent improvement – but, when they hit these targets, they were issued another challenge – *another* ten per cent – and they began to understand continuous improvement.

QUEST had faltered in the early stages until the CEO, Dan Hendrix, gave teams a proportion of the money saved. At that point, over ninety per cent of the teams in Interface's factories volunteered for the programme and the money was distributed according to the time each worker had spent on the project. The first three years of the QUEST programme saved US$67 million, by 2008, it had reached $262 million, or twenty-eight per cent of the then-cumulative operating income. None of this was accomplished by Interface on its own. Anderson was assisted by his ECO Dream Team, a group of world experts in sustainability he assembled to help him realize his ambitions for a greener company.

It is clear that employees *enjoyed* this process, as well as getting extra money in their pay packets for creative suggestions, so much so that the company has been voted 'best to work for' several times and has record-level low rates of turnover and absenteeism. Perhaps 'making history' is a more worthwhile aim than just making carpets. One employee, after hearing Anderson speak, wrote and dedicated to Anderson the following poem, which was recited at his memorial service.[13]

Tomorrow's Child

1
Without a name an unseen face
And knowing not your time and place
Tomorrow's Child as yet unborn
I met you first last Tuesday morn.

2

13. Anderson, *Business Lessons*, p. 272.

A wise friend introduced us two
And through his shining point of view
I saw a day that you would see
A day for you but not for me

3
Tomorrow's Child, my daughter-son
I am afraid I've just begun
To think of you and of your good
Though always having known I should

4
Begin I will to weigh the cost
Of what I squander what is lost
If ever I forget that you
Will some day come to live here too

Wisely managed employees can make their working lives a legacy.

Another major initiative involved suppliers. Fifty per cent or more of the value of many products is bought in from outside. If the supply chain is full of waste and poisonous substances, so will be the company's finished product. While cutting back solid waste through QUEST had been successful, the poisons and pollutants released into rivers, oceans and the air were far more extensive and, to reduce those, suppliers had to be persuaded to rid the supply chain of contaminants, which wasn't easy. Trust must somehow be created.

Many suppliers did not know what contaminants were contained in their products, some did not *want* to know, and many more had to inquire from *their* suppliers, who did not know or care either. For several years the company was frustrated in its efforts, then it hit upon a solution. It told its suppliers that a typical division was going to reduce the number of suppliers from twenty-eight to three. This announcement signalled that those suppliers who didn't cooperate would almost certainly lose the account but those who *did* would receive an order eight to ten times larger, so that taking trouble was well worth their while.

Federal and local government regulations were seriously out of date and completely unsatisfactory, so that doing what was merely legal was no use at all. The latest scientific findings were scrutinized and a list of forbidden and suspect ingredients drawn up. Dealing with a much smaller number of suppliers was considerably cheaper in terms of administration. Tests to detect suspect ingredients were sent to suppliers so that they could screen for themselves. A 'trust but verify' regime was instituted. Random checks were performed to check suppliers' claims, and relations severed with those who were untruthful. Interface finished up with a handful of trusted partners who were very concerned to retain their business and share goals with the company.

Far from this policy costing the company money, it saved it US$300,000 a year and the suppliers also benefited from much larger orders and were able to offer discounts. NGOs were contracted to perform life-cycle assessments (LCAs) to test some of the ingredients used and report any dangers. The Kyoto Protocol had asked for a seven per cent reduction in greenhouse gases by 2008, a goal the USA refused so indignantly that the Senate voted it down by ninety-five to zero, considering it a completely unreasonable figure. Meanwhile Anderson reduced Interface's GHS emissions by *seventy-one per cent* between 1996 and 2008, while sales increased by two-thirds and earnings actually doubled.

Revamping distribution to use less energy

Saving energy and protecting the environment are especially challenging in relation to the *distribution* of products. Interface accepts responsibility for how its products reach the customer, and the waste and emissions that result from doing so, but the company is directly responsible for only ten to twenty per cent of the carbon footprint left by one square yard of carpet; everyone else – the user, the installer, the distributor, all the way back to wells and mines – produces the rest. Shipping produces more pollution than any other function. Currently, for example, Brazilian iron is shipped to China, where it's made into products, those products are then shipped to California and ultimately end up in shops in New York.

Anderson found that sourcing supplies locally so as to reduce the distance they travelled saved so much money it was impossible to estimate! Switching from truck to rail for most of the journey saved seventy-five per cent of all thermal units (a measure of energy consumption), and even more could be saved in Europe. Using waterways, Dutch canals and the Rhine was over fifty per cent cheaper than train and far less polluting. Where trucking was unavoidable, UPS (a firm of endearment – see Chapter 7) was used. Their truck fleets use the Environmental Protection Agency's 'Smart Way Calculator'. This technology is part of the Smart Way Partnership with the Federal government and scores companies on their contributions to environmental goals. EPA's website credits the use of its calculator with having removed 50.12 metric tons of carbon dioxide from the US environment annually, saving 120.7 million tons of oil a year and leading to cost savings of US$16.8 billion a year.

Trucking accounts for twenty-seven per cent of all greenhouse gas emissions in the USA. Interface cut their emissions by four to eight per cent through using wide-based tyres, by a similar amount through using streamlined trucks, and by even more through using auxiliary power systems so that engines do not idle when stationary. Further savings are made by loading trucks evenly, and using lighter trailers and speed controls. A huge distributor like Wal-Mart has saved up to US$60 million a year using such methods, including the re-routing of trucks so they cover less distance. The computer programs involved borrow from nature by imitating the foraging behavior of ants, which always take the shortest routes to new food sources and leave a trail for other ants to follow.

Of all American truck-makers, only Subaru supplies partial zero emission vehicles (PZEVs). Subaru also sends nothing to landfill. To make up for the emissions still to be reduced, the company promises to plant trees equivalent to the number of miles travelled. Interface not only uses Subaru trucks itself but also gives preference to suppliers who do so. It sponsors non-profit-making environmental organizations to check on its own compliance, helping these to survive too.

Moving to renewable energy resources

But cutting waste and pollution is not the only step that businesses can take. Reducing and offsetting emissions can only take us so far; what is really needed is the development of renewable energy sources, which have the potential to change everything. The most obvious solutions are solar, tidal and wind power. All these are not simply renewable but everlasting, limitless and free. All we need is improved technologies to harness them and make them more affordable and accessible. Between 2006 and 2007, use of solar power increased by fifty-five per cent, and this figure continues to rise. China is currently responsible for seventy-five per cent of the world's solar energy production. Geographically, Africa is best placed to harvest the sun, and China, with its massive budget surplus and potential for strategic, long-term investment, is likely to get there first.

Although this technology is surely coming, we do not yet seem to be fully embracing it. The idea that nothing can be done until the price of solar energy approximates the price of fossil fuels is false as we shall see. As the price curves converge much can be done in the short-term. But it is also wise to think long-term of just what is at stake, because a very great deal is at stake.

Let us be conservative and say that it may take twenty years for prices to become comparable. But once that happens then *the price of energy will fall in perpetuity* as technologies to capture alternative sources of energy improve. Contrast that situation with the price of oil *increasing* more than twenty times since 1972, when the price of oil stood at US$3 a barrel. The point is that renewable energy is free, is owned by no one, cannot be monopolized and is abundant; the sun produces 173,000 terawatts of energy every day. The entire world population uses only fifteen terawatts a day.[14]

What we are heading towards is the 'tipping point' when renewable energy achieves cost parity with fossil fuels, after which the costs will start to fall rapidly.[15] Whoever gets there first will prosper exceedingly. But is there anything at all we can do about the situation *now*? Ray Anderson found plenty of renewable strategies that repaid him many years before price parity will be achieved. The most obvious reaction to high fossil fuel prices is to stop using that form of energy, and so Interface cut its fossil fuel costs by sixty per cent per square foot of carpet while simultaneously increasing its use of renewable energy by twenty-eight per cent.

When Anderson informed the company accountants that Interface was moving to renewable energy, they told him the investment would last seventeen years and not pay back for thirty-five, a calculation that tells us more about accountants than about renewable energy. What had they not factored in? They had overlooked marketing and customer reaction, for one thing. The University of California contracted Interface to recarpet all its schools and colleges, so impressed was it by Interface's environmental strategy. A series of demonstration projects held at several plants brought in the crowds and with them new customers – interior designers and architects.

It may not pay the single homeowner to install solar panels, but suppose a company, like Duke Energy in North Carolina, bought the panels in bulk at half-price, installed them free and shared the power with the home-owner? Suppose, like the city of Berkeley in California, the panels are provided free and the cost added to property taxes for the next ten years, boosting the value of the house immediately? What governments pay for surplus solar energy

14. For these facts and many more see Al Gore, *Our Choice*, New York: Bloomsbury, 2009, pp. 62–65.
15. Malcolm Gladwell, *The Tipping Point*, New York: Little Brown, 2000.

returned to the national grid can vary. A government might, however, decide that a generous tariff would turn a roof into a business and thus greatly increase the rate of installation. Duke Energy has a 'power station' consisting of 600,000 roofs attached to its grid. Under such circumstances solar energy pays *now*.

It is now possible in the USA to buy a solar purchasing power agreement (PPA) for commercial or private residences. Through a PPA you can site a turn-key solar power generator on your own premises without up-front payment, buy all the power you generate, incur no maintenance costs and deliver unused green energy to the national grid. The cost of this energy supply is already comparable to that produced by fossil fuels. Several companies have taken advantage of PPAs, among them Staples, Whole Foods (see Chapter 8), Wal-Mart and Kohl. For years economic growth has been negatively affected by climbing oil prices, which have recently fallen. An era of cheap, abundant energy, falling in price with every advance in technology, will change everything.

Substituting resource efficiency for machine efficiency

The economy has been in thrall to machine efficiency for centuries. We have steadily replaced human muscle with machine power and human judgement with programmed instructions. Software is much cheaper than a human being.

Yet a huge untapped source of cost-savings lies in increasing *resource efficiency*; that is, doing much more with much less material. A prime example of mechanical efficiency is a Formula 1 racing car. But even those who aren't Grand Prix fans may have sampled the surge of power as they step lightly on the accelerator and their car goes from nought to sixty in a matter of seconds. But did you know that ninety-nine per cent of a car's energy is spent on moving *itself* and only one per cent on moving drivers and passengers?[16] Such facts are scandalous in a world approaching the depletion of its natural resources, and to which the Chinese are adding 14,000 cars a day. Our children's children will marvel at our profligacy and the ruined cities that are our legacy to them. It's not just the car itself but the acres of tarmac and concrete that we've poured over our environment to support them, the respiratory diseases caused by carbon monoxide emissions and the lead released into the atmosphere.

What will it take to reduce this extensive waste of resources? It will take

16.   Paul Hawken, *The Ecology of Commerce*, New York: Harper Business, 1993, p. 73.

live *human* intelligence, imagination, skill, insight and innovation, not just in the R&D and design departments but *everywhere* in the organization. We need to imagine solar vehicles made of fiberglass travelling noiselessly to their destinations and using most of their energy to convey *us* not themselves, or perhaps pedal-powered vehicles nipping along at thirty miles per hour and giving their seated drivers much needed, life-extending exercise. We must use our brains, not just software full of pre-programmed instructions.

An emphasis on saving the environment would create a huge increase in 'green-collar' jobs. Anderson cites the equation below, which calculates the environmental impact represented by affluent countries:[17]

$$I = P \times A \times T$$

Here, I is Impact, P is Population, A is Affluence and T is Technology, and we have a straight-line rational calculation of the kind we objected to in Chapter 1. But suppose Technology became the *denominator*? Suppose Technology could instead *reduce* and divide the Impact of Population and Affluence? This is what Anderson's 'separator machine' accomplishes, stripping the back of the carpet from the front, so that each component can be recycled. This is what it means to manufacture a car, so that it can be taken apart in ten minutes and its materials recycled. Suppose many such technologies drove *resource* efficiency rather than mechanical, job-killing efficiency? In that circumstance, with this different approach to technology (T2), the equation would look like this:

$$I = \frac{P \times A}{T2}$$

Anderson commented on what this change would mean:

> T2 begins to put millions of unemployed people to work, increasing resource-productivity by using an abundant resource – labor – to conserve the natural resources that are in decline. Technology becomes the friend of labor not the enemy. Technology becomes part of the solution, not a prime mover behind the problem.[18]

We cannot leave this to simple market forces, under which labour will continue to be shed as a short-term fix. We have to exercise leadership, determine to be stewards of our environment and guide our nations by visions of what is

17. Anderson, *Business Lessons*, p.186.
18. Anderson *Business Lessons*, p. 190.

possible. Anderson quotes Paul Hawken, Amory Lovins and Hunter Lovins, members of his dream team:

> For all their power and vitality, markets are only tools. They make a good servant but a bad master and a worse religion. They can be used to accomplish many important tasks, but they can't do everything, and it's a dangerous delusion to begin to believe that they can – especially when they threaten to replace ethics or politics.[19]

In all this, evolution is our great teacher

A tree was recently felled in the Amazon rainforest and among the many insects that crawled out of it were fifty unknown to science. Any one of these may, for all we know, demonstrate extraordinary survival strategies from which we can learn, or be the key to curing a human disease. Yet we are destroying this treasure trove to create cattle ranches. Numerous species with which we once shared the planet are already extinct. We need to take stock and consider this loss.

Slime mould, which despite its name is a creature of amazing beauty beneath the microscope, undergoes an amazing process of sequential transformation. As a worm-like creature it wriggles along and plants itself in the ground like a weed, then it disperses itself in liquid droplets and then it reforms itself into a worm. When eaten by a bird, it passes through its digestive tract and is then deposited on rocks, whereupon it continues its erratic progress. It is thought to be older than the dinosaurs and may have something to teach companies whose average longevity has fallen to less than twenty years! Janine Benyus, a member of Anderson's dream team, is the author of the landmark book *Biomimicry*, a plea that we should mimic and be inspired by nature. Her description of its near-miraculous qualities is unforgettable:

> When we stare this deeply into nature's eyes, it takes our breath away, and in a good way, it bursts our bubble. We realize that all our inventions have already appeared in nature in a more elegant form and at a lot less cost to the planet. Our most clever architectural struts and beams are already featured in lily pads and bamboo stems. Our central heating and air-conditioning are bested by the termite tower's steady 86 degrees

19. Amory and Hunter Lovins Presentation at Global Business Network Conference in San Francisco, June 1994.

Fahrenheit. Our most stealthy radar is hard of hearing compared to the bat's multi-frequency transmissions. And our new 'smart materials' can't hold a candle to the dolphin's skin or the butterfly's proboscis. Even the wheel, which we always took to be a uniquely human creation, has been found in the rotary motor that propels the flagellum of the world's most ancient bacteria... Bioluminescent algae splash chemicals together to light their body lanterns. Arctic fish and frogs freeze solid and spring back to life having protected their organs from ice damage. Chameleons and cuttlefish hide without moving, changing the pattern on their skin to instantly blend with their surroundings. Bees, turtles, and birds navigate without maps, while whales and penguins dive without scuba gear. How do they do it? How do dragonflies outmanoeuvre our best helicopters? How do humming birds cross the Gulf of Mexico on less than one tenth of an ounce of fuel? How do ants carry the equivalent of hundreds of pounds in a dead heat through the jungle?[20]

Benyus describes the principles on which all nature works, stating that it runs on sunlight, using only the energy it needs; fits form to function and recycles everything; rewards cooperation and banks on diversity; demands local expertise and curbs excesses from within; and that it taps the power of limits. It is the last characteristic that needs explanation since humans see limits as a dare. Within eleven years of inventing the plane, after watching vultures in flight, we were using it to drop bombs on our own species. We need to see nature, and its limits, as our mentor. The whole notion of natural *resources* is obscene, Wes Jackson, director of the Land Institute, claims. Nature is a well-spring of ideas, a cornucopia of successful experiments which should inspire us. It is not something for us to extract and exploit.[21] We think of farms as factories for millions of standardized products, only to find that disaster haunts our monoculture:

> Having put all our eggs in one basket we are at nature's mercy, caught in the crosshairs of drought, flood, pests, hail and eroding soil. If anyone knows about being booted from the Garden of Eden it is farmers... It comes from an insistence on decoupling ourselves from nature, from replacing natural systems with totally alien systems, and from waging war on, rather than allying with, natural processes.[22]

20. Janine M. Benyus, *Biomimicry*, New York: Harper Perennial, 2002, p. 6.

21. Benyus, *Biomimicry*, pp. 291–292.

22. Benyus, *Biomimicry*, p. 18.

How are we doing, for example, in our 'heroic' fight against pests? Since 1945 the use of pesticides in the USA has increased by 3,300 per cent. America is deluged with 2.2 billion pounds of pesticides a year. As for the pests, they've *increased* by twenty per cent. Pesticide residue has made agriculture the most polluting industry in America. It is linked to leukaemia, lymphoma and other cancers, and nitrates in drinking water are implicated in the high miscarriage rate in farming communities.[23] Isn't it time we worked *with* our environment rather than against it?

Nature and evolution should inspire us to be more innovative. The scum of algae on the surface of a pond captures energy from the sun more effectively than our photovoltaic cells. We are less impervious to cold than duckweed. That we live at all is thanks to once-green plants storing energy from the sun. The sun is our umbilical cord, producing, among other things, 300 billion tons of sugar a year by photosynthesis – the world's biggest chemical operation. Evolution may be 'blind' but it has a 3 billion year lead on human invention. It has had much more time to work miracles and we should have the humility to learn from it.

Nature's biggest advantage over us is that, as Benyus says, 'it manufactures its materials under life-friendly conditions in water, at room temperature, without harsh chemicals or high pressure'. The inner shell of the abalone is twice as tough as our strongest high-tech ceramics. Instead of breaking like man-made ceramics, the shell deforms under stress and behaves like a metal. Spider silk, ounce for ounce, is five times stronger than steel. Mussel adhesive works underwater and sticks to anything without a primer. Rhino horn is self-repairing without having any living cells. 'Bone, wood, skin, tusks and antlers and heart-muscle – miracle materials all – are made to live out their useful lives and then to fade back, to be reabsorbed by another kind of life through the grand cycle of death and renewal.'[24] As Braden Allenby, AT&T's vice-president of research, reminds us:

> Economies are like ecosystems. Both systems take in energy and materials and transform them into products. The problem is that our economy performs a linear transformation, whereas nature's is cyclic… A leaf falls to the forest floor only to be recycled in the bodies of microbes and returned to the soil water, where it is reabsorbed by the tree to make new leaves.[25]

23. Benyus, *Biomimicry*, p. 97.
24. Benyus, *Biomimicry*, p. 276.
25. Quoted in Benyus, *Biomimicry*, p. 242.

The problem is that this return may take decades or even longer, so the results of our folly may be long delayed and thus unnoticed. If we foul up the earth now, future generations must pay. The good news is that at least some business people are catching on. Allenby continued:

> OK, what we have realized is that despite all the happy consequences of industrialization… we can't go on like this. The way we have been operating is unsustainable. There are three reasons for greening up your act. It's the right thing to do, it's the competitive thing to do and you'll go to jail if you don't.[26]

Janine Benyus explains that the term 'biomimicry' derives from *bios* meaning life and *memesis* meaning imitation. It teaches that nature must be our model and biology our metaphor so that a solar cell is inspired by a leaf. Nature must also be our measure of what is appropriate, what lasts and what works. Finally, nature must be our mentor: we should be less keen to exploit nature or extract from it and more prepared to value and learn from it. James and Roberta Swann, authors of *Bound to the Earth* note:

> Nature has evolved systems over billions of years that work in harmony with each other, that build from bare, rocky, thin soil, to lush, green forests. Without human intervention the processes of nature have evolved self-regulating forms of beauty, grace and efficiency. Our challenge is to learn how to honour them and be inspired by their truth to create new cultural values and systems.[27]

In the amazing interstices of our natural environment, the conscience of capitalism can be found.

We have touched on at least four principal integrities in this chapter that together constitute the conscience of capitalism in regard to the environment; these are summarised overleaf in Figure 8.2.

The person *plus* environment is the unit of survival. Where we see environmental stewardship as a necessity we are more likely to be inventive. Nearly everything will need to change. Instead of plundering the earth's resources we must return and recycle as much of these as we can, using fewer virgin resources. Instead of efficient machines replacing people, with 'green collar' intelligence we can learn to use physical resources more sparingly

26. Quoted in Benyus, *Biomimicry*, p. 282.
27. James Swann and Roberta Swann, *Bound to the Earth*, New York: Avon Books, 1994, p. 33.

and more efficiently, replacing things with people. Finally, the straight-line reasoning process we employ is really but an arc of the larger ecosystem, the natural cycles that regulate our earth's systems.

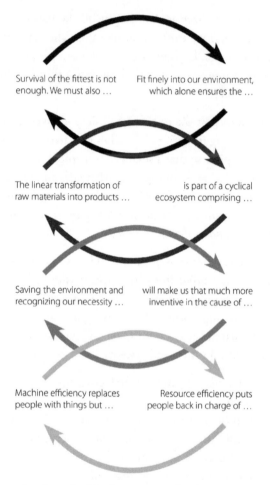

Figure 8.2 The unit of survival is the person *plus* the environment.

CHAPTER 9

The Global Alliance for Banking on Values (GABV)[1]

When enterprise becomes a mere bubble on a whirlpool of speculation (and) the capital development of a country becomes a by-product of the activities of a casino, the job of capitalism is likely to be ill-done.[2]

In Chapters 2 and 3 we were somewhat critical of the financial sector as a whole. Our major banks have lurched from crisis to crisis and as this book goes to press even the Bank of England has had to refer itself to the Serious Fraud Office. Billions have had to be repaid to customers for illegal activities. The Swiss office of HSBC has been involved in helping clients evade taxes. Payday lenders have had to be sharply curbed and have been shown to be predatory on the poorest in the land, sending out fake legal letters from non-existing law firms to panic their borrowers. It remains to be asked 'how can this situation be remedied?' Most assert that it is the *cultures* of these organizations which are at fault. So long as regulations are seen as hurdles to be surmounted or to be got around rather than values to be embedded and internalized, then a state of war exists between regulators and the regulated and the former will pick

---

1. This chapter features substantial input from Tom Cummings.
2. John Maynard Keynes, *The General Theory of Employment, Interest and Money,* *http://cas.umkc.edu/economics/people/facultypages/kregel/courses/econ645/winter2011/ generaltheory.pdf.*

off easier prey that are less well defended. Tax authorities, for example, find it much easier to go after you and me than an office bristling with tax-avoidance expertise. It makes better use of public funds to go after the careless and confused rather than the crafty and well resourced. Fighting the government to a standstill becomes a legal art. In contrast values are things we *want* to embody and strive to attain.

Here we will describe a new association founded in 2009, the Global Alliance for Banking on Values, notable for putting its agreed values above all other objectives. Our argument, circular as usual, proceeds by the steps shown in Figure 9.1.

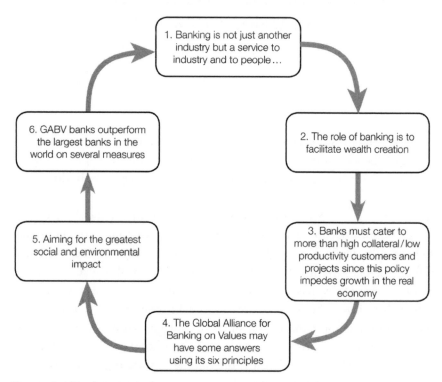

Figure 9.1 Banking on values

Is it possible to have values-oriented banks? Are these viable, or is it inevitable that banks must compete with those to whom they distribute funds? Ideals are all very well, but what would these cost us? Will those who lead through service be always small, weak and marginal? Is the status quo with banks being too big to fail or jail the only way? We should not assume that newer approaches to banking are outclassed or that profitability needs to be sacrificed to high ideals.

This was not true of the *Mittelstand* in Chapter 6, the Conscious Capitalism movement in Chapter 7 nor environmentally responsible companies in Chapter 8, nor the Cambridge Phenomenon in Chapter 10. In all these cases profits were needed to drive growth and we shall find that same is true of the alternative banking sector featured in this chapter.

1. Banking is not just another industry but a service to industry and to people

It is sometimes said that banks are just one more industry. As such they have an untrammelled right to profit just like any other business by competing for funds and for customers. But this proposition does not quite pass muster. If banks *distribute* funds to those *contributing* to our economy then they cannot at the same time be competing for such funds. You either supply funds or you receive them and if you supply funds then they pass through your hands before other companies can get to them. You are at the head of the line and you are in a position to take for yourself a proportion of the funds you distribute. There is no real limit on what you can squirrel away in this process. There are a few large banks and they constitute an oligopoly and they are taking more and more.

We saw in Chapter 1 that banks do not *create wealth* in any real sense of that term. Money cannot be made from money save by speculation, that is at best a zero sum game for the economy as a whole. To create wealth money has to be *transformed* into goods and/or services and then transformed *back* via customer revenue into more money than you began with. This does not mean that banks have no useful function. Lending and depositing make it possible to run a business and banks *facilitate wealth creation through their business and retail clients*. They play an important role. Their lending and their investment make enterprise possible. It is true that banks make money by leveraging their funds. They lend out multiples of the money that they hold in capital, but this assumes that assets will not lose value. If they do lose value leverage is reversed; banks *lose* multiples of what they initially leant or invested. In short, banks must rely on the wider economy growing or their leveraging turns against them when asset prices collapse. This is what happened in 2008 to 2010.

It follows from this that banks prosper as a result of wealth created in the 'real economy', that is, the sale to customers by suppliers of products and services demanded. Banks make *and* lose money by transactions that occur between them but they do not create wealth by this. There is the same amount of money as there was before. Given the fact that banks count on asset prices rising they are highly dependent on the real economy and they neglect this at their peril. Where they lose touch with genuine wealth creation we are all in trouble. It is from asset prices that they derive the paper products they sell.

2. The role of banks is to facilitate wealth creation

The proper role of the financial sector is to *support the underlying real economy.* If it is companies making things for customers which creates surplus value and if other transactions are largely zero-sum, then banks would be very wise *not* to compete with their customers, least of all in fraudulent ways, but rather to serve their customers faithfully and get a share of the wealth they create. *Banks are the helpers of industry* and a resource for individuals to save and to borrow. If banks are chiefly in it for themselves then the cost of capital will be higher and bank charges will be extracted by stealth to leave industries weaker not stronger and people out of pocket. In short banks should profit, but by *indirection,* by first serving industrial and other customers who will then switch their patronage to the best provider.

This process is assisted if banks are allowed to invest money in their customers. The long-term, low interest loans extended for many years by German regional banks to the industries in their *lander* were partly motivated by the investments the bank had made in their own customers, a process forbidden in Britain and the USA, but this *does* give the bank a sizeable stake in building industries rather than giving what they earn to shareholders. It is very much the approach of the China Construction Bank, among others. If the purpose of money is to create industry rather than the other way around, then the mission of the financial sector is to get funds to where these are most needed by entrepreneurs, manufacturers and innovators.

The job of distributors is to get funds in lavish amounts to the top contributors. Spotting the latest innovation and getting funds to it for rapid expansion is an important role. It is often thought that creativity is the new road to economic growth. This is only true in part. A nation can be very inventive as indeed Britain has been, yet fail to create an industry out of that inventiveness. The computer, penicillin, radar, the jet engine, the magnetic resonance scanner, the tilting train, the hovercraft and most recently graphene were all British inventions *but were developed for the market by others.* What creates wealth is establishing a global standard for your new product and exploiting this via mass-production. It is the *follow-up* of inventiveness that builds an economy and banks need to get money, a lot of it, to where a breakthrough has occurred and the real contributor is situated. China has taken out 2,200 patents on the uses of graphene. America has 1,700 and Britain, where it was invented, about 100![3] Part of Singapore's success, described in Chapter 5, was riding on the coat-tails of Western innovation by exploiting this in East Asia. You need to be first-to-market or your creativity will not be repaid by innovation. In the race-to-markets banks can play an important part.

3. Banks must cater not just to high collateral/low productivity customers and their projects since this policy impedes growth in the real economy

Wall Street and the City of London specialize in financial services and dominate this sector globally. Surely this is a good thing? Even if financial 'products' are not real products and lack the wealth-creating potential of the latter we should stick with what we do well and make the best of this, shouldn't we? The answer depends on the effect that a burgeoning financial sector has on the wider 'real' economy. Assuming the financial sector serves it well this is obviously an advantage but does it serve the real economy well or does it signally fail to do so?

A most disturbing paper for the Bank of International Settlements written by two American economists, Stephen G. Cecchetti and Enisse Kharroubi, has troubling conclusions. Its message is that financial sector growth crowds out growth in the real economy in several countries which they studied.[4] Indeed this would appear to be a global phenomenon. Aggregate productivity tends to fall when the financial sector expands and to rise when the financial sector slows or contracts. Why should financial booms act as a drag on growth? They estimated that had Ireland's financial sector employment remained flat in the four years from 2005 to 2009, instead of growing at 4.1 per cent annually, this would have shaved 1.4 per cent off the Irish economy's decline of -2.7 per cent in total factor productivity in the period after 2009. But why does this happen?

Assuming that banks are purely out for themselves and for their shareholders with scant regard for the nation or the community, then they would naturally

3. Will Hutton, *How Good Can We Be?* Little, Brown, 2015.
4. Stephen G. Cecchetti and Enisse Kharroubi, 'Why does financial sector growth crowd out real economic growth?' *Bank for International Settlements Working Paper*, no. 490.

lend their funds to projects with the highest collateral and hence the least risk, most of which have low productivity. Housing is a good example. A home is an asset easily repossessed and that, because of the housing shortage, is very likely to rise in value. Yet it produces little or nothing, so as money pours into a housing boom your loan is 'as safe as houses', but the productivity gain is modest to non-existent. Indeed, if funds are *not* advanced to high risk entrepreneurial projects because houses and other safe bets like credit cards have taken up all the slack then total factor productivity will fall. The simple crowds out the complex, the low risk crowds out the high risk, the routine replaces the innovative.

We must also consider the availability of skilled workers who are hired by an expanding financial sector and are therefore not available to entrepreneurs whose projects are usually high risk with low collateral. The bank attracts skilled employees into vanilla-type activities and so prevents entrepreneurs teaching them new skills in state of the art businesses. It is easy to assess the value of a house – you need only a surveyor – yet it is hard to estimate the potential of a new business. The risk of losing money is much higher. It follows that aggressive expansion of simpler propositions makes innovative industry harder to support. Low collateral start-ups are unlikely to get either the funding or the skilled employees whom they urgently need. Wealth creation and total factor productivity are likely to fall and the authors cite evidence that this has been happening. The UK especially has a crisis of low productivity brought about by this bias. An economy where everyone sits quietly in their houses and waits for these to accumulate value is very unlikely to be productive.[5]

This has an especially deleterious effect on manufacturing, which as we argued earlier creates the most wealth by creating wholes far more valuable than their components. The researchers found that the manufacturing sectors especially were harmed by booms in financial services, the distributors pushing aside the major contributors and those who sustained the working class. They concluded 'financial sector growth becomes a drag on real growth'. Additional research on thirty-three manufacturing industries in fifteen economies by Rajan and Zingales found that falling research and development among manufacturers correlated with expansion by finance industries. R&D was as much as two per cent down in the face of financial expansion.[6] Slowly growing financial sectors help raise R&D expenditures.

5.   Cecchetti and Kharroubi, 'Why does financial sector growth?'

6.   R. Rajan and L. Zingales, 'Financial Dependence and Economic growth', *American Economic Review*, 88, 1998, pp.559–581.

Since R&D is the major force behind innovation the rapid expansion of financial sectors would appear to damage innovation. Victims of an expanding financial sector mentioned specifically by the authors were aircraft, computing and electronics. There is even evidence that the expansion of finance favours selectively those with *lower* R&D, the less innovative. The researchers concluded that credit booms harm what we normally think of as the engines of growth – those that are more R&D intensive. That, together with the recent experience of the financial crisis, led them to conclude that there is a need to reassess the relationship between finance and real growth in modern economic systems.

Of course all this assumes that banks are exclusively out for themselves and have scant regard for the rest of the society or the larger economy. They look for the most profit from the lowest risks with the highest collateral. In this respect housing is perfect. The growing population and the chronic housing shortage in countries like the UK means that this largely unproductive sector is the darling of banks and the apotheosis of the consumption oriented society, a place to stash your loot. It certainly beats working! But has there arisen a challenge to self-seeking banks? To this subject we will now turn.

4. The Global Alliance for Banking on Values may have some answers using its six principles

The establishment of the Global Alliance for Banking on Values (GABV) coincided with the Great Recession of 2008. The emergence of a new constellation of banks that combined social, environmental and economics driven banking models was a timely response to the recession.[7] We will consider what influences gave rise to it and some earlier examples of banking which had values, *other* than its own capital accumulation and advancement, while still including these. The problem with predatory banking practices, of which we have lately seen so much, is that in the end a bank depends upon the prosperity of its clients and the wealth of its community. To exploit stakeholders is ultimately to spike your own guns. Your customers will deposit less and borrow less. Banking can have objectives in addition to its own advancement and the more it advances the goals of its society the better it does, as we shall see.

It is useful to distinguish between a conscious aim to benefit other parties and what is sometimes called 'enlightened' self-interest, or corporate social responsibility. This holds that you must first and foremost make money for

7. See www.gabv.org

your shareholders and only then will you be in a position to be generous to other people. Corporate Social Responsibility is something to keep your company's reputation high and win you political allies. It is something to be dispensed at the end of the day, if you wish to, if shareholders do not object too strenuously and if there happens to be anything left over. This attitude is shaped by what companies can legally do. It is not their money to dispose of in this manner and nothing more than a gesture will usually be attempted.

What we mean by 'values-based banking' is that the bank's purpose and reason-for-being is to serve its customers and its community and to continue doing this on an ever-expanding scale it must make profits and generate surpluses. In short, the service to society is an integral part of its strategy, *not* an add-on and not contingent on having enough to spare. An early exemplar of community centred banking was Frederick Wilhelm Raiffeisen (1818– 1888). He was civic minded and served as the mayor of three towns, lastly and longest at Huddesdorf in Germany.[8] Many banks in Europe still bear his name in such countries as Austria, Germany, Switzerland, Romania, Kosovo, Luxembourg and the Netherlands.

Raiffeisen was greatly influenced by the 'Starvation Winter' of 1846 to 1847 in Germany and set up the Association for the Procurement of Bread and Fruit, a famous benevolent institution, followed by the Rhenish Agricultural Cooperative bank. He promulgated his philosophy that poverty was the consequence of unilateral dependency on charities, on loan-sharks and on politicians. The only remedy was a group or union following the S Formula, Self-help, Self-government and Self-responsibility at the group level. Members must serve each other with a bank or credit union as the focus of their integrity and survival.

A second major influence on some of the GABV members is the philosophy of Rudolf Steiner (1861–1925), Austrian author of *The Philosophy of Freedom*. He sought to unite science with the human spirit and believed that spirit inhered in practical pursuits such as organic agriculture, education, medicine and the conduct of financial affairs. Much as in this book, he created bi-polarities, one of which was economic life, productive of material things at one end and the life of the spirit which produces ideas at the other end. Only when economic life is fused with ideas and only when policies mediate between these two poles, while protecting both, can human endeavour gain.[9]

He began his career as a literary critic and had an abiding admiration for Johann Wolfgang Goethe after whom he named his cultural centre.

8.   www.raiffeisenonline.ro

9.   http://en.wikipedia.org/wiki/Rudolf_Steiner

Like Fichte, mentioned in Chapter 6, his ideas grew out of German idealist philosophy. His lifelong quest was for a 'spiritual science', fusing the clarity of science with the passion of the spirit. His patron was William Waldorf Astor of Waldorf-Astoria fame and there are over 1,000 Waldorf schools in the world teaching Steiner's philosophy. There are thirty-three Steiner schools in the UK and Ireland alone.

Steiner was very much a social reformer and his book *Towards Social Renewal* is still widely read. He taught an ethical individualism. He quoted Goethe's belief that 'Thinking is an organ of perception, no more or less than the eye or ear. Just as the eye perceives colour and the ear sounds, so thinking perceives ideas.' To have banking without ethical perception would be unthinkable. He also taught that there were no limits for our appetite for knowledge. The more we know the more we want to learn. He is credited with being the father of organic farming methods. He posited a Fundamental Law of Social Life which put a sharp curb on selfish conduct.

> The well-being of a community of people working together will be greater, the less the individual claims for himself the proceeds of his work, i.e. the more of these proceeds he makes over to his fellow workers the more his own needs are satisfied, not out of his own efforts, but out of the work done by others.[10]

This statement is the antithesis of the Invisible Hand. We should think of others first and let their reciprocity serve our self-interest. He famously said that the community is mirrored in each human soul, each one of which reflects our communities. He called his philosophy 'anthroposophy', meaning essentially human-centredness, a spiritual world accessible by direct experience of human beings and subject to rational verification.

More recently two banks in Bangladesh have shaken up conventional banking. These are the Grameen Bank, the micro-lending bank, founded by Muhammad Yunus and the BRAC (Bangladeshi Rural Advancement Committee) Foundation, together with its bank. Both were initially sponsored by the Ford Foundation, but Grameen, which generated a profit for its owner-borrowers for twenty years out of twenty-three, moved to a self-funding basis and no longer applies to charities.

Muhammad Yunus is a Bangladeshi Muslim and his ideas have an affinity with Islamic Finance. He received his PhD in Economics from Vanderbilt

---

10. Richard Seddon (ed.), *The Fundamental Social Law, Selected Writings of Rudolf Steiner*, Bristol: Rudolf Steiner Press, 1993.

University and returned to teach in Bangladesh. On his first morning at his new university he found a mother and her baby who had died on his doorstep in the night. There was widespread starvation in the countryside. It came home to him forcibly that nothing taught to him in the USA had prepared him for this crisis. Economics had nothing to say about the *absence* of money only about its presence. The university was at Jobra Village several miles out of town so that students could not mount demonstrations against the military government. Yunus sent his students into the village to speak to fifty-seven poor women about their economic survival. He discovered that middlemen charged them thirty cents for the materials needed to make chair-backs and baskets and bought back the finished work from them for thirty-three cents, so that the women earned three cents for each batch or six cents a day. By the absurdly simple expedient of Yunus giving each woman thirty cents they were able to sell their products to the highest bidder and earn eighteen cents a day, enough to save their lives and that of their families. As Raffeisen had discovered more than a century earlier, the problem was dependency and loan-sharking. Unrestrained self-interest leads the poor to be preyed upon by the near-poor.

Yunus and his bank won the Nobel Prize for Peace in 2006, the first ever for a citizen of Bangladesh. President Obama presented him with the Medal of Freedom and the UN proclaimed 'the year of micro-finance'. Micro-finance has spread to eighty countries but the results are mixed and a closer look at what Yunus wrought, until the Bangladeshi government seized his company and removed him from control, will prove enlightening. We will consider his record up to 2010 when his enemies began to harass him. His achievements were remarkable and are explained in his books *Banker to the Poor* and *Building Social Business*.[11]

By 2010 his bank had 8.07 million borrowers serving 2,564 branches in 81,351 small towns and villages. He had disbursed a total of US$9.09 billion in loans, ninety-five per cent to poor women. His bank was owned by its borrowers, made profits and paid dividends. In addition he had disbursed US$113 million in scholarships, US$366 million in village phones and US$90 million in taking beggars off the streets. But his enemies were gathering and even affidavits from Hillary Clinton, Mary Robinson, President of Ireland and John Kerry could not save him. The loan-sharks were furious but so was the judiciary to which the sharks had once paid large bribes. On

---

11. Muhammad Yunus, *Building Social Business: The New Kind of Capitalism that Serves Humanity's Most Pressing Needs,* London: Arum Press, 2003

the grounds that the government had once given him a grant, not repaid, his bank was seized. He has been compared to Galileo persecuted by the Pope. A Norwegian inquiry into the misappropriation of their government's funds cleared him of all blame and pointed to perjured evidence against him.

But the really amazing statistic that awakens us to a future without poverty is *that he achieved a repayment rate of 97.5 per cent,* truly remarkable for a country beset with floods and disasters. Such a repayment rate is the envy of most banks, even those catering exclusively to the rich. How did he do this and how come wretchedly poor mothers repaid the bank with such extraordinary fidelity? There are several answers. First, the borrowers repay because they and their children may die if they do not. This is their one path out of poverty. If they repay $15 they can borrow $30 next time and then $60 and so on. They will rise to influence in their village and use their judgement to lend to those they trust. It is the intimacy of family-like relationships we examined in Chapters 4 and 6.

The second reason they repay is because they are usually mothers and the survival of their children is in their hands. The money they borrow will go straight to the nourishment of their family, not gambling debts or prostitutes. Moreover, loans are made on condition. Children must be in full-time education, the family roof must be in good repair, the outside toilet at least ten-feet from the house. This helps mothers to be more responsible and guards against both avoidable illness and the elements. But the most remarkable feature is that each borrower must have a support group of five co-signatories, usually women friends of the borrower. They are eligible to borrow at a later date *provided the borrower they are backing has repaid on time.* For this reason they will make sure she does, even lending her money themselves if necessary. They wish to qualify too. Yunus's description of a woman receiving a loan is moving.

> When she receives a $15 loan she is shaking. The money is burning her fingers. Tears roll down from her eyes because she has never seen so much money. She carries it like a delicate bird, until someone tells her to put it into a safe place. She is stunned. She promises she will never let down the institution that so trusted her. She will struggle to see that every penny is paid back. [12]

Yunus, like Raiffeisen and Steiner before him, saw that self-interest and altruism, far from being opposed, could be combined. The poor must be *helped to help themselves* He wrote:

12. Yunus, *Building Social Business*, p. 56.

The entire meaning of what Grameen has preached is that the poor are bankable, that one can lend to them on a commercial basis and make a profit, that banks can and should serve the disinherited of the earth, not only out of altruism but out of self-interest, treating the poor as untouchable, as outcasts, is immoral, indefensible but also financially stupid.[13]

We describe this virtuous circle in Figure 9.2.

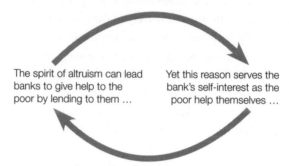

The spirit of altruism can lead banks to give help to the poor by lending to them …

Yet this reason serves the bank's self-interest as the poor help themselves …

Figure 9.2 Altruism and egoism reconciled

What Yunus has essentially done is reconcile spirit with science as Steiner prescribed. He has reconciled altruism with self-interest and lending with being repaid. The importance of repaying is not to be overlooked. The poor are poor not just because they do not *get* enough but because they cannot *give* enough, to family, to friends and to the bank. Just try watching your own children starve and being helpless to prevent this! The simple act of repayment, routine for many of us, is their path to empowerment, what enables them to join the human race and stand on their own two feet. Yunus put the blame for poverty squarely on the banking system itself, saying 'It is not that people are unworthy of credit, it is that banks are unworthy of people.'[14]

While Yunus accepted charitable donations in the earlier years especially from the Ford Foundation, he later decided to forgo all dependency on hand-outs, funding Grameen entirely from its own profits and becoming self-sustaining. He was well on the way to this when his company was removed from his leadership.

The BRAC Foundation is an economic and social development success story originating in Bangladesh but now working in eleven countries including Pakistan, Tanzania, Sri Lanka, Uganda, Liberia, Sierra Leone, Haiti, the

13. Yunus, *Building Social Business,* p. 102.
14. Yunus, *Building Social Business,* p. 6.

Philippines, Afghanistan and South Sudan. Its founder, Sir Dr Fazle Hasan Abed, began as a Bangladeshi social worker, returned to his country to rebuild it after the 1970 cyclone and turned his relief project into an international NGO employing 100,000 people with representation in 69,000 Bangladeshi villages. He has received the Ramon Magsaysay Award, the Clinton Citizen Award and the Olaf Palme Award. He has honorary degrees from Oxford, Columbia, Princeton and Yale, among others. The BRAC Bank and BRAC NGO helped found the Global Alliance.[15]

The truth is that it has always taken more than a driving self-interest to turn the world around. This is true even of America, the home of aggressive self-interest. The Nobel Prize-winning economist Joseph Stiglitz in his book *The Price of Inequality* quotes Cornel West:

> The great movements of America – abolitionism, civil rights movement, feminist movement, anti-homophobic movement – they did not argue that we needed self-interest properly understood. If that was the slogan black folks would be still in Jim Crow, something else was going on. Strong moral forces, strong spiritual forces, linked to stories – about a nation, in terms of national identity, in terms of what it means to be human, our connection to other countries. There's not going to be a matter of self-interest properly understood if it's not informed by very rich stories of the art of living, loving, serving others.[16]

Partly as result of the movements described above and partly as result of the near-collapse of the financial sectors in Wall Street and the City and our seeming inability to fathom what went wrong, there has arisen a whole new vision of finance. The Global Alliance for Banking on Values is one such example. By 2007 Triodos Bank had accumulated €3.2 billion assets under management by funding only businesses which it judged to be of social, cultural and ecological benefit to the world. Its current CEO, Peter Blom, then commenced a dialogue with like-minded financial institutions and banks to create an independent network to deliver social and economic development to people by serving their communities and the environment in a sustainable way. The Alliance is made up of banks from around the world that are determined to benefit humanity. It tries to answer the burning questions, such as, what is wrong with capitalism? What is the current crisis about? It aims to demonstrate via its Principles for Sustainable Banking that there is another path.

15. http://www.brac.net/
16. London: Allen Lane, 2012 p. 73.

Triodos, established in the Netherlands, has a presence in the UK, Belgium, Germany, France and Spain.[17] It gets its name from the Greek for 'three ways' which incorporates the 'triple bottom line' of People, Planet and Profit, first enunciated by John Elkington in 1994.[18] It makes a profit so it can serve people and the planet. Together with the BRAC Bank and ShoreBank Corporation it formed the embryo alliance. ShoreBank was a Chicago-based community development bank and was reconstituted in 2010 as the Urban Partnership Bank with branches in many US cities. A fourth founding bank was GLS in Germany. These banks pledged themselves to Thought Leadership by which they aimed to give to banks a social conscience and environmental awareness. They would express solidarity with those similarly engaged and bring together their CEOs to exchange ideas and best practices, new tools and new structures. Above all, they pledge themselves to 'A shared commitment to find global solutions to international problems.'[19]

At the end of 2014 the Alliance had grown to twenty-five member banks in Europe, North America, Latin America, Asia, Africa and Australia, all growing and all profitable, with combined assets under management of US$ 100 billion. They are situated in thirty countries and serve twenty million people. They include credit unions, sustainable banks and community banks. The aim of the Alliance is to grow to fifty members in the next two years and thence to 100 by 2020. Non-banks and corporations can become Supporting Partners. Members are invited based upon an assessment process undertaken by the Board of the Alliance. Members of the Alliance are listed below.

- Affinity Credit Union, Canada
- Alternative Bank Schweiz, Switzerland
- Assiniboine Credit Union, Canada
- Banca Etica, Italy
- Banco Fie, Bolivia
- BancoSol, Bolivia
- bankmecu, Australia
- Beneficial State Bank, USA

17. www.triodos.nl
18. See John Elkington, *Cannibals with Forks: The Triple Bottom Line,* Oxford: Capstone Books, 1999. Elkington is the founder and director of Volans.
19. See www.gabv.org

- BRAC Bank, Bangladesh
- Centenary Bank, Uganda
- Clean Energy Development Bank, Nepal
- Crédit Coopératif, France
- Cultura Bank, Norway
- Ecology Building Society, UK
- First Green Bank, USA
- GLS Bank, Germany
- Merkur Cooperative Bank, Denmark
- Mibanco, Peru
- New Resource Bank, USA
- SAC Apoyo Integral, El Salvador
- Sunrise Banks, USA
- Triodos Bank, Netherlands
- Vancity, Canada
- Vision Banco, Paraguay
- XacBank, Mongolia

The basic requirement for joining is a desire to improve the quality of life for everyone within a bank's orbit, but this must be achieved by adhering to certain key principles, to which we now turn.

Principle 1: Triple Bottom Line approach

The sequence of people, planet and profit (or prosperity) is important. You strive to improve the lives of your stakeholders and enhance their habitat but unless this turns a profit on a sustainable basis you cannot expand such activities or even sustain them. You must engage with people and with the planet but must also develop your strength to deliver even more over time. The intention to confer benefit must be deliberate, not incidental or accidental and your profitability is never a stand-alone objective but a means to better service delivery. Human needs are paramount and must be served.

In short, the triple objectives are integrated and reconciled. Your profits come from serving people and the planet and members must demonstrate that they are accomplishing this. It is genuine wealth creation in which all parties benefit. The Alliance uses the term 'the real economy' with great frequency. It tells us that they do not think of banking as an industry independent of others but as a service to them.

Principle 2: The Real Economy

Projects must be grounded in the community and serve the real economy. The value of grounding in the community was seen in Yunus's conditions for a bank loan: children in full-time education, roofs mended, toilets at a distance, each borrower vouched for by five friends. Banks which cannot afford loan officers often use village councils and elders. They lend their money to these and let them lend it in turn to the most trustworthy people in the village and of course their knowledge is much better than that of a loan officer asking applicants to fill out a form and sometimes coaching them to lie! Elders have years of experience in who can be trusted with money and who cannot. The communities of the poor are much closer and better informed. Village elders may prefer to repay from their own pockets in cases where they have made mistakes. They need to keep loans coming.

Generally speaking, poor people are much more community-oriented. They only have each other and frequently emancipate themselves as a group. Moreover, there is remarkable unanimity in what they need. Basic wants are much the same. They all need nutrition, a living wage, training, skills, etc. Any improvement in these touches millions of them. As Yunus found, it took only thirty cents apiece to triple the wages of the women he initially helped. *The poor pay more because they are vulnerable* and because they are preyed upon. Even the vestige of a fair deal leaves them considerably better off.[20] It cost Yunus very little to stop those women starving. Given their desperate circumstances, they will be fiercely loyal to any help that aids their survival.

It is interesting that the Alliance uses the phrase 'the real economy'. They clearly know that certain people do genuine work for others and that banks are there to facilitate this, not help themselves to the money. We will see that most of their work is lending and deposit taking in personal relations with customers, not the alphabet soup of derivatives or speculative ventures. That the Rabo Bank (not a member of the Alliance but operating in many ways with similar principles to Alliance members) emerged better from the recession than any other Dutch bank testifies to their devotion to the farming communities which they served and the relative absence of speculative activities. This leads us to the third principle to which Alliance banks must pledge themselves.

20. A point made by Muhammad Yunus and supported by C. K. Prahalad.

Principle 3: Banks must be client centred

You get to know and to support your customers long-term and seek to understand their business activities. In an industry where loans are sold on to second, third and nth parties, relationships are attenuating. They do not care what happens to you. Why should they? The digital revolution consigns the cashier to the scrap heap and reduces the customer to an electronic signature. The less you see of him/her the more money you save. Relationships are expensive and time consuming. For many, banking is a relationship with ATM machines and computers.

When Alliance members speak they insist that banks should not pretend to be heroes like the Masters of the Universe proclaimed by the world's leading investment banks. Banks are facilitators, but vital facilitators, in getting money to where it is most needed. 'We bring value to customers' lives', states one GABV video. 'We seek a zero-waste society' claims another.[21] Clearly these banks are the long-term partners of those interested in green energy, waste treatment, recycling, better farming methods, and so on. Shared concern for such causes means that customers cannot be exploited without damaging the cause which unites them with their bank. This is a super-ordinate goal to which your relationship is dedicated.

Principle 4: Long-term resilience

This principle refers to the possibility of sudden collapse when banks speculate, play the markets or rely on asset prices in an indebted economy. The traditional role of banks, lending money, taking deposits and managing funds is far less volatile than the fancy operations in the world's casino and trying to rig markets in your favour by bets that skew the odds. Genuine innovation is risky enough without additional gambles. Routine banking services need not be boring; if your customer is helping to improve the world there will be thrills enough. If you do not genuinely know your customer then all you have is a fair weather friend or a marriage of convenience. Given a dip in the market they will all run out on you, cut off your credit and call in their loans. Exclusive self-interest spreads like wildfire so that the whole system becomes volatile. Yet even in a recession customers still make deposits and seek loans. This sector of the market is far less volatile and far more sustainable. We will show numbers which suggest that members who later formed the Alliance survived the recession in far better shape than other financial institutions.

21. See videos on GABV website, www.gabv.org/

Principle 5: Governance is transparent and inclusive of all stakeholders

Alliance banks have customers and environmentalists on their boards that share information widely and report separately on each of the triple bottom lines, with information derived from customer activity and the social impacts these have made. For example, a few weekends each year, one of the alliance member banks, Vancity in Vancouver, Canada, organizes transparent 'Cash Mobs' for their members to 'swarm' to new and innovative businesses where the bank is an investor. For a new restaurant or small business this is a vital lifeline and kickstart for early cash-flow that can be used for reinvestment or dividends; for the community, it is a way to know where the social and environmentally minded businesses are springing up. What needs to succeed is *the entire ecosystem:* employees, suppliers, customers, contractors, the community and the environment. Benefits to such parties become a condition of the loan and are ethically and legally binding. Information is *not* sent exclusively to shareholders but all parties are kept informed. Growth occurs via a concerted push by all protagonists.

Principle 6: All five of the previous principles must be *culturally embedded within the banking organization*

They are not coerced into doing this by regulations, fines and penalties like those levied on our largest banks by the authorities, but make voluntary undertakings to achieve strategic aims which are the conscience and the character of the organization itself. All employees pledge themselves to bring this about by cooperative efforts. This is a challenge rather than an easy task and ways must be found to develop the human resources needed. This requires innovation not just by the bank's customers but by the bank itself in discovering best practices in this new field of endeavour and spreading the word. How cheaply it can lend depends on the successes of the path-finders and the adoption of these practices by others.

In a very real way this culture is the *mirror image* of the big bank culture, a phenomenon we discussed in Chapters 2 and 4. While large banks make money out of industry by milking the cash cow, the Alliance makes industry out of money and helps nurture star players. While large banks make money *directly* by wresting this from their own customers, the Alliance creates wealth *indirectly* by building up its community of stakeholders, taking their deposits and giving them loans. The large banks represent shareholder capitalism. The Alliance represents stakeholder capitalism.

Large banks compete promiscuously to take advantage of others; the Alliance cooperates to make the whole community ecosystem more resilient and self-sustaining. The large banks strive to make the whole world adhere to the Washington Consensus and the Anglo-American model of capitalism while the Alliance champions diversity and creates dialogues among nations, of which the recent Paris conference and the earlier Berlin Declaration was an example. The large banks exercise power *over* other players, appropriating the lion's share of the proceeds, the Alliance exercises power *through* other players, strengthening them and hence itself in a system of interdependence.

Alliance cultures also steer themselves by the use of reporting frameworks to measure degrees of success and impact and their levels of attainment. It is part of the culture that these 'non-financial goals' are met and then raised even higher in the period following.

5. Aiming for the greatest social and economic impact

It almost beggars belief that catering to people with *less* money could produce better returns than catering to people with *more* money and yet there is a 'Fortune at the bottom of the pyramid' as C. K. Prahalad, among others, has pointed out.[22] Populations may be poor individually but because of their sheer numbers poor people form the broad base of a pyramid so that social and economic impacts can be massive. If you drop your price by a few cents demand leaps from thousands to millions. For example the Aravind Eye Hospital in India removes the cataracts that grow over the eyes of tens of thousands of people. These patients have very little money. Yet a laser gun in the hands of a surgeon can remove these cataracts in a few minutes or less.

By setting up on an industrial scale the cost of the operation can be brought down to less than US$50 per person and middle class Indians and medical tourists are charged enough so that poor Indians are treated free and profits can still be earned. This operation also makes the previously blind person employable and releases the blind person's carer so the combined social impact is huge. Visitors fly in from the whole world to avail themselves of this service which costs more than US$1,000 for each eye in the West. A poor community makes for the leanest and the lowest cost production which can then attract everyone who earns more.

Or take the fact that salt loses its iodine content in transport. A cheap spray made by Hindustani Lever in India stops this loss for just pennies and some quarter of a million children are saved from being born with disabilities

22. C. K. Prahalad, *The Fortune and the bottom of the Pyramid,* Upper Saddle River NJ: Pearson Education, 2010.

due to insufficient iodine. How much money this saves the Indian nation is simply incalculable but it clearly contributes to its seven per cent plus growth rate. A disinfectant hand-soap also made by this company reduces typhus and cholera rates. Joint efforts by the government and the company to increase public hygiene through hand-washing may have saved hundreds of thousands of lives. The benefits are near-incalculable. Flush toilets, which we generally take for granted, are estimated to *double life expectancy.* A bridge across a river may save a million people and many businesses from taking a two-hour detour. It saves a community millions.

No wonder then that economic growth is so high in the early stages of economic development, when the first roads, railways and bridges are built. Which is the fastest growing economy in the world? The answer is NOT China, although its 7.40 per cent on such a large base is truly impressive. China is actually tenth. The fastest growing economy is South Sudan with 23.7 per cent. Also ahead of China are Ebola-ravaged Sierra Leone, 13.3 per cent, Paraguay twelve per cent, and Mongolia 11.80 per cent (the two latter have Alliance banks) Laos, 8.3 per cent, Liberia 8.1 per cent and Ivory Coast eight per cent (the latter two despite Ebola) while India and Tajikistan are level with China.[23] Economic growth also jumped after the Second World War in both Germany and Japan.

What all these have in common is *infrastructure building or rebuilding* (in the case of Germany and Japan). Like the bridge we cited, roads, railways, schools, hospitals and buildings multiply wealth. Buildings are at least three times more valuable with improved road and rail access and with proximity to schools, shops and hospitals. Any one of these developments serves an entire community but *collectively* they multiply each other's worth exponentially. To be a banker to a region with such growth rates could offer a bonanza to all concerned. Profitability is, if anything, more likely.

In Chapter 5 we looked at catalytic technologies, those which improve the performance of *other* technologies. Mobile phones are responsible for thousands of entrepreneurs, so no wonder Yunus distributed them free, in some cases. Ten people can use a phone for one hour a day for a very small charge and become ten times more effective than before. Generally speaking, infrastructure improves exponentially. A single pipe under large curb stones by the road edge can carry several utilities and the road does not have to be dug up at intervals to find faults, mend them and then repair the road! Faults can be traced electronically. The countable benefits are large but even more significant can be those that are incalculable because they touch all lives in the community.

23.   see www.economic.growthrates

An increasingly popular movement is *social impact investing*. The prime aim of the Alliance banks is to make the largest possible impact on the social environment and *then gauge the returns from this*. There is good reason to believe that looking at the social impact *first*, especially as this ramifies through the community, will give you a much better idea of the true returns from a given activity. Take companies listed on the UK's Social Stock Exchange. Accsys treats wood to make it last longer and doubles its useful life. This pays us in myriad ways, because wood is renewable, because alternatives lead to CO_2 emissions, because window frames and doors made of treated wood do not swell, rot, shrink or buckle, because trees renew our atmosphere, create oxygen and waste nothing. Indeed the benefits from this activity are almost immeasurable, even when what we *can* measure more than justifies what we do. HaloSource removes impurities from water, an increasingly scarce resource, so that the same water can be recycled several times and safely drunk. Given the danger to all wildlife by encroaching humans and increasingly turbulent conditions of drought and flood, such companies could save both human and animal lives.[24]

The Darden School of Business at the University of Virginia has set up courses on social impact investing as part of its MBA curriculum, an initiative sponsored by students, and this has been adopted by the Finance faculty. It is challenging other business schools to come up with ideal customers. Darden is the home of R. Edward Freeman whom we encountered in Chapter 3 and whose Olson Centre for Applied Ethics champions stakeholding. A report by the Monitor organization in 2009 estimated that impact investing would increase from US$50 billion to US$500 billion by 2019. It is well on its way. The Norwegian Norfund and Britain's Commonwealth Development Corporation are major world investors. According to GIIN (Global Impact Investing Network) Britain's Alternative Investments grew by 1,000 per cent in 2014. Philip Morris is busy suing poorer governments in the Third World for impeding its cigarette sales. There is a special fund created to stand up to them and to counter-sue using national cancer rates and associated costs to challenge their case.

Alliance banks have among their aims the social empowerment of communities. In 2015 it announced the launch of a Sustainability | Finance | Real Economies Fund (SFRE – pronounced Sapphire). 'SFRE is the first global open-ended investment company created to deploy substantial amounts of long-term capital to support the growing segment of banks focused on serving individuals and enterprises in the real economy whilst delivering a triple bottom line of prosperity, planet and people.' SFRE was initiated by

24. socialstockexchange.com

the Global Alliance for Banking on Values to meet the growth capital needs of values-based banks, and expand their impact and reach.[25] This fund was established solely for private capital and is independent of public development finance institutions. At its launch and celebration at the Paris meeting of Alliance members during March 2015, the Alliance announced that investors had already committed over US$40 million to SFRE. It is expected to reach US$100 million by the end of 2015 and has an ambition to mobilize up to US$1 billion over the next ten years.

SFRE is a Luxembourg based investment company, headed by CEO, Jim Prouty. MicroVest Capital Management, LLC acts as portfolio manager for SFRE investments. Key Partners include: Enclude Capital Advisory UK Limited which served as adviser to the GABV and acts as placement agent to SFRE; Crestbridge Management Company S.A. which is the Alternative Investment Fund Manager (AIFM); and Clifford Chance which serves as legal counsel.

6. GABV banks out-perform the largest banks in the world on several measures

Could it *possibly* be that this clutch of banks, of which few of us have ever heard, which are located, in many cases, in Third World countries, could out-perform the likes of Bank of America, JP Morgan, Goldman Sachs, Morgan Stanley, ING Bank, Deutsche Bank, BNP Paribas Citi Bank, HSBC, Credit Suisse, Barclays Bank, the Bank of China? Research sponsored by the Alliance is both extraordinary and encouraging.[26] Latest figures from the GABV show that the average Alliance member bank has a compound annual growth rate of 9.7 per cent in loans and 17.3 per cent in assets over the five years since the inception of the GABV in 2009. And employees in Alliance banks have grown from just over 22,000 to nearly 31,000 in the same period. Proof that the values-based banking approach is not only viable but sustainable.

Let us look at the very obvious advantages possessed by the world's largest banks. They can afford four to ten times the level of salaries, which the large banks insist are essential to prevent them going into a 'death spiral'.

---

25. SFRE Fund press release and press pack http://www.gabv.org/our-news/ sustainability-finance-real-economies.

26. 2014 GABV Annual Report http://www.gabv.org/our-news/the-gabv-launches-its-first-annual-report. See also: GABV Research: Real Economy – Real Returns: The Business Case for Sustainability Focused Banking, http://www.gabv.org/wp-content/uploads/Real-Economy-Real-Returns-GABV-Research-2014.pdf.

If large salaries are indeed essential to effective banking and to the adequate motivation of bankers then the GABV is, in comparison, a clutch of small-time visionaries who do not have a prayer of approximating the levels of performance and effectiveness of the big boys. Then there is the fact that large banks have a vast amount of market power. They can bet their multinational customers' money and if the risk stands up, add their own funds to this. Their stakes are large enough to skew the odds in their favour and create a rise in the share price so they can then sell. They are an oligopoly and can and do raise their charges. They organize and assist those *already wealthy;* a process that one might consider can hardly go wrong. They have the world's greatest achievers as their customers and on their side. They can afford the most up-to-date equipment and attract the best brains to work for them and buy up the best talent in the world. They have had Nobel Prize winning mathematicians working for them. Who could possibly match such financial acumen?

They have vast asymmetries of knowledge compared to their own retail customers and with small businesses. They obfuscate bank charges so these cannot be compared, have targeted naïve customers for their own gain, sold them 'protection' when there was nothing to protect and have received billions from taxpayers. They fund the election campaigns of Senators and members of Congress and employ five lobbyists for each law-maker. Surely comparing these powerful worthies with a bunch of tree-huggers and do-gooders is absurd. Was there ever so uneven a contest?

But we should not jump to hasty conclusions. Being located in places like Paraguay or Mongolia may not be a disadvantage given the national growth rates of their real economies. We saw in Chapter 2 that high pay-for-performance *lowered* innovation and that those with vision and meaning in their lives who were *intrinsically* rather than extrinsically motivated fared far better. We saw that large areas of the financial sector were zero-sum so that winners snatch money from losers but the sector as a whole does not gain. We argued that money cannot create money but must first be transformed into goods and services. Does it help to expand at a cost to the real economy when your derivatives and financial products are abstractions *from* and ultimately rely *on* that economy? When asset prices plunge so do the big banks! Does it help to have the mightiest multinationals on your side when these are bureaucratic, hated by much of the public and are losing jobs and market share to smaller companies which are more agile, as explained in Chapter 6?

Large banks do exploit customers and wrest their monies from them, but is that in their long-term interests? Would not smarter, nurtured customers borrow and save more? If the customers prospered would not the banks prosper too? If charges could be compared would not competition work better? If they failed to corrupt the judgement of legislators might bankers not adapt better to the future? If financial advisers are so brilliant why do over half of them fail to beat the Dow Jones averages? This has nothing to do with their personal failings, around half of them are bound to fail and *will always do so because the system is zero-sum.* Their cleverness is self-cancelling. The Nobel Laureate in mathematics may eclipse the Senior Wrangler. Speculation makes a loser of half the population, with casino owners taking a further cut. Why did Long Term Capital Management and its Nobel Laureate go bust? Is not a casino of *any* kind a huge waste of money and a trap for those addicted to money? Is defeating environmental laws in our long-term interests? As for receiving tax-payers' money, was this not for failure rather than success? All in all we might be rash in dismissing the Alliance and what it stands for in favour of the status quo.

In the results shown in Table 9.1 SFB stands for Sustainability Focused Banks and GSIFI stands for Global Systematically Important Financial Institutions. As we shall see, the former more than hold their own. We must judge GABV banks by what they hoped and aimed to attain when compared to the failings, as they saw them, of the largest banks in the world. There were four contrasts:

1. The support provided by the bank to the real economy.
2. The resilience of the bank in the face of economic challenges.
3. The returns provided by the bank to society, clients and investors.
4. The growth of the bank so that its activities expand its impact.

Large banks do not transparently report their speculative activities even to shareholders so there was no way of measuring the fact that GABV members did less of this. However it was possible to measure the extent to which all banks attended to the task of lending and taking deposits as a ratio of their total activities as a proxy for exposure to speculative activities. These differences were marked.

Table 9.1 Comparing the performance of SFBs (Sustainability Focused Banks) and GSIFIs (Global Systematically Important Financial Institutions)

		2013	2008	2003
Ratio of loans to	SFIBs	76.2%	76.0%	77.1%
total assets	GSIFIs	40.5%	38.8%	43.4%
Ratio of deposits	SFBs	80.4%	71.5%	71.4%
to total assets	GSIFIs	48.8%	42.0%	47.3%

It is clear from these figures that members of the Alliance 'stuck to their knitting', the basic job of the bank to take deposits and make loans to businesses and people, while for large banks this was less than fifty per cent of their balance sheets. The research covers the members of the Alliance on an individual basis throughout all years, even prior to the creation of the Alliance. They therefore exhibit the characteristics that led them to become a member of the Alliance. Note that in the financial bull-market up to 2008 large banks let their loan business fall five per cent and their deposit business fall five per cent, yet chastened by the recession this has climbed back nearly two per cent in regard to loans and to fully six per cent in regard to deposits. We also see that loans are stable for Alliance members while deposits climb steadily by nine per cent. This is evidence of less volatility and less liquidity risk.

We next turn to the subject of capital comparisons through key ratios. These are set out in Table 9.2.

Table 9.2 Capital comparisons between SFBs and GSIFIs

Capital comparisons		2013	2009	2003
Equity/total assets	SFBs	7.7%	7.3%	6.2%
	GSIFIs	6.6%	5.0%	5.2%
RWA/total assets	SFBs	60.9%	60.5%	not meaningful
	GSIFIs	39.8%	41.0%	
Tier 1 ratio/total assets	SFBs	12.4%	11.6%	
	GSIFIs	13.3%	10.1%	

SFBs hold more equity as a percentage of total assets which is considered safer. If banks put their own capital at risk, not just that of other people, they will behave more responsibly. The usual objection to this is that they will lend less but as we have seen, SFBs lend more and speculate less. GSIFIs fared slightly better until the bubble burst in the 2008 crash but then lost ground. Risk-weighted average measures the bank's own estimates of how much risk it is bearing, with US Treasury bonds given zero rating and sub-prime mortgages a much higher rating, although the models used up to 2008 gravely underestimated this risk. Risk models also fail to estimate the peril to the *entire system* and are widely criticized.

Risks also vary very much in quality. The risks taken by the SFBs are those of innovating and attempts to save the environment by as yet untried measures. Risks taken by large banks on say, junk bonds, are attempts to earn higher margins for shareholders. We see above that SFBs take potentially higher risks with no evident penalty, possibly as a result of their strong connections with their clients. Tier 1 is another measure of how much of one's own equity is at risk. Before 2009 large banks risked less of their own equity. Today they risk slightly more.

In Table 9.3 we turn to the subject of return on assets and again the SFBs acquit themselves well.

Table 9.3 Returns on assets

		2009–13	2003–13
Return on assets	SFBs	0.66%	0.68%
	GSIFIs	0.46%	0.58%
Standard deviation around mean	SFBs	0.16%	0.30%
	GSFIs	0.20%	0.35 %
Return on equity	SFBs	8.6%	9.2%
	GSIFIs	7.6%	10.3%
Standard deviation	SFBs	2.4%	3.7%
	GSIFIs	3.8%	7.9%

Return on total assets for the SFBs was also better than the GSIFIs at 0.66 per cent to 0.46 per cent. This was also true of the decade of 2003 to 2013, although the difference is smaller. The standard deviation from the mean is less for SFBs, pointing to the lower volatility of the latter. Volatility is a threat to sustainability.

Return on equity after the crash of 2008 is a full point higher for the SFBs, but the GSIFIs still did a little better in the run up to 2008, in the bubble that burst with the collapse of Lehman Brothers. Their overall score for the decade of 2003 to 2013 is one percentage point higher but that result needs to be considered within the context of much higher leverage and risk. Once again the SFBs are more sustainable with less volatility as shown in a standard deviation 1.4 per cent lower. Notice also how much better the SFBs rode out the crisis of 2008. Their standard deviation was only 3.7 per cent while that of the large banks was 7.9 per cent, over twice as high and a major shock to the global economy in which trillions disappeared. The Chinese and Islamic banks were also relatively stable at that time.

Finally we come to the growth figures for these companies. GSIFIs are already huge and it is probably harder to manage very big companies with representation in many nations. HSBC's latest scandal had to do with its recently acquired Swiss operations. Moreover, small companies are often in an early growth phase. So we might reasonably expect SFBs to be growing faster than the existing giants. Moreover *unless* SFBs grow fast they will mount but a feeble challenge to the status quo. If they are ever to change the dominant mode of banking in the world they are going to have to gather strength, a lot of it. Yet the numbers speak for themselves.

Table 9.4 Compound annual growth rates

		2009–13	2003–13
Loans	SFBs	13.2%	9.3%
	GSIFIs	3.8%	8.3%
Deposits	SFBs	15.3%	10.4%
	GSIFIs	4.9%	9.4%
Assets	SFBs	12.9%	9.0%
	GSIFIs	0.7%	8.5%
Equity	SFBs	13.8%	10.8%
	GSIFIs	8.6%	11.0%
Total Income	SFBs	8.5%	6.4%
	GSIFIs	6.5%	6.4%

Although it appears that the Alliance is mounting a formidable challenge we must beware of high growth figures on a much smaller initial base. A huge bank growing at three per cent could stay indefinitely ahead of a much smaller one growing at ten per cent. It could even be widening its lead. It is quite clear that if we were to regard only the figures on the right, those between 2003 and 2013, the SFBs are not growing fast enough to make any real difference and are probably falling further behind. Yet the figures on the left generated *after* 2008 tell a different story. *Loans* are nearly four times higher, deposits also. Assets are two and a half times higher and so on.

Moreover, it appears that the crisis of 2008 was very much a watershed. Since that date there has been a sharp rise in values-based banking and the movement has yet to break cover and make its appeal to the wider public. There has been little media attention thus far. It only *began* in 2009 with a few members and its progress to date has been impressive. On 23 October 2014, Alliance members collaborated online to add local voices from over twenty countries to the GABV's growing global movement through the I Am #BankingOnValues campaign.

This social media campaign was the first international awareness effort by the Alliance, combining online and offline engagement activities to prompt thought about the relationship between banking, the economy, the environment and society and stimulate conversation about values-based banking. Successes included more than 7,500 social media posts and 8.8 million impressions using the #BankingOnValues hashtag. The campaign had a high level of member participation with more than ninety per cent of Alliance members joining the conversation. I Am #BankingOnValues also garnered media attention in at least six countries and saw the launch of a new YouTube video with more than 3,600 views. Several members also held local events to complement the global campaign, furthering their own connections with their clients, members, shareholders and the wider public. This pilot campaign received very positive feedback and will run again on 22 October 2015.

It is not necessary that the larger banks be defeated or displaced by Alliance members. It is enough to establish that one can serve people, planet and prosperity without suffering *any diminution of earnings,* or even doing better. One can serve a higher good and make a difference through one's work without sacrificing one's own income and impoverishing one's own family. Nice guys need not finish last. *You can create wealth through serving more than yourself.* There is another way to live, to work and to invest and this is economically viable and ethically satisfying. That is surely the point.

Conclusion

This chapter has featured issues previously addressed in this book. This includes an orientation to creating wealth in the real economy and using money as a means to create industry (Introduction). It renews the vows of our Puritan ancestors to build God's Kingdom on this earth and turn his word into an ethical code (Chapter 1). It aims to curb our runaway individualism and addiction to abstract numbers indicted in Chapter 2. It qualifies the rights of shareholders with those of other stakeholders and aims to emancipate whole communities and their environments (Chapter 3). It is the mirror image reversal of our conventional values, putting the whole before the parts, the community before its members, sharing above gaining, power *through* customers above power *over* them. It extols personal and intimate relations in the manner of the fast-growing Chinese culture (Chapter 4).

It aims not to 'win' or 'beat' conventional banking at its own game but to *improve the game of banking itself* and have it serve the sustainable industry on which it relies (Chapter 5). Like the *Mittelstand* it has all the advantages of smallness and of being to human scale with admiration for feats of human growth and innovation (Chapter 6). Above all it *consciously* aims to improve human health and happiness by benefiting all stakeholders (Chapter 7) and has similar results to show. It is dedicated to the long-term, to Tomorrow's Child, to the preservation of our planet, to zero-waste and a more harmonious universe (Chapter 8). It seeks to use and promote advanced knowledge and creates an intelligent universe similar to the Cambridge Phenomena and its ever-crossing diverse disciplines (Chapter 10). We *must* direct funds to where these do most good and free King Midas from his golden tomb. Like all addicts, those hooked on money have found a poor substitute for being loved. The best distributors must sustain the very finest contributors. We started with John Maynard Keynes; let us end with him:

> The decadent international but individualistic capitalism in the hands of which we found ourselves after the war is not a success. It is not intelligent. It is not beautiful. It is not just. It is not virtuous and it does not deliver the goods.[27]

---

27. *National Self-sufficiency* (1933) Section 3. See also: Elizabeth Johnson and Donald Moggridge (eds) *Collected Writings of John Maynard Keynes*, Volume 11, Cambridge University Press, 1982.

CHAPTER 10

The 'Cambridge Phenomenon':
Pure science and filthy lucre

With few exceptions, entrepreneurs who start successful businesses don't do so to maximize profits. Of course they want to make money, but that is not what drives most of them. They are inspired to do something that they believe needs doing. The heroic story of free enterprise capitalism is one of entrepreneurs using their dreams and passion as fuel to create extraordinary value for customers, team members, suppliers, society, and investors.[1]

In this chapter, we look to the New Entrepreneurialism, which is based on ever-expanding knowledge. It is this that could reinvigorate the British and American economies. We will look at Cambridge University and take a glance at Harvard University. We have chosen these two because they reveal the underlying theme of a policy that could halt our decline: high status cultural activities must rescue lower status activities on which they depend.

If consuming is granted higher status than producing, then consumers have it in their power to champion favoured producers. If knowledge workers are of higher status than manufacturers, then the former should ensure that manufactured goods are full of knowledge. If 'pure' research is elevated above grubbing for money, then consider just how much *more* research you might do were the money more forthcoming! Wealth creation is a synthesis. Add the

---

1.   Mackey and Sisodia, *Conscious Capitalism.*

owners of silver mines to Aeschylus and Sophocles, add the Medici bankers to Michelangelo and Galileo, and the world is reborn.

If Britain and America, armed with the English language, can produce much of the world's theatre, films and broadcasting, and they do, then they also have the unrivalled power to make business activities once more noble, inspiring, exciting and adventurous. By showing wealth creation for what it is, the exercise of conscience, the bestowing of gifts on our fellow beings and the creation of climates of trust, they can push these values to the forefront of public consciousness. We could even recreate the visions in the minds of entrepreneurs, make them perform before our eyes and solicit crowdfunding (see Chapter 11) to help them take off. There is no want of excellent examples, as this chapter will show. Can we learn to celebrate wealth creation?

The city of Cambridge and its university is an example of total transformation within a third of a century. A very similar transformation is being planned at Harvard's Allston campus which, if successful, will alter higher education and its contribution to wealth profoundly. Cambridge was, until quite recently, a sleepy market town and a leading science university eight centuries old, which Britain's industrial revolution had passed by with barely the wave of a hand. It was rural, tranquil, near-monastic in its separation from the wider world. Many were determined to keep it so. Sir Arthur Marshall, founder of the airport at Cambridge, described the town as 'one of the last places in the world that anyone would consider for major industrial development'.[2]

As recently as 1950, William Holfor and H. Myles Wright, expert planning advisers to Cambridge County Council, recommended a 'resolute effort to slow down migration into the Cambridge district and to reduce the high rate of growth'. This proposal was endorsed by both county and city authorities. Henceforth, an Industrial Development Certificate would be needed before anyone could employ more than five people and many applications for such a certificate were rejected. The attitude that industry was a form of pollution could not have been more baldly stated. Scientist and novelist, C. P. Snow, quotes the Master of Jesus College when told that trains would henceforth run to Cambridge on a Sunday: 'It is as displeasing to God as to myself.'[3]

And yet, in 1960, a significant event occurred that would later turn the tide, Tim Eiloart, Rodney Dale and David Southward set up Cambridge

2.   Quoted by Kate Kirk and Charles Cotton, *The Cambridge Phenomenon: 50 years of innovation and enterprise*, London: Third Millennium Publishing, 2013.

3.   C. P. Snow, from the Rede Lecture *The Two Cultures*, Cambridge University Press, 2001.

Consultants. The Ministry of Supply had financed their degrees, so they could hardly despise industry. Their mission was to 'put the brains of Cambridge University at the disposal of the problems of British industry' – which was widely seen as failing. We should not be confused by the word 'consultant'. These were not the usual kind of consultants but experts in technology transfer to industry. They were advocates for a new form of development and their output was largely written reports including some designs and prototypes. [4]

These reports were prepared for the Ministry of Defence and for large engineering and manufacturing companies and described opportunities in the Cambridge area for economic development. Harold Wilson had been elected prime minister in 1964, and had popularized the sound-bite 'the white heat of the technological revolution', a curious phrase confusing steel-making with much cleaner information technology, but it nonetheless offered some encouragement. Wilson's Labour government donated computer-aided design (CAD) equipment to the university a few years later.

While Cambridge Consultants had been an able midwife at the birth of several companies, its young enthusiasts lacked management skills and profit motives. In 1972 it became part of US management consultancy firm, Arthur D. Little, from which it gained access to professional management support and international markets. Cambridge Consultants became Arthur D. Little's European HQ. In the meantime, two employees at Cambridge Consultants, Gordon Edge and Roy Hawkins, frustrated by foreign ownership, had established relations with the PA Consulting Group, as a result of which Cambridge won its second major advocate for technological development of the area. Edge then led a group leaving PA Technology (PAT), part of PA Consulting Group, in the mid-1980s when it refused to back spin-outs; companies which are independent in their business operations but connected by science and technology to their progenitor. Edge then founded Scientific Generics, the region's third 'consultancy'. The Technology Partnership was the fourth, two years later.

Another major spur to the development now known as the Cambridge Phenomenon was the development of the CAD Centre. Access to CAD equipment not only meant that companies could produce computerized prototypes, but also *simulations* of proposed ventures, which could be shared with employees, customers, investors and so on. All innovation is prone to error; after all, it is something being done for the first time. The more errors that can be caught and corrected at the simulation stage, the less costly they are to rectify. The CAD Centre was privatized in 1983 and bought out by its employees in 1994.

4.   Kirk and Cotton, *Cambridge Phenomenon.*

But the advocates of new technologies, written up in reports intended to precipitate action, were facing considerable frustration. For the most part their clients wanted to watch not to act, to be in touch and in the know but not in the lead. Even when monies were located and partners found the habit was to stall. The advocates for new science-based technologies began to take their own fervent advice and act on what they had long advocated. Cambridge Consultants is widely credited as being a major catalyst for the Cambridge Phenomenon. Today, 1,575 high-tech companies are located in the Cambridge area, employing 57,140 people; their total revenue is £11.8 billion and their combined value is £50 billion.[5] Unemployment in the area is less than two per cent. Wages are well above average, exports are booming and major corporations, including Microsoft and GlaxoSmithKline, have moved in. What dynamic has propelled the Cambridge Phenomenon? This chapter examines the drivers behind it.

In the first place values of pure vs. applied research which had been invidiously compared for centuries had to have their mutual revulsion healed. Lucre had to cease being filthy. It was consultancies beginning with scholarship, turning to advocacy and finally acting for themselves that helped to turn the tide. There had to be new ways of getting needed funds from distributors to contributors. Banks were not really up to it. Entrepreneurship is dogged by the failure of more than two thirds of its attempts. A way and a reason had to be found to persist.

When these efforts were harnessed to the collegial knowledge network of crossed and converging disciplines things began to move. A sleeping giant had awakened. The issues had been turned back to front. Now problems and opportunities vied with disciplines for the attention of highly educated persons. Education was not just about disciplines being developed but about opportunities being seized and problems solved with the help of several disciplines.

What makes Cambridge a potentially more interesting model than Silicon Valley or Route 128 around Harvard is that the clusters are more numerous and that the life sciences predominate, not just electronics. There is the possibility of thinking about business organically and developmentally and celebrating what is alive. As usual, our model is cyclical or actually helical since its elements are part of a growth process (see Figure 10.1, opposite). It reveals the order in which events unfolded. We will consider the elements of this cycle in turn.

5.   Elizabeth Garnsey, Powerpoint presentation at Institute for Manufacturing, Cambridge University, 2013.

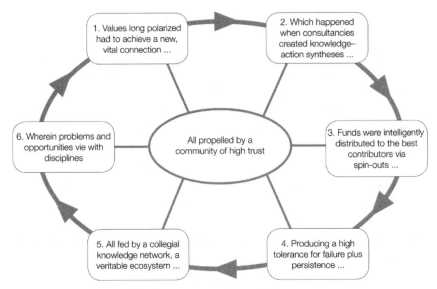

Figure 10.1 The growth of an inquiring knowledge system

Values long polarized at last connected

In October 1975, Richard Milner wrote an article in the *Sunday Times* describing Metals Research's move to Cambridge; the headline read 'Marrying pure science to filthy lucre'.[6] This attitude to business was not merely common but endemic. What kills innovation is one value determined to subordinate another so that they never fuse creatively. If researchers are 'too good' for money, they'll be starved of it.

Why is it that pure research is seen as so virtuous and money so filthy, and why did Oxford and Cambridge Universities allow a whole industrial revolution to pass them by, while for the most part disapproving of it? The poet Matthew Arnold called Oxford 'the Adorable Dreamer whose heart has been so romantic – a haven from the purely practical'.[7] C. P. Snow recalled that, at Oxford, 'we took great pride in the fact that what we did could not be of the slightest use to anyone. The more assured we could be of this the better.'[8] What contributes to this extraordinary bias?

6.   Kirk and Cotton, *Cambridge Phenomenon*.

7.   Matthew Arnold, *Culture and Anarchy* (1869), Oxford University Press, reissue 2009.

8.   Snow, *Two Cultures*.

It is derivative of the imbalances we examined in earlier chapters. If you value individuality above community and competition above cooperation (see Chapter 2), then pure research is perhaps the greatest freedom a scholar can enjoy. There is no requirement to cooperate, you can follow wherever your research leads you and be completely free from any expectation that you will give something back to the community. You have tenure, complete autonomy, and owe responsibility to your discipline and little else. It is a 'perfect' embodiment of freedom.

Cambridge is also a science university so that nature's universal rules are what the scholars are committed to uncovering, God's laws. This is a sacred quest for would-be saints investigating the celestial clock as we saw in Chapter 1. You are actually discovering the laws of the universe. There is nothing that should distract you from a task of such import, least of all the exigencies of daily life and the demands of commerce! Lesser beings must confine themselves to what will sell and to exploiting what has already been discovered. The pure researcher is the platonic guardian of universal forms. Unfortunately, conscience-before money leads to its antithesis, money-before-conscience, an attitude that characterizes the City and Wall Street. The idea that self-interest or disinterested discovery must be pursued at all costs, each without contamination by the other, tends to impede the funds needed for innovation.

There is no purer achievement than academic achievement, no freedom or individuality more perfect than the pursuit of your own hypotheses. The world is viewed from the top of the abstraction ladder. It is not too surprising that the wider world is seen as subverting a state of grace, that Cambridge has for centuries distanced itself from an otherwise sinful world. There are more Nobel Prize winners, nominated by their own disciplines in Trinity College than there are in the whole of France. You go 'up' to Cambridge or Oxford, dine if you are fortunate enough at High Table and then come 'down' when your studies are complete.

To be genuinely innovative, these paradoxes must be confronted and resolved. If you can discover a 'pure law' that is also of practical use, then you will not want for support and patronage. And there is no limit to the money that will be showered on you and which can be used in part to again pursue pure knowledge.

We have to break the habit of mind that consigns applied knowledge to a vulgar collaboration with commerce. It is as legitimate to start with a problem or an opportunity as to start with a discipline, especially as problems and opportunities *cross* disciplines.

Figure 10.2 The reconciliation of pure and applied knowledge

There is another major paradox underlying our educational system that greatly reduces its innovative capacity. The vast majority of university courses are *discipline-centred*. Nobel Prize winners, for example, are nominated by their disciplines. Academics are judged by their contribution to their discipline and by their articles in refereed journals. Knowledge grows out of disciplines and is *then* applied to a problem. But there is an alternative approach: why not start with the problem or opportunity and then ask several disciplines to assist you? Problems and business opportunities are not generally confined to one branch of knowledge. To some extent professional schools already do this but still tend to stay within their professions like law or medicine. One reason the Cambridge Phenomenon has flourished is that entrepreneurs can borrow from several disciplines within the university to find what they are looking for.

After all, the economy is many things: sociological, psychological, anthropological, scientific, technological *and* economic; looking at it through just one lens makes little sense. Moreover, more and more products and technologies, such as bio-medicine and gene-mapping, are multi-disciplinary; medical, biological and chemical knowledge in one package. Likewise, environmental challenges need multiple disciplines to work together to find solutions. Disciplinary studies are *half* the answer. Problem and opportunity-centred studies form the other half. The whole issue is shown in Figure 10.3.

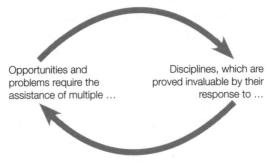

Figure 10.3 Several disaplines solving problems and responding to opportunites

Harvard University recently embarked on a major experiment, which, if successful, will change education profoundly. Its new Allston campus will be entirely given over to cross-disciplinary studies organized around projects such as, 'How to make the US economy more innovative'. Such a project might borrow from a dozen disciplines, examining the profile of the problem and then hire staff from various graduate schools, picking those with the needed expertise. The Allston campus will also be situated next to the business school.[9] A huge surge in innovation can result from making disciplines equal partners with societal problems and opportunities. Solving the international problem with addictive drugs, for example, requires at least a dozen disciplines working as one because the problem is psychological, therapeutic, international, political, economic, legal, medical, criminological, sociological, military and ethical (most drugs originate from developing or conflicted regions of the world).

One interesting aspect of the Cambridge Phenomenon, and Silicon Valley and Route 128 around Harvard too, is how relatively few businesses originated from *within* the university and were spun out by university departments. Some, such as the Cavendish Laboratory and the School of Engineering, contributed several start-ups, but on the whole it was industries in the *vicinity* that reaped the benefits of the knowledge generated within the university. The university is a multi-disciplinary resource from which entrepreneurs take their pick. Most of the cross-disciplinary work is *around* not *in* the university, a situation Harvard plans to alter.

What can happen when technology consultants achieve novel syntheses

The Cambridge Phenomenon has, from its beginnings, found a way to cultivate the entrepreneurial spirit. An entrepreneur – the word is French and originally meant an impresario or theatre director – 'takes a stand' (*preneur*) 'between' (*entre*) various parties and brings them together. The entrepreneur was first said to be a coordinator, then a 'risk bearer', in cases where the parties might not agree, and finally the 'uncertainty bearer'. Entrepreneurs have also been described as arbitrageurs, who bought low and sold high.[10] The

---

9.   See http://news.harvard.edu/gazette/tag/allston/ and http://evp.harvard.edu/allston

10.   Alan Barrell, David Gill and Martin Rigby, *Show Me the Money*, London: Elliot and Thompson, 2013. There is a good series of definitions of entrepreneurship in the first few pages.

economist Joseph Schumpeter saw the entrepreneur as an innovator amid a 'gale of creative destruction' and this definition is the one that has stuck. The entrepreneur is our chief contributor, the person who conjures wealth out of nothing, who rubs ideas together and creates something that never existed before and which people will pay for.

What is unusual and distinctive about the Cambridge area is the role played by 'technology consultants', particularly those at Cambridge Consultants, PA Consulting Group (PA Technology, in particular), Scientific Generics and the Generics Group, The Technology Partnership (TTP), Sagentia and Plextec. These companies have organized entrepreneurs into a cohesive group force.[11] Advances in science and technology create business opportunities and specialists in a particular field are the first to grasp this. A large number of high-tech companies in Cambridge were set up by post-doctoral researchers, who were perhaps in the best position of all to recognize such opportunities.

The MBA model of business education will not do for this purpose. The notion that you can 'master' business administration (or *any* business!) in two years or less by reading written cases may be among the more hubristic claims of professional education. The conspicuous lack of MBA graduates in Silicon Valley, Cambridge science companies and similar hotbeds of innovation speaks for itself. Business schools serve large corporations and divide their teaching modules according to organizational functions – marketing, finance, human resources and so on. Big business is generally weak in innovation in part because of departmental rigidity and in part because it has money to lose while start-ups have next to nothing to lose and jump in at the deep end.

The genuine innovator first needs to be in thrall to their speciality. Tracing the ascent of burgeoning new technologies is what technology consultants do and Cambridge has all such information to hand. For example, The Technology Partnership's ongoing venture in three-dimensional printing of objects involves several clients who pay to stay in touch. They may potentially jump in as partners on a new development. The entrepreneur must be aware of new technologies and the products they make possible; they need to constantly be on the leading edge.[12]

As technology advances and becomes ever more complex, the mental capabilities of the solo entrepreneur may not be enough. Groups of people are better able to pore over the possibilities and identify those ventures worth trying. It was this that gave rise to the 'soft start' initiated by Cambridge

11. Kirk and Cotton, *Cambridge Phenomenon*, pp. 49–52.
12. Personal communication with TTP, 2013.

Consultants. They were funded to look into a possibility for clients who turned out to be a lot less daring than the consultants. If the client fails to see the potential in the results, then the consultant company can exploit the opportunity itself. The great advantage of being paid for working on technology road maps and future developments is that you soon become even wiser and keener than your clients. Companies that outsource their R&D are making Faustian bargains in any case, as new ideas are seminal to the enterprise. The technology consultants have more genuine enthusiasm for a new technology than have their clients. The consultants are closer to the developments, and can identify the moment when this reaches the commercialization stage.

If the client loses interest, the consultants may proceed on their own. Alternatively, they may set up a joint venture with the client, who usually has more money. In reality, the consultant has found a way of being paid for imaginative and constructive thinking. The consultant's contract may even extend to advising on the fine details. Can the client's intellectual property be protected? Could they set up in the Cambridge science park? Who should be contacted for investment funds? Is enough skilled labour available? By the time all these questions have been answered, the consultants are ready to take the plunge. No wonder that many consultancy staff resign at some point in order to take charge of new start-ups themselves. They thought it up. They watched the technology grow – now they want to do it.

Funds are intelligently distributed to the best contributors via spin-outs

In Chapter 1, we identified banks as distributors and industry as contributors. The greatest surge in economic growth has occurred when distributors get funds to the most brilliant contributors of that period. It is beyond the knowledge and means of most loan officers to spot who the outstanding contributors are, especially in the highly complex fields of recently emerging science. They suggest you mortgage your house! This is where the spin-out becomes a form of intelligence.

Over time new models to fund innovative enterprise have evolved. One of the founders of Cambridge Consultants, Gordon Edge, later went on to establish Scientific Generics and perfected the art of the spin-out. The development of any technology tends to produce off-shoots; sometimes a small group of employees will become enamoured of such an off-shoot, resign as a whole group and take the knowledge and ideas with them. This is sometimes called a spin-*off*. The parent company loses valuable people and valuable information and so the spin-off is seen as a nasty surprise or even a threat. The trick lay in making the spin-*out* purposeful and deliberate.

Edge proposed that spin-outs be anticipated, deliberately cultivated and made profitable for parent and offspring alike. He believed the parent company should research the opportunity and invest in the spin-out, be a customer for it if that were possible and help support the endeavours of a new crop of talented young people. Note how close this model is to the family ideal we discussed in Chapters 4 to 6. It is a process of procreation, with generations of products and founders following each other in rapid succession. In place of a family tree is a technology tree, a body of knowledge joining them all together as the science branches out.[13]

Such friendly spin-outs had, of course, happened before, probably many times, but Edge was notable for turning them into a policy. Scientific Generics would branch out by extending many small units from the core technology they had selected. These units would comprise face-to-face primary groups, to human scale, connected by the science they shared in the manner of the 'hidden champions' we discussed in Chapter 6 and anchored by trust. It was also a way of giving the company's younger people the entrepreneurial opportunities the founders had already enjoyed. When last encountered, Scientific Generics was launching hydrogen-powered batteries for computers. The Cambridge Phenomenon has engendered literally hundreds of spin-outs, accidental and deliberate. It is now how most new companies are formed in Cambridge, that is, as part of a network of intellectual relationships. The 'parent' of course knows the technology of which the 'child' is an offshoot and is in a much better position to know what its prospects are and to afford the funds needed to spin it out. The competence of the people being spun-out is also well known. They used to work for their sponsor.

The kind of cross-disciplinary creative problem solving that goes on within a consultancy was described to us by Gordon Edge himself. We filmed the interview, so the passage below is verbatim and illustrates the expert resources from which the university can draw and then connect together, a new *unity* amid a very wide *diversity*:

> What we did, and I did in particular, was to create a group of people from the university who shared their views – biologists, physicists, mathematicians, plant geneticists and engineers, etc. – and we spent

13. Personal communications with Gordon Edge, April 2008, and with Elizabeth Garnsey of the Institute for Manufacturing at Cambridge University.

a whole day together thinking about our problem. The breakthrough came when one of my colleagues, a biologist stated, 'What we are trying to do in this case is to understand how light is absorbed by a medium. The Japanese have gone the dye route. Why don't we see how nature does this?' One of the people there was a zoologist and he said, 'I know of some work being done in Sweden with the nocturnal moth.' This by definition flies at night and it is very important to its survival that light is not reflected from its eye, or it gets picked off by predators.

He went on, 'If we can understand how nature has managed to eliminate reflection from the eye then that will allow us to maximize absorption of light on a plastic surface.' We then set out to model the eye of this moth, which allowed a colleague of mine, Bob Pettigrew, to create what was at that time the largest intraperometer in the world. This is a way of casting a pattern of light on a surface. We were trying to create a pattern roughly equal to the wavelength of light itself, that is, 500 nanometres, a fraction of the size of a human hair.

When we did this, we found that the polycarbonate suddenly became black. We sent off several specimens to our client, who telephoned us a few days later to say 'we can't get the dye off'. We told him, 'there is no dye'. The material is black because it has absorbed all the light that falls on it. And so we created a huge industry in affordable CDs based on the views of biologists, zoologists, physicists, engineers, etc.[14]

This passage makes it very clear that technology consulting is entrepreneurial in spirit; it engages a multiplicity of viewpoints to solve ongoing challenges. It creates unity out of diversity, as shown in Figure 10.4.

Figure 10.4 The role of consultants in forging new creative unities

14. Filmed interview with Gordon Edge. April, 2008

The Cambridge Phenomenon holds some important lessons. The money contributed by those keeping watch on what was happening has diminished as a source of consultants' income over the years. However, investing in companies spun-out from technology consultants has increased considerably. In 2000, forty-two spin-outs had emerged from Scientific Generics,[15] it is probably at least double that figure today. Most technology consultants now have investment portfolios, and they are in a *very* good position to know who and what is likely to be successful.

In the early days of technology consulting, tales of heroic risk-taking by banks were plentiful. This isn't much in evidence today. One of the more ingenious schemes for raising money was set up by TTP. It involved all employees taking out personal loans from their banks, pooling the money and TTP giving everyone shares in the company. It has been owned by its employees ever since, and is highly profitable. Employees who leave can retain or sell their shares, but lose voting rights. TTP recommends this structure to its clients. Employee share ownership is part of the stakeholder ethic we examined in Chapters 3, 5, 6 and 8. Investors, employees and customers are in close alliance.

Take-overs by big companies aren't uncommon but they're rarely successful. The cultural gaps between the start-ups and the large companies that acquire them are, in many cases, too large to bridge. Olivetti came to the rescue of Acorn and the BBC Micro Computer but was not able to revive them. Hewlett-Packard paid over US$10 billion for Autonomy, only to write down the investment a few months later. The potential of smaller acquisitions is frequently misunderstood. Better ways of funding start-ups has to be found – and this is happening.

Much greater success has been enjoyed by angel investors. The name derives from Broadway and the wealthy individuals who backed theatrical productions, but the impulse favours innovation, even at great risk to the investor. Unlike venture capitalists, business angels aren't using their investment specifically to make money but are trying to encourage new enterprise as an end in itself. Many, such as Hermann Hauser of Amadeus Capital Partners, are serial entrepreneurs who have sold their own companies and have developed excellent judgement regarding what works and what does not. While their aim is not usually to get rich – there are easier ways – they cannot afford to lose very much and, for this reason, form angel syndicates (of which the Syndicate Room is an example), whereby a large number of people make relatively small contributions under expert advice and agree to share the risk between them.[16]

15. Segal, Quince and Wicksteed, *Cambridge Phenomenon Report*, 1985, 2nd edn, 2002.
16. Segal, Quince and Wicksteed, *Cambridge Phenomenon Report*, Vol. 2.

Angel investors also make suggestions and dispense advice and are more likely to invest if these are heeded. Between them angels have broad and deep experience of the kind of businesses they help to sponsor. The Great Eastern Investment Forum holds bi-monthly meetings on topics of interest to investors and twice-yearly presentations by companies hoping to start up. More than 100 potential investors attend. Each company is given a ten-minute slot in which to pitch, and a room for the whole day in which to talk to those who show an interest. A 2000 report claimed that as many as one-third of presenting companies obtained seed capital of £4–£5 million.

The Cambridge Angels were founded by Richard Samson and Doug Richard, two Americans who were introduced to each other and to local opportunities by Alan Barrell, entrepreneur-in-residence at the Judge Business School.[17] Since starting in September 2001, they have invested £16 million, largely in early stage seed funds. IQ Angels, an investment partnership for high net worth individuals, recently sold companies to IBM and Google.

When asked about the constraints of being located in Cambridge, the main problems people cite are poor infrastructure and expensive housing – almost no one mentions lack of access to capital. According to the 2009 East of England Technopole Report, 'Cambridge is one of the top four regions in Europe in terms of total institutional investment into innovative start-ups, and is number one in Europe for investment per capita.'[18] In this one region, at least, money is reaching the people who really need it and can put it to best use. The situation is illustrated in Figure 10.5.

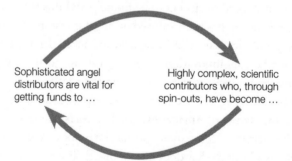

Sophisticated angel distributors are vital for getting funds to ...

Highly complex, scientific contributors who, through spin-outs, have become ...

Figure 10.5 Getting funds to the most sophisticated contributors

Distributing funds to where the real talent lies is essential, and who better to do this than those who have excelled in the past and those who the science involved?

17. Personal communication. See also Kirk and Cotton, *Cambridge Phenomenon*, p. 60.
18. http://www.stjohns.co.uk/wp-content/uploads/2011/11/EastEnglandTechnopole.pdf

Producing a high tolerance for 'failure' plus persistence

It is axiomatic that most innovative products fail and most start-ups do not survive. Even the Cambridge Phenomenon has had many casualties. Of the nine companies cited in 1984 as the 'making' of the Cambridge Phenomenon, most have not survived.[19] So why do people persist despite the high failure rate?

The persistence of entrepreneurs and inventors is legendary. We mentioned in the Introduction that Josiah Wedgwood never stopped innovating. Thomas Edison famously stated that he hadn't failed, he'd merely discovered one thousand reasons why his light bulb wouldn't work. The Dyson vacuum cleaner involved over two thousand prototypes. Perhaps 'failure' is an essential part of the development of new products and technologies.

If you are a post-doctoral researcher, as many founders of Cambridge start-ups were, then you know with some certainty what elements of a project have failed and what have not. The science and the technology to which you have dedicated much of your life have *not* failed and continue to develop apace. What has happened is that a particular product using the latest developments has for some reason attracted insufficient revenue at this time. This could be because the product is ahead of its time or because the market has insufficient information to appreciate the potential of the product. Perhaps the appeal was not clear enough or was misconstrued.

Academics are very used to such set-backs. It is one thing to know, but quite another to put what you know at the disposal of others. That you need to persist until you are fully understood is obvious; the underlying science has been tested and verified step by step. You are not wrong, you have a potentially invaluable technology, but you have failed to communicate its potential. If markets do not see this now, they soon will, but perhaps in another form. Failure to exploit must not be confused with failed research. The computers produced by Acorn and the BBC Micro 'failed' to match the appeal of the Apple I. In reality there were a number of contributing factors: the USA has a much larger and more demanding market; California legislators approved a free Apple for every public school, provided that school purchased a second; a new mass market was created that shut imports out; and Apple was pitched in terms of personal liberation from IBM, the rebellion of a defiant citizenry against a corporatist ethos.

Such products are also rarely 'one' item, but a synthesis of many innovative parts. Many of the features of Acorn and the BBC Micro were ahead of those of Apple – and those who created them were still in town. Hermann Hauser and

19. Segal, Quince and Wicksteed, *Cambridge Phenomenon Report*, Vol. 1, p. 21 and personal communication with Bill Wicksteed.

Andy Hopper, co-founders of Acorn and the BBC Micro, are very much still active. Within a few years parts of Acorn had found their way into ARM, which designs chips for customers across the world. Now worth £12 billion, it is the largest and most successful company within the Cambridge Phenomenon and is among the UK's top 100. Two 'failed' companies became the power behind the centrifuge that spun out many more. A particular product might be dead, but not the people who made it, not its individual features and components, not the software designed for it and not the science that helped create it. These can all live to fight another day. Acorn has had numerous offspring – fifty-one 'children and grandchildren', in fact, as illustrated in Figure 10.6. Not bad for a company that had apparently 'failed'.

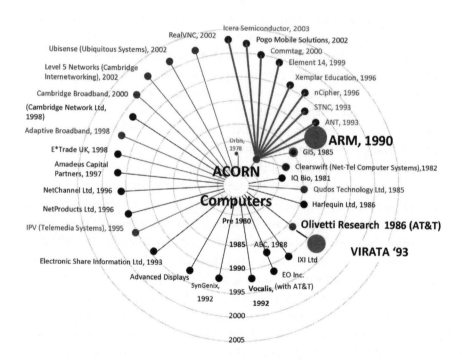

Figure 10.6a Commercially independent, scientifically joined: the spin-out. Diagram designed by Elizabeth Garnsey, to whom the authors owe the spin-out/spin-off distinction.

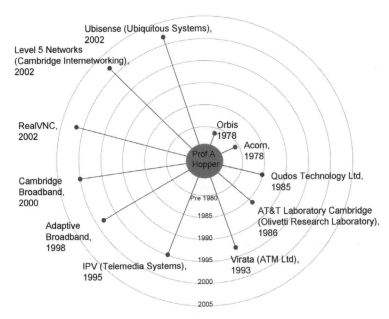

Figure 10.6b Hermann Hauser and Andy Hopper as progenitors

Hermann Hauser and Andy Hopper spun out all these companies between them, 'scattering their maker's image through the land,' as Dryden might have put it. All are extensions of their founders' thinking. The spin-out is a powerful dynamic. And importantly, although products are spun out or away from the parent company, they retain their connection, their common parentage and their roots in science. Unfortunately, the habit of only doing the designing in Cambridge persists; ARM designs the chips, but the rest of the process is done elsewhere. To fully develop the economy, this issue needs to be addressed unless the whole working class is to be abandoned.

The knowledge involved in science-based entrepreneurship is multi-layered. There is the science (level 1); the burgeoning technology (level 2) growing out of the science, the particular application offered for sale (level 3); and the response of customers and markets (level 4). Failure, if it occurs at all, is usually at levels 3 and 4, which is readily correctable and doesn't shatter the integrity of the science or the technology and new opportunities will arise with later versions of the same technology.

In this sense 'failure' becomes a vital part of the learning process. We learn most and fastest from *negative feedback*. Rather than a bad thing, negative feedback can be viewed as something surprising that leads us to rethink our approach. Getting a product ready for market is an *error-correcting process*; each improvement brings you closer to what the customer wants. The ditty below is much cited in Silicon Valley:

The road to wisdom, yes it's plain
And easy to express
You err and err and err again
But less and less and less.[20]

This suggests yet another paradox that the Cambridge Phenomenon may have resolved: reconciling two approaches to progress. Science is advanced by the method of hypothesis and deduction, sometimes called 'if–then'. If the science and technology are right, then the performance should follow. It is all very rational. But then there is also a type of logic that plunges in at the deep-end, causing waves, turbulence and errors, which are subsequently corrected by swift action until the customer is happy. It is a serious mistake to see these errors as failures. Errors are the road to faster learning. Understanding what the customer wants is often a subjective mystery, sometimes requiring more psychology than technology. You must guess, take the plunge and then keep correcting until the product fits the customer.[21]

However rational your science and brilliant your technology, it takes a *second* kind of logic to discover whether, and how much, the customer wants it. The first logic is based on the university as a refuge from the world of commerce, a place that is pure, single-minded and uncontaminated by external social forces such as money. The second logic is that of precipitous action in a world of endemic uncertainty; where something new is being tried the risk of failure must be faced and dealt with. The two logics are illustrated in Figure 10.7.

While science advances by hypothesis and deduction ...

Commerce advances by trial, error and successive improvements ...

Figure 10.7 The error-correcting system compliments the hypothetico-deduction system

20. Attributed to Piet Hein, quoted by Michael Schrage, *Serious Play*, Harvard Business School Press, 1999, p. 11.

21. W. Edwards Deming is the chief proponent of the error-correcting system, see *Out of the Crisis*, Cambridge: MIT Press, 2000. When Americans scorned him he trained the Japanese.

All fed by a collegial knowledge network, a veritable ecosystem, wherein problems and opportunities vie with disciplines

There is an ancient system of residential colleges at Cambridge. Students, live, work, eat and study in their colleges and go out during the day to be engineers or historians in their different faculties. Their studies may also be supervised in their college. The Master of Queens' College, Lord Eatwell, described the situation to us:

> Cambridge has silos but she also has this remarkable piece of medieval genius called colleges and what is extraordinary about colleges is that people meet, eat, talk, study and work together. For example, in this college we had a young plant geneticist sitting down at lunch with a number theorist, a pure mathematician. She was describing a problem in genetics which she could not solve and he said, 'I can do that.' They wrote a paper together which became the top science paper of the year in genetics. That would not have happened in a university without colleges because they would never have met each other.[22]

Cambridge colleges are based on a series of courtyards and quadrangles and it is virtually impossible for staff and students not to meet each other on a day-to-day basis, either walking about, in the library, the common room, at meals, in the chapel, in gardens or in meeting rooms and on sports fields. It gives a new meaning to collegiality. We have seen throughout the preceding chapters that conviviality plays a large role in wealth creation, as do communities of trust. Success depends critically on finding support, friends who will tell you the truth as they see it and people you can rely upon in helping you realize your goals.[23]

Networks are a vital clue to the success of the Cambridge Phenomenon. These are knowledge-specific connections that help to bring together elements of new products and services in original combinations. Networks are informal, ad hoc and have no hierarchy. The standing of various members depends on the value of their contributions to the aims of the network. They attach or detach members at will as their mission develops. An additional member to a network

22. Lord Eatwell, filmed interview, 2008.
23. Teresa Amabile investigated helping patterns at innovation and design firm IDEO; she found these highly correlated with innovation, see 'IDEO's Culture of Helping', *Harvard Business Review*, January–February 2014, pp. 55–62.

of 100 will create as many new relationships, and this increases exponentially as the network expands. Any one of those new relationships could lead to a breakthrough. Knowledge is stored in these relationships, so people are aware of what information others have, which facilitates knowledge sharing.

Perhaps the greatest virtue of a network is that any person within it can become a *hub*; that is, the person through whom most of the information flows and to whom most opportunities are communicated. Suppose you provide more valuable information than anyone else. If so, you will very shortly start *receiving* more valuable information than anyone else, which you can relay back to interested people, further increasing your influence within the net. In one sense you are competing with other members of the net by having more information to hand than anyone else. But such competition relies on you *cooperating* with the largest number of net members. What a network does is reconcile the values of competing and cooperating.

Here, the person who gives the most information also receives the most information, and this benefits not just his or her ability to compete with other networkers but benefits the entire network. The consequence is co-opetition or collaborative competing. This is how a 'knowledge culture' such as the one that underlies the Cambridge Phenomenon is established and enriches itself.

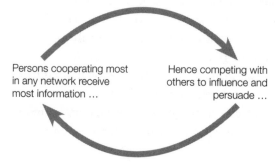

Persons cooperating most in any network receive most information ...

Hence competing with others to influence and persuade ...

Figure 10.8 Competing and cooperating reconciled

Networks form within *clusters* and are one of the main reasons industries cluster in the first place (as discussed in Chapter 5). What is distinctive about the Cambridge Phenomenon is that, rather than having one dominant cluster, like films in Hollywood and electronics in Silicon Valley, it has at least *five* clusters: engineering, electronics, healthcare and biosciences, software and telecommunications. Having a number of clusters is important because, over time, two or more clusters will tend to converge and the interactions between two initially diverse bodies of knowledge are more likely to be innovative. To be innovative you need to make new and original connections, which tend to emerge from combinations of clusters. The Human Genome Project, for example, emerging from clusters in the UK and the USA has made gene-mapping possible. This opens up the potential for customized medicine, which could have a major impact on medical diagnosis and the sale of medical devices. There is a cluster forming at the Allston campus at Harvard to explore this further.[24] Some diseases share many of the same symptoms and certain illnesses not caught early enough can be fatal. If your gene map is available, diagnosis is both faster and much more accurate and you can be monitored at far lower cost than by medical examination. Gene-mapping provides a challenge for the software, information technology and medical scanning industries. Cambridge is very fortunate to have access to Addenbrooke's Hospital, a teaching and research hospital of some renown, where new devices can be tested.

Chapter 5 introduced the notion of 'horizontal' or catalytic technologies that join other technologies and products. Clearly, software, electronics, engineering and telecommunications are 'horizontal' and improve *other* technologies. Where these are developed, they improve infrastructure in general and pay off across the board.

Specialized networks are often established in innovation centres and science parks, sometimes known as 'incubators'. St John's Innovation Centre in Cambridge offers assistance to start-up companies, including patent applications, tax advice, periodic reporting, postal and parcel services, telephone service, sources of funding and bank finance, routine administration, introductions to local resources, meeting rooms, a prestigious address, lunch facilities, business assistance, accounting and book-keeping, colleagues in the same boat and periodic lectures on subjects of common interest. It is hard to innovate on a shoestring budget, and to have such support given at cost frees you up to strategize, network and imagine. St John's even provides debt counselling for those companies that can't pay their rent.[25] Science parks offer similar services to tenants. You may be yards from a joint venture partner with a source of funding next door.

Throughout this book we have disputed that the prime aim of the innovator and the entrepreneur is to make money. The success of the Cambridge Phenomenon suggests that money-making can hardly have been the prime objective of most protagonists. Consider the career path of most of the prime movers. They were for the most part academics with doctoral or at least master's degrees and were engaged in post-doctoral studies. Had

24. Discussion with Professor Clayton Christensen at Harvard, June 2008.
25. Visit to St John's Innovation Centre and information from their brochures.

their aim in life been to become rich, it is difficult to conceive of a more roundabout way of getting there. When they began their studies and showed promise, the technologies that they eventually championed had in many cases yet to be invented. The stipend of a post-doctoral fellow is modest, to say the least. Would anyone whose aim was to make a fortune spend their life in or around a university with fellow academics? It is hardly conceivable.

Propelled by a community of high trust

We come finally to the centre of the diagram shown in Figure 10.1. Where a community is dedicated to the discovery and advancement of knowledge it is very likely to be high in trust. Indeed deceit or lying strikes a mortal blow at the process of generating knowledge. You are betraying not just colleagues but your discipline and your students, the knowledge you are passing on to the rising generation which will far outlast you. Academics have higher goals without having to invent these. Since they construct their edifice piece by piece and design by design, an inability to trust the work of colleagues would spell ruin to the joint endeavour. At stake is much more than anyone's reputation for honesty but the integrity of work in the public realm and open to scholars worldwide. A false report could waste years of work by scholars everywhere who had relied upon it. Knowledge may be the only immortality we have, our sole legacy to others. You cannot take it with you but you can leave it behind as a gift to your field.

The point is *not* that the purveyors of knowledge are better than the rest of us. They have their scandals too. The point is that their joint task is next to impossible unless their colleagues can be trusted. It follows that knowledge-intensive business is likely to reciprocate this trust if only from fear of the alternative, a lie that festers at the root of some problem and prevents its solution. If we all believe in some vital branch of science then we can believe in each other and better serve this superordinate goal that stands between us.

While the Cambridge Phenomenon gives us hope it surely is not sufficient to rescue the economy. It remains stubbornly cerebral. ARM may be worth billions but it only *designs* chips. It does not make them. While other cultures pay wages to those actually producing things, UK workers are nowhere in evidence and wages will continue to stagnate until this changes. The economy is leaving more and more of us behind as it grows more complex. This situation has led Professor Mike Best at the University of Massachusetts to warn his fellow Americans *against* following the Cambridge model:

We run the risk of turning into Cambridge, England; we'll have isolated clusters of the very best university research and a number of small R&D firms but not the downstream production, service and support jobs that make a vibrant economy. We will create all the new ideas – but others will get too much of the benefit.[26]

Yet there are reasons to be upbeat. To paraphrase Irish playwright George Bernard Shaw, we must go beyond seeing things as they are and asking 'why?' We must see things as they never were and ask 'why not?' But in fact the first question prompts the second. Why not create man-made materials as light and strong as the spider's web, as resilient yet as tough as the abalone shell, as light-absorbing as the eye of the nocturnal moth, as finely fitted to its environment as the clown fish, as photosynthetic as algae? The earth and its living systems should be our inspiration and the experiments of evolution should be our mentor.

26. Quoted by Elizabeth Garnsey during a presentation at the Institute for Manufacturing, Cambridge University, November 2013.

CHAPTER 11

Can crowdfunding bring conscience back to capitalism?

There is a very recent development which properly executed promises to remedy the faults of finance-dominated capitalism as set forth in this book. If you do not already know about the rise of crowdfunding, sometimes called crowdsourcing or peer-to-peer lending, then you soon will.

According to NESTA, the National Society for Science and the Arts, the British Charity specializing in innovation, the phenomenon of crowdfunding is undergoing exponential growth. Moore's Law once proclaimed that computing power doubled every eighteen months at a speed which was making us dizzy and could transform our economy. Yet crowdfunding is currently doubling in size *every two months*! This is roughly ten times as fast as the rise in computer power. Equity crowdfunding grew by 410% in 2013 and Forbes Online expects its value to reach US$2.5 billion by early 2015. A recent World Bank Report estimated the current level of crowdfunding to be US$4.86 billion, but predicted that in the developing world alone this would reach $93 billion by 2025, an estimate that appears conservative in the light of recent statistics and looks like being dwarfed by the developed world. On a world scale there are an estimated 469 new projects per day.[1]

In the first quarter of 2014 more than four million backers pledged US$350 million. A new crowdfunding project is launched every three minutes. Globally,

---

1. See NESTA website and Forbes Online 'Is Alternative Finance now Britain's fastest growing industry?' 7 November 2014.

crowdfunding doubles every sixty days. In the UK, which is some way behind the US, crowdfunding grew 350 per cent in January 2014, as much again in February, and in March the growth exceeded the combined rate for the previous two months. The UK government has a Crowdfunding Forum. Worldwide there was a 101 per cent increase in crowdfunding in the first quarter of 2014 with the US and its more mature market growing at 76.8 per cent, or over 300 per cent for the year.[2] The USA is still by far the largest market, launching 14,853 pledges per day compared with only 1,109 in the UK. (A pledge includes some monies which are never collected because not enough people subscribed to a project and it failed to reach its all-or-nothing target.)

Every venture launched requires a 'platform' which helps prepare the offering and reaches out to its potential investors on the Internet. It also enforces legal requirements. Kickstsarter, BanktotheFuture, Indiegogo, Seedrs, CrowdFunder UK, Crowdcube and Prosper.com, the Lending Club, Gofundme and KIVA are among the best-known platforms. KIVA features Third World entrepreneurs, cites the number of times they have repaid their loans and explains why they want an additional loan and what they will do with it. Colleagues of ours have loaned for several years without incurring a single bad debt. The Syndicate Room specializes in high-tech, knowledge intensive start-ups of the kind examined in Chapter 10 with expert advice from angel investors. The size of the 'crowd' which actually backs the project varies with different platforms. Kickstarter has an average of 535 backers for every project funded, while FundRazr has only thirty-eight. Crowdcube raised an average of US$316 million per project with 114 backers. Kickstarter has just raised US$13.2 million to fund Coolest Cooler, a portable freezer for picnics. Clearly the numbers involved and the amount raised varies widely.

There are three different varieties of crowdfunding. There is rewards crowdfunding in which those who pledge money get a reward greater than their contributions where the launch is successful (where the offer is undersubscribed their money will not be collected). The rewards offered by a film-maker like Spike Lee might include tickets for seats at the premier of the film and the champagne dinner which followed. Persons backing the launch of a high-resolution 3-D printer might be able to lease one free for a month and be instructed in its use, a scheme which would add to publicity as the backer showed it off to his or her friends and printed objects for them as gifts.

2.   Here as in much of the rest of the chapter Hampden-Turner is indebted to Alan Barrell, a close friend, an angel investor and enthusiast for CF.

In equity crowdfunding the contributors get equity shares according to the size of their stakes. One might think this was the most obvious and popular solution, but legal scrutiny is much stricter where shares are involved and the SEC is having trouble drafting legislation that protects small investors. Many use rewards to avoid legal hassles. Sharing your good fortune is the best way when success is very large and unforeseen. For example Occulus Rift gave rewards to its backers and then sold its company to Facebook for US$2 billion. The backers received rewards much smaller than the money made by the founders and they naturally resented the deal.

In donation crowdfunding nothing is given back to investors save the knowledge of how their donations have been used and the benefits conferred. Those who donate do not expect to gain personally. Many charities are turning to these methods. The figures cited thus far refer to rewards and equity approaches only. Donations are not very different from charitable giving and are not included here.

At first glance crowdfunding might appear to be little more than an additional form of raising capital. Yet in truth it is a very different way of conducting business with very different value premises and, if it continues to rise in prominence, it will alter the conduct of commerce most profoundly. Because it explains the idea and vision behind the project it can be seen as an act of imaginative conscience which seeks an echo in the hearts and minds of members of the crowd and draws them into a network of high-trust and shared enthusiasm.

While an Initial Public Offering appeals to the pocket-book and promises a stream of income, the crowdfunded pitch speaks to the heart and mind of enthusiasts for particular new developments in music, film, arts, sciences, health, games, medicine, etc. It appeals to a whole spectrum of values including social, economic, professional, compassionate and aesthetic. After an IPO is launched the company is too often transformed into little more than a money-machine with quantity as its god, but the early days of a new venture are full of hope, idealism and social benefit. To get investors involved at these *early* stages will transform the image of capitalism and give it the idealistic aura that many of its innovative feats deserve. What begins in genius can all too often end in greed. We need to mine the depths of enterprise where the founding inspirations lie. Investors can take pride in helping life-saving and world-saving technologies achieve their initial lift off. Where the investor is the midwife at the birth of a new technology and takes pride in delivering a new product, then capitalism is significantly changed for the better. We might give shares bought at this early stage voting rights greater than those who jumped on the bandwagon at a later stage.

In this chapter we will consider thirteen advantages of crowdfunding.

1. Crowdfunding sells an ideal not an existing product or service

Crowdfunding appeals to investors in the crowd on the basis of an ideal of service *to* that crowd: 'Give me the money and I promise to supply this.' Unlike the normal sale of shares there is no extant business or flow of revenue. There is, as yet, no product and no service. What is on offer is an *ideal* that could, with sufficient funds, become a reality. In no other form of capitalism are so many people asked to participate so broadly at such an early stage in the process. They help bring a viable notion into reality with high degrees of enthusiasm for a jointly sponsored outcome. There are perhaps fifty to one thousand people without which this new enterprise would not exist. These constitute a flying wedge, too many and too enthusiastic to be ignored. Early stage enterprises have never before had such wide support and so many friends. It needs high confidence to launch a new enterprise and the funds and good wishes offered by the crowd are a strong vote of confidence.

2. The combining of ideas into a new ideal is the true source of wealth creation

We need to remind ourselves what it is that *creates wealth*, as opposed to just making *money*. Appropriating the funds of another person may make money for the winner but creates no wealth. Wealth is created when two or more ideas or elements are put together and the ideal combination of these is more valuable than were the prior ingredients, so for example, a delicious meal is worth more than a bag of groceries, or a microchip is simply metal and silicon in a purposeful design yet we might owe our lives to the air-bag it inflates in our vehicle in the event of collision, or to the vents it seals when the car hits water.

In crowdfunding the entrepreneur tells the audience just what s/he plans to *combine* and the happy result expected from this. They either agree to help or they do not. But the *process of creating wealth* has been explained to them and awaits their approval. Something humdrum and lacking originality is unlikely to be proposed and even more unlikely to be approved. Crowd-funding depends for its impact on the startling originality of the idea and/or the nobility of the ideal and upon the mutuality of the entrepreneur and the crowd. It constitutes a joint venture to improve our society. It is an invitation to the crowd to embrace diversity, to think of things that might be and ask 'why not?'

3. When ideals vie with rival ideals they grow increasingly ambitious

What is likely to happen when competition grows hotter for available funds on an Internet platform like Kickstarter, Seedrs, Crowdcube or Indiegogo? Clearly each venture will strive to make itself more attractive and to win more adherents. Promises of really significant values are likely to escalate. Suppose you have been studying algae which absorb energy from the sun very much more efficiently than photovoltaic cells and you have developed a new substance that mimics this. This would be likely to have a strong appeal to those concerned with the environment, but not all the crowd is so minded. Why stop at that? Why not also promise employee share ownership, wellness initiatives to keep employees healthy (which have proved far cheaper than intervention after they fall sick). Why not promise wages above the industry average and productivity levels which more than pay for this? Why not promise modest differentials between the highest and lowest paid and win the support of persons championing equality. Why not give work and training to single mothers, equal wages and salaries to women and train the unemployed to produce your new technology?

The point we are making is that ideals are not singular and the crowd will have many different convictions between them, so the more points you can score with members of the crowd the better will be its response to your proposal. The more policies you can think of that help stakeholders to serve your envisaged company the wider will be your appeal to the crowd and the more funds will be forthcoming. Instead of redistributing money via the taxation system after the fact, you 'pre-distribute' resources *before* the fact and government takes less income in taxes. When customers are buying what they want they are *also* advancing multiple causes you stand for.

4. The numbers of failures and losers is reduced

Crowdfunding almost certainly *reduces* the failure rate for start-ups because ideas which the market finds insufficiently attractive will fall at the first fence before anyone loses their money. All-or-nothing fundraising is by far the most popular alternative and does not collect the money if the instigator does not get all s/he asked for. The disappointed enthusiasts may have been saved from folly. The response or non-response of investors is in effect a *market test of the venture itself*, much stricter than the question 'would you buy this?' If the crowd is prepared to *invest* then being a customer, an employee or a supplier are much easier options. Asking for investment funds is more ambitious than asking for customers and sets the bar higher. If investors show a lead, customers, suppliers, employees and well-wishing stakeholders are likely to follow and you have mobilized a group of supporters from the very start of your venture. You have a crowd of fans rooting for you.

Kickstarter reports that over thirty per cent of its ventures succeed in raising sufficient funds, which means that some sixty per cent are stopped before their instigators suffer serious loss by putting a product out there which insufficient people want. Were the failure rate to halve then entrepreneurship could take off in a big way. Those who were under-subscribed could try again and their persistence could pay-off. Those not subscribing might be asked why and what additional values would need to be put forward for them to reconsider.

We tend to use the word 'competition' loosely for any attempt to show what we can do in comparison to others. In fact there are major differences in the kinds of competition and in their social impacts on society. We must distinguish between *comparable* efforts to succeed, where one effort can be numerically compared to another as in a football game or grades in a classroom, and *incomparable* efforts to succeed, where the achievements are so different that comparing them and choosing 'the best' is meaningless and a waste of time. The first of these produces losers. Indeed the Hollywood starlet chosen from among twenty other contestants for a starring role produces nineteen losers. We tend to applaud her and forget the rest. The second kind of competition produces valuable distinctions which enrich our society through their variety

What is notable about much innovation is that it is *so* different from any other innovation that comparisons are pointless. We can of course compare the price of two books, one about a pet ginger cat and another about mountain landscapes in western China, but this comparison grossly simplifies and obscures the virtues of each. One is reminded of Oscar Wilde's jibe about 'A man who knows the price of everything and the value of nothing.' The great advantage of crowdfunding is that it *extols the incomparable,* that the success of one idea in no way reduces the success of another and invidious distinctions are not called for. Indeed, should one venture succeed spectacularly the crowd would swell and its readiness to invest in yet more ventures would *increase.* There is no finite pool of money to grab before other people get it. Every successful launch increases the chances for success of those which follow. You have only to delight and surprise with your originality. It is logical to wish all contestants well and to rejoice in their feats of excellence.

5. Ambitious promises made in public are binding and must be redeemed

One of the advantages of making a public pledge on the Internet for the virtues of your venture is that those supplying funds will keep you to the promises you made. Were they to feel betrayed they might dump their shares, the price would fall and replacement funds might be difficult to find. Just as marriages are strengthened when vows are made in public, so investors have a right to expect you to deliver what you promised before so many witnesses. Moreover, investors are potentially *organized* by the platform which solicited their funds initially and can talk to each other about how well pledges have been met. A Dutch proposer was recently turned down after it was revealed that he was cheating on his wife. If she could not trust him why should they? All concerned are conscious of how and why the company is coming into existence and want undertakings to be met.

Those not keeping their promises can have their words read back to them, their indebtedness to their early backers re-emphasized. Crowdfunded companies will in all probability acquire a 'Greek Chorus' of those who helped them take off and who will comment publicly on their conduct. There could be online dialogues on the subject of corporate probity. There could be reports from the field when practice goes awry. Crowdfunded companies would be wise to restate their *intentions* and correct their mistakes as and when these are reported to them.

6. The appeal for funds simulates the actual launch

We saw earlier that simulating and modelling what you plan to do both reduces the likelihood of failure and provides a low-cost trouble-shooting system. The crowdfunding process *simulates* the launch of an enterprise. The appeal to backers is like the dress rehearsal for a coming performance. Any lack of enthusiasm will be apparent and those who are attracted but left with doubts can communicate what those doubts are. The venture can be modified and relaunched once the doubts have been addressed. Several platforms promote this process of feedback and modification, which gives innovative people a chance to *play* with ideas and improve them.

People need to feel good about the process of innovating, and bankrupting yourself and your family at the first attempt is a severe discouragement. Timely simulations can be fun and avert losses.

7. Crowdfunding does what banks find difficult: getting access to specialized groups

Crowdfunding is at its strongest where banks are weakest. What does the average loan officer know about the prospects of a film festival in Brooklyn? You need to appeal to film fans and professionals. What does he or she know about an electrical appliance that absorbs the heat of the sun and makes coffee or cooks porridge for breakfast the next day? You need to know about heat-absorbing polymers. The scientific knowledge needed to appraise such an opportunity is held within hard to access knowledge communities and by persons with esoteric skills. However, such people know each *other* and can constitute a crowd.

Moreover, there are thousands of groups with a cause that has won their fierce allegiance, often because they or someone dear to them has suffered. Those who suffer from autism, multiple sclerosis, bipolar disorder, diabetes, infant cot death, asbestos inhalation, dementia, Asperger's syndrome, malnutrition, obesity, alcohol, spinal injuries, the onset of genetic cancers, drunk drivers, are much in need of investment funds. These number in the hundreds of thousands and are highly committed to an alleviation of the suffering with which they live even where a cure is not possible. Such conditions may need to be better *managed*. Those involved would invest considerable sums in anything promising to assist their cause. In many cases such groups already offer counselling and advice and products could help these services survive and prosper. Banks are busy with funding safe real-estate, where the property can be repossessed and have neither the expertise nor the inclination to be of help.

8. How does CF compare with venture capitalism?

Given the existing skills and track record of venture capitalists, is there any reason for crowdfunding? VCs have done a creditable job in Silicon Valley and their sober calculations may be better than the psychology and herd mentality of crowds. Surely savvy financiers know better than fans of the latest craze? Certainly VCs have an important role to play, but they also have some limitations.

An investment by venture capitalists is usually based on the judgement of a market by one or two people, while a crowd IS that market or is a close approximation of it. It takes a crowd of satisfied people for an enterprise to succeed. Moreover the VC has borrowed investment funds from a bank and is relending at higher rates of interest. Not only is the cost of capital higher than with most crowdfunding, but the VC is in some hurry to get his or her money back and repay the bank. This will enable the backing of new projects. One condition of funding from a VC is to put the financier on the board and do as s/he wishes and a very common wish is for a quick sale to a larger company and curbing the influence of the original founder and entrepreneur. The VC wants to cash in on the first wave of innovation even if that pre-empts the second wave.

The motive of many VCs is almost exclusively financial. They are in their job to make money and what happens to the enterprise after the VC has made a quick exit is of negligible concern. Many sales are made too soon and dilute the influence and the genius of the original founders and reduce the value of the enterprise to its sale price. Unlike the Crowd the VC is not concerned with the founding ideals of the company surviving for any length of time. It is sold off to the highest bidder whether they understand the potential of the enterprise or not. The long term potential of the founder's vision is often lost. The acquirer is certainly wealthier but are they better informed?

9. CF makes possible fate-sharing and gain-sharing among stakeholders.

What CF produces is a sense of shared fate and shared gains between investors and other stakeholders. The first investors, the first employees, the first suppliers and the first customers all contributed to the success of the company at the critical moment of its birth. Without the presence of every one of them there would be no company. Because A discovered B who knew C and D the company became possible. Rather like the veterans of foreign wars, they shared the same experience of peril and came through it. Between them they co-created a surplus not there before and they engaged each other. They helped to put two or more meanings together and created a larger reality. It can be an unforgettable experience for those involved.

We saw earlier that the chances of an ordinary start-up making it to viability were but one in five. It follows that those who *do* survive owe their economic lives to one another. What crowdfunding can do is forge unbreakable bonds of mutual respect among protagonists. It can be the beginning of great things. Instead of fighting for ever more over a common pool of cash, so that what one party receives the others must forgo, you agree in advance to take a percentage of anything created between you, sharing the gains of joint enterprise. You jointly build your future.

It is for this reason that crowdfunding is so potentially powerful. There is always a shortage of money but there is often an abundance of *ideas*. Discussing ideas and combinations of ideas to form ideals is not haunted by economic scarcity. Indeed one can agree to share the proceeds of an innovative breakthrough according to the hours put into the joint discussions. You are talking about what might be co-created in the future and an abundance you have agreed to share. If I sell a piece of candy for one dollar in the school yard, I can have the dollar OR the candy, not both. It is a straight exchange. But if I sell an idea to a crowd of friends in the school yard I have the money *and I retain the shared idea* from which we all might benefit. Because crowdfunding operates in the realm of ideas it transcends scarcity.

10. Drama, narrative, meaning and superordinate goals

In a process called an 'elevator pitch' an entrepreneur has one minute to persuade the rich investor in the elevator to consider a proposition even as the elevator ascends. In a business plan he or she must convince an often unimaginative person to imagine. No wonder funds are often hard to generate! But suppose the ideas in the head of entrepreneur could *dance before our eyes*? Suppose entrepreneurs could show the product in action, what it accomplishes, how customers might use it and adapt it, the results it would generate, how it would benefit users and what else it makes possible? Crowdfunding using film animation on the Internet can do all these things and is extremely persuasive. It does not do this in one minute before one rich person but could potentially reach hundreds and be replayed while they decide.

Every innovative idea is a story and as the idea struggles to be born a dramatic narrative can be woven around it. If the challenge is to convince investors and other stakeholders then moving images with sound can accomplish this much better than the rushed words of some geek in an elevator to a person regularly hit upon.

Crowdfunding starts as a drama. The prime instigator aims to do this and that but cannot succeed without assistance. Who stands ready to help him/her? The initial pitch is a narrative, albeit an unfinished one. The narrative has meaning and direction. It is dedicated to higher purposes and superordinate goals. With enough help the story will unfold. Britain and the USA create many of the world's novels and dramatic narratives. If we can turn innovation into the grand cultural narrative for a whole nation then we can potentially regain leadership of world enterprise, which is currently slipping away from us. We need to turn our entrepreneurs and social entrepreneurs into heroes and come to their aid. Let them tell us what they have conceived so we can help these ventures come true. Let our press and media give us blow-by-blow accounts of dreams that were transformed into new realities.

11. When will CF be featured on mass-media, especially TV?

Some complain that much crowdfunding is small-time, a concert or film here, a motorcycle rally there, mere games for hobbyists and cranks. But if crowdfunding is working well on the Internet consider how much *more* influential it could be on television, with audiences in the millions. It is a mixture of reality TV and staged performances with large doses of imaginative visions of a future, very different from our current business. Moreover it invites the participation of the audience which could be aroused nationwide to support worthy initiatives.

A ninety-minute prime-time show with six pitches for funding could feature animated proposals, together with their impact on society and the environment. Celebrities could endorse proposals and experts could testify as to the science behind them. It could reach an audience of millions. The amount of money pledged could be announced live, together with promises to spend it well. Getting on the programme in the first place would require expert selection to guarantee entertainment *and* economic effectiveness. Networks might congratulate themselves on the number of successful launches. They might choose to invest in their protégés in addition to taking the five per cent fee for their launch.

The BBC already has a good record with Children in Need and with the earlier Live Aid concerts. Crowdfunding is potentially superior to charity because it gives the cause a way of supporting itself long-term, like the Grameen Bank, which stopped taking grants from foundations and made profits from its service to poor women so it could expand that service. But it is commercial television and cable stations that could do the best out of this. Instead of commercials about imagined cures for aging, stain removal and indigestion, they could collect a proportion of the investment money pledged by their audiences and specialized channels could pitch specialized products. Instead of turning us all into passive consumer trainees, it could turn us into active and bold adventurers, placing carefully calculated bets to improve the human condition.

The fees from launching new products could become an important source of income for the media, including national newspapers, currently in economic trouble. They would not be 'corrupted' by this since the ventures are in their infancy, not powerful advertisers but hopeful aspirants to which the media was drawing our attention and inviting our support. Newspapers might feature supplements full of ambitious business plans to which journalists lent their support and contributed their research.

Our TV programmes would be less interrupted by the usual foaming nonsense. We might actually receive information about an enterprise which *mattered*, rather than foolish, empty blandishments about the noises made by milk being poured on breakfast cereal and the groans uttered by people who have over-indulged themselves and need indigestion remedies! The messages on new potential enterprises might even be important to the future of our societies.[3]

In the famous Hawthorne Experiment, productivity climbed week after week, until it reached nearly forty per cent above the starting point. One powerful reason was that the women involved were no longer assembling telephone relays, a routine, soul-destroying job, they were discussing and researching, with the help of Harvard academics, *how relays might better be assembled.* They were taking part in a world-changing experiment with many attentive visitors and spectators.

As productivity climbed more and more admiring visitors came to observe the process and the women were given increasing autonomy lest the extraordinary gains disappear. Above all they saw themselves as being 'on stage', characters in an ongoing drama where the leaders set the scene.[4] There is no inherent reason why such meanings cannot be present in nearly every workplace. We are born to learn and discover and our place on the frontiers of knowledge needs to be celebrated and turned into never-ending stories of daring accomplishment.

In creating such narratives and acting these out, Britain and the USA have incalculable advantages. They already entertain much of the globe and the English language is a boon to such enterprise. We should not be teaching from dry, abstract business cases but from high dramas. We should be able to tease out the elements of non-stop innovation from the elements of creating a story; the two forms of creativity probably illuminate one another. A novel is built around narrative individualism in which David Copperfield for one became 'the hero of my own life'.

3. A wonderfully witty and vivid denunciation of our 'culture of foaming nonsense' is by the cartoonist Osborne in *The Vulgarians,* New York Graphic Arts Inst., 1963.

4. Fritz Roethlisberger and William Dixon, *Management and the Worker*, Cambridge: Harvard University Press, 1939.

12. Small losses with huge potential gains: Tapping into gambling fever

An important feature of crowdfunding is that each member of the crowd has a relatively small stake in something that *might* become very big indeed. The odds on a Kickstarter project taking off are roughly the odds on betting on the favourite in a horse or dog race, somewhere between 6–4 and 3–1 against, although getting enough money is no guarantee of eventual success. Not only does the population at large have an appetite for gambling at longer odds than these but it is prepared to lose money on an epic scale *so as to buy excitement*. It is well established that bookmakers take *at least* fifteen per cent of all losing stakes and casinos in Las Vegas much more than this. That people gamble on a vast scale testifies that the *prospect* of gain is attractive in itself and persists even in the face of near-certain losses over time. It seems that *irregular rewards* are more tempting than regular ones. Sensible gamblers do not bet more than they can afford to lose and enjoy the hope of gain as they watch or attend the event they gamble on.

Crowdfunding could prove every bit as attractive without the gross exploitation of the gambling community which currently occurs. Most *would* still lose but enough would win at long odds to keep the excitement up and the wagers coming. Moreover, gamblers would *gain* on aggregate, which might quadruple participation. Quite apart from the thrill of long odds many people would regard even a small chance of improving the human lot as worth betting upon. If, like Martin Luther King, we have a dream, then even an outside chance of that dream being fulfilled is worth our stake and unless we hazard we cannot win. Nothing good comes easily. We have to take risks on the reciprocity of others. Someone must be the first to search for a response from others and somewhere among the crowd enough of such people may be found.

Were we to try out new ideas when they were still highly uncertain then the culture would be a first-mover in hundreds of fields. Even if we often failed we would still *learn* and try again, as better information accumulated. Those who make a splash understand the turbulence that then ensues better than those on the sidelines. You become an expert on your own near-miss, on what you *should* have said to potential backers and buyers.

13. We are looking at nothing less than the radical democratization of capitalism

We are supposed to be living in a democratic nation, but with five lobbyists from the financial sector in the USA disbursing millions to members of Congress, our ability to influence our legislators is very unevenly distributed, while the sponsoring of attack ads ends up by persuading us of the villainy of all concerned in politics as the mud begins to stick. Never before has the electorate been so widely disgusted by the whole spectrum of politics. We need positive messages with hope for the future, which is where crowdfunding comes in. The truth is that most of us do not invest at all, but leave this to a tiny band of professionals who concentrate our funds in large organizations with market power. The resulting pay-off is our sole concern and theirs. Much of this money is wrested away from rivals or from customers. Society is less and less enriched by this process.

The most democratic aspect of current capitalism is the ownership of our homes and this is highly privileged through mortgage interest deduction. Unfortunately, this tends to emphasize owning as opposed to doing, and to creating wealth, and privileges the old over the young. We sit fast in our homes with our possessions all around us and celebrate consumption rather than production. Banks prefer to sponsor housing above all else. It is safer and easier. A very important advantage of crowdfunding is that it reverses this bias towards a nation of rent-seekers. It favours imagining, innovating and contributing over possession and rent-collecting.

We suffer from the reigning doctrine that the purpose of industry is to make money while neglecting the reverse proposition that the purpose of money is to make industry. We need look no further than China for the success of this second proposition. It even borrows – too much we claim – to boost investment, while our multinationals sit on unused trillions. What crowdfunding does is encourage millions to invest in ideas they cherish, to rebuild Western industry and see it grow. To quote John F. Kennedy, it asks 'not what your country can do for you but what you can do for your country'. It reawakens America's and Britain's productive pasts, their dedication to spiritual goals.

But above all it *democratizes capitalism* by encouraging millions to invest who have either never invested before or never chosen their own investments with ethics, innovation or social purpose in mind. Moreover they can now invest in their viable dreams, not in oligopoly suppliers and their powers to appropriate the earnings of other people. The Age of Innovation has dawned. We can see it growing in proximity to our major universities. We urgently need to give our most creative people a hearing and get funds to those who impress us. Crowds of eager supporters can realize their ideals. 'The market place for ideas' has long been a dream to aspire to. It may at last be within our reach.

How might crowdfunding learn from the themes of some of our chapters? In the Introduction we argued that values were really *differences* and until we encountered people whose values were different from our own we could scarcely understand ourselves, much less them.

We also featured the 'first tycoon' Josiah Wedgwood. He reached far into the past by conjuring up the beauties of Greek and Roman antiquity and far into the future by championing the then unpopular cause of American independence. He joined science to business and the Staffordshire potteries to the Chinese art of making porcelain. Despite his origins in a small Protestant minority sect he reached out to the royal houses across Europe. His own Unitarian 'crowd' aspired to nothing less than the world spiritual unity of Christendom.

Crowdfunding places its audience in front of a torrent of new ideas and invites them to sponsor those which attract them most. It is a very diverse and stimulating place to be and extremely out of the ordinary. If you wish to encounter value differences then here is the spot you should occupy. The mountain is searching for Muhammad, the crowd is looking for creative leadership, the community is cherishing its more innovative members.

In Chapter 1 we introduced the Protestant values that pushed Britain, the USA and much of the West into centuries of industrial leadership. We saw values as rule-based, methodical, written ways of building heaven on earth. We saw life as an individual narrative, a pilgrimage and a learning journey in the service of divine authority. Just as Christian, in *The Pilgrim's Progress,* heard 'the trumpets sound for him on the other side' so there is a crowd or Heavenly City somewhere which will grasp what we stand for and have laboured to create. But we need to persist in our quest and have faith in our creative endowments, eschewing easy options. America's founding fathers and men like Wedgwood were built of this sterner stuff. We need to embark on creative quests and dangerous journeys of our own.

In Chapter 2 we asked whether some of these heady values had recently become hubristic. Is economics *really* a universal science? Who deputized us to become world policemen? Is our financial system *too* specific, abstract and analytical? How can trillions of dollars just disappear and were they there in the first place? The great advantage of crowdfunding is that a written 'gospel' speaks potentially good news to a faithful community of particular people, fellow pilgrims in the land of doubt and sorrow, yet also of eternal hope. These people embraced the ideals of the individual before they ever became products or services. He or she was always innovative but thanks to the crowd never isolated, always expressing selfhood but never predatory or selfish. Crowdfunded initiatives are a flying wedge of individuals plus an enthusiastic crowd of sponsors. They have been waiting for someone to lead them.

Chapter 3 argued that wealth was in fact created by *stakeholders working together.* Tilting the field of play towards maximizing the enrichment of just one party, the shareholders, was a mistake. This was because there was no money for shareholders to collect *until* employees and suppliers had delighted customers and received their revenues. Trying to give shareholders more and other stakeholders less, leads to self-harming strategies. With crowdfunding the stakeholders are there from the very start, are deeply committed and are not lightly put aside. Moreover, investors in many cases ARE employees, partners, suppliers, customers and the community of those with stakes. They are members of the same crowd, committed to the same aims and there to see that promises are kept.

Crowdfunding does *not* go down the route recommended by Milton Friedman, that the only responsibility of business is to make money for shareholders; it rather supports Mackey's axiom that money is the route to creating wealth for all stakeholders, including shareholders, who will have their generosity repaid. The motives of investors are constructive, not extractive. They want to help create something that was not there before.

Chapter 4 explained how the Peoples' Republic of China was relegating us to the slow lane. The tight, cohesive 'crowds' of the Chinese diaspora with their Confucian values had found a new goal in life, not just the family dynasty but the nurture of their ancestral home, a triumphant return to their roots. A very diverse diaspora is returning to China and creating a cosmopolitan mix of values. Moreover, allowing world markets into China had opened up East Asians to Western influences. Not only had East met West, but communism had encountered capitalism and the result was not the nuclear holocaust many had feared but the fastest surge of economic growth the world has seen! In those terrifying gaps between systems lay not just danger but opportunity, as the Chinese characters from 'crisis' proclaim. You must jump across the ravine to get the other side

The traditional values of Taoism have made a reappearance with Yin and Yang in harmony with one another and the Middle Kingdom as the hinge of the world order. Crowdfunding has the same stress on relationships, on intimacy and informality hosted by a constant stream of new ideas. Indeed China constitutes the crowd listening very attentively to new initiatives from the West and mobilizing around these with amazing speed and great enthusiasm. We desperately need the high morale of such crowds, their hopes and aspirations, their emphasis on agreement rather than disagreement, their positive attitude to the technology they are sponsoring, their aim to engage fellow employees rather than control them.

In Chapter 5 we saw that Singapore is hosting outstanding multinational companies, which provide jobs, goods, markets and education for the people of Singapore. Singapore has acted as the crowd, welcoming input not so much from entrepreneurs but from established and successful multinational companies, chosen by their government for their enlightened treatment of stakeholders. It has used Western individualism to inform its own community and universal Western science to educate its people.

It is relentlessly pro-business and does everything to support international initiatives. It is a prime example of a country with a largely Chinese culture which has embraced Western ideas and encouraged these to infiltrate the crowd. Together with Hong Kong, Taiwan and South Korea it demonstrates that East–West *hybrid economies* are fast-growing and highly competitive. Although Western ideas must be strange to its people it has borrowed these wholesale and demonstrated that difference, especially that between East and West, is a great teacher.

Because of the shortage of space in Singapore, companies compete to be located there and must make and keep promises to their host. Among the promises they make is to sustain all domestic stakeholders, employees, suppliers, customers, lenders, the community and the environment. They must also join a cluster. In return the government will introduce them to local resources, coach them and advise them. The government, much cheaper than most Western governments but much more influential, *does* favour certain businesses above others. But this favour is not towards political cronies but towards *knowledge*. Products with more extensive ideas and knowledge inside them are preferred to those with less. Crowdfunding has the means to make similar distinctions. It entertains a range of exciting prospects and chooses the best.

In Chapter 6 we learned that many virtues of capitalism were hidden from our gaze because we were largely conscious of companies which boosted our shares or sold us consumables. We tended to ignore privately owned and business-to-business companies without recognizable brands, most of whose output was exported. The *Mittelstand*, especially common among German-speakers in Germany, Switzerland and Austria contained many companies with business units sufficiently small that intimate, face-to-face relationships were the norm and bureaucracy was rare.

All this reminds us of the adage, 'small is beautiful' and that where organizations can retain their human scale their people are more likely to be innovative, loyal, hard-working, trusting, professional, discipline-oriented and dedicated to quality and customers alike. They are more concerned with the meanings of what they make. They are more innovative as measured by patents per head; train their people more assiduously; provide longer-term employment; are more accepting of women and more likely to promote them; more oriented to the long-term; and more supportive of the local communities in which they are located.

Crowdfunded companies would likely share many of these virtuous characteristics. They are as yet small or medium-sized. They are of human scale, are born out of intimacy and enthusiasm around new ideas and are frequently initiated by professionals who shared the same discipline and the same knowledge and sought to serve a common cause. They will often be business-to-business and constitute clusters and supply-chains in which the crowd of special customers plays an active part. They are dedicated to innovation and human development and find their loyal customers from within their crowds. They have the fierce loyalty of those mobilized around ideas essential to their future and the industry of those fully absorbed in what they are doing.

In Chapter 7, we looked at conscious capitalism. We saw that it took a veritable crowd of stakeholders working with each other to create a company conscious of all the benefits it can confer on others and on itself. We saw that companies that created wealth were *synergistic*. For example, they paid their employees more than average for that industry and spent more money on their training but got all these costs back and more from *higher levels of productivity* and sales per square foot. It could be proved statistically that they gave more to employees, customers and suppliers while receiving *even more* in return. What crowdfunded companies have to persuade their investors is not only that they are offering a new and better product but that they are producing it in a way that develops employees, delights customers and nurtures suppliers. It is not simply that being loved by your stakeholders is gratifying but it pays off in profits. Investors must be convinced that service is the best kind of leadership, that those who give the most will subsequently receive the most.

Crowdfunding begins as a pure consciousness shared with other would-be stakeholders. Before there is even one product or one sale there is shared meaning, higher purpose, superordinate goals and all the characteristics that distinguish loved companies.

In Chapter 8 we looked at the environment and how to sustain it. Since nature itself consists of many cycles we need to mimic this. Pollution, waste and resource inefficiencies stretch all the way from the raw materials supplied initially to the distribution and installation of the product itself. What is required is an entirely *new business model*, a redefinition of profit and loss, not just products designed to have several lives and to be easily disassembled and recycled, but a new look at the process of making and distributing the product.

All this makes crowdfunding even more important since it alone goes to the very origin of a product and service and the ideas from which it springs. To go to the roots of industry means starting out in a new way with a better idea of something created to be sustainable in the first place. Crowdfunding is in at the birth of a new kind of economy and can ask its investors to hold it up to a new set of standards, a triple bottom line that cites people, profits and planet. We need to put a price on wiping out whole animal species or loss of fresh water supplies. The big advantage of crowdfunding is that the business philosophy comes first and the product/service is its extension. Within the crowd will be enough people who care so that companies losing their founding principles will be weeded out. The pledge to sustain the environment will be honoured.

One of the most cherished ideas of capitalism and its advocates is that it constitutes a 'marketplace for ideas'. Switch on your TV and you see that it is closer to a culture of idiocies! But crowdfunding puts seminal ideas and their flowering at the very heart of their propositions. The marketplace for ideas could come true at last. Let sustainable ideas win our allegiance over unsustainable ones. Because crowdfunding writes down what its enterprise is all about, it revisits the early Puritans who extolled the word of God. We do not simply serve human wants but human needs, not just people but societies and civilizations. We do not just live to eat but eat to live and serve humanity.

In Chapter 9 we followed the fortunes of the Global Alliance for Banking on Values which like CF puts values and ideas first and funded those projects with the greatest social impact which were most likely to enhance people, planet and profit – in that order. We saw that money was a service *to* industry, that banks were servants to their customers[5] and could grow as these grew. Banks should prosper by *indirection* through the growth of their clients, the same purpose as motivates the crowd.

We come finally to Chapter10 concerning Cambridge and Harvard and the growth of high-tech industry in these areas. Here we saw that some of

---

5. Fons Trompenaars and Ed Voerman, *Servant Leadership Across Cultures,* Oxford: Infinite Ideas, 2009.

our best brains despised business as 'filthy lucre' and extolled pure research paid for out of our taxes. This is partly the fault of business itself which has told us 'money has no conscience' and has gone a long way in its conduct to exemplify this. However, the money that pays for pure research has to come from somewhere and despising it only reduces the flow. To the extent that science can be turned to commercial ends it will be eagerly sponsored.

Indeed, we might expect the university, dealing as it does in information, to take crowdfunding to its heart. There are signs that this is happening. Cambridge features The Syndicate Room in which panels of experts recognize promising developments in science and commend these to their less expert but civic-minded followers. NESTA has reported on the advice of angel investors. It found not only that their advice profited investors but that the returns were above average.[6] All this occurs despite the fact that angels are thinking chiefly of the innovative process not about making money. Unlike Venture Capitalists angels put their own money in what they recommend.

The great advantage of crowdfunding is that entrepreneurs and founders tell us not simply about *what* they plan to supply, but *why* they are doing this, what this means to them and also *how* they aim to it and the people who must be engaged along the way. The benefits can be enumerated, the ramifications itemized and the changes to the social system described. Where founders make clear their good intentions the crowd can help them attain these. Founders will not always succeed. They will sometimes fall short of their promises but if their good intentions are believed the crowd will report failures and provide counsel on the subject of remedies.

It was Arnold Toynbee in his *A Study of History*[7] who observed that civilizations are made by their own creative minorities. Where these are tolerated, which happens only on occasion, and where sponsorship goes to a group of geniuses, a priceless heritage may arise. It typically lasts but a short period until fear of novelty peaks and some 'bonfire of the vanities' intervenes and ends it all. Crowdfunding promises to give minority 'crowds' of around five hundred to a thousand people vast powers of innovation. This is unprecedented in human history. The sheer diversity of knowledge makes this astounding variety the phenomenon of our times and elevates innovation to the most important of human virtues. Something understood and championed by only a few score of people can still benefit millions.

6. http://www.nesta.org.uk/

7. Arnold Toynbee, *A Study of History*, with D. C. Somervell, Vols. 1–6, Oxford: Oxford University Press, 1946.

What human beings ultimately seek is to be loved. We can confine this realization to small family enclaves in an arid desert of business-as-usual, where you 'never give a sucker an even break' and grab all you can from other families. Alternatively, we can take pleasure in what we have bestowed on our fellow human beings. Lenscrafters, the US eye-glasses manufacturer has worked with OneSight for over twenty-five years to provide free eye exams, prescription glasses and eye care to underserved communities in forty countries. Their work has literally transformed the lives of millions.

Why do such policies need to be exceptional?

CHAPTER 12

The prospects for a progressive capitalism

Here we will summarize some of the main lesson from this book and suggest some policy alternatives. We need to turn around the economic growth strategies of the UK, Europe and the USA before bitterness festers, before they turn on the immigrants who could save them and start to blame each other for national decline. There is not much time.

Lesson 1: Values, meta-values and circular reasoning

There are values and meta-values. Meta means 'about' so that some values *link other values together.* For example integrity is a meta-value integrating other values. 'Inspiring' in the sense of 'breathing life into' other people and other values is a meta-value. Meta-values are linkages, so that *diversity* needs to be integrated with *inclusion,* or a society will come apart. The individual needs to be integrated with the community and rules need to cover would-be exceptions or the rule of law breaks down. If these pairs of polarities are severed severe disruption will follow, as was illustrated in Chapter 2. Values are *not* things like coins or jewels. If 'diamonds are a girl's best friend' why did Marilyn Monroe kill herself?

Contrasting values *grow together* so that the individual serves the community and the community nurtures the individual. Money helps create industry and industry helps to make money. We can consume more if we (or someone else) produce more. Error allows us to correct, decentralization allows us to centralize information from such activities and we risk our money to secure more than we started with. *All such reasoning is circular or cybernetic* as are the natural cycles of the universe we inhabit. To claim that industry is a mere means to make money, or that communities exist to encourage individuals, introduces a cultural bias, however reasonable this may sound. Every means is also an end as the circle revolves.

Capitalism is a versatile system of amazing breadth that can extol slavery and also help end it, bankroll fascism and halt it in its tracks. However, this cornucopia of benefits has received ridiculously narrow, single minded and selfish interpretations. It is time we unlocked its wider and deeper meanings and showed what it can accomplish. The earlier chapters tried to do this.

Lesson 2: Creating wealth is not just making money

We have fatally confused the making of money with the creation of wealth. Money is all too easily appropriated from other people's pockets to render them poorer. Society as a whole gains nothing from this but loses from the friction involved. In the game of speculation slightly more than half the population will always lose, no matter how smart they are. In comparison, wealth creation has us *giving* to our customers but *getting back* even more than we initially gave. Wealth is created by *indirection*, by first so delighting another that they offer you more. But money is usually made by *direction*, by calculated predatory conduct that outwits an adversary. This simply empties one pocket to fill another and if it grows our economy at all, does so at the expense of other, poorer economies. It is the source of exploitation.

Wealth is created when values are joined by meta-values, when for example workers receive higher wages for being more productive so there is more money or value for everyone. Customers provide more revenue that is shared between employees and investors. Wealth is also created when products do not die and go to waste but become a cradle for another product. We create wealth when we give customers not just what they want but what they *need* to be better off, for example healthy bodies, longer lives, better nutrition and a fairer society. Wealth is generated when values mingle and fuse so that the whole product dwarfs the value of its constituents, for example, an air-bag expanding between a toddler's head and the wind-shield in a car crash is an intervention of priceless value to the parents.

We need to ask ourselves whether banks create wealth to any realizable degree and what price we are paying to the Kings of Capitalism for distributing our money to various industries. Banks do indeed have a role in the economy. They *facilitate wealth creation by distributing money to major contributors.* In this process much money is siphoned off from the rest of us. Does handling money entitle banks to the lion's share? It is the *contributors* they supply, not the *distributors,* who actually create wealth. We saw that the Global Alliance for Banking on Values could leave everyone better off by making powerful social impacts in communities in need of this. It is possible to make the world a better place AND profit personally from doing so.

Lesson 3: The increasing irrelevance of politics

Politicians have rarely stood lower in public esteem than they stand today, whether in America, the UK or Europe. What has gone wrong? In part this is down to the fiercely adversarial invective which politicians hurl at one another, compounded by the work of shock-jocks and attack ads. Some of this mud sticks and it amounts to a race to the bottom, to voting for the least feared and objectionable. Another reason is their helplessness before global turbulence which they can do almost nothing to calm. They talk about 'making one thing absolutely clear' but offer very little clarity and much doubt. We are being tossed on the waves of change and claims to be 'in charge' are laughable. Politicians resemble a man waving his fingers over a player-piano on which the tune has been pre-programmed by unseen persons. They are not the authors of the music at all.

Yet the chief reason for their chronic failure is that their rhetoric tears apart the fabric of our economy instead of binding and healing it. In truth, wealth is not created by managers *or* workers but by both helping each other. Making employees easy to fire in the name of flexibility weakens the feedback loop. Miserable employees without recourse will not produce enough. It is not a case of less government and more private enterprise or vice versa but of government *serving* private enterprise which serves government and pays its taxes. Empowering shareholders or empowering managers are not alternatives but complements. Of course some progressive education is silly and some traditional forms of teaching archaic, but progress derives from strict disciplines coming together creatively and progressively. Turning education into a tug-of-war between ideologies is to disrupt and destroy. Every minister of education has a new pet theory and is gone in a few years leaving chaos in his wake.

The ideologies of Right and Left are poisonous to an economy that needs both points of view. Each party brandishes half the answer but rejects the other half. Within each polarized extreme *there are no answers remaining.* You can empower shareholders but they cannot create wealth by themselves. The power of labour can do nothing by itself, it needs to be well managed so as to be the source of innovative ideas. Bribing employees to conform and handing out money incentives for obedience is counter-productive. At least trades unions had visions of a better world and felt passionate about their work. Locked within its cage each ideological polarity becomes sterile. Every political problem can be blamed on the sins of your adversary who must be banished to the opposition; but this is no solution, just a debate, or at worst a shouting match. Prime Minister's Question Time has no real questions and no real answers. How is anyone to learn anything? US cable stations screen it for entertainment where it vies with re-runs of *I Love Lucy*.

Democracy was, at its inception, a great boon. We stopped killing each other and started debating in front of audiences who chose the winner. But the structure of industry is NOT the structure of debate. Viable solutions are not polarized but reconciled. It is not freedom *or* regulation, but regulations protecting freedoms. It is not government getting tough with industry or industry heroically resisting, but industry *voluntarily* behaving in more ethical ways because it is morally and practically better to do this. Complying under threat is usually ineffective. It is not being tough or tender but being tough on the problems and tender with the people involved. It is not equality *or* excellence but treating other forms of excellence as equals so that you can choose the right combination for the issue at hand. It is not high standards so that more fail or lowered standards so that more of the under-privileged succeed, but standards that lead students to excel. Political parties lose the plot between them. The linkages are destroyed.

Perhaps the biggest mistake is that the British, the Americans and the French have one party supporting labour and the other supporting investors and top managers, when the whole point of industry is to enrich one another and the wages employees earn buy the goods which companies make. Bargaining over a finite pool of money is inevitably a zero-sum game. What labour gets the investors forgo and vice versa. The answer as we shall see is to bargain over wealth yet to be created by joint efforts.

The main hope for a change is in bipartisan parliamentary committees studying such subjects as high-tech innovation, renewable energy, resource saving technologies, the future of manufacturing and banking reform. They should make agreed statements of policy and defend them from the partisans on each wing of politics. Politicians should not be taking money from entrenched interests but helping smaller companies to survive and grow. Ideology is a lazy way of thinking and totally without originality in which all problems are blamed on the belief system of your opponents! In a curious way these convictions are self-fulfilling.

Paul Watzlawick asked us to imagine two sailors standing up in a small sailing dinghy, holding onto ropes attached to the mast at waist height but leaning one to the left and one to the right in an attempt to keep the craft on an even keel. The cartoon is captioned 'Two sailors trying to steady a boat that was steady to begin with'. Each believes and is *right to believe* that were he to lean at less of an absurd angle and stand closer to the mast then the extreme angle of his opponent would capsize the boat in that direction. Give labour what it demands and the company is finished! Yield to management demands and productivity will dive! (There is some evidence for this). Each ideologist has trapped his opponent into leaning so far out that his behind is almost in the water, while shrieking abuse and imprecations at the absurd posture of the other. It is neither dignified nor very effective. No wonder politicians are in trouble. No wonder we call journalists hacks. What is there to vote *for*, the least offensive? We need politicians to help us solve problems and grow the economy.

Lesson 4: Immigrants – our saviours or our nemesis?

We have seen in this book that immigrants were the making of many economies. The USA, Australia, Canada and New Zealand are all world-leading immigrant economies. The Chinese diaspora was, as early as the seventies, the world's third largest economy and has since inspired China. Many ethnic groups in the USA are wealthier and better educated than the country at large. The self-esteem of Jewish adolescents who reported anti-Semitic taunts was actually *higher* than those who did not recall such abuse. Their families and communities seem to have rallied around the victims.

What is it that immigrants have that overcomes the prejudices against them? They have at least two points of view or social contexts, the one they brought with them and that of their adopted land. Too many of us have just one. Immigrants must strive to include their diverse views with our own. It is when cultures collide that we learn – not only about others but about ourselves. Values are *differences* and immigrants know all about the differences they encounter daily. They can encompass different points of view.

Immigrants are also more likely to be *individualistic*. They have broken ties and moved away from old attachments, but they are also more likely to be *communal,* since their economic futures depend upon a network of fellow migrants and maintaining their close support. They are prepared to work harder for less in order to survive. That they better understand other differences between say, sellers and buyers, is not unexpected. We saw that where East meets West in Singapore, Hong Kong, Taiwan, South Korea and Malaysia the economies tend to be strong. These populations have also learned from both sides. Since birth rates have fallen in the affluent West we *need* educated immigrants to make up for this.

Of course immigrants are not always successful. Some are crippled by prejudice or by culture shock, or bring cultural practices with them that clash with majority values (female genital mutilation, for example). Moving from one culture to another *makes you or breaks you* and anti-immigrant feeling is easily aroused by the numbers of broken strangers, many in prison, some unemployed, claiming benefits or before the courts. Depending on their social class, indigenous citizens may encounter more losers than winners and generalize from this. Those who are different will not always be included. Tolerance is not enough. We should *learn* from immigrants. Why are Ismaili Muslims so affluent, so peaceable and so charitable to the poor? Why did Islamic banking suffer so much less than other banks in the recent recession? What is the role of their banks in their communities?

Lesson 5: The power of intrinsic motivation

All great feats of imagination, creativity, innovation and commitment come from deep within us. They are intrinsic. Money rewards which are extrinsic are a 'hygiene factor'. Frederick Herzberg referred to that which *motivates us by its absence not by its presence.*[1] Where people *lack* money and receive less than they feel they should they can think of little else. They become enraged, embittered and non-compliant. Whole political movements are born of this resentment. But where people get enough to live on and need no longer worry about survival then *intrinsic motivation takes over* and it is this that drives excellence, good work for the sake of itself, not for money. Having enough unleashes us for higher goals and avocations. Your unrealized potentials take over your life. Gallup found that a self-fulfilling job was among people's greatest yearnings but that only a minority of us were so engaged.[2]

1.   F. Herzberg, B. Mausner, B. Bloch-Snydermann, *The Motivation to Work*, New York: John Wiley, 1959

2.   Gallup, 28/10/2008, http://www.gallup.com/poll/150383/majority-american-workers-not-engaged-jobs.aspx

The notion that those engaged in business need large bonus payments to keep them motivated is almost certainly false, save in cases where the work is so boring and arduous that employees must be 'compensated' for an otherwise dull life. Getting funds to the most innovative people in your society is important work needing fine discrimination and there is no reason why bankers must be bribed with huge pay-outs for doing this. Banking offers thrills a plenty as you watch your protégés grow. The Global Alliance for Banking on Values puts concern for people and planet first and made above average profits by doing this. Simply handling money does not entitle you to the major cut.

But what is most serious is that huge bribes and bonuses act like a castrating knife. They metaphorically kill our capacity to procreate and leave living legacies in our wakes. That extrinsic incentives kill innovation and reduce cognitive, problem-solving skills has been revealed again and again, yet the Apostles of Money and the Monks of Mammon refuse to take this on board. Money is the source of abject conformity to those in authority over us who seek to buy our obedience. It is responsible for the neglect of customers, the sidelining of personal judgement, the eclipse of conscience, the compounding of erroneous decisions and driving whole companies over the cliff edge. It is largely responsible for our roller-coaster economy and our famous imitations of Gadarene swine.

Almost everyone should be fulfilled by the work they do and if this is not happening the employer is losing out on a massive scale. We have just one life and should be filling it with everything we can. If the employee has not grown more useful, better informed and more resourceful in their work then the company's time is being wasted along with the employee's life. All it takes is fitting the task into a wider context with greater meaning, about which we will have more to say presently.

Lesson 6: How organized consumers and investors could turn things around

We highlighted a major problem in Chapter 2. Our society and its individuality has become more oriented to consumption than to production. We would rather play than work and the money we earn goes preponderantly into consumption. Self-indulgence has overwhelmed self-restraint. Yet the secret of positive change is to use such biases to our advantage. Consumers could help turn our society around by the patterns of how they consume. Our purchases can become more discerning of the conduct of companies which can be rewarded or punished in the market place.

There is nothing to be ashamed of in wanting to wash our clothes, clean our houses, alleviate colds and headaches, but why leave it at that? Companies employ thousands of people and we should care about the morale, the fulfilment, the equality and the satisfaction of their employees. Organized women shoppers, who are the majority in any case, could demand that companies reveal the ratio of male to female wages and invite the most equal of companies to put this information on their packaging and advertising. If market shares began to shift women would be promoted in a hurry! Unilever for example has a mostly good record in such regards and we should 'buy' this enlightenment when we shop. *The One Hundred Best Companies to Work For* is published annually and we should make sure their sales increase as a consequence. Why not reward the companies who grow their people? They do us all a favour. The product will probably be better in any case, but there is so much more to life than eating breakfast cereal!

Published information about responsible companies need not stop there. What proportion of this product was recycled, How much more does the CEO earn than the average employee? If Whole Foods can grow to a US$ 12 billion company on a ratio of nineteen times more, then is not 350 a bit obscene? Why not reproach such greed, which is in any case a ludicrous over-estimation of *any* one person's powers? Of course companies would not always be truthful but NGOs have already arisen to make independent assessments, as we saw in Chapter 8 and the social responsibility of companies would become part of their strategies, where customers demanded this. It *pays* Nestle to assist its own coffee growers so let the company benefit twice, from better suppliers and grateful consumers. It *pays* Johnson and Johnson to keep its employees in good health so let it too benefit twice, from its own wisdom and from our gratitude.

Organized consumers would be powerful stakeholders. In the Age of the Internet there is no excuse for not publishing comparative data on what companies are doing or not doing and those holding out would be beset by rumour and anonymous complaints by employees and ex-employees. Being a good corporate citizen could become essential to survival. Benefiting shareholders exclusively at the expense of others could be a thing of the past. Legislation might not be needed.

Many products are much of a muchness. There is little difference between the many writing pads, ball-point pens, shoe-polishes and baking powders on offer. But the very fact that the products are mundane in themselves gives us a chance to produce them in more socially useful ways, with deserving people and achieving additional objectives. Just as crowdfunding sells the idea behind the product so social marketing can sell ideas attached to an otherwise mundane product, like package delivery. If UPS can help put its drivers through college then just imagine the host of benefits companies might confer in the process of growing their people. Why not produce 'Just Pens', from an outfit trying to get justice for those who cannot afford it? Organized consumers could have vast powers if they would just mobilize them. We could discover how many days it took a company to pay its suppliers. We could count and publicize the number of businesses which ran out of cash as a result and perished. We could award 'scalps' to late-payers and 'crowns' to quick-payers. We could celebrate 'the best friend of small companies' and recommend them to others. And of course government has the power to do the same.

Political and social movements could organize mass switching from one energy supplier to another, from one insurer or lender to another, according to their treatment of stakeholders. The time and the nuisance of switching would be carried by the movements, representing thousands at a time and saving costs. Even conservatives would concede that we were aiding market forces and making competition work. Companies could have their market shares boosted or eroded according to the responsibilities they accepted.

In addition to organized consumers there are spontaneously organized investors. Stephen Foley, has written of the hedge fund titan Paul Tudor Jones who has started a project named Just Capital, which will rate companies on the social justice of their actions.[3] Given the issues raised in this book justice, in the sense of balance and weighing different viewpoints 'justly' before combining them, should pay off handsomely. Productive human relationships are fair and just. Just Capital is researching and polling how the American public wants its corporations to behave. It will then produce a Just Index of the corporate conduct of more than 1,000 leading companies. In the USA the Global Sustainable Investment Alliance, not to be confused with the GABV featured in Chapter 10, has found that the proportion of professionally managed investments that considered ESG factors (Environmental and Social Governance) had risen from 21.5 per cent to 30.2 per cent in just two years. These are expected to be in a majority by 2020.

S&P Dow Jones now runs 130 ESG equity indices and these have grown more than fifty per cent in the last two years. MSCI Inc. the US provider of

3.   Stephen Foley, ' "Just Index" sets sights on market solution to inequality', *Financial Times*, 23 March 2015.

stock-market indices and portfolio analysis tools has more than 130 ESG equity indices for investors who wish to do more than profit. This has also grown fifty per cent since 2013 and has now reached US$25 billion. Just Capital promises to be the first large fund 'driven by the attitudes and beliefs of the public', instead of experts or activists in search of profit alone. It has polled 20,000 Americans, many in focus groups and found that fairness to workers has become a major issue, higher even than large top salaries. The US Securities and Exchange Commission is arguing with itself as to whether to endorse indices that disclose the ratio between CEO salaries and average earnings.

Lesson 7: Stakeholders united in prosperity

We saw in Chapter 7 that wealth was created ten times more effectively when all stakeholders worked to help each other. What we suggested in the previous section was that consumers help all stakeholders, the employees, suppliers, investors, the community and the environment. They could even help the government to collect taxes by listing avoidance schemes and dubious claims to have intellectual property in South Sea islands. The pressure exerted by consumers would actually *improve* the performance of the companies. They would be speaking for all stakeholders. Even shareholders would gain from such a broad alliance, as Chapter 7 showed. It should not be difficult to generate scores for the *satisfaction of all stakeholders* and companies might choose to steer themselves strategically by such scores. A composite index of stakeholder satisfaction could be published for each company and would prove far more effective than bottom lines.

This should remind us of another important point. Success belongs not to single companies, which might have gained at the expense of their customers, their employees, their suppliers or a devastated environment but to the entire ecosystem surrounding that company which prospers, if at all, *with the assistance of all stakeholders*. We all generate wealth together. A single dissenting voice can bring down the whole system, as when customers revolt, employees strike, suppliers go belly up, or the government names and shames a company and the press has a field day.

Lesson 8: Limits on size – the value of intimacy

A message of major importance in this book is that units of a smaller scale are often more ethical, more effective and more innovative than giant corporations and vast bureaucracies. The idea that virtue inheres in size and that the large should be helped to gobble up the small is an extremely suspect premise. Just because larger companies *can* buy smaller ones does not mean that they should do this or that it is in our interests that they do so. The evidence from America is that small businesses are still liked and admired by most of those polled but that big businesses are, for the most part, despised and distrusted. Nor do bigger businesses absorb the virtues of the small when they acquire them. The 'Bear hug' may squeeze the life out of the small acquisition. Generally speaking taking 'ownership' of the genius of an entrepreneurial firm is a very doubtful process. It is not easy to possess the creativity of others. Such genius is either given freely or withheld and if the founders are turned off then value vanishes.

We need to see companies as families, a trait we saw in Chapter 4 on China. It is within the intimacy of close human relationships that people grow, dare, aspire and inspire. Chapter 6 revealed how much more innovative and developmental were the hidden champions or *Mittelstand,* all companies of limited size. Yet what really needs to be of human scale is not so much the company but the *business unit.* Many hidden champions operated in a dozen or more countries yet each unit was small enough for everyone to be on a first name basis, and the unit *organized itself through shared excitement around chosen products and goals.* This is the secret of the kinds of organizations that develop their stakeholders. Wealth creation relies heavily on the quality of relationships and it is these rather than individuals who create wealth. Even Steve Jobs needed customers and the brighter these were the better. The hackers are a vital part of the equation.

There is a curious metaphysical pathos about the inevitable onset of bureaucracy to which Max Weber testified. Must people become roles and positions, their discretion captured by job descriptions, their minds punctuated by bullet points, their heads hunted by specialists, their promises written into contracts, their day divided into time-sheets, their thoughts rendered as bullet points and their lives dedicated to shareholders they neither meet nor engage. Are we all just units of social capital? Are we all human resources, alive, but otherwise no different from other physical and financial resources? The view taken here is that our humanity is the organizing spirit of everything or we might as well pump copying fluid into our veins. Organizations should be the incubators of human development or they lose their purpose and direction. We render this world more humane, prosperous and aesthetic or we are nothing of any consequence.

The more informal, spontaneous, affectionate, supportive and understanding we can be the better. These are family values but they shouldn't be left at home, we need them in the workplace. All help explain why China is overtaking us apace and why values linked together in systems create wealth for all participants. Even big corporation can recreate this spirit within teams. Jack Welch famously created GE's work-out groups, teams given challenging problems to discuss with the goal of finding coherent solutions. Towards the end of his reign he was implementing nearly seventy-five per cent of all team solutions *substantially unchanged.* The membership of each team was a microcosm of the problem to be solved. A team is just large enough to be a community and just small enough to allow individual members to shine and to lead.

As Margaret Mead once remarked, 'Never doubt that a small group of thoughtful, committed, citizens can change the world. Indeed, it is the only thing that ever has.' In what Burke called a little platoon we grow our humanity. There may be no better experience in life than being the heroine or hero to one's intimate acquaintances. This *private* popularity is the key to our confidence and our integrity, while *public* popularity is fools' gold. Famous actresses overdose on nights when a third of the male population of the USA would have given their eye teeth for a date with them. Mass attraction does nothing to alleviate despair. We need to be loved and respected by those close to us whom we know well.

We should consider allowing small, creative companies to be taken over only with their agreement and give employees six months to find alternative sources of support. The quarrel between Hewlett Packard and Autonomy is a lesson for us all. It is near-impossible for an established company to understand the potential of a fledgling company outside the context of an ongoing friendship between them. Once relationships break down millions vanish and only bitterness remains. The true value of Autonomy lay in the mind of the founder and unless this was willingly shared and understood, the value of the company was inevitably written down. Searching for villainy is a waste of time – 'only connect'.

Lesson 9: Wealth is created by the quality of our relationships

Our stress on individualism and on owning our own property as individuals obscures a most important truth. *Wealth is created by the quality of our relationships,* by what we share with one another. This is especially true in an age of information. I can sell a bar of chocolate for a few cents in the school yard but on receiving the money I must forgo the chocolate. In that sense there is economic scarcity. But what if I sell information? Then I receive money *and keep the information* although it is now shared between us. The scarcity has vanished. The case for attending college is marginal if you look at individual monetary gains from doing so, but the gains are undoubted if you consider that you might enrich your relationships with anyone you ever met for the rest of your life including spouse and family. We have not appreciated life in the round until relationships are fully considered.

Wealth-creation depends on relationships between leaders and subordinates, among fellow employees, between suppliers and customers, between trainer and trainee, between company and contractors, between government and private enterprise, management and workers and between all the players in the industrial ecosystem. The strongest bonds of all are forged between those who co-create products and services. They are like veterans from the same trenches. They faced, if not annihilation, then that of their shared project. They survived thanks to one another.

But it is not just relationships among people that are vital *but the combinations of their ideas.* We cooperate *at* competing, and compete to see whose ideas it might be best to cooperate around. We *risk* our money in the hope of *securing* more of it. Fortune favours the prepared mind, so that *intention* leads to happy *accident. Exceptions* form the basis of revised *rules.* Our parents *ascribe* status to us when we can only gurgle, yet we can go on to *achieve* this. The simple act of *borrowing* and later *repaying* can lift a poor mother out of wretchedness. What we *centralize* is information about *decentralized* activities. We have seen that the *poor* have a potential for *prosperity.* We could go on indefinitely. What creates wealth is relating these concepts.

All that each one of us has to work with is *our end of the relationship* which is why we should not argue endlessly about whose fault a problem is but try something different at our end. If an executive is paid three times more than her secretary then it might be wise to hold her seventy-five per cent responsible for the ensuing relationship. If the executive has trouble retaining secretaries then she is not doing what she was paid for in this respect. If just one person leaves a ten-person company, then nine relationships are lost in which information is stored. We not only know, *we know who knows.*

Lesson 10: Superordinate goals and higher purposes

It might seem that many of us are doomed to do mundane tasks whose only benefit lies in what we can buy with the money earned. Running a large supermarket like Whole Foods is typical of the work on offer to many people and it might seem insufficient to keep the mind alive. Yet it is possible to see beyond the task to the wider context, like the stonemason who realized he was helping to build a cathedral and serving his God in the process. Perhaps taking charge of the vegetable counters at Whole Foods is as small time as some of the new potatoes on sale, but even so, the company was thinking of higher purposes and superordinate goals as we saw in Chapter 7.

All employees are called 'team members' because it is in the intimacy of these that we find our worth. These teams were, among other things, dedicated to a better diet for children, one that would rescue them from obesity and sustain an active life. Employees work to give all customers a longer life-span through more nutritious eating and dedicate themselves not just to what customers *want* but to what they *need*. Employees may volunteer to serve in more than seventy nations abroad making micro-loans, their expenses for living and working paid by the company. As with IBM this is seen as a form of leadership training and successful volunteers are regarded as showing a sense of adventure and greater potential. Employees may also work in the local community as company volunteers, a scheme which John Mackey, Whole Foods' founder and CEO sees as repaying him many times over in community appreciation.

The company demands from its suppliers the highest levels of animal welfare, the avoidance of depleted stocks of fish or animals, humane methods of slaughter and the local sourcing of vegetables to save energy and assure freshness. Employees help select local charities to which a percentage of one day's purchases will be donated and it is suggested they encourage their supporters to turn out to shop on that day, a strategy which unites egoism with altruism and helps both stakeholders. Great pride is taken in the new companies Whole Foods has helped launch with test markets in different regions of the country and day by day uptake of different product varieties are fed back to the producer. It takes great pride in every start-up it has nursed to life, lending it cash-flow in any crisis. There is great intrinsic pleasure in such activity. You rub together two ideas or more and create a fire. The power large retailers have to grow small companies is vast. We should celebrate such nurturance and reward it.

Lesson 11: William Blake's world of innovation

We have stressed how important it is to connect, to relate, to nurture and to grow. We have seen how diversity provides us with ever new elements to bring into the combination. But what matters most of all is that the *combination be innovative.* This is the only possible path for a highly educated economy. Everything that is routine can be more cheaply made elsewhere and by outsourcing we impoverish our own working class. Anything new and useful commands a high price at least for a short period until others catch up. We must innovate or die.

Innovation is not narrow but broad, very broad. If Toyota can get scores of *implemented* suggestions from each of its factory workers then so can we. If it pays a company to have its workers *think* for half an hour or more at the end of the day and decide what new processes should be tried out next day, then clearly their thoughts are of value. Moreover the next day's work becomes a way of *testing your hypotheses* and you are a person, not just a pair of hands and a blue collar. Your work has the meaning you brought to it. Just as it once took a mere child to announce that the emperor was naked, so good ideas have no respect for formal hierarchy. They speak out of turn.

A creative combination may not be merely twenty per cent more valuable than its constituents, but five hundred times as in the Portland Vase cited in the Introduction, enough to enrich everyone concerned. Innovation is almost certainly a form of logic, a theme with endless variations, a circle of contrasting values, always departing only to return, like Janus the Roman god of arrival and departure. What is it about ideas so *diverse* that no one has thought of *combining* them, so *strange* that never before were they *familiar? We believe that innovation is to be found in the midst of profound dilemmas and between sometimes bitter conflicts,* like that between capitalism and communism which the Chinese may have brought to an end with a prospering economy. We believe that if Muhammad Yunus can get 97.5 per cent of loans repaid by dirt-poor Bangladeshi women and then award them profits from this, that almost *anything is possible,* however seemingly improbable. We saw that twenty-five banks all dedicated to sustainably helping their stakeholders could perform at least as well as banking giants.

We believe that innovation can bloom in the most unlikely places on earth; that necessity is indeed the mother of invention; and that gold emerges from the heat of the refiner's fire. Innovation requires that we mix *equality* with *excellence, association* with *distance, vertical* with *lateral* thinking, the *serious* with the *playful, preparation* with *good fortune, blindness* with *watchfulness, low costs* with *premium value, lines* with *circles, separation* with *symbiosis, conflicts* with *reconciliation,* and *inspiration* with *perspiration* for ever more.

A person who saw all this but is too often dismissed as a mystic was William Blake. He argued that opposites were complements and that contraries are positives. 'I was angry with my friend, I told my wrath my wrath did end.'

Bring these contraries together and we would 'cleanse the doors of perception'. He famously wrote, 'I will not cease from *mental* fight, nor shall my sword sleep in my hand, till we have built Jerusalem…' For him mental fight was the answer to physical force and its brutality. He was an admirer of the French Revolution blazing at that time. 'Tyger, Tyger burning bright, in the forests of the night', was his celebration of its passion. He was once arrested for defending it.

But he had sensibility enough to realize that the tiger's passion was but part of the answer. We needed the 'marriage of heaven and hell'. God had made both the lamb and the tiger and these could be reconciled by creative consciousness and its mental fight. We must pull the world's conflicts into our own souls and let these contend. If a communist government can work with a market economy what is *not* possible, and why does that combination seemingly surpass all other economies?

Blake was especially infuriated by Newton's world of dead objects measured by dividers, even as the muscle-bound giant placed his bare bottom on the beauties of nature all around him. The sculpture he drew of this is famous. Blake wrote to a friend, 'May God us keep from Single Vision and from Newton's sleep.' Out there in the wider world was context after context, vision after vision, pattern after pattern, song after song which combined innocence with experience. Things were not just 'out there' in a world silent, colourless and dead, they were 'in here' in a beautiful environment of endless re-conception and imagination. Colour, beauty and fragrance is not 'out there' but within our human sense impressions, in the way we perceive the universe.

SPECIFIC ——————————————————— DIFFUSE

Figure 12.1 Newton as depicted by William Blake with his bottom seated on flora and fauna while he concentrates on small details, objects and measurements. The world of abstractions is dead, shrunken and notational.

Lesson 12: Circular thinking among the cycles of nature

We must learn to think as nature moves and as our earth has evolved, in cycles: lunar cycles, oxygen cycles, ocean cycles, rock cycles, cycles of the seasons, of day and night, sleeping and waking, work and rest, procreation, successive generations of people and of products, lifecycles and so on. Only if we think this way can we eschew the barbed harpoons which were stuck into *Moby Dick* and cease despoiling our environment and crushing nature's secrets beneath bulldozers. Given that scientists have found substances inside scorpions and other deadly insects that can be used as healing medicines, to 'conquer' anything that threatens us is a poor option.

To think in circles is to combine contrasts: past and future, ideal and real, possibilities and actualities, risking in ways which make your money more secure, freedom and subsequent responsibility for that freedom. The more deeply you relax at night the higher your energy the following morning. Jet lag comes from our bodies being out of synchrony with our sleeping-waking, lunar cycles. We must search in order to find. We must not just ready-aim-fire, but ready-fire-aim. Where the last shell landed informs us where to point. We err and correct. We discover what customers want by successive approximations to their ideals.

We saw that many cultures, especially those in East Asia turned our Western values *back to front*. How dare they? How very sinister! But circles have no one starting point, no back which is not also a front and no front that is not a back, no end that is not a means and no means that is not an end. Depending on how we view a model of a double helix, the figure becomes the ground and the ground the figure, the text becomes the context and vice versa. To grasp these different contexts and points of view is to be king of what we survey, which is why at least some immigrants succeed despite our very real animosity towards them. This is why the Taoist, Yin-Yang symbol is so powerful in the context of China and East Asia. It is a circle of eternal return with entry at either point.

What environmentalism can do for us, regardless of how dire are the threats to our planet, is to *reconceive and reinterpret the creation of wealth in its entirety*. Every machine or product can be manufactured for easy disassembly once its useful life is over; its separate ingredients can be recycled so as to save virgin resources and two or three new lives can be made out of its seeming 'decay' as the grave of one product becomes the cradle of another. We are talking not just of product innovation but of *process innovation* in which new toxin-free supplies are more healthily manufactured, distributed and installed, with sources of energy which are renewable and our god is once more the sun, from which much of life flows.

We must mimic nature, especially evolutionary experiments millions of years in the making, which combine luck with selection, change with continuity, cooperation with competition, disruption with equilibrium and survival with fitting finely into the natural scheme of things. These wondrous designs should fill us with awe and the tree of life should become our talisman. The way some animals co-evolve with the help of others should inspire us. The irony is that this is immensely cost-saving and hence profitable. Resource efficiency will repay us many times over and will leave this earth as a legacy to our grandchildren in a better condition than we found it. The degree of non-stop innovation that environmental responsibility demands is truly mind-blowing and we should derive enormous satisfaction from its delivery. We can leave more abundant lives in our wake.

We have to rethink banking from the ground up. Dollars, pounds, yen, etc. are by themselves sterile things. Money needs to be poured into the *real economy* and there be turned into wealth-creating innovation. We need banks to search for genius contributors and ensure that these get the help they need. Helping the poor and destitute can pay off handsomely *but only if this is not your chief motive.* Even micro-loans stop working if your chief aim is not to nurture your clients but to profit your bank. Ceasing to exploit the poor will by itself win you millions of grateful adherents. In the world of basic, ever-improving infrastructure are hidden sky-high levels of economic growth. Nurturing banks can fuel such growth. What grows an economy is building and sustaining its industrial and natural ecosystems and getting stakeholders to help one another. The Global Alliance could become a consultant-banker on global economic development, dispensing not just money but its own principles.

Finally crowdfunding, deriving as it does from the realm of ideas, can potentially deliver the advantages cited in every chapter of this book, circling between imaginative individuals and intelligent, supporting crowds. These can make ideals real, turn money into creative endeavour, use cash to co-create a better world, vote with their pocket books, invest in their fondest dreams, make the word of God into a reality as the early Puritans aspired to do, and assemble values into an imposing edifice. What might a Progressive Capitalism look like? There follow some imagined possibilities, some but not all of which will fail.

Headlines and scenarios from 2020

The manifesto of the new coalition

'Don't just make money, create wealth!' This looks like being the watchword of the new Australian coalition government. 'We must serve others *and* ourselves in that order.' Parliamentary committees are under strong pressure to create bi-partisan public policies on such topics as funding innovation, reviving manufacturing, increasing productivity, nurturing and paying suppliers, re-industrializing the economy and social marketing by organized consumers. Support for these imperatives is to be removed from adversarial politics and public slanging matches.

The USA celebrates its ten thousandth 'B Corporation'

Benefit Corporations, pledged via their by-laws to benefit all stakeholders, officially welcomed their ten thousandth beneficial member today. Originally developed by a group of Californian entrepreneurs, B corporations are dedicated to a community-oriented capitalism. While the number of companies *claiming* to serve stakeholders is probably several times that figure, the B-lab together with State authorities are active in certifying the companies whose strategies are deemed genuine. The public is warned not to believe 'greenwash' and spurious claims to ethical policies. Only companies willing to be independently certified can be trusted.

The National Association of Beneficial Organizations not only claim that their stakeholders have higher levels of satisfaction but that their return on assets is higher than average for companies in general. They have signed a formal pact with the League of Ethical Investors and have gained endorsement from the National Council of Churches. Negotiations are underway with Banking on Renewable Energy and with Social Impact Investors. WGBH Boston's Public TV Channel is sponsoring a contest for the Social Entrepreur of the Year. All-in-all, caring capitalism is on the march and dismisses allegations of communist sympathies.

Thirty-nine American states have now passed legislation favouring B Corporations. These include reductions in property taxes, lower corporation tax, access to local government contracts and the right to accept donations from the community. The members' charter claims that their long-term objective is to harmonize profit-making with charitable objectives.

King Charles announces new knighthood

A new order of knighthood has been proclaimed by King Charles III. The Order of Servant Leadership is to be conferred on persons for sovereignty-through-service to their society. 'All human beings make mistakes,' said an announcement from the Palace. 'What is important is that we keep trying to serve as best we can. I have convictions which I have no intention of keeping to myself. Our nation needs the controversy of those determined to leave their mark. It is a question of ethics, not politics. From now on your monarch will pose questions to his people to which answers must be found.'

'Blasphemy' say angry evangelicals

An angry group of evangelical clergy has denounced a report by a group of bishops of the Church of England entitled 'Immortality through Innovation'. It refers to innovation as a path to the immortal and as leaving a legacy to humankind. It speaks of this as a divine calling. There are special objections to its final paragraph put forward by three female bishops, which states: 'Christ, whether we think him man or God lives *de facto* in the hearts of millions and may do so for eternity.' Describing this as 'an attack on divinity and a sop to secularists,' critics denounced the deliberate blurring of the sacred nature of the Christian faith.

Ten million visitors to the Exhibition of the Future

Amsterdam has welcomed the ten millionth visitor to the Exhibition of the Future. Originally scheduled for two months in the summer it has now been extended to November and may last indefinitely. More than eight hundred booths show animated films of developments from innovators and entrepreneurs. Fifty countries have contributed to the exhibition with China providing ten per cent of all exhibits. These visions are in search of backers and all have patent protection. A spokeswoman explained that a big advantage of the exhibition was the ability of exhibitors to show products and services *in action*, inside and outside, making impacts on customers and sustaining the environment. 'This is vastly more persuasive than a written report. The ideas come to life before your eyes so you can share the creator's enthusiasm. Every new product or service is an adventure.'

The new Europe-wide Ministry for Productivity

It is now generally accepted that much of Europe has a crisis of lagging productivity. The answer, according to the experts, is gain-sharing and fate-sharing with employees and with trades unions. This has been adopted by the European Parliament. Wealth is shared *before it is even created* to remind us of the creativity within all of us. Organized workers are entitled by agreement to fifty per cent of any gain in the input-output ratio created by their cooperation with managers, who along with shareholders get the other fifty per cent. This ensures that both wage rises and share-price rises are paid for through productivity increases. All workers will confer with one another for at least half an hour a day to plan experiments in process innovation the following day. It is pre-distribution not re-distribution, explain the experts. Employees become engaged with the company by using their brains and then testing their hypotheses. No one knows more about waste, duplication and stupidity than the person actually *doing* the job!

'Invest in Innovation' reaches a TV audience of twelve million

The BBC's ninety-minute programme 'Invest in Innovation' has reached an audience of twelve million according to official figures and has raised £2.5 billion for sixty projects. Excitement reaches fever pitch as the pledge of contributions, limited to £500 per person, reaches astronomic figures, as the entrepreneurs in question thank the live audience and celebrate on stage. Each contributor receives non-voting shares in an attempt to extend the genius of founders and leave them in charge of their own creations. Objections that this 'shallow entertainment' would lead to 'ersatz companies' which 'died in a matter of weeks' have not been borne out. Fewer than thirty per cent of the new companies have ceased trading, well below the average for start-ups and largely due to the careful work of selection panels who have picked some notably non-photogenic personalities in whom they had business confidence. There is still controversy over involving celebrities in making endorsements but as one producer argued: 'If your entrepreneurs are not feted they will take a back seat. Is that what we want?' In any case this looks like becoming a dream. As one punter put it, 'I never thought I would see a form of gambling that pays most of the people most of the time. It is too good to be true.'

Following the BBC's lead, The Leuven Triangle, of the Netherlands, Belgium and Germany, which includes the towns of Eindhoven, Leuven and Aachen, are planning a TV show featuring products created in this area, one of the most innovative in Europe. Details of the programme are still under wraps. While the British are more inventive, the Triangle has brought more products to market and emphasizes fast development backed by German banks.

100 welfare consortia in Scotland

A Scottish experiment in welfare consortia, backed by its secessionist government, is thriving. Consortia consist of around 100 recipients of welfare who voluntarily pool their entitlements so as to earn over £2 million per year in entitlements per consortium. The average consortium receives forty-one per cent of its income from welfare payments. Members volunteer in their communities but may accept additional payments where their work has exceeded expectations. To date, forty children's playgrounds have been created, twenty five parks have been designed and planted, and over five thousand meals have been cooked and served to the hungry using waste food. There have been forty-three prosecutions for female genital mutilation discovered by consortium members and fifty-six women's refuges have received protection. Two thousand carers have received respite care. All consortia are non-violent but have been given mobile phones on which to record threatening behaviour or criminal activities. Up to thirty able-bodied citizens can be turned out in a matter of minutes to see off threats to the community. Ninety-year old Shaun McTavish told me 'this is how communities used to be'.

Glasgow City Council will give a local consortium fifty per cent of its savings on the energy supplied to public housing made possible by insulation installed for free. Being paid for the success of your work stimulates improvement, explained a council member. They will receive more in the end than they would on any contract. 'Nothing is worse than paying people to do nothing,' explained Hamish McGregor at the University of Edinburgh. 'They are trapped between the welfare bureaucracy on the one hand and zero-hour contracts for casual labour on the other, looking keen for would-be employers and like a certified slob for their welfare officer. It is a good definition of hell-on-earth. We have nowhere to go but up!'

Every consortium is legally obliged to get twenty per cent of its eligible members into paid work each year. They do *not* compete for minimum wage jobs but create new endeavours and new roles. Entrepreneurs may use their free labour for four months but must then offer at least fifty per cent of those who volunteered paid employment. There are huge advantages in first showing what you can do and then being paid later on. Taxpayers are sponsoring these people and they should give back as much as they can.

The age of social marketing is upon us (an article in the *New York Times*)
Social marketing tends to unite the political left and right. What the right likes about it is that it is a market solution. Customers voluntarily reward corporations for good conduct without the need for government to interfere. What customers want they should get. More good can be done by corporate efforts than by redistributed taxes. The left likes social marketing because it looks after people, especially workers and employees, and the runaway self-interest of greedy companies is sanctioned in the marketplace. You have to work for *all* stakeholders otherwise they will punish you for neglecting social responsibility to employees, the environment, suppliers and the community.

Organized consumers can get anything they want, the promotion of women, non-polluting packaging, transparent prices, self-fulfilment in the workplace, decent wages for employees, better nutrition for customers, etc. Companies benefit *twice* from the positive response of the social marketplace and from the fact that treating people better pays off in spades. Stakeholders are more engaged and creative in their work. The trick is to *reward those companies behaving best* which inevitably punishes those behaving badly but is pro-business not anti-business.

In time, organized consumers will rate products according to the ongoing conduct of companies which make them. Some will be starved of employees, customers and government contracts until their behaviour improves. Huge discrepancies in salaries, firing employees and hiring them back as contract labour at lower wages, raiding pension funds, dumping waste in Third World countries can be sanctioned while IBM's private peace-corps and Unilever's campaigns for better nutrition can be extolled. Thanks to the Internet every company has a Greek Chorus rejoicing or wailing in its wings. It has to manage its reputation very carefully indeed. Once the best companies start to promote social benefits in their advertising, others must follow. Nestle's help to its coffee growers is part of its global strategy and it pays that company even without customer gratitude, but mobilizing that gratitude would help still more.

Conclusion

This concludes our exposition. Let us end it as we began, with the nature of values. These must be enjoyed in their diversity and contrast but also be reconciled into one integrity. William Blake argued that contraries were positives. He stated that Heaven and Hell must be joined in marriage. Hell is a seemingly menacing dichotomy. The twin horns of the devil, the cloven hooves, the half-goat, half-man, the fiend who quotes scripture. But virtue is reconciliation and without the menace of those opposites there would be nothing to marry and to connect. Virtue makes an integrity from shattered pieces of vice. Blake put it well in *The Marriage of Heaven and Hell*:

> Without contraries there is no progression. Attraction and repulsion, reason and energy, love and hate are necessary to human existence.

Bibliography

Amabile, Teresa, 'Motivating Creativity in Organizations', *California Management Review* and 'Creativity under the Gun', *Harvard Business Review,* August 2002.

Amabile, Teresa, Colin M. Fisher and Julianna Pillemer, 'IDEO's Culture of Helping', *Harvard Business Review,* Jan–Feb 2014, pp. 55–61.

Anderson, Ray C., *Business Lessons from a Radical Industrialist,* New York: St. Martin's Griffin, 2009.

Ardagh, John, *Germany and the Germans,* London: Penguin, 1991.

Arnold, Matthew, *Culture and Anarchy* (1869), Oxford: Oxford University Press, reissue 2009.

Barrell, Alan, David Gill and Martin Rigby, *Show me the Money,* London: Elliot and Thompson, 2013.

Bateson, Gregory, *Steps to an Ecology of Mind,* (updated edition) Chicago: University of Chicago Press, 2000.

Bell, Daniel, *The Contradictions of Capitalism,* New York: Basic Books, 1976.

Bellah, Robert, *Habits of the Heart,* Berkeley: University of California Press, 1985.

Bennett, Milton J., *Basic Concepts of Intercultural Communication,* London: Nicholas Brealey, 2013.

Benyus, Janine, *Biomimicry: Innovation Inspired by Nature,* New York: Harper Perennial, 2002.

Blankert, Jan Willem, *China Rising; Will the West be able to Cope?,* Singapore, World Scientific, 2009.

Bogle, John C., *Enough: True Measures of Money Business and Life,* Hoboken NJ: John Wiley, 2009.

Bock, Chan Chin, *Heart Work: Stories of how EDB steered the Singapore economy from 1961 to the 21st century,* The Singapore Economic Development Board, 2002.

Bootle, Roger, *The Trouble with Markets; Saving Capitalism from itself,* London: Nicholas Brealey, 2012.

Carse, James P., *Finite and Infinite Games,* New York: Ballantine, 1986.

Carson, Rachel, *Silent Spring,* Boston: Houghton Mifflin, 1962.

Cassidy, John, *How Markets Fail: The logic of economic calamities,* London: Penguin, 2009.

Cassidy, John, *Dot con: the Greatest Story ever Sold,* London: Bloomsbury, 2003.

Chang, Ha-Joon, *23 Things They Don't Tell You About Capitalism,* London: Penguin, 2010.

Chen, Ming-Jer, *Inside Chinese Business,* Boston: Harvard Business School Press, 2003.

Chesbrough, H. W., 'The Era of Open Innovation', *MIT Sloan Management Review,* (44)3, 2003.

Child, John, *Organizations: A guide to problems and practices,* New York: Harper and Row, 1977.

Christensen, Clayton, *The Innovator's Dilemma,* Boston: Harvard Business School Press, 1997.

Chua, Amy and Jed Rubenfeld, *The Triple Package: What really determines success,* London: Bloomsbury, 2014.

Clifton, Jim, *The Coming Jobs War,* New York: Gallup Press, 2011.

Collins, James C. and Jerry I. Porras, *Built to Last,* London: Century, 1994.

Collins, James C., *Good to Great; Why some corporations make the leap and others don't,* New York: Harper Business, 2001.

Cooper, George, *The Origins of the Financial Crisis,* Petersfield: Harriman House Ltd. 2008.

Cooperrider D. L., D. Whitney and J. M. Bedford Stavros, *The Appreciative Inquiry Handbook*, Heights OH: Lakeshore Publishers, 2008.

Deming, W. Edwards, *Out of the Crisis,* Cambridge: MIT Press, 2000.

Dent, Harry S, *The Roaring 2000s Investor,* New York: Touchstone, 1999.

Dolan, Brian, *Wedgwood: The First Tycoon,* London: Viking, 2004.

Dunlap, Alfred J., *Mean Business,* New York: Random House, 1996.

Elkington, John, *Cannibals with Forks: The Triple Bottom Line,* Oxford: Capstone, 1999.

Ellen MacArthur Foundation, 'Towards a Circular Economy', *Macro Economics Reports,* vol. 3, 2013.

Elliott, Jacques, *The Form of Time*, New York: Crane Russak, 1982.

Erikson, Erik, 'Identity and the Life Cycle', *Psychological Issues,* vol. 1 no.1.

Evans, Harold and Gail Buckland, *The American Century*, London: Jonathan Cape, 2000.

Ferguson, Niall, *The Ascent of Money,* London: Penguin Books, 2012.

Fisher, Roger, *Getting to Yes*, Harmondsworth: Penguin, 1990.

Ford, Jonathan, 'The Money Monster', *Prospect,* November, 2008.

Frank, Robert H. and Philip Cook, *The Winner Take All Society*, London: Virgin, 2010.

Freeman, R. Edward, *Stakeholder Theory: The state of the art,* Cambridge: Cambridge University Press, 2010.

Friedman, Milton and Rose Friedman, *Free to Choose,* New York: Avon, 1981.

Fukuyama, Francis, *The End of History and the Last Man Standing,* New York, Free Press, 1997.

Fung, Yu-Lan, *A Short History of Chinese Philosophy*, London: The Free Press, 1976.

Garnsey, Elizabeth and Paul Hefferman, 'clustering through spin-out and attraction', *Regional Studies* (39) 8, November 2005.

Gladwell, Malcolm, *The Tipping Point*, New York: Little Brown, 2000.

Gray, John, *False Dawn: The Delusions of Global Capitalism,* London: Granta, 2009.

Gordon, Seth, *Tribes*, London: Piatkus, 2008.

Gore, Al, *Our Choice: A plan to solve the climate crisis,* London: Bloomsbury, 2009.

Hall, Edward T. and Mildred Reed Hall, *Understanding Cultural Differences,* Yarmouth, Maine: Intercultural Press, 1990.

Hampden-Turner, Charles and Fons Trompenaars, *Building Cross-Cultural Competence,* Chichester: John Wiley, 2000 pp. 123–159.

Hampden-Turner, Charles and Fons Trompenaars, *Mastering the Infinite Game,* Oxford: Capstone, 1997.

Hampden-Turner, Charles and Fons Trompenaars, *The Seven Cultures of Capitalism,* London: Piatkus, 1995.

Handy, Charles, *The Second Curve: Thoughts on Reinventing Society*, London: Random House Business, 2015.

Handy, Charles, *The Age of Paradox,* Boston: Harvard Business School Press, 1988.

Hawken, Paul, *The Ecology of Commerce,* New York: Harper Business, 1993.

Hawken, Paul Amory Lovins and L. Hunter Lovins, *Natural Capitalism,* London: Little Brown, 1999.

Hayek, Friederich A., *The Road to Serfdom,* London: Routledge, 1944.

Heskett, James L., W. Earl Sasser and Leonard A. Schlesinger, *The Value Profit Chain,* London: The Free Press, 2003.

Hofstede, Geert, *Culture's Consequences,* Beverly Hills: Sage, 1980.

Hurst, David K., *Crisis and Renewal,* Boston: Harvard Business Review Press, 1995.

Hutton, Will, *How Good Can We Be?* London: Little, Brown, 2015.

Hutton, Will, *The State We're In,* London: Jonathan Cape, 1996.

Jacques, Elliott, *The Form of Time,* New York: Crane-Russak, 1982.

James, William, *Essays in Pragmatism,* New York: Haffner Publishing Co., 1949.

Johnson, Elizabeth and Donald Moggridge (eds.) *Collected Writings of John Maynard Keynes,* Volume 11, Cambridge University Press, 1982.

Jones, Jeffrey M. 'Americans most confident in the military', *Gallup Politics,* June 2011.

Jones, Owen, *The Establishment: How they got away with it,* London: Penguin Books, 2015.

Kaletski, Anatole, 'Bankers are masters of the universe again', *Financial Times,* 8 September 2010.

Kao, John, *Innovation Nation,* New York: Free Press, 2007.

Kao, John, 'The World-Wide Web of Chinese Business', *Harvard Business Review,* vol.71 no. 2 March–April, 1993.

Kaplan, Robert S. and David P. Norton, 'The Balanced Scorecard: Measures that drive performance' *Harvard Business Review,* January 1992.

Kay, John, 'The Kay Review of Equity Markets and Long-term Decision-Making', The Department of Business, July 2012.

Kingston, Maxine Hong, *The Woman Warrior,* New York: Vintage, 1975.

Kirk, Kate and Charles Cotton, *The Cambridge Phenomenon: 50 years of innovation and enterprise,* London: Third Millennium Publishing, 2013.

Koestler, Arthur, *The Act of Creation,* New York: Macmillan, 1964 and London: Hutchinson, 1976.

Kohn, Alfie, *Punished by Rewards,* Boston: Beacon Press, 2008.

Kosman, Josh, *The Buyout of America,* New York: Portfolio Penguin, 2009.

Kotler, Philip, *Confronting Capitalism: Real Solutions for a Troubled Economic System,* New York: Amacom, 2015.

Kotter, John and James Heskett, *Corporate Culture and Performance,* New York: Free Press, 1992.

Krugman, Paul, *The Great Unravelling,* New York: WW Norton, 2005.

Kynge, James, *China Shakes the World,* London: Weidenfeld and Nicholson, 2006.

Lambert, Richard, 'Business seeks a convincing story to bring back growth', *Financial Times*, 15 October 2013.

Lanchester, John, *Whoops! Why everyone owes everyone and no one can pay*, London: Penguin Books, 2010.

Lawler, Edward E., *High Involvement Management*, San Francisco: Jossey-Bass, 1986.

Leach, Edmund, *Levi-Strauss*, London: Fontana Modern Masters, 1976.

Lesieur, F. G. (ed.), *The Scanlon Plan*, Cambridge: MIT Press, 1958.

Lesmoire-Gordan, Nigel, Will Rood and Ralph Edner, *Introducing Fractals; A Graphic Guide*, London: Icon Books, 2009.

Levi-Strauss, Claude, *Structural Anthropology*, London: Penguin, 1979, p. 51–57.

Lewis, Richard D., *When Cultures Collide*, London: Nicholas Brealey, 1996, pp. 36–51.

Luce, Edward, 'Anglo-Saxon Trumpeting will strike a hollow note', *Financial Times*, 6 January 2014.

Luce, Edward, 'Caught between apathy and anger' (Capitalism in crisis), *Financial Times*, 14 January 2012.

Lux, Kenneth, *Adam Smith's Mistake*, Boston: Shambhala Books, 1990.

Mackey, John and Raj Sisodia, *Conscious Capitalism: Liberating the Heroic Spirit in Capitalism*, Boston: Harvard Business School Press, 2013.

McCrum, Dan and David Gelles, 'Activist investors celebrate banner year', *Financial Times*, 24 December 2012.

McDonough, William and Michael Braungart, *Cradle to Cradle*, New York: Northpoint Press, 2002.

McClelland, David, *The Achieving Society*, Princeton: Van Nostrand, 1961, p. 203.

Mahizhnan, Arun and Lee Tsao Yuan, *Singapore: Re-engineering Success*, New York: Oxford University Press, 1998.

Mandelbrot, Benoit B., *The (Mis)Behaviour of Markets: A Fractal View of Risk, Ruin and Reward*, London: Profile Books, 2005.

Maruyama, Magorah, 'New Mindscapes for Future Business Policy and Management', *Technological Forecasting and Social Change*, 21, 1982.

Maslow, Abraham, *Towards a Psychology of Being*, New York: Van Nostrand, 1962.

Mason, Paul, *Meltdown: the end of the age of greed*, London: Verso, 2009.

Mayer, Colin, *Firm Commitment: Why the corporation is failing us*, Oxford; Oxford University Press, 2013.

Moore, James F., *The Death of Competition*, New York: Harper Business, 1997.

Mulgan, Geoff, *The Locust and the Bee: Predators and creators,* Princeton: Princeton University Press, 2014.

Naisbitt, John and Doris, *Innovation in China: The Chengdu Triangle*, Beijing: China Industry and Commerce Associated Press, 2012.

Naisbitt, John and Doris, *Chinese Megatrends: The 8 Pillars of the New Society*, New York: Harper-Collins, 2010.

Nohria, Nitin, *Handbook of Leadership Theory and Practice,* Boston: Harvard Business School Press, 2010.

Ogilvy, Jay and Peter Schwartz, with Joe Flower, *China's Futures: Scenarios for the World's Fastest Growing Economy*, San Francisco: Jossey-Bass, 2000.

Ogilvy, Jay, *Many Dimensional Man,* New York: Oxford University Press, 1978.

Peston, Robert, *How Do We Fix This Mess?* London: Hodder and Stoughton, 2012.

Peters, Tom and Robert Waterman, *In Search of Excellence,* New York: Harper & Row, 1982.

Piketty, Thomas, *Capital in the twenty-first century*, Harvard University: Belknap Press, 2014.

Pink, Daniel, *Drive: The Surprising Truth of what Motivates Us,* London: Canongate, 2009.

Plato, *The Apology,* available at www.bartelby.com/2/1/1.html.

Plender, John, 'Capitalism in Crisis', *Financial Times*, 9 January 2012.

Plender, John, 'Recession has revived labour's struggle', *Financial Times*, 12 January 2014.

Porter, Michael, *The Competitive Advantage of Nations,* New York: Free Press, 1990.

Porter, Michael, *Competitive Strategy*, New York: Free Press, 1980.

Prahalad, C. K. and Venkat Ramaswamy, *The Future of Competition,* Boston: Harvard Business School Press, 2004.

Prahalad, C. K., *The Fortune at the bottom of the Pyramid*, Upper Saddle River NJ: Pearson Education, 2010.

Rachman, Gideon, *Zero-Sum World,* London: Atlantic Books, 2010.

Rachman, Gideon, 'The West is losing faith in its own future', *Financial Times*, 10 December 2013.

Rajan, R. and L. Zingales, 'Financial Dependence and Economic growth' *American Economic Review*, 88 pp.559–581, 1998.

Redding, Gordon S., *The Spirit of Chinese Capitalism,* New York: Walter de Gruyter, 1990.

Reich, Robert B., *Aftershock; The Next Economy and America's Future*, New York: Random House, 2011.

Reich, Robert B., *Tales of a New America*, New York: Times Books, 1987.

Roethlisberger, F. and William Dixon, *Management and the Worker*, Cambridge: Harvard University Press, 1939.

Rostow, Walt W., *The Stages of Economic Growth*, New York: Vintage, 1968.

Sainsbury, David, *Progressive Capitalism: How to Achieve Economic Growth, Liberty and Social Justice*, Biteback Publishing, 2014.

Saxenian, AnnaLee, *Silicon Valley's New Immigrant Entrepreneurs*, San Francisco: Public Policy Institute, 1999.

Schrage, Michael, *Serious Play*, Boston: Harvard Business School Press, 1999.

Scott, Bruce and George C. Lodge, *US, Competitiveness and the World Economy*, Boston: Harvard Business School Press, 1985.

Sculley, John, *Odyssey*, New York: Doubleday, 1991.

Seddon, Richard (ed.), *The Fundamental Social Law, Selected Writings of Rudolf Steiner*, Bristol: Rudolf Steiner Press, 1993.

Senge, Peter, *The Necessary Revolution*, London: Nicholas Brealey, 2008.

Simon, Hermann, *The Hidden Champions of the 21st Century*, New York: Springer, 2009.

Sisodia, Rajendra S., David B. Wolfe and Jagdish N. Sheth, *Firms of Endearment*, Wharton School Publishing, 2007.

Smith, Adam, *An Inquiry into the Wealth of Nations*, London: Penguin, 1984.

Smith, Adam, *The Theory of Moral Sentiments*, 1759. Available online at Google Books.

Snow, C. P., *The Two Cultures*, Cambridge: Cambridge University Press, 2001.

Stephens, Phillip, 'Nothing can dent the divine right of bankers', FT.com, Philip.Stephens@ft.com.

Stiglitz, Joseph E., *The Price of Inequality*, London: Allen Lane, 2012.

Swann, James and Roberta, *Bound to the Earth*, New York: Avon Books, 1994, p. 33.

Tett, Gillian, *Fool's Gold. How Unrestrained Greed Corrupted a Dream*, London: Abacus, 2010.

Thurow, Lester C., *The Zero Sum Society*, New York: McGraw Hill, 1980.

Tillich, Paul, *The Courage to Be*, New Haven: Yale University Press, 1952.

Tillich, Paul, *Love, Power and Justice*, New York: Oxford University Press, 1958.

Toffler, Alvin, *Future Shock*, New York; Bantam, 1970.

Toynbee, Arnold, *A Study of History*, Vol.1–6, Oxford: Oxford University Press, 1946.

Trompenaars, Fons and Piet Hein Coebergh, *100+ Management Models: How to understand and apply the world's most powerful business tools*, Oxford: Infinite Ideas, 2014.

Trompenaars, Fons and Charles Hampden-Turner, *Riding the Waves of Culture,* London: Nicholas Brealey, 3rd edn, 2013.

Trompenaars, Fons and Maarten Nijhoff Asser, *The Global M&A Tango,* Oxford: Infinite Ideas, 2010.

Trompenaars, Fons and Ed Voerman, *Servant-Leadership Across Cultures,* Oxford: Infinite Ideas, 2009.

Turner, Adair (now Lord Turner) 'Mansion House Speech', 22 September 2009, http://www.fsa.gov.uk/library/communication/speeches/2009/0922_at.shtml

Walzer, Michael, *The Revolution of the Saints,* Cambridge, Mass: Harvard University Press, 1965.

Weber, Max (with Peter Bahr and Gordon C. Wells), *The Protestant Ethic and the Spirit of Capitalism,* London: Penguin, 2011.

Wicksteed, William, *Cambridge Phenomenon Report,* Cambridge: Segal, Quince and Wicksteed, 1985, 2nd edn 2002.

Wilkinson, Richard and Kate Picket, *The Spirit Level; Why Equality is Better for Everyone,* London: Penguin 2010.

Wolf, Martin, *The Shifts and the Shocks,* London: Allen Lane, 2014.

Wolf, Martin, 'Britain's Economy should not go back to the Future', *Financial Times*, 13 April 2013.

Wolf, Martin, 'Britain's needlessly slow recovery', *Financial Times,* 6 December 2013.

Yao, Yang and Linda Yueh, 'The China Model and its Future', *China: Twenty Years of Reform and Development*, Peking University Press, 2010, available on *Foreign Affairs Online,* February 2010.

Yang, Yeo, 'Beijing Consensus or Washington Consensus: what explains China's economic success?', *Developmental Outreach,* April, 2011.

Young, Hilary, *The Genius of Wedgwood,* London: Victoria and Albert Museum, 1995.

Yunus, Muhammad, *Building Social Business: The New Kind of Capitalism that Serves Humanity's Most Pressing Needs*, London: Arum Press, 2003

Yunus, Muhammad, *Banker to the Poor: The Story of the Grameen Bank,* London: Aurum Press, 2003.

Zeng, Ming and Peter J. Williamson, *Dragons at Your Door,* Boston: Harvard Business School Press, 2007.

Zhang, Haihua and Geoff Baker, *Think Like the Chinese,* Sydney, Australia: Federation Press, 2012.

Acknowledgements

Charles owes most of all to the person to whom this book is dedicated. Gregory Bateson. He was my unauthorized mentor and inspiration when I lived near his home in California. He taught me that values are not things, but differences or contrasts related to one another in a dynamic balance. When I examined the notes to our chapters I realized I had hardly credited him at all. But the reason is simple. His ideas have so shaped mine that I have lost awareness of the distinction between us. He taught me to think in circles, not in lines, so as to comprehend the nature of the wholes of which we are all parts. He described the 'double-bind' or the dilemma that makes or breaks us and holds the possibility of imprisonment or of innovation on its far side. He described the growing split in the structure of ideas that can break apart our values and cultures like rotten sticks (see Chapter 2). Although he died in 1980 his thoughts have animated my co-authors and me ever since. He preferred questions to answers. This book is an attempt to give life to some of his ideas and to suggest some answers. My sense of tribute was reawakened by an excellent film on her relationship with her father by Nora Bateson, entitled *An Ecology of Mind*.

I owe to Fons Trompenaars a thirty-year partnership and some five books based on his research. Because of his support I have been free to think and write from 1985 onwards. How many of us have the privilege of thinking and writing thoughts in the order we wish and building these into an edifice? I could not have been more fortunate in a partner for life. Having internalized the way we both think he could have dispensed with me and earned more himself. He did not.

Several people have read chapters of this book and put me right on their subject. I am grateful to Hermann Simon for helping me grasp the significance of *Mittelstand* (Chapter 5) as the hidden champions of so many economies. I am indebted to Neo Beng-Tong in keeping in touch with Singapore and East Asia

317

in general (Chapter 6). He has been a faithful friend. Peter Hiscocks, himself a formidable entrepreneur, helped me understand the Cambridge Phenomenon of which he is a part (Chapter 10). Raj Sisodia and John Mackey introduced me to the Conscious Capitalism movement at a San Francisco conference in 2013. R. Edwards Freeman at the University of Virginia helped me understand the values behind stakeholder theory which he has championed for most of his life. Martin Gillo has been most valuable as a colleague, a co-presenter and a friendly critic and has read my views on Germany.

I owe a great deal to Alan Barrell, entrepreneur in residence at the Judge Business School, an amazing entrepreneurial networker and angel investor. His help to me has been unflagging and I learned the possibilities of crowdfunding mostly from him (Chapter 11). Thanks to Alan I met the late Gordon Edge whose views on interdisciplinary innovation are presented in Chapter 10. He also introduced me to Charles Cotton, author of *The Cambridge Phenomenon,* Johnathan Milner of Abcam and Peter Taylor of the employee-owned Technology Partnership, all of whom showed me great kindness.

I am grateful to Professor Raymond Abelin, my ex student at Cambridge. The two of us developed the Entrepreneurship and Innovation Program at Nanyang Technological University, which went on to be widely acclaimed and much imitated. I was greatly invigorated by shooting a film on innovation, which he directed. The way he sprang to life on the set was wondrous to behold. We should all be the directors of our own thoughts and lives. Although the film itself became a victim of a protracted legal dispute the experience of shooting it was memorable and we got to interview Professors Clayton Christensen, Teresa Amabile and Howard Stevenson, all at Harvard. Clayton was especially kind and his memorable words on disruptive innovation are reproduced in Chapter 5. I once taught with Robert Reich in La Jolla and although our acquaintance was fleeting I treasure what he says and writes. I talked at some length with Will Hutton on a flight to Malaysia and have enjoyed and admired his books since then. His review of my work in the *Guardian* was generous.

I owe a deep debt to Peter Senge at MIT, where he made me a visiting scholar on two occasions, and gave me renewed hope in system dynamics. His book *The Fifth Discipline* was an inspiration. John Kay was head of the Centre for Business Strategy where I worked at the London Business School and I have followed his writing and reports ever since. That I was made a Senior Visiting Fellow there I owe to Arie de Geus, my boss at the Scenario Planning Department at Shell. He was the first to roundly endorse my dilemma theory and his own writing on planning to learn is first rate. I need to thank the Judge Business School for putting up with me for eighteen years, especially Paul

Judge, Christopher Loch, Marc de Rond, Peter Williamson, Shai Vyakarnam, and Shaz Ansari. I am also grateful to my friends and supporters at the Institute for Manufacturing at Cambridge, especially Elizabeth Garnsey and her spin-out diagrams (Chapter 10), and Bill Wicksteed and his exposition of the Cambridge Phenomenon. Helen Zhang was a great help on the subject of China, as was the head of the Needham Research Institute, Professor Jianjun Mei. Steve Evans is brilliant on the environment and his own hydrogen car.

Raymond Madden, now at the Asian Institute of Finance in Kuala Lumpur supported me as best he could when Dean at a business school best forgotten. He has been the client of our company over the years. I was encouraged in my circular thinking by Jamie Butterworth of the Ellen McArthur Foundation and wish their campaign well. I am grateful to the Li Ka Shing Foundation that awarded me a Hutchinson Visiting Scholarship to China in 2003, while I was at Cambridge. Chapter 4 on China owes much to that visit. The third author of this book, Tom Cummings, has done much to help me over the years and convinced me that the Global Alliance for Banking on Values (Chapter 9), was worth including. Our company, Trompenaars Hampden-Turner, was acquired by KPMG in the Netherlands and we owe much to the support of Mark Spears, the Global Head of People and Change, Robert Bolton in Canary Wharf in London and their counterparts in the Netherlands, Erik Schut and Harold de Bruijn. Thanks to this partnership we hope these ideas will be championed.

Many thanks to Peter Blom, chair of the Global Alliance for Banking on Values and Managing Director of Triodos Bank. Peter has built on the vision and impulse of the four founders of Triodos and has been a great mentor and supporter of the ideas in Chapter 10. David Korslund and Linda Ryan of the GABV have also helped to clarify the essential points of the alliance, and its value as an emerging banking alliance.

Finally, our publisher Richard Burton, who has published several of our previous works, encouraged us hugely with his reception of this book's proposal and we are grateful for the detailed help of Rebecca Clare in getting everything ready for publication. Writing is lonely work and Richard's faith and judgement and Rebecca's patience, kindness and diligence are much appreciated.

There is nothing like composing this acknowledgement to remind us three just how much we owe to others and to each other. The runaway individualism of our culture needs desperately to be countered and this short account should remind us all of the value of knowledge communities and of shared ideas. Our thanks are extended to all mentioned.

Charles Hampden-Turner (ChuckHT@aol.com)
and Fons Trompenaars (fonst@aol.com), July 2015

Index